ALL DAT
NEW ORLEANS

ALL DAT

NEW ORLEANS

Eating, Drinking, Listening to Music, Exploring, &
Celebrating in the Crescent City

MICHAEL MURPHY

PHOTOGRAPHS BY RYAN HODGSON-RIGSBEE

THE COUNTRYMAN PRESS
A DIVISION OF W. W. NORTON & COMPANY
INDEPENDENT PUBLISHERS SINCE 1923

For information about permission to reproduce selections from this book, write to
Permissions, The Countryman Press, 500 Fifth Avenue, New York, NY 10110

For information about special discounts for bulk purchases, please contact
W. W. Norton Special Sales at specialsales@wwnorton.com or 800-233-4830

Manufacturing by Versa Press
Production manager: Devon Zahn

The Countryman Press
www.countrymanpress.com

A division of W. W. Norton & Company, Inc.
500 Fifth Avenue, New York, NY 10110
www.wwnorton.com

978-1-58157-413-5 (pbk.)

10 9 8 7 6 5 4 3 2 1

CONTENTS

What happens in Vegas may stay in Vegas, but what happens in New Orleans goes home with you —**Laurell K. Hamilton**

INTRODUCTION
TO THE INTRODUCTION
How to Use this Book

Prior to telling you what this book is (or was intended to be), I'll begin with how to use the book.

The key to reading *All Dat* is to put it down. Unless you are the most vapid, platitudinous person on the planet, and you come to New Orleans just to check off your list that you (1) ate a beignet at Café DuMonde, (2) took a selfie next to a busker who was pretending to be a statue (hint: in the photograph you're both going to look like statues), and (3) spent a night on Bourbon Street because you think you sort of have to when you come to New Orleans, then you're going to completely miss the essential lessons this city and this culture has to teach you.

New Orleans is not about bucket lists or following someone else's opinion (including mine) as to where to eat or drink, or which musical performers to see. This is a city where you're supposed to join the parade, not just watch one from the curb. This is a city where you should talk with as many people on the street or seated next to you on a streetcar and not have your nose buried in a guide book or some travel app loaded onto your phone.

Unlike New York City, where I lived for 27 years and where visitors are warned not to stare up at the skyscrapers because that's a telltale sign you're a tourist, here you want to be seen as a visitor. Stand on a street corner or, look lost while fiddling with a map. New Orleanians will come up to you and ask you if you need help. As they answer your immediate questions about direction needs, they'll also shower you with unjustifiable opinions about where to eat and hear music, as well as details about if there are any upcoming parades or festivals, where they went to high school, and offer at least ten reasons why we should fire the LSU football coach. Again.

New Orleans is a city for participating, not just reading about its history or looking at its sights from a tour bus window. Each chapter of this book has an active verb used as the title, Eating, Drinking, Exploring, or Fitting In. I added the chapter Shopping with some reservations. I want you to know about Boutique du Vampyr, the only brick and mortar vampire shop in America. I feel you need to know where you can buy authentic voodoo charms or potions and not the made-in-China stuff that clutters much of the French Quarter.

But the best way to "do" New Orleans is not to fill up your suitcase with consumer knickknacks and doodads, but to fill up your mind and your soul with one-of-a-kind experiences.

INTRODUCTION

To get to New Orleans you don't pass through anywhere else.

—Allen Toussaint

2018 marks the 300th anniversary of New Orleans, or what you might call the city's Triennial or Tricentennial or Tercentenary celebration, depending on which of the almost never-used terms you choose to use. Choose carefully, because you won't get to use it again for another 58 years, when the whole United States celebrates its own 300th birthday.

Yes, New Orleans is 58 years older than the country. That's if you accept the story that is was first founded in 1718 by Jean-Baptiste Le Moyne de Bienville, the explorer from Montreal. Bienville is said to have selected the site because it was relatively high ground in an otherwise swampy area prone to flooding. The sharp bend in the river, right about where Café Du Monde has been shoveling beignets since 1862, serves to form a natural protective levee. The site that became New Orleans was also adjacent to the trading route used by Native Americans and trappers as portage between the Mississippi River and Lake Pontchartain, and it was a safe distance from Spanish or English settlements down river. With this pocketful of reasons, Bienville claimed the land and named it La Nouvelle-Orléans in honor of the then Regent of France, Philippe II, Duke of Orléans.

But Rene-Robert Cavelier, Sieur de La Salle, also from Montreal by way of Rouen, France, was actually here 36 years prior. He came across the Atlantic to set up trade with Native Americans; his brother, a Jesuit priest, came to convert them to Christianity. After expeditions to Erie, Pennsylvania (called either the Gem City or Dreary Erie) and Louisville, Kentucky (home of a wax statue of Colonel Sanders decked out in a suit really worn by the real Colonel Sanders—who's not really a colonel), La Salle's journeys brought him all the way down the Mississippi.

In 1682, he buried a metal plate and a cross claiming all the land at the base of the Mississippi River for the king of France. French explorers buried lead plates all over North America. The first was one planted at Conewago Creek, Pennsylvania. These plates claimed the land for France that was already occupied by various Native Americans. It'd be like some family from Germany coming into your house and placing stickers on pieces of your favorite furniture that said, "This is MINE"—only the stickers would have read "Das Ghent MIR."

La Salle set out to return to New Orleans in 1684 with 300 colonists to establish and develop the city. Of the original four ships that carried them, one was seized by pirates, another sank, and a third ran aground. La Salle and his congregation then wandered on foot, looking for his plate through swamps infested with poisonous snakes and yellow fever-carrying mosquitos. They never found it. When the original 300 had been whittled down to 36 survivors, they killed La Salle on March 19, 1687, and started walking back to Montreal. I doubt they made it very far.

There's a story that a fisherman in the 1930s actually found the metal plate 240 years later but, not being able to decipher the inscriptions, he melted it down to use for fishing weights and buckshot.

Fast forward 300 years and, with considerably less fanfare or historical significance, I arrived in New Orleans. Like so many others, on my first visit I was immediately seduced by New Orleans' unique, some might say twisted charms. The actor John Goodman said of his first time in the city, "If I could put my finger on it, I'd bottle it and sell it . . . I came down here originally in 1972 with some drunken fraternity guys and had never seen anything like it—the climate, the smells. It's the cradle of music; it just flipped me. Someone suggested that there's an incomplete part of our chromosomes that gets repaired or found when we hit New Orleans. Some of us just belong here."

New Orleans was so unlike anywhere I'd ever been before. Musician Sunpie Barnes claims that, "It takes 30 seconds to fall into New Orleans and realize you're in a different place." The John Goodman and Sunpie Barnes quotes are joined by many others at the back of this book, where I collect what I consider the 300 best things ever said by New Orleanians or about New Orleans. I, myself, am fond of saying (far too often) that New Orleans is as far as you can get from America while you're still in it.

This city is different in every way. If you're a lawyer in California, New York, Texas, Oregon, or anywhere else, you can't come here and practice law. We are still, today, living under the Napoleonic Code. You'd have to learn a whole different set of laws.

Women could own property, run businesses, and vote here in the 1700s, while the rest of the United States didn't catch up until 1920—except for Oklahoma, where women got the vote in 1919, 200 years after Louisiana.

In Louisiana, and nowhere else, slaves could buy their freedom, based on Spanish rule after they acquired Louisiana in 1762. As a slave, the older you got, the less it cost to emancipate yourself, because you could do less work. The Spanish slave code introduced the practice of *coartación* (co-are-TA-see-on); this policy of self-purchase originated with the Spanish perception of slavery as an unnatural human condition.

Six years before the Civil War, a full 20 percent of the population of New Orleans was comprised of ex-slaves, who actually lost rights after the Civil War. The introduction of new and constrictive Jim Crow laws took away freedoms that black people in Louisiana had formerly possessed.

For some, the city is old, disorderly filled with cracked plaster, sagging balconies, and busted up sidewalks. A loggerheaded tourist once asked me in a derisive tone, "Why is everything so *old* here?"

For the rest of us, New Orleans is a seductive vortex, the singular place where we feel most at home. Those who choose to love New Orleans (most of us fiercely) willingly overlook or forgive the city's faults. As writer and blogger Eve Kidd Crawford says, "The city can be flaky as hell. The boil orders issued hours after everyone has consumed the unboiled water. The potholes. The basic inability to provide any kind of bureaucratic service with even the slightest degree of efficiency. If New Orleans were a person, he would get his power cut off a lot because he just forgot to pay the bill. He would have vodka in the freezer but no milk in the fridge."

In 2014, after publication of my first book, *Eat Dat*, I was speaking on a panel at the annual Tennessee Williams Festival. One panel member, whom I'd never met, was restaurant owner and local icon Dickie Brennan. After the panel, I came over to introduce myself. During our greeting, Dickie mentioned how our beloved city absolutely deserved a great tome, or doorstop of a book to be published for our 300th anniversary. A lightbulb went off over my head.

I still believe New Orleans deserves a true chef-d'oeuvre. This book is not it.

As one who's lived here only since 2009 (although I'd been coming once or twice a year ever since I first came to New Orleans in 1983), I wouldn't dare to try to be the spokesperson for the city on its 300th. The NOLAier Than Thou crowd would have my Yankee non-Catholic hide. While I'm not a native born, or what locals might tag me as a "come-here" rather than a "from-here," I am most definitely an enthusiast for New Orleans, perhaps even an apostle spreading the gospel of this most unique city.

All Dat is intended to be my much more modest version of the tome Dickie Brennan envisioned. There will be no full color photographs of The Louisiana Purchase, a document now housed in the Cabildo, nor reprints of the handwritten manuscript of *A Streetcar Named Desire*. No recipe cards from Mme. Bégué, the first lady of chefs. I hope that book does get published. I'll buy multiple copies.

Instead, *All Dat* is what one reviewer of an earlier book described as "a love letter from ex-pat-yat Michael Murphy." Ex-pat-yat is a phrase I coined in the book to describe the great many people who first come to New Orleans, get completely seduced, and have to live here amongst the Yats. Ex-pat-yats include Brad Pitt, John Goodman, Sandra Bullock, musicians Beyoncé and Jay-Z, Jimmy Buffett, Meschiya Lake, writers Sherwood Anderson, Andrei Codrescu, Richard Ford, and of course Tennessee Williams, plus a huge number of everyday people. Poet Andy Young intended to spend the weekend here en route to Austin, Texas from her home in West Virginia. She's now lived here 10 years.

One preface note: the facts and stories laid out over the next few hundred pages I have either experienced directly or heard from at least two sources. But all histories are at least partially fictionalized by what the writer puts in as well as leaves out. There's a phrase we use in New Orleans: *never let the truth get in the way of a good story*. It is also a Southern tradition to embellish. I once sat with the late novelist Pat Conroy when he spoke to a room of would-be writers. He asked, like the good Southern writer he was, "Why use just one adjective when you can use six?"

Each (more or less) fact-filled chapter of *All Dat* uses an active verb as the header.

As stated earlier, New Orleans, more than anywhere I've ever been, is a city about participating. It's the tourists with too much money on their hands who buy seats in the stands to watch a Mardi Gras Parade from the distance of cordoned-off bleachers.

The chapters Eating, Listening, and Creeping Around are repurposed material from my previous books, *Eat Dat*, *Hear Dat*, and *Fear Dat*. The chapters Drinking, Shopping, Rooting, Reading, Exploring, Fitting In, and Celebrating are all-new material and provide a much more comprehensive picture of New Orleans. Because of the success of the first Dat books, my publisher approached me to do a book on our history of cocktails and current bar scene called *Drink Dat*. I backed away because I'm not much of a drinker. I like my alcohol to taste as much like Hawaiian Punch as possible. Elizabeth Pearce is The Man when it comes to drinking in New Orleans. Elizabeth is a cocktail historian and guide for her Drink & Learn tours. She helped create the cocktail portion of the Southern Museum of Food and Beverage, has appeared on the Travel Channel, and has written the lively and anecdotal *The French Quarter Drinking Companion*. I hooked up The Countryman Press and Elizabeth. *Drink Dat* is now available to be bought and read with delight.

LUMINS OF NEW ORLEANS:
Lafcadio Hearn

Humans of New York is a hugely successful blog and best-selling book featuring interviews and portraits collected on the streets of New York City by photographer Brandon Stanton. With each chapter of *All Dat*, I am attaching a sidebar story of a New Orleanian I consider a signature representative of our ebullient and sometimes twisted vibe. I'm calling these portraits "Lumins of New Orleans," with Lumins being short for Luminaries. (And then I'll pray for a fraction of the 16 million followers Brandon Stanton has built up on Facebook.)

I'd wager a good eight out of ten New Orleanians know Lafcadio Hearn, but I would bet the houses I can no longer afford that very few people outside of New Orleans know of him. He is the New Orleans equivalent of Thomas Jefferson or John Adams or Benjamin Franklin. Only rather than crafting a declaration of independence, Lafcadio wrote a lasting declaration of New Orleans' enduring weirdness. He has been dubbed "the inventor of New Orleans."

Hearn, who was born in Greece, was abandoned by his mother and raised by Irish relatives who shipped him off to the States at

There is also a chapter called Bonking, which covers New Orleans' complex sexual history from Storyville through the evolution of Bourbon Street to the Neo-Burlesque of today. Bonking has a back story. In addition to being a synonym for shagging, screwing, and fornicating—bonking is a sports term meaning a precipitous fatigue and loss of energy, or "hitting the wall," as they call it in endurance sports. Remedies for sports-related bonking include a brief rest, ingestion of food or drink.

If you ever hit the wall in your real, day-to-day life, New Orleans is the perfect remedy for the other kind of bonking. Come take a much-needed respite and eat our food, drink our Hurricanes, Sazeracs, and Huge Ass Beers, listen to our live music, or just sit awhile and chat up whomever is seated next to you on a park bench or streetcar seat. Eating, drinking, listening, exploring, and bonking in New Orleans can restore your soul.

The city can drive a sober-minded person insane, but it feeds the dreamer. It feeds the dreamer stories, music and food. Really great food.
                                                        —Andrei Codrescu

age 19. In Cincinnati, he took odd jobs, lived in a stable, read voraciously, and eventually became a self-taught writer. He started penning profiles for the *Cincinnati Enquirer*, but was forced to leave Ohio for New Orleans in 1877, when he broke a state law by marrying a biracial woman.

Drawn to others on the fringe, Hearn and New Orleans formed a perfect marriage of misfits. His exotic stories about his new adopted city became regular pieces in *Scribner's, Cosmopolitan*, and *Harper's Bazaar*. It was Hearn who first reported on the the folklore of the unique local cuisine in his verbosely named book, *La Cuisine Creole: A Collection of Culinary Recipes, From Leading Chefs and Noted Creole House-wives, Who Have Made New Orleans Famous for Its Cuisine*. It was Hearn who also detailed for outsiders the customs of New Orleans–style voodoo. And it was Hearn who painted word pictures of New Orleans as the most exotic city in America. He wrote, "There are few who can visit her for the first time without delight; and few who can ever leave her without regret; and none who can forget her strange charm when they have once felt its influence."

As a person who grew up in Ohio, I take special joy in another of his turns of phrase about New Orleans: "Times are not good here. The city is crumbling into ashes. It has been buried under taxes and frauds and maladministrations so that it has become a study for archaeologists . . . but it is better to live here in sackcloth and ashes than to own the whole state of Ohio."

Ever the wanderer, Hearn moved to Martinique, then settled in Japan. His former NOLA neighborhood grew seedy and his residence became a dingy flophouse. The property was eventually bought and restored by NFL Saints linebacker Pat Swilling. Richard Scribner, an LSU professor, then took ownership and through his efforts the house (1565 Cleveland St.) was designated a historic landmark and added to the National Register of Historic Places.

CHAPTER 1

Eating

Where We Live to Eat Rather than Eat to Live

"To understand New Orleans, you have to understand the food."

—**Ray Cannata**

Any presentation about All Things New Orleans needs to begin with food. There's a local joke that we have lunch just so we can talk about dinner. Restaurants, chefs, and even waiters and oyster shuckers are firmly established as the heart, soul, and essential part of New Orleans' culture.

Before stumbling into any of our numerous restaurants in town, though, it's worth acquainting yourself with our food traditions and signature dishes. This first of the two eating chapters can be viewed as New Orleans' culinary anthropology. Here will be portraits of our cuisines and histories of our signature dishes. And we have a lot of signature dishes here. Appearing on an episode of *The Tonight Show* after the Saints won the Super Bowl, Jay Leno asked quarterback Drew Brees to name as many signature New Orleans dishes as he could in 15 seconds. Drew responded, "Charbroiled oysters, fried oysters, oysters Rockefeller, oysters Bienville, po'boy sandwiches, shrimp Creole, shrimp tasso, fried shrimp, meat pies, red beans and rice, jambalaya, turtle soup, gumbo, anything fried or blackened." He of course didn't have time to mention beignets, bananas foster, bread pudding, muffuletta, etouffee, boudin, andoullie, barbecue shrimp—which is a dish with no barbecue sauce—pralines, stuffed mirliton, grits & grillades, trout meunière, yakamein, calas, Doberge cake, and King Cake (which you should only eat during Mardi Gras season).

When dining out in New Orleans, you can get great Israeli food at Shaya, voted Best New Restaurant in America 2015 by both *Esquire Magazine* and the James Beard Awards. Casa Borrega, run by the ebullient Hugo Montero, is one of the best Mexican restaurants I've ever eaten at. And since Isabel and Manny Ochoa-Galvez's place, La Macarena, is the only El Salvadorian restaurant I've ever been to, I will likewise call it the best of its kind.

Our food culture is founded on four pillars: Cajun, Creole, seafood, and the lesser-acknowledged Vietnamese. (There are 15,000 Vietnamese in the New Orleans area, more than anywhere else in North America.) Before the fall of Saigon, there weren't 15,000 Vietnamese in all of America.

Most visitors coming to New Orleans want our "authentic" Cajun-Creole food, as though Cajun and Creole are the same thing. They are not.

Cajun

A quick definition of Cajun is that the word is a mutated version of Acadian. There's one story (probably not true) that someone here misunderstood a person being described as Acadian and they heard "A Cajun." When France owned Canada, many French settlers plopped down in the region called Acadie. The area is now Nova Scotia and part of Newfoundland. After the French and Indian War (1754–1763), the conquering British tried to force the inhabitants to swear allegiance to the king of England. This would have also required renouncing their Catholic faith. When most refused to do so, the British exiled just under 12,000 residents. The deportation has many names, from Le Grand Dérangement to the Great Upheaval. Many of these Acadians made their way to Louisiana, which was both French and Catholic. When they arrived in New Orleans, they were not well-received by the French who, unlike the Cajuns, were actually *from* France and had already been living here for the previous 40 years. So most of the Acadians settled out in the Bayou Country of southwest Louisiana. If you want "real" or "authentic" Cajun food or Cajun music today, you are best served about an hour or two outside New Orleans in places like Houma, Thibodaux, Breaux Bridge, Opelousas, and Ville Platte.

Cajuns were trappers, farmers, and fishermen. They ate whatever they caught or harvested right outside their front door. To make it edible, Cajun food is highly seasoned.

Because Cajuns were not wealthy, they tried not to waste any part of a butchered animal. Cracklins are a popular snack made by frying pork skins. Boudin, a signature Cajun food, is created from the ground-up leftover parts of a hog after the best meat is taken. Trust me, boudin is much better than it sounds.

As much as *what* they eat, rural Cajuns are known for *how* they eat. Cajuns view food as the chance for a community get-together.

A boucherie is a pig-slaughtering party where Cajuns gather to socialize, play music, dance, and eat meat with side dishes of meat. They use every last bit of the animal, including organs and variety cuts in sausages and the less accessible bits in the head known as head cheese.

The crawfish boil is a celebratory event where Cajuns boil crawfish, potatoes, onions, and corn in large pots over propane cookers. Lemons and small muslin

bags containing a mixture of bay leaves, mustard seeds, cayenne pepper, and other spices are added to the water for seasoning. The results are then dumped onto large, newspaper-draped tables and eaten by hand.

There aren't many authentic Cajun restaurants in New Orleans proper, but those that are can be considered holy ground. Paul Prudhomme, born and raised outside Opelousas, effectively put Cajun food on the international map with his best-selling books, TV shows, and signature restaurant, K-Paul's Louisiana Kitchen. Rayne, Louisiana, a city of under 8,000 residents in Acadia Parish and nicknamed the "Frog Capital of the World," was home to two current master Cajun chefs in New Orleans: Isaac Toups of Toups' Meatery and the soon-to-be-opened Toups South, plus the James Beard Awards favorite, Donald Link. Link has won five James Beard Awards, including Best New Restaurant in the South 2007 (Cochon), and Best New Restaurant in America 2014 (Pêche).

Creole

Creole is a word that has been used so many different ways that it's almost lost its meaning. Creole derives from an old Spanish word meaning "mixture of color." A tight definition is a person born in colonial Louisiana (1718–1803) to foreign-born parents who spoke French or Spanish or learned to speak those languages after they arrived. It does not (necessarily) mean a light-skinned person of mixed race.

Food-wise, the often-repeated formula of Creole cooking is 75 percent French, 20 percent combined Spanish, Italian, German, and Irish, and 5 percent Indian and African. But I heard a presentation by the brilliant Lolis Eric Elie where he argued passionately and effectively that West African food traditions contributed far more than 5 percent to Creole cuisine.

Most New Orleans cookbooks define Creole cuisine as the food of French settlers attempting to recreate the tastes of their homeland using what was available here in the bayous and swamps of Louisiana. Many ingredients in their European recipes simply weren't to be found here. From the Native Americans, French cooks learned about filé powder (ground sassafras leaves) and hominy (a corn kernel staple). Creole cooking also blended flavors and ingredients introduced by other European and African immigrants.

The first Creole cookbook was the verbosely named *La Cuisine Creole: A Collection of Culinary Recipes, From Leading Chefs and Noted Creole Housewives, Who Have Made New Orleans Famous For Its Cuisine*, written by Lafcadio Hearn in 1885. We forgive Lafcadio his excess because his words elsewhere helped create the image of New Orleans as an exotic locale that still draws millions of tourists every year. Beginning in 1900 and spanning sixteen editions, *The Picayune's Creole Cook Book* was called "the ultimate cook book on Creole cuisine," and the "most notable among early-twentieth-century food writings." These two books form the foundation of the hundreds of imitators you see stacked up in every bookstore and most gift shops in New Orleans.

A far too simple line can be drawn dividing Cajun as the food of country people from Creole as the food of the city people. There are some near-not-quite truths in that statement. Creoles, for the most part, ate domesticated animals—chicken, duck, cow, and pig. Cajuns ate what they caught in the wild—gator, turtle, rabbit, possum, squirrel. Creoles generally used fresher ingredients, chosen at the market almost daily. Cajuns came to the market only three or four times a year, when they brought their furs and crops to sell, and would then smoke and store their meats. Now, that's a broad and historical statement. Don't be thinking you're getting "old" food if you eat at a Cajun restaurant tonight.

Seafood

Seafood is at the heart of both Creole and Cajun cuisine. The Gulf area is blessed with an abundance of sustainable shrimp, oysters, crawfish, blue crab, soft-shell crab, redfish, drum, speckled trout, and catfish—oh, and gator, if you want to group it as seafood. I have heard that New Orleans produces one-third of all seafood consumed in America. (But when I tell that to people in Seattle or Boston, they reply, "Yeah. We say the same thing.") I can write, without question, that 90 percent of the crawfish eaten each year comes from Louisiana, that we catch between 100 and 120 million pounds of shrimp per year, and that in a blind taste test consumers chose Louisiana oysters over all others 85 percent of the time.

New Orleans has a wealth of seafood restaurants and oyster houses: GW Fins, Drago's, Deanie's, Red Fish Grill, Oceana, Pêche (my personal favorite), Acme (a tourist favorite, but not mine), Felix, and the incomparable oyster house Casamento's. But you can get decent seafood in every restaurant in New Orleans. Even our steakhouses, like Chophouse and Dickie Brennan's, have at least three seafood entrees.

Vietnamese

New Orleans has the best Vietnamese food in North America, period. Vietnamese chefs, restaurants, and groceries have operated here since 1976, after the arrival of the Vietnamese immigrant-exile population following the fall of Saigon. New Orleans is very much like Saigon in terms of weather, topography, as well as having some French history associations thrown in. Like most any American city, a certain group of immigrants came over, then their cousins and neighbors joined them, and suddenly, bam, Boston has a significant Irish population. New Jersey becomes equal parts Russian and Italian. Cleveland, where I grew up, is strongly Polish and Slovenian-Czech. When Vietnamese immigrants arrived, carrying family recipes, they set up shop in communities on the edges of New Orleans East and on the West Bank.

In 1976, To Hong Duc opened the first Vietnamese restaurant in the area, Hong-Lan. A year later, Hai Nguyen came from Saigon to open his restaurant in a suburban strip mall. He closed it 2 years later—not because he didn't have enough customers, but because he had too many. *The Times-Picayune* said of his experience: "The American Dream began to turn into a nightmare." Nguyen quickly grew weary of working 18-hour days to serve the long lines outside his front door.

If you cross the bridge out of New Orleans over to the West Bank, via a bridge commonly called the Crescent City Connection, you'll find Gretna and Terrytown, where many Vietnamese immigrants first settled. There are a number of outstanding Vietnamese restaurants in the area—Pho Bang, Kim Son, Hoa Hong 9 (or Nine Roses), and Tan Dinh, to name just a few. The best story comes from the eatery Pho Tau Bay, where American-born GI Karl Takacs fell in love with Vietnamese food during the war and then fell in love with Tuyet, the daughter of the owner of his favorite Saigon restaurant. He married Tuyet, learned cooking from her family, and now mans the kitchen at Pho Tau Bay. Dong Phuong Oriental Bakery, in New

Orleans East, is a restaurant, bakery, and caterer, and considered to be the makers of the best bahn mi (called Vietnamese po'boys) in the city. Dong Phuong's bakery supplies the baguette-style bread for nearly every Vietnamese restaurant in the area.

Since I wrote *Eat Dat*, Vietnamese restaurants have become much more of a presence on the East Bank, which includes the French Quarter and Garden District. Among my favorites are Ba Chi Canteen (7900 Maple St.), Nine Roses's new location in the French Quarter (620 Conti), plus the exceptional Vietnamese food from inside a quick take-out spot with cheap booze and lottery tickets, Eat Well (2700 Canal St.). My absolute favorite is Lilly's (1813 Magazine St.), where Trinh "Lilly" Vuong serves the best pho I've ever tasted.

Gumbo

We take gumbo very seriously here. At the back of my first book, *Eat Dat*, I crafted an appendix where experts like food historian and radio host Poppy Tooker, author and former director of The Southern Foodway Alliance Sara Roahen, noted food writer and restaurant critic Ian McNulty, and founder and director of The Southern Museum of Food & Beverage Liz Williams, among others, listed their opinions as to our Best Jazz Brunch, Best Fried Chicken, Best Po'boys, etc. When I asked these experts to name where to eat the Best Gumbo, most responded "My House."

More than just food experts, the entire breadth of New Orleanians take gumbo seriously. Disney discovered this when they posted "Tiana's Healthy Gumbo" on their *Princess & the Frog* Facebook page. Their version had no roux and added ingredients like quinoa and kale. Disney's nonsense was pulled after mere hours when they received comments like, "THIS RECIPE IS AN ABOMINATION. THIS IS NOT GUMBO. Really though, tomatoes, kale, and quinoa? Have you BEEN to Louisiana? I shouldn't be this offended but boy are my panties in a bunch," and "I've never seen a recipe before that actually made me mad. and this recipe right here makes me mad enough to wanna punch a baby . . . right in the face," and "No roux. Tomatoes? Kale? Seriously. Go home Disney, you're drunk." These are the nicer comments I could print without my book being banned in several library systems.

The basis of all gumbo, and most every New Orleans dish, is a roux. The phrase "First, you make a roux" has prefaced so many recipes in Louisiana cooking that it has become a cliché. Paul Prudhomme devotes four pages in his cookbook, *Louisiana Kitchen*, just to making a good roux and includes two full-color pages with photographs of the different stages of roux. Marcelle Bienvenu's decades-old classic book is titled *Who's Your Mama, Are You Catholic, and Can You Make a Roux?* Then there's a local joke: "Q: How does a Cajun make love? A: First they make a roux . . ."

Roux is the basic ingredient in not just gumbo, but in much of traditional

Cajun and Creole cooking. Making a roux seems to be the simplest thing in the world. One cookbook lays out the recipe very starkly: "Make a roux with equal parts oil and flour to desired color."

It's far from that simple. Do you choose vegetable oil, or lard, or butter? What color for your roux are you looking to achieve? The choices are white, blond, peanut butter, pecan, milk chocolate, fudge, bittersweet chocolate, mahogany, red black, noir. For many, the darker the roux, the nearer to the Holy Grail of the Black Roux. However, the closer you get to black, the closer you flirt with the disaster of burnt sludge.

Do you cook on the stovetop or in the oven? Do you stir constantly or consistently? High heat for a short amount of time or low heat for a long time? Family members have been cut out of wills over disagreements here. Making a roux in the microwave is (or should be) punishable by prison time.

Traditional roux was done by very slow cooking. Paul Prudhomme said his mother used to make a roux that cooked for several hours. Most contemporary cooks use higher heat and constant stirring in a shorter amount of time. A butter-based roux needs to be stirred at low to medium heat. Vegetable and peanut oil can withstand higher heat, so a good dark roux can be made in a shorter amount of time. All recipes will include the instructions, "Stir like hell!"

In addition to oil and flour, the recipe must include New Orleans' take on the Holy Trinity: onions, bell peppers, and celery. Then you can pretty much add anything. Gumbos are made with shrimp, crab claws, crawfish, oysters, chicken, duck, smoked sausage, or Andouille sausage, and Leah Chase is known for her vegetarian gumbo, Gumbo Z'Herbes, made with a variety of greens like spinach, collards, mustard, chard, turnips, cabbage, parsley, or scallions.

Pretending to know where gumbo originated is another opportunity to start a food fight. The original *Picayune's Creole Cook Book* (1900) claims, "Some sources say it [gumbo] derives from the Choctaw word 'kombo,' which means sassafras. Whatever the source, gumbo is based on the French soup Bouillabaisse." Lolis Elie has argued gumbo lacks any connection at all to the seafood soup of France. Gumbo does, he states, have much in common with the okra soups and stews that are commonly found in Western Africa. He adds, the word gumbo is derived from gombo, the word for okra in many Bantu languages, not Choctaw.

New Orleanians are passionate about our food. Don't mess with our recipes and never ever insult our cuisine. *GQ* food critic Alan Richman is now a man much and forever hated here. He came to New Orleans after Katrina and questioned what was worth restoring or rebuilding. Richman dismissed roux as pretty much just cornstarch and added that most of the residents are too drunk to care about what they're eating. The city struck back. Poppy Tooker said she wanted to toss the arrogant little turd into a back room with the Neville brothers. Food critic Brett Anderson wrote,

"Richman's story is a weakling's idea of what it means to be tough." New Yorker Anthony Bourdain became our top defender. He nominated Richman as "Douchebag of the Year" and later named one of the chapters in his book, *Medium Raw*, "Alan Richman is a Douchebag."

But no one got hit upside the head more than actress Kara Elders. In 2014, *The New York Times* ran a piece that included this quote by the C-level actress: "New Orleans is not cosmopolitan. There's no kale here."

This simple but stupid statement by the largely unknown actress (Kara is best known as the voice of Rita in *Flushed Away*—the Dutch version) launched immediate and passionate responses. By the end of the same day the kale article appeared, *The Times-Picayune* demanded a correction. By the next day, the blog site nola.eater.com had compiled a map showing the (many) places you could eat kale in New Orleans. Rouse's, the Louisiana-based grocery store chain, tweeted, "We actually offer many varieties of kale: organic, lacinato, red, green, baby, whole bunch, cut bags, and more." By the weekend, several restaurants were running "kalegate" specials and social media lit up with attacks on Kara using Instagram #kalegate and mean tweets @NOLAKale.

Jambalaya is kinfolk to gumbo and uses similar sausages, meats, seafood, vegetables, and seasonings. However, gumbo includes filé powder and okra, which are not common in jambalaya. After browning and sautéing the meat and vegetables, rice, seasonings, and broth are added and the entire dish is cooked together until the rice is done.

Étouffée is a third version of basically the same ingredients. A difference is that étouffée uses exclusively seafood and, rather than cooking with the rice, like a paella, here the mix is poured over the top of cooked rice at the end.

Po'boys

For visitors, po'boys are probably equal to gumbo in terms of must-try foods. The po'boy sandwich originated during the transit strike of 1929, when 1,800 unionized streetcar drivers and motormen left their jobs and protested in the streets.

Brothers Bennie and Clovis Martin were former streetcar operators who opened their hole-in-the-wall Martin Brothers' Coffee Stand and Restaurant in the French Market. They watched an extended and brutal strike. When the transit company attempted to run the cars using "strike breakers" from New York, jeering crowds stopped them. More than 10,000 New Orleanians gathered and watched strike supporters disable and burn the first car operated by a strike breaker.

The Martin brothers sided with their striking friends and former co-workers. They promised, "Our meal is free to any members of Division 194. We are with you till hell freezes, and when it does, we will furnish blankets to keep you warm." They are claimed to have said, "Get them poor boys some food," thus giving the New Orleans staple its name.

They also hooked up with local baker John Gendusa to create a new type of French bread with even ends, rather than rounded ones, measuring a huge 40 inches end to end. This innovation allowed for half-loaf sandwiches of 20 inches as well as the 15-inch standard, which would become one of the signatures of the New Orleans style po'boy.

At least that is the common and often retold story of the po'boy. There was an article written by James Karst that appeared as I wrote this book, titled "The Messy History of the Po'boy," that called into question many points in our accepted tale. There may be evidence that Benny and Clovis sold po'boys years before the strike. Another tale insists the po'boy was not named after striking rail workers but after the hard-pressed farmers of St. Bernard Parish, who gathered daily on the curb along North Peters Street with their produce in the back of a truck. Jazz great Sidney Bechet wrote in his autobiography about sending out a young Louis Armstrong and a drummer, Little Mack, in 1910 to get some beer and "those sandwiches, Poor Boys, they're called—a half a loaf of bread split open and stuffed with ham. We really had good times." In 1917, the Comus Soda Fountain on Common Street and St. Charles Avenue advertised an oyster sandwich for 10 cents. The exact wording of the ad touted the "four delicious fried oysters in a toasted, buttered French loaf with piece of pickle, wrapped in sanitary wax paper sealed bag, for 10 c." The ad also said, "We

Po'boy Disassembled

keep them hot and ready to take with you." Sounds an awful lot like po'boys to me. Maybe, we have to scale back the claim that Bennie and Clovis were the only ones who gave po'boys their name.

But here's the thing: Do you care more about the veracity of the history of po'boys, or how they taste?

In New Orleans today, if you ask a local, "Where's your favorite po'boy place?" you're likely to receive a response: "What do you mean? For roast beef po'boys, I go to R&O in Metairie. For shrimp it'd be Parkway, High Hat for oyster. Sammy's does a Southern fried chicken with grilled ham and Swiss cheese (basically chicken cordon bleu on French bread). And if not for the slew of health code violations, I'd definitely be in line for the slow-roasted duck po'boy at Crabby Jack's."

For me, my soul aligns with Guy's Po-boys (5259 Magazine St.). Guy's is basically one guy, Marvin Matherne, who bought the restaurant from the original guy, Guy Barcia, vowing not to change a thing. The fates have tested Marvin's oath, as the place has burned down twice, and most recently had a truck crash through the front window. No one was injured.

Just to show you how much love our community has for Guy's, after the crash, five competing po'boy places—Parkway Bakery, Tracey's, Parasol's, Killer PoBoys, and Ye Olde College Inn—threw a fundraiser and block party where patrons paid $15 to get a wristband that entitled them to taste sandwiches made by the five and get a bag of Zapp's chips and a soda. The Hot Club performed music. All proceeds went to help Marvin get back on his feet. Marvin is sort of the Brett Favre of po'boy makers. His boyish "love for the game" is overwhelmingly clear as he chats up his customers while lovingly making po'boys in the open kitchen. In some ways, Guy's Po-boys is quintessentially New Orleans. It's been repeatedly knocked down by disasters, but it always gets back up.

While I will forever love Guy's, my taste buds probably have to favor Killer PoBoys, which has two locations (219 Dauphine, nicknamed Big Killer, and 811 Conti, at the back of the Erin Rose Bar, or Little Killer). What both Killers have that the others don't is a bona fide chef. Cam Boudreaux worked the kitchens of two classic restaurants, The Delachaise and Arnaud's, before setting his sights on making the best po'boys on the planet.

As a chef, he knows how flavors work. His shrimp po'boy is Vietnamese-style seared shrimp stacked with pickled vegetables and Sriracha aioli. The Dark & Stormy is a pork belly marinated for 12 hours in Steen's Syrup, real ginger, and dark rum. It is, quite simply, spectacular. He offers a vegan option comprised of roasted sweet potato medley with black-eyed pea and pecan spread. Cam calls them "internationally inspired." He adds, "All the meat is all-natural, hormone- and antibiotic-free, and we've been adding as much fresh, local produce when we can." Rather than the Leidenheimer Baking Company French bread of nearly every other po'boy spot

Marvin Matherne   Ian McNulty

in the city, Killer PoBoys are served on rolls from Dong Phuong Bakery. And the best thing I've ever tasted there was not a po'boy at all, but the smokiest, porkiest-tasting, but nonetheless completely vegetarian smothered greens.

Muffuletta

New Orleans' other sandwich is the muff"U"letta, though it's sometimes pronounced muffa"O"letta or muff"A"letta. I used to think I was hearing or pronouncing it wrong, then realized there are just a bunch of local dialects and all are acceptable variations.

The name of the sandwich comes from the bread, known in Sicily as "muffuletta" (pronounced "muffuLETta"). Salvatore "Tommy" Tusa, proprietor of the Central Grocery, believes that the bread was named after a baker in Sicily. Central Grocery opened in 1906, and is considered the birthplace of "The Original Muffuletta," though Tusa's own mother remembers that as many as five or six Italian bakeries sold the sandwiches from carts in the French Quarter earlier than that. Tusa maintains, however, that his grandfather, Salvatore Lupo, Central Grocery's founder, was the first to sell the sandwich pre-assembled, saving the workers some time on their lunch hour.

The sandwich is a combination of cured meats (traditionally ham, pepperoni, mortadella, salami, and/or capicola) and cheeses (provolone, Swiss, and/or mozzarella), dressed with the ever-important olive salad with chopped garlic and carrots, and served on large round bread with sesame seeds. At most places, a half of a muffuletta is enough to feed two people.

The story goes that the muffuletta was the solution for when workers used to stroll down the French Market, grabbing bits of meat from Bavarian butchers, cheese from Italians, and bread from French bakers to shove together in a manageable and affordable lunch.

There are several slight variations and, of course, tempers flare as to what constitutes a "real" muffuletta. Central Grocery serves their sandwiches cold. In fact, I suspect they are made hours or even days before you stand in line to pick up their muffulettas, which are tucked inside saran wrap. Personally, Central Grocery's would not crack my Top Five Muffulettas in New Orleans. Two doors down Decatur Street is a better spot, Frank's. Their muffalettas are heated with a signature toasting method. Innovative chef Phillip Lopez, owner of New Orleans' Square Root restaurant, insists, "It is a cold-cut sandwich. It is meant to be served and eaten cold!" James Beard Award-winning chef Donald Link disagrees. "I like the cheese to be a tad melty, and I think heat brings out the flavor more in the meat because it renders the fat and brings out the juices."

Link's take, served at Cochon Butcher, I consider to be the best in the city. All of their meats are cured in-house, and the olive salad is also made on-site. I'm a near-equal fan of the muffuletta served heated in Napoleon House, if just for the pure pleasure of sitting inside the historic spot. Mandina's in Mid-City serves theirs on French bread, rather than the round muffuletta bread. Luizza also uses French bread, and coats it in garlic butter. Purists dismiss sandwiches that use French bread as "Frenchulettas," as in, not the real deal.

Hot sauce

Any arguments about muffulettas or gumbo pale in comparison to the spats that can break out over hot sauce. In New York, you cannot be both a Yankees fan and a Mets fan. It's not allowed. In North Carolina, you have to choose between UNC Tar Heels and the Duke Blue Devils. Here in New Orleans, you're either a Tabasco fan or Crystal's Hot Sauce fan. Most restaurants will have both bottles on the table next to the salt, pepper, and Sweet N' Low packets. They don't want to start a fight.

There are literally hundreds of hot sauce brands you can buy in New Orleans; CaJohn, Emeril's, Frank's, Scorned Woman, Cholula, Ring of Fire, Da Bomb, Chile Today-Hot Tamale, Louisiana Gold, Acid Rain, Ass in Hell, Bayou Love, Bayou Passion, Bayou Pecker, Crazy Bastard, Crazy Good, Mad Dog, Lucky Dog, Slap My Ass and Call Me Sally . . . and I could go on. But only Tabasco and Crystal have acquired superstar status.

Tabasco, created in the late 1860s by Edmund McIlhenny, may have been the first hot sauce ever. However, recently, word of one Colonel Maunsel White surfaced, whose "Concentrated Essence of Tobasco Pepper" supposedly predates McIlhenny by 4 years. Nasty rumors have circulated that Eddie McIlhenny borrowed, bought, or even stole the recipe from Colonel White. Tabasco created a Myths page on their website to dispel the rumors officially, though they're now curiously putting qualifying phrases in their copy like, "according to family tradition," seemingly just in case any of Col. White's heirs seek recompense.

Edmund McIlhenny, food lover and avid gardener, was given seeds of *Capsicum frutescens* peppers that had come from Mexico. He sowed the seeds in his home soil on Avery Island (about 2 hours from New Orleans). After the Civil War, the cuisine of New Orleans got briefly bland and monotonous, either because during Reconstruction, residents couldn't afford better ingredients or because of the stultifying influences of the Puritan Northerners (houses should be white, clothes should be black, food should avoid Satan's beckoning of flavor).

This was an ideal time for McIlhenny to introduce his flavor-enhancing spices. He made his sauce by crushing the reddest peppers from his plants, mixing them with Avery Island salt, aging this "mash" for 30 days in jars and barrels, then blending the mash with French white wine vinegar and aging the mixture for another 30 days.

Hot Sauce   TODD COLEMAN

He sold his strained concoction in discarded cologne bottles. In 1868, when he started to sell to the public, he ordered thousands of new cologne bottles from a New Orleans glassworks. He labeled the bottles "Tabasco," a word of Indian origin meaning "damp earth" and also a region in Southern Mexico. His new sauce became so popular that McIlhenny quit his job as a banker to devote his full time to making and marketing Tabasco Sauce. His first year, he sold 658 bottles at $1 apiece. Nearly 150 years later, the company ships 3.2 million gallons of hot sauce every year to 165 countries across the world. Tabasco labels are printed in twenty-two languages.

In 1923, Alvin and Mildred Baumer produced the first bottle of Crystal Hot Sauce at their plant on Tchoupitoulas Street. For many, including me, it is the superior sauce. Crystal sells to only seventy-five countries, but their 3 million gallons shipped each year come close to Tabasco's 3.2 million. You can buy Crystal Hot Sauce in 7-gram packets (fast-food ketchup-sized), or 6-ounce, 12-ounce, or 32-ounce bottles. For people serious about their hot sauce, you can also buy gallon jugs.

"We believe we sell flavor and not heat," said Al Baumer, Jr., son of the creators and current company CEO. Crystal's SHU (Scoville Heat Units) is not revealed by the company, while Tabasco's standard sauce is pegged at 2,500, with their kicked-up varieties reaching as high as 5,000 SHUs. The SHU measurement was the creation of pharmacist Wilbur Scoville, who devised a method of calibrating the amount of capsaicin, the chemical compound that stimulates chemoreceptor nerve endings in the skin, particularly the tongue, that is present in a dry unit of mass. In other words, he figured out how to say just how hot shit is. There are many brands that run hotter, a lot hotter, than Tabasco's 5,000 SHU. Endorphin Rush Beyond Hot Sauce is 33,390; Dave's Gourmet "Insanity Sauce" is 95,000; DaBomb is 119,000; and then there's the just-silly Mad Dog (3,000,000), Magma (4,000,000), and Blair's 16 Million Reserve, the hottest hot sauce on the planet. Blair's 16 Million Reserve is an extremely collectable sauce, with only 999 bottles ever made and discontinued after 2006. We wonder if they stopped because the thousandth bottle would ruin the "on the wall" song or because of hot sauce-related deaths. The SHU of Blair's is 16,000,000, naturally. These sauces aren't about flavor. They're about drunk college boys on a dare.

In hot sauce competitions, Tabasco won the Huffington Post's Hot Sauce Death Match. Crystal didn't make it out of the first round. But then *Cook's Illustrated* rated Tabasco dead last. Their tasters described it as "flavorless," "vinegary," "out of balance"—even "vile." You're just going to have to jump in, taste each for yourself, choose your personal winner, and then get ready to rumble.

Beignets

Perhaps our least exotic signature food has, for reasons I'll never understand, catapulted to become New Orleans' #1 food attraction. At Cafe Du Monde, the lines are painfully long to eat the one and only thing they serve: beignets. Hint: The Cafe is open 24 hours. The best time to go is 3:00 a.m. when there's no line.

A beignet is nothing more than a deep-fried square of dough, cooked very quickly at intense heat (Cafe Du Monde uses cottonseed oil, which can reach much higher temperatures—420 degrees—than vegetable or peanut oil) and then covered in powdered sugar. Hint: Unless you have a first-rate deep fryer at home, don't buy a souvenir box of beignet mix. Otherwise, you'll just end up with ill-shaped hunks of goo.

The other thing to note is to eat them while they're hot. Do not bring a bag back to your hotel room. Do not buy a bag on your way back to the airport to bring home for the kids. Once your feet hit the pavement on Decatur Street outside Cafe Du Monde, they're barely edible.

Quite frankly, beignets are nothing more than New Orleans' take on funnel cakes from up North or sopapillas from the Southwest. Cafe Du Monde is far and away the most popular place to wolf down three to a plate. They've been serving them since 1862. However, beignet cafes on Royal Street and Bourbon Street are practically the same, as are the ones served on the breakfast menu at the Hilton Riverside hotel, or, my personal favorite, Morning Call in City Park, which is also open 24 hours. I prefer Morning Call simply because they have powdered sugar shakers on the tables. You get to choose how much to use dusting your fried bread, rather than being presented with beignets covered in the small mountains of powdered sugar as in all other locations.

To accompany your beignets, Cafe Du Monde serves chicory coffee. The coffee is served Black or Au Lait, the latter meaning that it is mixed half and half with hot milk.

Coffee first came to North America by way of New Orleans back in the mid-1700s. The city remains the #1 American importer of coffee, bananas, and chocolate.

The taste for coffee with chicory developed with the French during the Revolution (1789–1799). Coffee was scarce during the war, so they were forced to use chicory as a coffee extender. Chicory is the root of the endive plant, a type of lettuce. The plant is roasted and ground, then added to the coffee. Chicory coffee became the New Orleans norm during our own Civil War (1861–1865). What better way for the Yankees to try to bring the South to its knees than by cutting off their supply of coffee?

The Cafe Du Monde website states chicory softens "the bitter edge of the dark roasted coffee. It adds an almost chocolate flavor." Quite frankly, to most, it actually *adds* a bitter edge. But, once used to it, chicory coffee becomes ambrosia. It is how we want our coffee served.

Sno balls

New Orleans sno balls are a different food group. Sno ball stands and shops are as ubiquitous in New Orleans as nail salons everywhere else. Places like Plum Street Snowballs and Pandora's have their intensely loyal fans. But, as far as iconic spots, there really is only one, Hansen's Sno Bliz. First opened in 1939, Hansen's is now run by the founder's granddaughter Ashley (profiled in this chapter). They received the

King Cake

2014 James Beard Award as an American Classic, joining other iconic food stops like Peter Luger Steakhouse in New York and Primanti Brothers in Pittsburgh.

King Cake

King Cake is meant to be eaten during Carnival Season, what you call Mardi Gras. It is not meant to be eaten any other time of the year. So if you storm out of Gambino's, Randazzo's, or Haydel's Bakery because they don't have king cake in June or July, please know that to us you just came off looking as ridiculous as if you were outraged by a store not having snorkels and sunscreen in December.

Each king cake has a tiny baby inside (generally plastic, but it's possible the baby might be made of porcelain or even gold). Or, I should write each cake used to have a baby inside. Lawyers have seen to it that modern king cakes have a baby packed separately next to, but not in, the cake. You can insert the baby at your own litigious risk. The tradition of King Cake Parties has evolved over time, but generally the "lucky" person who receives the slice of cake with the baby inside is expected to continue the festivities by having the next King Cake party, or at least purchasing the next cake.

Originally, king cakes were a simple ring of dough with a small amount of decoration. Today's king cakes are much more elaborately decorated with a variety of toppings, but still almost always feature the traditional Mardi Gras colors of purple, green, and gold. Inside the cake, fillings now range from the traditional cream cheese filling to mascarpone cheese, salted caramel, pecans and caramello, chocolate ganache, blueberries and other fruit, plus uniquely individual versions like Aunt Sally's Croissant Almond Queen Cake and Cochon Butcher's obscene Elvis King Cake. The Elvis, like the King of Rock 'n' Roll's favorite sandwich, has marshmallows, peanut butter, bananas, and bacon. Rather than the traditional baby, the Elvis comes with a plastic pig.

Doberge cake

Doberge cake is a New Orleans food every bit as indigenous as po'boys or jambalaya, just not as well-known. I have never once been asked, "Where can you get the best Doberge?" or "Where do the locals go for Doberge?" It's six or more thin layers of cake alternating with custard or pudding, and covered with buttercream or a fondant shell. The flavors are most often chocolate, caramel, or lemon. The New Orleans Doberge is a variation of the Austrian/Hungarian Dobos cake. Beulah Lechner originated Doberge in her bakery shop, which opened in 1933. Joe Gambino bought the name, recipe, and retail shop in 1946.

Pralines

You need to know, and I'll tell you more than once: here it's pronounced PRAH-leenz not PRAY-leenz. We'll humor you if you call our streetcars "trolley cars" or if you butcher the pronunciation of Tchoupitoulas Street. But say PRAY-leenz and you might just as well have said you like Nashville's music better than ours, or that you're an Atlanta Falcons fan.

The praline originated in France. There, it was an almond dusted in sugar. It was consumed to cleanse the palate between courses. In New Orleans, there were no almonds, so pecans took their place. There's a saying in New Orleans: *anything worth doing is worth overdoing*. So rather than a dusting of sugar, we use heaps of brown sugar with butter and butter and butter to make a caramel-colored patty that's so outrageously sweet, it'll make your teeth hurt.

There are hundreds of places to buy pralines all over town. The best-known are Aunt Sally's, Southern Candymakers, Laura's, Leah's, Loretta's, and Magnolia Praline Company, but every grocery store, drugstore, gas station, and your hotel gift shop probably has them as well. Aunt Sally's is the most popular because they're a block from Cafe Du Monde and make their pralines on a hot stove right in front of you. Southern Candymakers wins the most awards and was ridiculously voted the

Tyrone "Big Chief Pie" Stevenson

third-best "restaurant" in New Orleans on Yelp back when I wrote my earlier book about our food. I mean, they're good, but better than Bayona, Commander's Palace, Galatoire's, Cochon, Shaya, and the other 1,400 restaurants? I personally only look at Yelp and Trip Advisor to see if anyone's written good or bad things about me, never to take their advice.

The differences between all these praline palaces are paper-thin. I'd never be able to tell the difference in a blindfolded taste test. I am, nonetheless, partial to Leah's (714 St. Louis) because it has better stories and history. Originally named Cook's Confections after its owner Cecil Cook, the shop opened in 1933. In 1944, Cook sold his praline company to Leah Johnson, and it became known as Leah's Southern Confections, and eventually, Leah's Pralines. Leah's niece, Elna Stokes, is the present-day owner, and she runs the shop with her daughter Suzie. Every time I have been inside Leah's Pralines, Suzie has been told by at least by two customers how beautiful her eyes are.

Leah's Pralines is the oldest continually operating family-owned praline shop in New Orleans. They haven't changed the recipes nor the cooking methods in over 70 years. Inside the shop, there's an old photo of Leah, a former fashion model, draped elegantly across the old stairs that still stand in front of you. I've heard there are other photos of Leah, in all her elegance, presiding over the front of the shop in haute couture.

Old brass cooking kettles are still used in the back. The shop has two ancient W. M. Crane & Company Vulcan Candy stoves, an original marble slab-topped tables, two (now antique) chairs, one Howe platform scale, a Toledo Computing Scale, a Hobart Candy Mixer, and a more recent treasure, a photograph of chef Tyrone Stevenson by the front door.

He is pictured in his lavish Mardi Gras Indian costume as his alter-ego, Big Chief Pie of the Monogram Hunters. Tyrone, a.k.a. Big Chief Pie, joined Leah's Praline's as the company's candymaker back in 2007. "He's become as much a part of this place as the candy he makes," says Elna Stokes.

Snack foods

Every city or region has its distinctive snack foods, often ambrosia for those who grew up eating it and nearly inedible for those who didn't. These include fried cheese curds in Wisconsin, Halfpops in Washington, Berger Cookies in Baltimore. Where I grew up, it was Win Schuler's cheese spread and Vernors ginger ale.

Here in New Orleans, even our snack foods come with full-blown stories.

Barq's

Edward Charles Edmond Barq was born in the French Quarter in 1871. His father died when Ed was 2 years old, an event that sent the family to Nice, France. There, Ed learned the art of creating chemical flavors from masters in Paris and Bordeaux. Later, to avoid being drafted into the French military, Ed returned to New Orleans with his brother, Gaston. In 1890, they opened Barq's Brothers Bottling Company in the French Quarter. The brothers bottled carbonated water with various flavors. The most popular, initially, was their orange-flavored soda, called Orangine, which won the Gold Medal at the 1893 World's Fair in Chicago. Their sodas had more carbonation and less sugar than the other early sodas like Vernors (America's first soft drink) and Coca-Cola (the company that likes to think it was the first), and, unlike the others, they had caffeine.

When they created what was to become their signature flavor, they were forbidden from calling it "root beer" because the Hires Company sued Barq's, claiming that they owned the rights to the words "root beer" exclusively. The inability to use the phrase "root beer" pushed the Barq boys to create their bare-to-the-bones, but delightful, slogan, "Drink Barq's. It's good." The company did eventfully win the right to call their drink what it was, but then almost immediately dropped any root beer references in 1938 when the federal government banned caffeine in root beer. Rather than remove caffeine, Ed Barq simply changed the name of his drink from Barq's Root Beer to just Barq's.

Believing his soda was good enough to sell itself, Barq's always had tiny advertising budgets. The beloved slogan, "Drink Barq's. It's Good," was emblazoned on clocks and the frames of chalkboards (where daily lunch specials were handwritten) given away to restaurants. The logo was also etched on pencils and rulers handed out to schoolchildren.

Then the inevitable happened in the merger-happy 1990s: Barq's was acquired by Coca-Cola. Almost immediately, committees of business-casual pencil pushers met in their Atlanta-based glass-walled offices to market-test and PowerPoint the wonderful "Drink Barq's. It's Good" slogan out of existence. After intensive planning meetings, undoubtedly some with "out of the box blue sky splitballing," they now use the even more banal "Barq's has bite!"

However, Barq's executed a clever contract by which Coca-Cola obtained the rights to market and bottle Barq's, but not to make the syrup. By contract, Coca-Cola has to purchase the syrup for the root beer from New Orleans. Also according to the contract, all bottles sold in Louisiana have a different logo, imprinted with "Copyright Barq's, Inc." And all the bottles sold here are not stamped "Barq's has bite!" but instead stamped with the original slogan, "Drink Barq's. It's Good!"

Zapp's

Ron Zappe graduated from Texas A&M University with a degree in industrial engineering and became a distributor of pumps and other oil-field equipment. But his four companies went bankrupt during the 1980s oil bust. As Zappe was sitting around, trying to figure out what came next, his wife came home from the grocery store with a bag of kettle chips. He'd never before tasted the thicker, sturdier, caramelized flavor of kettle chips and fell so immediately in love that he chose to dedicate the rest of his professional life to making them.

The banks did not share his enthusiasm. The first ten lenders he approached "all laughed me out of the office," Zappe recounted. "The eleventh finally gave me my start. I never gave up. That's the secret."

Zappe bought the former Faucheux Chevrolet dealership in Gramercy, just outside New Orleans, where he began making his own thicker-cut, kettle-fried potato chip cooked in peanut oil. Appearing on Oprah, he retold Zapp's Chips' inauspicious beginnings: "We made chips on the showroom floor and teenagers would park outside, watch us like a movie, and do a lot of kissing."

Zappe's first creation, the Spicy Cajun Crawtator, was introduced in 1985 as the nation's first spicy Cajun chip. They now sell a huge variety of flavors such as Voodoo,

Sour Cream and Creole Onion, and Cajun Dill Gator-tators, Hot N' Hotter Jalapeño, Salt & Vinegar, Mesquite BBQ, Baby Back Rib, Sweet Pimento Cream Cheese and the most recently introduced Drago's Charbroiled Oyster, one I have not yet had the nerve to try. They have also marketed limited-edition chips such as Mardi Gras, Who Dat (in honor of the Saints), and Tiger Tators (Crawtators packaged in an LSU-designed bag). Some other flavors didn't catch on. "We did a Key Lime flavor. That was one of our most limited editions," Zappe said. Twice they've tried pizza flavors that just didn't take.

One of the chips' slogans was, "It'll make ya want to kiss your horse . . . or spouse . . . or both." Not sure what that means exactly, but I get the spirit of the comment, so Tru Dat.

Hubig's

September 9, 2016 was a red-letter day in New Orleans, when all non-diabetic residents let out a huge, "Thank you, Jesus!" Haydel's launched their own version of Hubig's pies. Hubig's pies had been more than a snack food—more like a daily sacrament. They'd been deep-frying handheld pies in New Orleans since 1922, when Simon Hubig opened his bakery in a small Bywater warehouse.

An average of 25,000 Hubig's pies were baked every day, offered in their top-selling year-round flavors of apple or lemon, along with peach, pineapple, chocolate, and coconut, and seasonal flavors such as blueberry, strawberry, sweet potato, and banana.

(Louisiana does, by the way, lead the nation in diabetes. Not exactly shocking considering how we eat.)

Each small pie, which looks like an empanada, was individually wrapped in a glycerin pack, hand-stamped with a label identifying the flavor and also featuring Hubig's rotund chef mascot, Savory Simon.

The pies were endcapped and counter-packed everywhere: gas stations, convenience stores, grocery stores, hardware store check-outs. If you were arrested in New Orleans, you'd even get a Hubig's with your state-issued bologna sandwich. The Orleans Parish Jail was their #1 customer.

Then on July 27, 2012, the inconceivable happened. A lard-fueled fire broke out in the bakery, leaving it completely destroyed. The early rumors reassured the public that Hubig's would quickly be rebuilt and return to making and shipping pies. However, as weeks turned into years, the two owners could only seem to agree on suing the company that maintained their fire suppression system, and argued about everything else. Letters to the editor and personal ads showed an increasing sense of loss, in some cases near-panic, as it appeared that Hubig's may never come back.

LUMINS OF NEW ORLEANS:
Ashley Hansen Springgate

There is no one more representative of New Orleans than Ashley Hansen Springgate. Her heritage combines food, plus tradition, plus a natural *joie de vivre*. She is the third-generation owner of Hansen's Sno-Bliz (4801 Tchoupitoulas St.).

Hansen's Sno-Bliz is (for me and many, many others) one of the most sacred spots in New Orleans. Each year since Ernest and Mary Hansen first opened the doors in 1939, they repaint the number of years they've been in business on the side of the building. Hansen's has reached deep into its 70s throughout three generations.

Ashley Hansen began working at her grandparents' shop when she was 15 years old. Her twin sister would go to leadership camps each summer, but the painfully shy Ashley would hang out with her grandparents, learning their trade along with life lessons. Ashley says it was her grandmother who taught her how to overcome her shyness. "She would stick me at the counter and I would just smile," Ashley recalls. "She would tell me 'Just say what I say and you'll be OK.' She could talk to anyone. To this day, I still channel her."

2005 was a horrible year for Ashley. Her mother died in March, then her dog died, then the family lost both houses in the hurricane. Nine days after Katrina, her grandmother Mary passed away at the age of 95. Her grandfather Ernest lasted only 6 more months without her. In life, her grandparents were inseparable. After working right next to each other all day, they still wouldn't go for an evening walk or to the local K&B grocery without each other.

Like so many in this city hit by hurricanes, floods, and oil spills, Ashley responded to her setbacks by getting back up, shoving a figurative chiclet where a tooth used to be, and got on with it.

She re-opened her grandparents' shop and has been running the stand ever since. That means mopping the floor every day, creating or tending to their thirty-seven flavors of homemade syrups every morning (most of the flavors are still based on recipes created by Mary), serving customers from 1:00 to 7:00 p.m. every day except Monday, and counting the cash drawer each evening.

Each day, she is surrounded by history in the form of yellowed newspaper clippings, old Polaroids of customers who now bring their kids or grandkids there, and the renowned ice-shaving machine, custom-built by Ernest in 1934 and which has a full patent from the U.S. government.

Ernest, a machinist by trade and absent-minded-professor-like tinkerer, built the machine just for family use. It creates a fluffy ice cloud that no other sno ball stand can match. Mary started dragging the ice-shaving apparatus to the street, where she'd sell flavored syrups for two cents. Their home-made gourmet syrups are both richer and more complex than the jarringly sweet store-bought flavors of most other stands. I call them the nectar of the gods. For me, their best flavor is the limeade with ginger, topped with sweetened condensed milk . . . but I also really like root beer with can cream, or what they call the Brown Pelican . . . and I am nuts for satsuma orange with vanilla bean . . . and . . . heck, I like 'em all. My daughter is strictly a wild cherry girl, the wilder the better. Ashley's current

favorite is the ginger-cayenne. Her 4-year-old likes blueberry and cardamom. Clearly, you're going to have to come more than once.

When you go to Hansen's (not *if*) you have to be prepared to stand in line. Whether there are thirty people waiting to be served or just three, you'll probably be standing a good 30 to 40 minutes. And that's kind of the point. Hansen's motto, posted on their website and ancient interior signs, states, "There are no shortcuts to quality!"

In addition to the best sno balls on the planet, the no shortcut motto also refers to the quality conversations and the sharing of baby pictures you're likely to experience while waiting in line.

In 2014, Hansen's Sno-Bliz received the food industry's highest honor: the James Beard Foundation Award designating them an "American Classic." Even this highest of praise didn't change things much; after a quick trip to New York to receive the award, Ashley was right back behind the counter. "This is so much fun, I don't really consider it a real job," she says.

Food writers like Ian McNulty jumped in as first responders with articles like, "Craving a Hubig's Pie? These Alternatives Might Interest You." Readers were directed to try Bud's Broiler, a local burger chain, which sold hot fried pies in apple, peach, and cherry flavors. Award-winning chef Donald Link had "pocket pies," but with a tangy sour cream dough and a dash of moonshine in his sugar glaze. Treo's chef, James Cullen, created a fried apple pie, imbued with a subtle hint of cayenne and finished with vanilla-flecked crème anglaise and fresh mint. But please—when you crave something like a Moon Pie or a Twinkie, anything with a dash, a subtle hint, or flecked crème anglaise just won't do.

Haydel's Bakery finally threw us a lifeline with their debut of New Orleans Hand Pies. They are similar in size and shape to Hubig's. They are glazed and bagged individually, just like the old Hubig's. The only difference is that the new pies are baked rather than deep-fried. Hayden's launched with four flavors—apple, lemon, chocolate, and cherry—and sells its pies in Fleurty-Girl shops as well as their bakeries.

Something . . . stranger

Other New Orleans snack foods are probably best left to the locals. While I have never seen anyone chewing and sucking on raw sugar cane, apparently just a few decades ago, it was commonplace. Sugarcane is actually something of a super-hero among plant foods. The juice has an abundance of vitamins and minerals. These nutrients add up to a supremely health-promoting food that has been studied for its role in fighting cancer, stabilizing blood sugar levels in diabetics, assisting in weight loss, reducing fevers, clearing the kidneys, preventing tooth decay, and a host of other health benefits. Seems like maybe we should bring this tradition back.

Even today, you'll see hand-painted signs all over town, pitching special prices on the far less healthy traditional treats like turkey necks and pig knuckles. I've heard of, but have never dared to try, a local treat where you get yourself some pig's lips and a bag of chips. Open the bag, toss in the lips, shake it all up, and you're ready for some fine eating. This is called living low on the hog.

This second, or emergency back-up chapter about Eating will highlight our restaurants and noted chefs—albeit a very limited number of our restaurants and noted chefs. At the time of Katrina, New Orleans had just over 800 restaurants. Today, there are over 1,400. The restaurant scene is absolutely exploding.

In *Eat Dat*, I profiled only 205 restaurants. The back cover of that book claims over 250, but they lied. You know how over-zealous those copywriters are. (I actually think I wrote the back cover copy.) Here, in a single chapter, I am forced to write about only 75 restaurants. I will focus on ones I consider our best, plus a few iconic spots like Mothers and Acme that I don't particularly like, but I know some readers would react with hysterics if I left them out.

We, of course, have many chefs in New Orleans. It is impossible to choose any one chef as best of the bunch.

Emeril Lagasse is probably our best-known nationwide, despite the fact that he is from Fall River, Massachusetts. His cuisine sort of straddles the line between Cajun and Creole (with a dash of Portuguese). Many members of the food mafia have never liked Emeril, finding his fame, big personality, and catch phrases (like "Kick it up a notch" and "BAM!") offensive. To understand what I mean by "food mafia," think of the imperious food critic Anton Ego in the cartoon *Ratatouille*. I recall a critic from *The New York Times* bashing the food that this critic tasted during the taping of his Food Network show, as though dishes thrown together in between commercials had any relationship with what you'd be served in Emeril's restaurants.

After working at a Portuguese bakery in his home town, Emeril developed his skills in Paris and Lyon, France. Then in 1982, Lagasse replaced Paul Prud-homme as executive chef of the famed New Orleans restaurant Commander's Pal-

ace. He opened his own first restaurant, Emeril's, in 1990. Located in New Orleans' underdeveloped Warehouse District, the menu fused elements of French, Spanish, Caribbean, Asian, and Lagasse's native Portuguese cuisine. He was instantly well-received by patrons and critics alike. Emeril's was named Best New Restaurant of the Year by *Esquire* magazine.

In ensuing years, he has been chosen as "Chef of the Year" by *GQ* magazine, "Best Southern Chef" by the James Beard Foundation, received the "Distinguished Service Award" from *Wine Spectator*, "Executive of the Year" from *Restaurants & Institutions* magazine, and was named one of *People* magazine's "25 Most Intriguing People of the Year." In 2013, Emeril was named the Humanitarian of the Year by the James Beard Foundation for his dedicated efforts to further the culinary arts in America, as well as his philanthropic work supporting children's educational programs through the Emeril Lagasse Foundation. He now has thirteen restaurants throughout America. Meril (424 Girod), named after his daughter, is the most recent, opened Fall 2016.

Emeril did take some unjustified hits in the local press when he kept his commitments to a book tour and did not rush back to New Orleans after Hurricane Katrina.

For a while, it seemed as though John Besh would replace Emeril as New Orleans' most honored hash slinger. Besh has a mini-empire of twelve acclaimed restaurants. His restaurant, August, was one of three nominated for the 2013 James Beard Award for Best Restaurant in America. Thanks to the clear New York bias of the judges, he was nudged out by Dan Barber's West Village restaurant, Blue Hill.

Unlike Emeril, John Besh did rush back to the city immediately after Katrina, and was seen in photographs posing like Washington crossing the Delaware, boldly riding boats through flooded streets like the ex-Marine he is, showing off his really good hair.

Probably the hottest chef in New Orleans right now is one who John Besh brought to New Orleans from Israel by way of Philadelphia to work in Besh's restaurant, Domenica. Alon Shaya won the 2015 James Beard Award as Best Chef: South and then went on to win Best New Restaurant in America for his own spot, Shaya.

While Shaya won the James Beard Award for Best New Restaurant in America 2015, Donald Link's Pêche won Best New Restaurant in America 2013. New Orleans wins a lot of James Beard Awards, and Donald Link takes home a lot of them—five and counting, at press time.

Over the years, Link has opened Herbsaint, a contemporary take on the French-American bistro; Cochon, a spot for true Cajun and Southern cooking; Cochon Butcher, a tribute to Old World butcher and charcuterie shops; Pêche Seafood Grill, the seafood restaurant I consider our absolute best; and Calcasieu, his private event facility.

Link was brought to New Orleans by master chef Susan Spicer to serve as her sous chef at Bayona. She partnered with Link to open Herbsaint in 2000 before he fully took the reins. While I may be starting an argument with some New Orleanians and risk complete dismissal from others, I consider Susan our resident genius. She has been inducted into the James Beard Foundation's Who's Who of Food & Beverage in America and was also inducted into the Culinary Hall of Fame. She is also rumored to be the model for the character of Chef Janette Desautel in the HBO series *Treme*.

While he has fewer national awards than the previously mentioned five chefs, I am a huge fan of the wildly creative and unconventional Chris DeBarr. Over the last 20 years, he has made a name for himself, introducing duck fat fries at The Delachaise, as well as pasta made from beets (that you'll swear is pasta) at Green Goddess. He's just returned to New Orleans after a 3-year hiatus.

A superstar chef you most likely don't know is Gerard Maras. He is our Yoda or Zen master. Many chefs you do know were influenced or trained by Maras. Like many top chefs in New Orleans, he passed through the kitchen in Commander's Palace before setting up the ongoing menus for new restaurants that became institutions—Mr. B's and Ralph's on the Park among them. Maras was an advocate for the freshest ingredients simply served decades before "farm to table" was a term, let alone a trend.

Today, he is semi-retired on his produce farm across the lake, but he does teach classes at the New Orleans Cooking Experience as well as private lessons, and does some catering for (really) special occasions.

It would require me to write an entire book, maybe a boxed set, to do justice to all the honored chefs of New Orleans. In addition to the aforementioned New Orleans chefs, the James Beard Award has also been bestowed upon Leah Chase, Willie Mae Seaton, Sue Zemanick, Ryan Prewitt, Tory McPhail, Stephen Stryjewski, Anne Kearney, Jamie Shannon, Justin Devillier, and Frank Brigtsen, I will refrain from writing like a raging Facebook post or Trump tweet about the deep injustice I feel that Austin Leslie never received the honor. As Calvin Trillin wrote of his fried chicken, "It tasted as if it were made from chickens that have spent their entire pampered lives strolling around the barnyard pecking contentedly at huge cloves of garlic."

One star chef many non-New Orleanians erroneously consider a New Orleanian is the late Justin Wilson, he of the red suspenders and the "I gawr-own-tee" catch phrase. Justin was born in Tangipahoa Parish, Louisiana and died in Pike County, Mississippi. He's a country boy, and was as much a comedian and Cajun storyteller as he was a cook. Folks who grew up in New Orleans cringe at the mere memory of his baked eggs made with creme de menthe, and would want me to make sure you were aware his recipes are no more New Orleans than Britney Spears (hailing from McComb, Mississippi) is New Orleans music.

Over the next pages, I'll organize about seventy-five of our noteworthy eateries by neighborhood.

French Quarter

Acme Oyster House 724 Iberville St.

Let's start with one eatery I consider our most over-hyped. It seems that everyone who visits New Orleans eats at Acme on their first visit. There's always a line. If it's too long, catty-cornered across the street is Felix Oyster House, two doors down is Bourbon House, and just around the corner is Red Fish Grill. All three have raw oyster bars and are better than Acme. They just need a better PR person or a neon sign to compete with Acme's "Waitress Available Sometimes."

Acme shucks and serves 10,000 raw oysters a day, every day. They encourage oyster gluttony with their fifteen-dozen challenge. If you eat fifteen dozen oysters in an hour, you don't get them free (as I think you should, like The Big Texan restaurant's 72-ounce steak in Amarillo), but you do get your name placed up on the wall.

There's nothing terribly wrong with Acme. It's simply that their checkered tablecloths, the canned chipperness of the servers, the fact that most everything is fried, fried, and fried, and that they'll serve you crawfish out of season (shipped in frozen from California), combine to makes the place feel like a New Orleans version of Applebee's or T.G.I. Friday's.

Antoine's 713 St. Louis St.

Antoine's is the oldest restaurant in America (owned by one family). Many of our oldest, biggest, longest claims come with a qualifying phrase, just as we claim Canal Street is the widest street in America. As you're about to argue, "But what about . . ." we'll chip in, "The widest street in America. Of course there are wider avenues and boulevards." Union Oyster House in Boston (1826) is the oldest restaurant—but it's had several owners.

A city block in size, Antoine's is a labyrinth of fourteen dining rooms, each with its own unique history. The Mystery Room got its name during Prohibition. Patrons would go through a door in the ladies' restroom to a secret place and return with a coffee cup filled with illegal booze. When asked where they'd gotten alcohol, the response was, "It's a mystery to me." The Japanese Room was designed with Oriental motifs. The red walls of the Rex Room are lined with memorabilia from notable past diners like General Patton, the Duke and Duchess of Windsor, President Roosevelt, Judy Garland, Pope John Paul II, and, lest we forget, Don Knotts.

It was actually founder Antoine Alciatore's son, Jules, who made the restaurant an institution. Jules served as apprentice under his mother for 6 years before she sent him to France, where he studied in the great kitchens of Paris. He had a talent for creating new dishes, such as his invented Oysters Rockefeller, Oysters Bienville, and Trout Marguery.

Arnaud's 813 Bienville St.

French wine salesman Arnaud Cazenave opened his restaurant in 1918. Like Antoine's, Arnaud's also has fourteen different dining rooms, but bests Antoine's in one respect by having six different menus: the A La Carte Dinner Menu, Sunday Brunch and Jazz Menu, French 75 Menu, Table d'Hote Menu, Dessert Menu, and Speakeasy menu. Arnaud's also has live jazz music and a Mardi Gras Museum that most closely resembles Liberace's closet.

In 1978, 60 years after opening, Arnaud's was acquired by Archie and Jane Casbarian. Casbarian sought to return Arnaud's to the roots from which it had strayed by both restoring the property and reinvigorating the cuisine. The restaurant is currently best known for its crab cakes, veal tournedos in mushroom sauce, and crawfish tails in brandy/lobster sauce.

As an added treat, you can buy a plaque placed above a table, marking it as your own, for only $10,000.

Bayona 430 Dauphine St.

Bayona is, without question, my favorite restaurant in the Quarter. Owner and chef Susan Spicer is pure genius. She and her restaurant have won about every award available. She's received the James Beard Award, the Mondavi Culinary Excellence Award, the Ivy Award, and was inducted into the Fine Dining Hall of Fame. In 2010, Spicer was also inducted into the James Beard Foundation's Who's Who of Food & Beverage in America, followed up by her 2012 induction into the Culinary Hall of Fame.

Bayona's cuisine is Northern African, Mediterranean, French, and sometimes Asian. She likes to experiment. Spicer may change the menu as often as twice a year because she wants to keep growing as a chef.

Even her dishes that sound terrible are delicious. My wife ordered and then tried to foist on me a nasty-sounding peanut butter and duck sandwich. After my lengthy protestation, I finally tried it and it was—fantastic. I then thought to myself, "Idiot! What's Thai food but chicken or duck with peanut sauce?"

In addition to the food, Bayona has the #1 best receptionist in New Orleans. Laurie Kaufman is an absolute delight and can hold court in conversations on just about anything. In a city filled with personalities, receptionists like Laurie or phone reservation attendants like Jimmy Boudreaux of Commander's Palace help to make your visit even more memorable.

Bourbon House 144 Bourbon St.

Located close to Canal, at the end of the first block of Bourbon Street, the huge floor-to-ceiling plate-glass windows look out on tourists dressed in questionable fashion with feather boas and Mardi Gras beads out of season. But you'll be dining a few blocks before the serious riffraff and perpetual smell of vomit on New Orleans' most infamous street.

Dickie Brennan opened his restaurant in 2002 and serves respectable versions of many Creole standards like seafood gumbo or barbecue shrimp, plus a few signature spins like the Plateaux de Fruits de Mer, a selection of shucked oysters, Gulf shrimp, assorted seasonal seafood salads, and marinated crab fingers. There's a large oyster bar, unfortunately framed by a huge plasma TV.

The restaurant is as much known for its extensive and impressive selection of small-batch and single-barrel bourbons as its food. The Frozen Bourbon Milk Punch should be as famous as the more popular Hurricanes, Grenades, and Huge Ass Beers found farther down the street.

Cafe du Monde 800 Decatur St.

Cafe Du Monde has been shoveling fresh hot beignets buried beneath enough powdered sugar to suffocate a cat since 1862. The 24-hour stand has become, I think inexplicably, the #1 food attraction in a city of over 1,400 restaurants, many of them serving meals you will remember fondly 3 months from now. Still, if you have to go, I recommend going at 3:00 a.m. No lines.

Central Grocery 923 Decatur St.

This is another place where, like Acme, there's always a line. I say that wherever you see a line in New Orleans, don't go. We can do better.

Salvatore Lupo, a Sicilian immigrant, opened the grocery store in 1906 and (it is said) famously invented the muffuletta to feed the Sicilian and Italian truck drivers driving produce to the French Market. The muffuletta is layers of Genoa salami, ham, mortadella (similar to baloney), provolone cheese, and olive salad with garlic and chunks of vegetables served on a large round bread studded with sesame seeds. Here and in other places serving muffulettas, you generally will be more than filled up by just half a sandwich.

Now, just because they were invented here doesn't mean Central Grocery's are the best muffulettas. The staff at Central Grocery is often less than welcoming. And for God's sake, don't snap a photograph inside their hallowed store or you'll be snapped at as though their sandwiches were in the Witness Protection Program.

Clover Grill 900 Bourbon St.

Company Burger on Freret Street has the best burgers in New Orleans. Camellia Grill may have the longer history and the more stylin' waiters. But Clover Grill, open 24 hours, is my favorite burger joint. Located on the other side of the Velvet Rope (that marks where the girls-gone-wild, frat-boy party section of Bourbon crosses over—literally—into the LGBT section), Clover Grill is as eccentric as the people who dine there. The late-late night is the best time to go for food and people watching. You can sit at one of their eleven (not ten or twelve) counter stools or try to slide into a jammed-in table with wobbly legs. You'll be greeted by a conversational, only slightly intrusive, often androgynous waiter or waitress wearing a "We love to fry and it shows" T-shirt. Your burgers will be fried under a hubcap to keep the grease in. There are a variety of clocks on the wall displaying the current time in distant lands like Baton Rouge and Chalmette (i.e., the same time as New Orleans). If you can pull it off, try to steal the menu on the way out. Clover Grill's menu is embedded with quips like, "We're here to serve you and make you feel better-looking than you really are," and "Have character, don't be one." They also serve a very good omelette first concocted "in a trailer park in Chalmette, Louisiana"—at least that's what the menu claims.

Coop's Place 1109 Decatur St.

Depending on your sensibility, Coop's Place is either cozy or cramped, hole-in-the-wall chic or Kitchen Nightmares shabby. It is an experience no matter what, as drunks sing along (poorly) to the jukebox with a chorus coming from the noisy video poker machines and balls banging away on the pool table. While it feels like a place serving day-old grilled cheese sandwiches, Coop's menu is surprisingly broad and even more surprisingly quite good. Many feel their jambalaya is the best in New Orleans. They also serve fried alligator bits that have actual flavor and are not merely something you'd eat on a dare. They do a decent redfish, a much more than decent duck quesadilla, and tasso that's smoked in-house.

The Court of Two Sisters 613 Royal St.

The restaurant was once the governor's mansion in 1732 and later the residence of Emma and Bertha Camors, for whom the restaurant is named. Royal Street bears the nickname Governor's Row because several governors, state Supreme Court justices, and one president, Zachary Taylor, have lived on the street. The "two sisters" never spent a day in the restaurant business. They owned a notions shop on this very spot and died there within 2 months of each other in 1944. They lie next to each other at St. Louis Cemetery No. 3. Their pictures are posted together on the walls of the restaurant. Joe Fein bought the historic location in the '60s and converted the space into a restaurant, but honored Bertha and Emma with the name.

The Court of Two Sisters offers respectable versions of Creole standards like Oysters Rockefeller, roast duck, and a bowl of gumbo. Their famous buffet has eighty items. But the draw is primarily the intensely photogenic old-world courtyard with original gaslights, flowing fountains, and the largest wisteria plant I have ever seen. It blooms in April if you're planning your trip around The Court of Two Sisters courtyard. There's also a strolling jazz trio 7 days a week.

Doris Metropolitan 620 Chartres St.

Doris Metropolitan is yet another tale of New Orleans' seduction. Restauranteurs Itai Ben Eli and Doris Reba Chia had successful ventures, first two Doris Butchers in Israel, then Doris Metropolitan restaurants in Costa Rica and California. Chia came to New Orleans simply as a vacationer to rest and take in the sights. By the fourth day here, he called Itai and said, "Get over here."

They were convinced New Orleans had the creativity and culinary chops to embrace the type of restaurant they wanted to execute and chose to open here rather than their planned new location in Miami. Doris Metropolitan's trademark steaks are dry aged a minimum of 21, and up to 31, days. But it's considerably different from Ruth's Chris, Chophouse, Dickie Brennan's, and other area steakhouses. In addition to the aged New York strip and ribeye, they offer Brazilian cut picanha and a slow-cooked whole beef rib known in Hebrew as *shpondra*. The appetizers are Mediterranean-inspired, with carpaccio, sweetbreads, a calamari salad with chickpeas and saffron potatoes arranged over an eggplant purée, and roasted "baladi" eggplant, dressed with pine nuts and tahini paste.

The front window displays cuts of raw meat as reverently as Tiffany's shows off fine diamond jewelry and watches.

Galatoire's 209 Bourbon St.

Galatoire's was founded in 1897 by French immigrant Jean Galatoire and moved to its current location on Bourbon Street in 1905. Five generations of descendants of Jean Galatoire owned the Creole restaurant until 2009, when they sold controlling interest to Todd Trosclair, who, in turn, sold his interest to New Orleans businessman and political candidate John Georges.

Galatoire's

There have been some other changes over the years that regulars have found quite disturbing, such as when they converted from shaved ice for their drinks to cubed, and when they removed the double set of French doors at the entrance that had previously served as a sort of decompression chamber between diners and the riffraff on Bourbon Street.

Inside, the feeling of tradition is embodied in the mirrored walls, tiled floor, slow-moving paddle fans, and white linens. Each table is set with its own glass water bottle, plus bottles of Tabasco and Worcestershire sauce, and bowls full of lemon wedges—specifically designed for fine-tuning a Bloody Mary. You'll be served by waiters in tuxedos, who were all male until recently.

The restaurant proudly took no reservations until Galatoire's created an upstairs dining room in 1999. You don't want reservations. You want to be downstairs with New Orleans aristocracy and waiters who have been working there since the Earth cooled. The waiters are as much a reason to dine at Galatoire's as the Trout Amandine. Veteran waiters here are not a luxury but a necessity in order to decipher, interpret, and advise you on the five-page menu that has well over 100 options. While the regulars know the difference between creamy Shrimp Maison and spicy Shrimp Rémoulade, they may need help choosing between Trout Marguery and Trout Meuniere.

For the street-level main dining room, patrons continue to stand in long lines on the sidewalk, often sweltering in their suits. Men must wear jackets. If you don't have one, there's a rack of ugly, high-polyester-content ones waiting for you.

Friday lunch is their signature, almost iconic, meal. Both Tennessee Williams and Truman Capote had their special tables where they sat for Friday lunch and drank their way into Friday dinner. Marian Patton Atkinson was a Friday lunch regular, usually joined by Mrs. Henri Viellere, known to her friends as Peachy. The ladies now have a bronze plaque, identifying "their" table.

If you stroll by Galatoire's at 8:00 a.m. on a Friday, you'll usually see college students and homeless people sitting on the sidewalk in front of the restaurant. They are being paid as place holders so that when the real diner shows up 4 hours later, they can walk right in. There are many tales of the famous and well-heeled, from Mick Jagger to U.S. senators, trying to jump the line and being turned back. When French leader Charles de Gaulle visited New Orleans, he was furious about standing in line at Galatoire's and so accosted the maître d': "Do you know who I am?" They replied, "Why, yes, Mr. President. But do you know where *you* are?"

Gumbo Shop 630 St. Peter St.

The Gumbo Shop serves seafood okra gumbo and chicken andouille gumbo every day of every year (and on some days, if you're lucky, duck and oyster gumbo) and has been doing so for more than a hundred years. Practice makes perfect. *New Orleans Magazine* chose the Gumbo Shop as the best place for gumbo multiple times, and the *Best of New Orleans* picked them as the best gumbo in 1999, 2000, 2001, 2002, 2003, 2004, 2005, 2006, 2007, 2008, and 2009, a winning streak to rival Red Auerbach's Boston Celtics. They serve much more than gumbo, offering covers of all the Top 40 hits: jambalaya, red beans and rice, shrimp creole, crawfish étouffée, and blackened fish. *Where* magazine chose Gumbo Shop for its Best (overall, not just gumbo) New Orleans Cuisine award.

GW Fins 808 Bienville St.

Zagat rated GW Fins as Best Seafood Restaurant in New Orleans. *Forbes* tagged GW Fins as one of the Top 10 Seafood Restaurants in all of America. *Esquire* magazine designated GW Fins one of America's Top 20 Best Restaurants, seafood or otherwise.

They print a new menu every day to take advantage the freshest fish they can find, whether it's local standards like oysters or redfish or the best, sometimes exotic, catch from around the world: lobster dumplings with fennel and tomato, Chilean sea bass braised in a hot and sour shrimp stock and served with sesame spinach, cashew- and peppercorn-crusted swordfish, king crab from Alaska, bluenose bass from New Zealand, or New Bedford sea scallops served with mushroom risotto and mushroom butter.

But here's the important thing: While the fish on your plate might be coming from New Zealand or Chile, most likely it was swimming yesterday.

K-Paul's Louisiana Kitchen 416 Chartres St.

Paul Prudhomme passed away in the Fall of 2015. He, more than anyone, put Cajun food on the culinary map. There are those that consider him right up there with Julia Child or Alice Waters as one of this country's most important chefs. His original idea was to do lunch only Monday through Friday, have fun, serve good food, and take a lot of vacations. Eleven best-selling books, three videos, 130 TV episodes, and a line of Magic Seasoning Blends sold in more than thirty countries later, it didn't turn out that way.

As I sat with Chef Paul one day in his test kitchen, he said that he regrets nothing. He is, after all, a millionaire. But, when he looks back, his perfect moment in time was back when he was still a "nobody" in a modestly sized restaurant. His wife Kay was still alive and blithely working the small front room, and Paul was in back cooking, tasting, and knowing that every dish sent out was perfect.

K-Paul's now seats over 200. It is best known for blackened fish—rum, yellowfin tuna, or redfish (the latter he made so popular, the fish nearly went extinct)—and also for other signature dishes like the blackened beef tenders with debris sauce, bronzed fish with hot fanny sauce, and sweet-potato pecan pie. A special treat at K-Paul's is their open-air kitchen where you can watch as your dinner is prepared.

Killer PoBoys 219 Dauphine St. and 811 Conti St., inside Erin Rose Bar

I used to feel the difference between the best po'boys and the also-rans was paper-thin. Parkway Bakery usually won "Best Of" competitions, many swear by Domilise's, I myself preferred Guy's. Cam Boudreaux has changed all that. A former chef in Delachaise and Arnaud's, Cam ventured out on his own to take po'boys to a higher level. As ballyhooed in the earlier Eating chapter, he has succeeded. Cam's detailed description of how they make just one of their po'boys underlines what his talent and passion bring to the table: "We marinate the pork bellies in the flavors of the Dark and Stormy rum cocktail, because rum, ginger, and pork sing so well together. Although, traditionally the cocktail is made with very dark rum, we use Old New Orleans Cajun Spice Rum mixed with Steen's Cane Syrup (another great product) and copious amounts of fresh ginger. The addition of the cane syrup gives that molasses aroma and body that is present in the cocktail, while the ginger creeps with a pleasant bite, balanced with the heady aroma of rum. After a rub of kosher salt and a massage of marinade, we let the bellies ride for at least 12 hours in the cooler, and then gently roast them, cool them, and eventually slice and glaze them with more of that killer sauce for each po'boy. Glazed, hot, and sticky, we dress the belly up with a squeeze of fresh lime, our mellow house aioli, and a crunchy and pleasantly sour lime cabbage slaw."

The same attention goes into everything they make. But beware their potato salad. It's great, but made with so much intense Zatarain's mustard that it will knock you back a step or two with the first bite. His smothered greens are quite simply and emphatically the best I've ever had.

Mr. B's Bistro 201 Royal St.

Mr. B's, a Brennan restaurant, has been recognized by *Food & Wine, Gourmet,* and other magazines for having the best barbecued shrimp and best gumbo ya-ya, as well as being the best business lunch spot of New Orleans. Internationally known Paul Prudhomme and local legend Gerard Maras helped open Mr. B's Bistro in 1979. The Brennans had a hunch that the public would support a laid-back alternative to their higher-end restaurants, Commander's Palace and Brennan's. Mr. B's is definitely not casual, however. It has the clubby feel of a place where business deals are made and legal documents signed. They are best known for their barbecued shrimp, which comes with garlic-enriched butter, a hot towel, and a bib to protect a businessman's tie. They also serve one of the better gumbos in town.

Muriel's 801 Chartres St.

Many French Quarter restaurants are haunted by tourists. Muriel's is haunted by Pierre Antoine Lepardi Jourdan. Pierre built his dream house, now used as Muriel's, and then crushingly lost it in 1814 when he wagered his home in a poker game. Before having to vacate the premises, he committed suicide on the second floor. The current waitstaff set a place for Pierre on the second floor every night. Pierre's ghost is said to move furniture around and now and again hurl glasses against the wall.

While this all might make Muriel's seem like a tourist trap for goth kids, it is actually a classic and sophisticated Creole restaurant with a wrenchingly beautiful view of Jackson Square from the second-story balcony. The interior rooms on both floors are opulently furnished with gold leaf or deep red walls. The Chart Room has a massive dark wooden bar.

More than the beautiful rooms and, yes, even more than Pierre, the food should be the #1 reason to go. Muriel's does classic Creole dishes, often with their own spin, like a sauteed redfish amandine with rich sweet-pea mashed potatoes or filet medallions drizzled with cabernet demi-glace and blue cheese wontons.

Napoleon House 500 Chartres St.

Where I'd be hard-pressed to name just one place to get the best gumbo, I have zero hesitation writing the best surroundings in which to eat it. The Napoleon House was the former home of Nicholas Girod, our third mayor. It was originally set aside for Napoleon Bonaparte to come live and basically rule as King of New Orleans, part of a local plot to rescue the French leader from exile in St. Helena. He never made it.

If you think Havana, Cuba, or Venice, Italy, are beautiful (as I do), Napoleon House is the most beautiful place to eat and drink in the city. Its sagging, cracked plaster walls, courtyard, and winding staircase make it the epitome of "faded splendor." The menu is an eccentric mix of comfort foods: panini focaccia, hummus tahini, tapenade and feta, a Reuben, and what many think is the best muffuletta in New Orleans.

Esquire magazine wrote that the Napoleon House might be the best bar in America. They are known for a cucumber-garnished Pimm's cup, a nineteenth-century gin-based drink. I cannot think of a better place to willfully waste a rain-soaked afternoon than knocking back Pimm's Cups and eating a little red beans and rice inside Napoleon House.

NOLA 534 St. Louis St.

Emeril Lagasse opened NOLA to serve as a casual alternative to Emeril's in the Warehouse District. Of his four New Orleans restaurants (Delmonico Steak House in the Garden District being the third), NOLA serves his boldest flavored dishes. As a transplant from Fall River, Massachusetts, Emeril has definitely embraced the New Orleans credo, "Anything worth doing is worth overdoing." Please know in writing that I do not mean your meal will be overcooked nor overly fussy and architectural. Dishes at NOLA have an abundance of (artfully) assembled flavors. Why have mere oysters when you can try his almond-crusted oysters with bacon brown sugar glaze, melted Brie, and rosemary fennel apple slaw? Why eat mere duck, when NOLA serves hickory-roasted duck with whiskey caramel glaze, buttermilk cornbread pudding, haricots verts, fire-roasted corn salad, natural jus, and candied pecans?

Palm Court 1204 Decatur St.

The exposed brick walls, bentwood chairs, ceiling fans, and old mirrored mahogany bar make you feel that you've stepped into a nineteenth-century New Orleans restaurant. But in fact, Nina Buck opened Palm Court in 1989. They serve crispy fried crawfish tails, Creole gumbo, and shrimp potato cakes as appetizers with red beans and rice, garlic chicken, Shrimp Ambrosia, Oysters Bordelaise, and crawfish pies as entrees. Their #1 draw has not been the food, though, but the variety of jazz musicians performing each night. The large band stage with an old Steinway piano is a splendid venue for the Crescent City Joymakers, Topsy Chapman and Lars Edegran, Thais Clark, Sam Butera and the Wildest, Juanita Brooks, and until recently, the irreplaceable Lionel Ferbos. Before he passed away in 2014, Lionel Ferbos performed each Saturday night. At 103 years old, Mister Lionel was the world's oldest working jazz musician. After his passing, the restaurant, almost as if giving me a sales pitch, told me, "We still have two 90-year-olds in the band."

The Pelican Club 312 Exchange Place

In 1990, owners Richard Hughes and his wife Jean Stinnett-Hughes transformed a neglected nineteenth-century French Quarter townhouse into an elegant three-dining-room restaurant with a large bar area. Each room has its own ambiance. There's the more traditional dining area decorated by antique prints and burnished Louisiana cypress, while another aims for a more contemporary feel with paintings by modern New Orleans artists and dramatic black-leather banquettes against cream-colored brick walls.

Their menu underscores Chef Phillip Lopez's claim that "New Orleans is over a thousand restaurants with one menu." But their barbecue shrimp, crab and corn bisque, baked oysters, crawfish étouffée, and crab and shrimp rémoulade over fried green tomatoes are so well prepared that The Pelican Club is, for me, definitely a Top 10 restaurant in the city.

R'evolution 777 Bienville St., inside The Royal Sonesta Hotel

R'evolution opened in the summer of 2012, a joint venture of award-winning chefs John Folse and Rick Tramonto. In Chef Folse's case, I feel I should add "legendary," he being the son of a Louisiana fur trapper who learned how to cook so he wouldn't have to work in the swamps, and now widely seen as Louisiana's longtime and leading ambassador for the region's cuisine. Since 1970, he's been a chef overseeing Lafitte's Landing, a destination rural restaurant and an institution as a training and testing kitchen. He's the author of a definitive and authoritative (and 50-pound) tome, *The Encyclopedia of Cajun & Creole Cuisine*. Chef Tramonto is likewise a prolific cookbook author and James Beard Award-winning chef, who came to New Orleans after already attaining star status in Chicago's restaurant scene with his two restaurants, Trio and Tru.

Before opening R'evolution, the two master chefs researched and delved into Louisiana history, exploring the region's culinary heritage. The corn and crab bisque and the crabmeat-stuffed frog legs, Chef Folse says, are inspired by the cuisine of Louisiana's Native Americans. Salumi platters are a tribute to the Italian kitchens. Beer-battered crab beignets presented with four rémoulade sauces and filled with velvety cream cheese from Folse's dairy are a refined riff on French beignets.

The pair also hired probably the best-educated staff in New Orleans. Chef de cuisine Chris Lusk has a degree in psychology from Stephen F. Austin University. Executive sous chef Erik Veney has a bachelor's degree in comparative religions from the University of Virginia. The result as a whole is a very imaginative reinterpretation of classic Cajun and Creole cuisine. In remarks at the ribbon-cutting ceremony, New Orleans mayor Mitch Landrieu called it the most important new restaurant to open here in the last 50 years.

Sylvain 625 Chartres St.

The small, intimate Sylvain is easily overlooked in a relatively quiet section of Chartres Street. Owner Sean McCusker, a transplanted New Yorker, and chef Alex Harrell, who's been cooking in New Orleans restaurants since 1998, created a place more "new" New Orleans fare than the neighboring old school Quarter restaurants. You will not find standards like barbecued shrimp or trout amandine—there's not even a gumbo. Sylvain does serve beef cheeks, pan-fried pork shoulder, and a brussels sprout and hazelnut salad. I'm probably a behind-the-scenes joke among the waitstaff because I order the same thing every time I go: Chicken Liver Crostini and Fried Eggplant and Burrata. My only complaint about Sylvain is that for a small, intimate restaurant, it is surprisingly loud. But that might make it the perfect place to take someone you don't want to listen to all night long. You can lean in, nod, and simply pretend to hear what they're saying while chowing down.

Tableau 616 St. Peter St.

Tableau is a new addition to the Brennan's empire. Dickie Brennan opened his three-story restaurant in 2013. "Opened" might be too passive a word for the loving way the restaurant came about and its attention to historic detail. "We're here for one reason," says Dickie. "I read in the paper one morning that Le Petit Theatre was canceling the season and going to close because of finances. We just couldn't lose the oldest community theatre in America." So he worked up a business plan to keep Le Petit open while taking on some of the building's space (and rent) to create a restaurant that would also serve to draw in theatergoers for before-the-play meals.

"We've pulled the original drawings for that building, and it had a full balcony, so we were able to add a full balcony back with Vieux Carré approval," Dickie says. A restored grand staircase spans three stories of the restaurant, connecting private dining rooms, the balcony dining area with a view of Jackson Square, and the courtyard seating.

The menu, developed by Chef Ben Thibodeaux, has likewise been intensely researched. Tableau offers courtbouillon, a traditional New Orleans seafood stew with Gulf fish, shrimp, oysters, and crabmeat in a rich broth served with popcorn rice. Thibodeaux discovered that 100 years ago, Leidenheimer baked a football-shaped sourdough bread, which the restaurant serves today. Other dishes do get contemporary updates. Tableau has a French onion soup, which is traditional, but adds new touches, cooking it with andouille and Abita Turbodog beer. They have a lineup of ten sauces made daily, including hollandaise, béarnaise, lemon-caper butter, meunière, New Orleans barbecue shrimp sauce, and amandine.

Tujague's 823 Decatur St.

Tujague's is the second-oldest continuously open restaurant in New Orleans (since 1856). Tujague's will admit "continuously" presents a problem, as they were once closed for 3 hours, "but it didn't work out." Their 140-year-old guestbook includes the signatures of Franklin D. Roosevelt and Ty Cobb. Brothers Steven and Stanford Latter bought the restaurant in 1982. Neither had any restaurant experience, nor had either even been inside Tujague's before the purchase. Sanford, who eventually sold his shares to Steven, saw the purchase as strictly an investment property. Steven envisioned a sort of Cheers for the French Quarter. He lined the rooms with memorabilia and historic photographs of old menus and previous owners from the original Guillaume and Marie Abadie Tujague to Clemence Castet. Miss Clemence ruled the dining room and the kitchen with an iron skillet and fist. Frustrated with her staff, she often brought food from her kitchen to the tables herself. Tujague's is best known for the beef brisket with Creole sauce and the Chicken Bon Femme, a classic New Orleans dish that is heavy with garlic and parsley. While they may not beat out Antoine's as the oldest restaurant, their long cypress stand-up bar is the oldest, not just in New Orleans, but all of America. Above the bar is the beautiful, massive mirror brought over in one piece by sailboat after having hung in a Parisian bar for 100 years.

Bywater and The Marigny

Arabella 2258 St. Claude Ave.

Owner Mowgli Pierlas says Arabella takes their food seriously, but not themselves. There is a playfulness to the decor (check out the bathrooms), a sincere goofiness to their titles (Mowgli calls himself the owner/dishwasher and that is literally what he does—in addition to making pasta) and to the names of the entrees, like Marco Pollo (a chicken dish), The Spaghettisburg Address, and the Lambotomy. But underneath the fun, Mowgli also serves the freshest (like rolled in front of you fresh) and best-tasting pasta in New Orleans. And you pay like $6 to $12, rather than the $30 to $40 you could pay for this quality elsewhere. Most of the menu is create-your-own, with such a huge variety of house sauces and ingredients, their website claims "you could eat here every day for the rest of your life and never have the same dish twice."

I ordered the Lambotomy for the title alone and then, of course, sampled from everyone's plate. The lamb, feta cheese, and fresh basil over roasted red pepper rigatoni with a spicy red pesto sauce had some serious heat, but it was also the best pasta dish I've had in New Orleans . . . ever.

Bacchanal 600 Poland Ave.

Friday lunch amongst the regulars at Galatoire's is one kind of distinctly New Orleans dining experience. An evening meal out back at Bacchanal, seated under string lights and tiki torches, listening to live music as the sun sets, is another. Bacchanal opened as a neighborhood wine shop in 2002. The front room is still a wine cellar, where you're greeted by exceptionally friendly hipster clerks, and where you pick up your beverage (wine, water, or carbonated fruit drink) and, if you want, one or more cheeses from the coolers. (You should want.) The exceptionally friendly hipster clerk will also take your cheese and give you a numbered stand to post on your table. (Don't worry, your cheese will be returned to you on a board with all sorts of accompaniments like olives, almonds, chutney, and toast slices.) After that, you leave the wine room and go out back to a window where other exceptionally friendly hipster clerks will give suggestions and take your food order. They give you another numbered stand to post at your increasingly crowded table. Most menu items are small plates like smoked trout salad with apple, manchego, and buttermilk vinaigrette ($8) or the too-good-to-be-true bacon-wrapped dates, chorizo, pequillo peppers, and roasted tomatoes ($8). Even the larger plates, like an exceptional pork chop served on a bed of arugula, white anchovies, parmigiano-reggiano, and balsamic vinegar is only $12. With orders placed and number stands in hand, you then pick out your table either out back or, on oppressively hot nights, upstairs by an indoor bar with air-conditioning.

There will be live music with lunch and dinner. Gypsy jazz groups are sort of standard. But on Monday nights, the incomparable Helen Gillet plays.

The "Bacchanal Experience" came about after Katrina. The wine store opened its backyard as a dining spot for a variety of chefs displaced from their own flood-damaged kitchens. Soon, it became an iconic Sunday night event. Now it has a permanent kitchen and its own chef, Joaquin Rodas, making it a classic contemporary bistro in a unique setting. On a clear, warm night, Bacchanal's backyard is the place to be in all of New Orleans.

Bao & Noodle 2700 Chartres St.

Doug Crowell, a former chef at Herbsaint, opened Bao & Noodle because he couldn't find the food he wanted in New Orleans. He married into a family from New York City's Chinatown and they taught him how to make their favorite dishes. Crowell doesn't claim he's making 100 percent authentic Chinese recipes—just the dishes his father-in-law taught him. It is absolutely nothing like any Chinese food I'd ever had in New York, San Francisco, or Guangzhou.

After New Orleans restaurant reviewer and gifted writer Ian McNulty kept praising Bao & Noodle in *The Advocate* and on the radio, I finally went there. Everything was fantastic. The beef soup, the lamb shank (which fell off the bone just by looking at it), dan dan with pork, bao with pork floss—everything. I'd never heard of the unfortunately named "pork floss" before. Turns out, what sounds like a painful dental appointment is pork so finely shredded that it melts in your mouth like a savory cotton candy.

The only kinda-sorta downsides are the bare bones decor, naked light bulbs, and amateur-hour cartoons sparsely placed and taped to the walls, plus the music. For our meal, our *entire* meal, P. J. Harvey yowled in the background. I used to be a P.J. Harvey fan, but "Down by the Water" doesn't hold up 20 years later much better than "Ina Gadda Da Vida."

The Country Club 634 Louisa St.

Housed in a historic Italianate cottage in the Bywater, The Country Club has been a neighborhood secret for over 35 years. Chef Maryjane Rosas has worked for Donald Link, but is largely self-taught with a fine intuitive understanding of how flavors work. You can have a wonderful small-plate meal of her house-made boudin balls or Canjiquinha Brazilian pork and corn grit stew, eaten in your choice of the parlor room with the grand hardwood walk-around bar or by the luscious green-backed cabana lounge and pool or on the breezy front veranda.

The Country Club used to be clothing optional, but the NOPD shut that down. They still offer a Sunday Drag Brunch, though.

Elizabeth's 601 Gallier St.

A *New York Times* review best summed up the appeal of this essential New Orleans joint: "The thing to love about Elizabeth's is that somebody there tried to make bacon better."

That somebody was Heidi Trull, another in the long history of expat Yats (people who pass through New Orleans, get seduced, and move here). Heidi is a Carolina girl, raised in Sumter, where New Orleans' only Civil War general, P. G. T. Beauregard, started the war. She received her culinary degree in Charleston and after finishing school, worked in fine restaurants in Savannah, just across the border. But on her first visit to New Orleans, after ravishing several of the city's great restaurants, she told her husband Joe, "I'm not leaving!" And she didn't. She and Joe took jobs with Emeril's NOLA restaurant, and then she went off to the Windsor Court Hotel. Joe stayed on as NOLA's dessert chef for 10 years. Finally in '98, Heidi opened her own restaurant, Elizabeth's, in the then-funky Bywater neighborhood where tourists never ventured. Bywater is still funky, but now tourists go primarily to eat at her restaurant. Elizabeth's has received rave reviews in publications like *Gourmet* and *Southern Living*.

Her motto was "Real Food Done Real Good," which still hangs on the rusted sign above Elizabeth's corner door at the intersection of Gallier and Chartres. The exterior is plastered with other hand-painted signs like a folk-art painting of a steaming cup of coffee saying, "Eat here or we both go hungry," or another sign with the inscription, "Eat . . . Relax." The interior walls are every bit as plastered with folk art, mostly the "Be Nice or Leave" paintings of Dr. Bob.

The artwork gives the place a roadhouse appeal, but it's the food that's been causing pilgrimages to Bywater by Uptowners and out-of-towners. Elizabeth's serves classic grits and grillades, fried chicken livers with pepper jelly, banana-enhanced sweet potato casserole, and the two signature items, calas and praline bacon. Calas is a traditional Creole dish: deep-fried, cinnamon-seasoned rice fritters, creamy on the inside and dusted with powdered sugar. They're kinda like beignets—only better. Elizabeth's is one of a few (maybe two) New Orleans restaurants still serving calas. But their signature item is the praline bacon—prepared by dragging bacon through chopped pecans and brown sugar with pork fat and then baking it. It's hell on the arteries, but heaven for the soul.

Heidi and Joe moved back to Carolina after the birth of their son. Elizabeth's has since gone through three sets of owners. The first two owners were wise enough to keep on Chef Bryon Peck. Then, in 2011, Chef Bryon Peck became owner Bryon Peck.

Franklin Restaurant And Lounge 2600 Dauphine St.

I sometimes complain about restaurants blaring ten-year-old hits like Beyoncé's *Single Ladies*. When I last ate at Franklin, the airwaves carried an even older hit, *Play That Funky Music White Boy*, performed by Wild Cherry in 1976. But, in my unjustifiable opinion, there is a date when a song crosses over from out-of-date to retro-cool. Franklin keeps their music at background level, and the song was integrated with Brian Eno-sounding ambiance music and other songs to create an eclectic but not ironic-hipster mix.

The entire experience at Franklin successfully straddles the line between cool and trying too hard to be cool. The interior is smartly broken up between high tables and low. A beautiful screened wall in a sort of Asian pattern breaks up the space so that you are practically sitting on top of the diners next to you, but it doesn't feel so. A large lamp, probably picked up at a yard sale, makes the front-most table feel homey. Small, glowing candles make most other tables feel intimate. There is a painting the size of an efficiency apartment that looks like Nicole Kidman drowning and yet miraculously doesn't scream for attention.

The menu is dominated by small plates that combine unique flavors, but again, with just enough restraint that they're not showing off. Judging by reviews and online comments, the avocado tempura with crabmeat seems to be their signature dish.

For our money, the avocado tempura was quite good, but didn't even crack the top three. The quail appetizer with a savory bread pudding was practically perfect. We loved the crab soup, served cold in a gazpacho with crostini, and when it came to the entree of duck with figs, julienne vegetables, and a sauce that was plate-lickable, we were tempted to climb up on the table and roll around on the dish.

Every Sunday, the Franklin hosts a sort of pop-up brunch from 11:00 a.m. to 2:00 p.m. with chef Baruch Rabasa of Atchafalaya and the short-lived Meson 923. His Chilango NOLA brunch serves Mexican dishes like bacon-wrapped pork loin in roasted corn, poblano relish, and hominy puree. We've not yet eaten the Sunday Brunch, and so therefore have not yet been tempted to roll in the poblano relish and hominy puree.

Kebab 2315 St. Claude Ave.

Benjamin Harlow and Walker Reisman became interested in doner kebab sandwiches while traveling Europe with a professional theater company. In most cases, kebabs are made with lamb (but sometimes veal, beef, or chicken) that has been slowly cooked on a turning rotisserie, marinated in its own juices, then cut vertically into very thin shavings and wrapped inside a flatbread and dressed with tomato, onion with sumac, pickled cucumber, and chili. You might consider it a Turkish po'boy. Anthony Bourdain called them "a throbbing missile of love."

Here, the variety of meats are combined with house-pickled cucumber, tzatziki and zhug, a cilantro-based Israeli hot sauce, and served in homemade bread (like the best bread ever). For vegetarians or anyone needing a meat time-out, they also serve hummus and falafel sandwiches.

We had one of about everything on the menu and the dark meat chicken doner kebab, the lamb gyro, and the falafel were all equally good in unique and differentiated ways. But the best thing we ate was, surprisingly, the fries. The Belgium fries, crafted with techniques learned in Germany, are drizzled with aioli and come with a small container of homemade (best-ever) ketchup.

The only downside was the artwork on the walls. A few decent pieces were overwhelmed by a lot of art you wouldn't hang on your fridge even if donated by homeless children in wheelchairs. Some of the space was recently and thankfully given over to the Mystic Krewe of the Silver Ball for a combination showroom and game room of their collection of pinball machines.

Pizza Delicious 617 Piety St.

When people used to ask where to get good pizza, I would most often answer in my snotty, ex-New Yorker refrain, "Chicago or New York." I'd tried all the local Reginelli's, Theo's, Rocky's, Slice, Naked Pizza, Louisiana Pizza Kitchen, Magazine Pizza, and Big Pie brands that at least one person or publication had tabbed "The Best" and none were better than "just OK." Pizza Delicious has changed all that. Transplanted New Yorkers Mike Friedman and Greg Augarten met at Tulane. Both had fallen in love with New Orleans but missed their native "real" pizza.

"We'd always be excited when a new pizza place would open, hoping that maybe it would be 'the one,' but it never really was, sadly. We were looking for love in all the wrong places," Friedman recalls. The two decided to do it themselves, even though neither knew anything about making pizza. Said Friedman, "We just decided to make pizza one night ourselves. It was our first time. We found a good dough recipe in a cookbook and gave it a try." They began experimenting with recipes in a community kitchen in Bywater. "While we weren't experts in making pizza, we were definitely experts in eating it."

A Kickstarter campaign allowed Pizza Delicious to grow from a one-night-a-week place, where they sold slices out of a window in a house, to a full-time, brick-and-mortar pizza parlor. The cast of HBO's *Treme*, mostly from New York and

Baltimore, held a blind taste-test pizza competition. Now, New Orleans finally has an answer to the question, "Where should I go for good pizza?"

Red's Chinese 3048 St. Claude Ave.

To serve as their street sign, Red's Chinese uses two-inch adhesive backed letters (black on gold) bought from an Office Max or Office Depot. More than easy to overlook, the sign is virtually impossible to see from the street. Even after being there more than once, I've driven straight past the restaurant and had to turn around. Look for the much more conspicuous signage on the second story market "GROCERIES–ICE–TAQUERIA–MEATS."

Once inside, Red's staff looks like a tattooed road crew filling in potholes on the interstate. Even dressed in all white, they still look like they've been ridden hard all day and put up wet. The decor is basic, not much more luxurious than a Subway or Popeye's. Then there's the handwritten chalkboard menu, so jammed with entrees and written in a style more often seen on prescription pads, such that you may start to wonder if Red's Chinese is really some mobster's money-laundering operation. Stay calm and order on. Ask for a printed menu.

You don't come for the ambiance (which frankly *does* appeal to me); you come for the food. The fare is as "authentic" to Chinese food as FOX News is fair and balanced. Owners and chefs Tobias Womack and his wife, Amy Mosberger, exuberantly ignore any traditional Chinese dishes. Womack learned cooking alongside James Beard Award-winning chef Danny Bowien of Mission Chinese restaurant in San Francisco. *The New York Times* said Bowien "does to Chinese food what Led Zeppelin did to the blues."

After becoming a weekly, then daily customer at Mission, Womack became staff and traveled cross country to work at the new Mission Chinese Food in New York City. He was later fired by Danny Bowien after a passionate fight about Sichuan peppercorns. They each take their food very seriously.

Tobias and Amy came to New Orleans and have established what is, in part, an homage to Bowien. The Kung Pao Pastrami, a signature dish at Mission, is a feature at Red's, but with a Louisiana twist by adding the local Holy Trinity of onions, bell peppers, and celery. Many items on the menu will mimic Bowien's impulse to use fresh ginger, scallions, peppercorns, and pickled anything, to add extra spice.

Red's is relatively inexpensive. A plate of Craw Rangoons, which replaces crab with local crawfish filled with cream cheese, horseradish, lemon, honey, and creole mustard, is only $8. The pig ear terrine is only $6. Mapo Dauphine, which is braised pork shoulder, silken tofu, black eyed peas, in Ma La broth and served over rice, or the Confetti Rice, which is filled with strips of either catfish or chicken, carrots, crunchy green beans, egg, and sweet Chinese sausage, are under $15.

St. Roch Market 2381 St. Claude Ave.

St. Roch Market is not a restaurant but a swank food court, 100 times (maybe 200) better than any you'll find in a mall or airport concourse. The market was originally built in 1875, but lay vacant and shuttered for the 10 years following Hurricane Katrina. The earlier St. Roch Market was where shoppers would come to pick up produce, seafood by the pound, and fresh eggs just laid by backyard chickens. This was the pre-grocery store era.

The revitalized market is open and airy. The original twenty-four steel columns supporting the 30-foot ceiling have been painted, along with the entire interior, with the brightest shade of white known to man or dentist. There are thirteen vendors lined up along the long sides, with tables for dining in center court. Among the vendors is Micah Martello, a New Orleans native who returned to be a part of the new market after he spent several years running the King Creole food truck in North Carolina. St. Roch's is the perfect fit for Micah, who has said, "I hate the restaurant business, but I love being a chef." His signature dish is the shrimp and grits, which won him the North Carolina Food Truck championship. King Creole also serves a decadent crawfish poutine, mixing crawfish with french fries, cheese curd, and a roast beef gravy, as well as crawfish ceviche with plantain.

Kayti Chung-Williams is one stall away, but far from a local. She was born and raised in Korea. She met her husband in Louisiana and her food business, Koreole, is a fusion of her food culture with his Creole one. You can order the Koreole fried chicken (with ginger), the bibimbap bowl (vegetables, choice of meat, a fried egg and sauce), or Japchalaya (Andouille sausage, vermicelli noodles, and vegetables).

Chef Tunde Wey's food stand, Lagos, serves his family's traditional Nigerian dishes like frijohn, which is fish with coconut in a red tomato and pepper sauce.

Kristopher Doll was brought to New Orleans by James Beard Award-honoree Donald Link to help open Cochon Butcher in 2007. He has gone on to create charcuterie programs for other area chefs. His St. Roch stall, Shank Charcuterie, is Doll's first space of his own.

There are two seafood stands. Brandon Blackwell and his wife Jen Sherrod-Blackwell run Elysian Seafood. He, a former sous chef at Upperline, and she, former manager of Martinique Bistro, sell fresh local seafood. Melissa Martin and Effie Michot serve raw oyster, pickled shrimp, smoked fish, and marinated crab claws at their stall, The Curious Oyster Company.

St. Roch Market has a produce booth and JuiceNOLA, which sells cold-pressed juices and salads made from items chosen from the produce booth. There's a home-style baker, the Sweet Spot, and the Coast Roast Coffee Company for cups of coffee or espresso. Befitting a New Orleans food market, Ali Mills' Mayhaw Bar sells cocktails, regional beers, and wines by the glass or bottle.

The market is not without controversy. Some have labeled it a "yuppie food court" and testament to unwanted gentrification. Six people in hoodies were caught on camera late one night spraypainting the outside walls and breaking windows. Others, like me, love it and went there three times in their first week.

If you're more like me, the market opens for coffee and pastries daily from 7:00 a.m. to 11:00 p.m. Vendors start serving at 9:00 a.m.

Treme

Dooky Chase 2301 Orleans Ave.

Until recently, owner and chef Leah Chase, now into her 90s, could always be seen going from table to table. She famously chastised President Obama when he visited her restaurant on the campaign trail. The president got a double barrel of "Oh no you don't!" from Miss Leah as he raised a bottle of hot sauce toward her gumbo. Don't mess with her recipes. Many consider her gumbo z'herbes, a meatless gumbo created for Catholics to observe Lent, to be the best gumbo in New Orleans. In a taste test performed by area restaurant critics and chefs, her fried chicken was chosen New Orleans' Best.

Leah Chase, a.k.a. the Queen of Creole, has been working the restaurant since 1957 (the restaurant's been there since '41). "I thought I was going to be the cute little hostess," she recalls, but was shoved back into the kitchen. Prior to working in the kitchen, Leah's training had consisted of managing two amateur boxers and being the first woman to mark the racehorse board for local bookies. Since then, this largely self-taught Creole chef has won practically every award. She's been inducted into the James Beard Foundation's Who's Who of Food & Beverage in America. She was honored with a lifetime achievement award from the Southern Foodways Alliance. Miss Leah won the 2016 James Beard Lifetime Achievement Award. She has honorary degrees from Tulane, Dillard, Our Lady of Holy Cross College, Madonna College, Loyola, and Johnson & Wales University. The Southern Food and Beverage Museum has a permanent exhibit named after her.

In addition to some of the best food in New Orleans, Dooky Chase also has a storied history. During segregation, blacks and whites could not eat together—except at Dooky Chase. Miss Leah knew no one would be arrested at her restaurant or a riot would break out. Therefore, all civil rights meetings in New Orleans took place inside. Her walls are also lined with one of the best collections of African-American art in the country. She's been collecting paintings since the '50s. Some artists would trade paintings for food.

As a self-taught chef, Miss Leah never measures an ingredient. She does measure the results, though, and has very strong opinions about the basics of Creole cooking, never hesitating to pronounce "That's not Creole," about someone else's dish. The gumbo at the Dooky Chase Restaurant contains crab, shrimp, chicken, two kinds of sausage, veal brisket, ham, and the perfect roux. "Not a real dark roux," she says. "That's more Cajun." She steadfastly holds that the roux must be the perfect color and texture and that the cook has to stand guard at her pot to make that happen. "Don't give me that sticky, gooey stuff." Miss Leah has many other rules: Onions and seasoning must be cut very fine. They cannot float. Beans can't float either. Okra has to be cooked down, i.e. to death. Cabbage has to be smothered. And for God's sake, onions and garlic and green peppers, the holy trinity, had better be in there.

Li'l Dizzy's 1500 Esplanade Ave.

If you watched HBO's series *Treme*, you've seen Li'l Dizzy's. In David Simon's obsessive need to make sure viewers in-the-know knew he was in-the-know about New Orleans, there was a scene filmed in Li'l Dizzy's, a local in-the-know kind of place, about every other episode. Owner Wayne Baquet's restaurant roots run three generations deep. His dad ran Eddie's. His sister opened up Paul Gross Chicken Shack. Wayne has opened a total of eleven restaurants and ran Zachery's in Carrollton for 13 years. All of the family restaurants were known for their fried chicken. After 40 years in the restaurant business, Wayne sold Zachery's to take a step back, immediately felt restless, and stepped back in, opening Li'l Dizzy's in 2004. The Creole filé gumbo served at Li'l Dizzy's is the same gumbo that his family has been serving for decades. It starts with a premade, seasoned, dry roux mix that Wayne and his father developed so that they could reproduce the essence of their gumbo anywhere they ventured.

Willie Mae's Scotch House 2401 St. Ann St.

Willie Mae's Scotch House is mid-cycle, transforming from beloved local hangout to being a place where locals stop going because the lines are too long, jammed with tourists seeking "authentic" New Orleans food where "the locals go." The Food Network and the Travel Channel aired segments on Willie Mae's within 6 months of one another. Since then, everything has changed. The two TV networks are loaded with shows that highlight locally favorite joints, of course forever destroying that vibe immediately after broadcasting the segment. The difference between those TV shows and my books, where I also seek to highlight local treasures, is that so few people read books, my influence wouldn't amount to a single peppercorn in Guy Fieri's Flavor Town.

Willie Mae's basically has two items, fried chicken and fried pork chops, from which to build a meal with red beans and rice, white beans and rice, butter beans, green beans, simmered okra, and tomato. Her fried chicken comes from a mysterious recipe she's never revealed. Willie Mae's won an "America's Classic" award from the James Beard Foundation, which recognizes local restaurants that carry on the traditions of great regional cuisine.

Months after she received the Beard award, the restaurant was destroyed by Hurricane Katrina. Three years of volunteer efforts and more than $200,000 in private donations brought Willie Mae's Scotch House back into business. When NPR visited to do a story on Willie Mae's, the radio crew asked Kerry Seaton, current owner and Willie Mae's granddaughter, what was in her secret batter. She responded, "Well, I keep the batter wet. There's salt . . . and pepper . . ." The interviewer interrupted: "There's gotta be crack cocaine in here somewhere." It's just that good.

Mid-City

Angelo Brocato's 214 N. Carrollton Ave.

Sometimes when you enter Angelo Brocato's, the place is pure magic. The magic is not only their original Sicilian-recipe gelatos, which are all excellent and include two types of Pistachio (they are very Sicilian), Baci, Torroncino, and a great seasonal Louisiana Strawberry (much sweeter than traditional strawberry); not only in their other traditional Italian desserts like Zuppa Englese, Cassata, Italian fig cookies, spumoni, and cheesecake (I think the best in New Orleans); and not only for the cozy Old World feel created by slowly turning ceiling fans, an archway of lightbulbs over the serving counter, rows of apothecary jars filled with candies, glass-topped bistro tables, and century-old portraits of Angelo himself on the wall; but the true magic is produced by their customers. On certain nights, the parlor is filled with families with kids blended with heavily tattooed and pierced hipsters and topped with 80-year-old Italian men who shuffle up to the counter using canes or walkers to have their mini-cannolis and double espresso, as they've been doing since Jesus was a juvenile. On such nights, you feel like you've been cast as an extra in *Cinema Paradiso*.

The original dream began in Palermo, Italy, where a young Angelo Brocato began an apprenticeship in an elegant ice cream parlor. He immigrated to New Orleans and worked on a sugar plantation, trying to save enough money to open his own parlor. In 1905, he opened Angelo Brocato's Ice Cream Parlor, a replica of Palermo's finest emporiums, and one of the city's first sit-down parlors.

A century later, the business is still run by his family, and everything is handmade daily on the premises. When you order the cannoli, the cone-shaped shell is spoon-filled with a ricotta cheese and sugar mixture right there in front of you and dipped in crushed pistachio nuts.

Blue Oak BBQ 900 N. Carrollton Ave.

Ronnie Evans and Philip Moseley, friends since grade school in New Orleans, worked together in a joint located in that haven for top barbecue: Vail, Colorado. On their way back to New Orleans, the two did a BBQ road trip through actual top barbecue towns like Austin and Lockhart, Texas. They became disciples of old-time pit BBQ and German techniques.

They opened their first New Orleans spot in 2014 as a pop-up inside Chickie Wah-Wah, a bar and music club. Two years later, they found their own storefront in Mid-City and have been serving a packed house ever since. You most often see The Joint picked as New Orleans' "best" barbecue. For me, it's not even close. Blue Oak is far and away our premier barbecue spot.

I've had one "just OK" meal here where everything that night had too much heat, even the mac 'n' cheese. But, I've also had five, six, or seven great meals here. My #1 favorite is the Doobin Lubin, a chopped brisket, house-smoked sausage, slaw, pickles, and BBQ sauce on a brioche. Nearly as good are their BBQ egg rolls, avocado deviled eggs, chili-glazed brussels sprouts, finished off with sweet potato bread pudding.

I've never had it, but I hear the smoked burger (house-ground brisket/pork patty, with caramelized onions, cheddar cheese, BBQ sauce, and pickles) is pretty special.

You can also get in your exercise and walk off the heterocyclic amines (HCAs) and polycyclic aromatic hydrocarbons (PAHs) because Blue Oak has become so popular, you're most likely forced to park blocks away. Of course, if you're eating BBQ, you probably aren't all that focused on heterocyclic amines (HCAs) and polycyclic aromatic hydrocarbons (PAHs).

Crescent City Steak House 1001 N. Broad St.

This is a classic, old-fashioned steak house, offering the same menu since it opened in 1934. Founder and owner John Vojkovich, an immigrant from Croatia, was the first to bring prime beef to New Orleans. Crescent City serves steak and only steak; your choice of rib eye, filet (wrapped in bacon), strip sirloin, T-bone, or an enormous porterhouse meant for two or three people. All meats have been dry-aged on premises. Steaks come to your table sizzling in butter, a Crescent City Steak House style that has become the tradition in New Orleans. Sauteed spinach, peas, mushrooms, and broccoli au gratin are served as à la carte sides. The potatoes—au gratin, french fries, German fries, Lyonnaise, Braebant, cottage fries, and shoestring—are all hand-cut, individually prepared, and almost as much a signature item as the steaks.

Slowly turning overhead fans and antique chandeliers grace an old pressed-tin ceiling. There are small curtained private booths with four-tops inside, off to the side of the dining floor, where one can imagine business deals done decades ago, or perhaps rubouts and hits were ordered. *Playboy* magazine tagged Crescent City one of the Top Ten steak houses in America.

Liuzza's 3636 Bienville St.

Hurricane Katrina turned out to be the least of Liuzza's owner Michael Bordelon's problems. After closing the refurbished Liuzza's one night, Bordelon was struck by a speeding drunk driver. He spent a week in a coma and a month in the hospital, and rehabilitation continues for the brain trauma he suffered. A week after the wreck, Shanette Bordelon Edler, Michael's sister and co-manager of the restaurant, died of cancer at age 59. The neighborhood pulled together to create a fundraiser, Liuzza Palooza. The festival was located a block from the restaurant where signature small dishes were served (like Drago's famed charbroiled oysters) and top musicians (like Rockin' Dopsie & the Zydeco Twisters and the Creole String Beans) played, alongside cooking demos and kids' activities. Liuzza Palooza drew 4,000 people and raised $130,000.

Founded in 1947, Liuzza's has changed hands several times since the original namesake owners. It has remained through all the changes a cash-only, comfort food, beloved neighborhood joint, where drinks are served in large frosted mugs. They do a decent po'boy, but are better with their fried pickles, Spinach Lougia (spinach with garlic, olive oil, and chicken stock), Crawfish Telemachus (crawfish cream sauce over pasta), or Eggplant St. John (eggplant medallions and pasta topped with shrimp and artichoke sauce). More years than not, Liuzza's is chosen as "Best Neighborhood Restaurant" in the *Gambit* Weekly Poll. Liuzza's is also where the John Goodman character in HBO's *Treme* chose to have his last meal before committing suicide.

Liuzza's by the Track 1518 N. Lopez St.

What few visitors could guess and most locals don't know is that the two Liuzza restaurants (about 15 minutes apart) have no affiliation. Jack Liuzza opened a combination grocery store, bar, and bookie joint by the Fair Grounds Race Track (the oldest continuously running horse track in America) in 1936. His grandson, also named Jack, converted it into a grill in 1965. Then, in 1996, Billy Gruber bought the restaurant. Over the years, the Gruber family has run a number of New Orleans cafés. Billy's Creole gumbo is a special (and secret) recipe, one that's a nod to his mother's Boudreaux Cajun heritage. Starting with a nearly black roux, Billy layers locally made sausage, cooked-to-order seafood, and a (secret recipe) mixture of thirteen seasonings. They also serve garlic- and horseradish-spiked roast beef, slowly simmered corned beef, (secretly seasoned) sausage, and a renowned barbecued shrimp po'boy, with sautéed shrimp and the restaurant's own (secret) version of the rich, peppery, butter-infused New Orleans BBQ sauce.

Lola's 3312 Esplanade Ave.

It's peculiar that, in a city once owned by Spain for 40 years, there aren't more Spanish restaurants. There are at least three French-influenced restaurants per block.

Angel Miranda opened his first Spanish restaurant, Altamira, in the Warehouse District in 1980. The restaurant closed a few years later. His second attempt was in '94 when he opened Lola's, named after his mother. The restaurant rests on Esplanade, along what was called "millionaire's row," where the wealthy Spanish citizens lived with well-to-do Creoles. This time his restaurant was un gran éxito.

Lola's serves authentic Spanish food (not Mexican, not South American, not Latin Isles). They serve a great paella and even greater pisto. Pisto is a portobello mushroom stuffed with eggplant, peppers, onions, squash, tomatoes, and garlic, and served with black beans, rice, and asparagus. Paella, as you probably know, is a garlic and saffron rice dish teeming with shrimp, fish, calamari, scallops, mussels, and vegetables. To say that Lola's dishes are garlic-friendly is a gross understatement.

Personally, I think Lola's serves the best Spanish meals I've ever had. If I were a native of New Orleans, that might not be saying so much. But I lived nearly three decades with easy access to a cluster of great Spanish restaurants in Newark, New Jersey. I've eaten at Sagres, Casa Vascas, Forno's, and Coimbra. Lola's is better.

Mandina's 3800 Canal St.

Mandina's started out as a corner grocery, this one run by Sebastian Mandina, an immigrant from Salaparuta, Sicily. His sons, Anthony and Frank, who had been born on its second floor, converted the family business to a full-scale restaurant. Anthony's son Tommy took over in 1975; he, too, had been raised in the apartment above the restaurant. Tommy is now semi-retired, while his daughter, Cindy, runs the restaurant today, thanks in part to Harry Connick, Jr. Cindy had been working at the restaurant since she was 8 years old, bussing tables. She started writing checks to vendors when she was 11. Becoming the fourth generation to run Mandina's was about the furthest thing from her dreams and desires when she got her master's in business administration from Loyola. But then she was leafing through an in-flight magazine during a trip to Hawaii when she was stunned to read Harry Connick, Jr.'s comments about her family's restaurant. He said their dishes were those "you can get anywhere. It just tastes better there." The article woke Cindy up to the realization that Mandina's was part of the soul of New Orleans and more than just an old pink-painted joint. "I always thought of Mandina's as just a neighborhood restaurant," Cindy said. "Dad went to work. Mom was home raising the kids. Dad came home. That was it. Who knew?"

Katrina took a toll on the place. When the contractor started to peel back some outside damage for repair, he realized the 72-year-old restaurant was in much worse shape than he'd thought. He said, "It was only standing because of grout, God, and gravity." Tommy Mandina was ready to throw in the towel, in spite of the protests of his regular customers. "I'm done," he said. "This is going to be too hard and take too long." That's when Cindy said, "I want to do it."

Cindy oversaw Mandina's return to being a place frequented by both natives and tourists. Noel Cassanova, a regular for 60 years, characterized the clientele: "At the bar, you had the bookmaker standing next to the district attorney standing next to the guy who runs the hospital. Later on at night, you'd have a couple of police captains in there. It was unbelievable." Once again, people are lined up outside for their it-just-tastes-better-there Catfish Meuniere, Trout Amandine, grilled shrimp over pasta Bordelaise. Don't worry, the line outside moves quickly, which is surprising because most of the waiters inside decidedly don't.

McHardy's Chicken & Fixin' 1458 N. Broad St.

In a town with Dooky Chase, Li'l Dizzy, Fiorella's, and Willie Mae's Scotch House, it's saying something that an in-and-out counter joint with no tables is part of the Best Fried Chicken discussion. McHardy's gives everyone else a run for their money, though. The money required at McHardy's is far less than at other places. My family ordered the ten-piece chicken, fried shrimp, red beans and rice, cole slaw, potato salad, and lemonade (all made in-house). We got change back from $20.

"We marinate the chicken once and then again in another solution, so the seasoning permeates all the way through to the bone," says owner Kermit Mogilles. "It goes through four or five different steps before it hits the oil." The result is chicken that is highly seasoned without being too spicy, is always fresh and exceptionally lean, giving each piece more crunch and less grease.

You can buy the five-piece box for only $3.14 or the suitcase-sized 100-piece for $62.80. At Mardi Gras time, they sell a lot of the 100-piece boxes for parade viewers, averaging about 3,000 pieces a day, which requires them to open up the restaurant at 5:00 a.m. to serve the seasonal surge.

Then, there's the resilient history of McHardy's. They were looted after being flooded following Hurricane Katrina. Kermit also lost his Gentilly home to the flood. But he and his wife, Albi, repaired the restaurant and, with the help of family members, reopened in January 2006. Five months later, a fire from a power surge devastated the restaurant once again. As the ruins smoldered, he told people that perhaps this was the end for McHardy's. It was then that Melvin Jones, a friend and regular who ran a local ministry for people overcoming addictions, showed up on his doorstep with a small army of ex-addicts who happened to have professional carpentry, electrical, and plumbing skills. They rebuilt the restaurant at no cost.

The restaurant's rebirth and then re-rebirth make it characteristically New Orleans.

This is a city that was 80 percent burned down in 1788, and 80 percent under water in 2005. It has survived the oil bust of the 1980s and the BP oil spill of 2010. New Orleans is a city filled with people like Kermit Mogilles who, when knocked to the ground, get back up to join the next parade.

Parkway Bakery & Tavern 538 Hagan Ave.

Parkway has been a neighborhood landmark since 1911. German baker Charles Goering, Sr. ran Parkway Bakery for the first 11 years, then Henry Timothy, Sr. purchased it with the intent of continuing to run it as the neighborhood bake shop until he added the recently invented "poor boy" sandwich in 1929 to feed the workers at the nearby American Can Company. A flood briefly closed the bakery in 1978. A more devastating setback occurred when the American Can Company closed in 1988, taking much of Parkway's customers with it. They reduced the bakery hours, and then in 1993, closed the doors of Parkway for good.

Jay Nix lived next door to Parkway. He saw the bakery as a cornerstone of his neighborhood, and hated to see it vacant. So in 1995, he bought it, with no intention of reopening the bakery, but to use the space as storage for his contracting business. Nix kept encountering people with stories to tell about growing up with the bakery. In 2003, Nix finally decided to follow the voices on the street and rumblings in his heart to reopen the Parkway Bakery. Nix's nephew, Justin Kennedy, moved to New Orleans later that year and jumped in as the untrained but enthusiastic chef. "The first day we opened, people were lined up," Justin remembers. "It's just been amazing how close the people are to this place. It's more than a sandwich shop here. People come here and even before they buy a sandwich, before they eat their roast beef, they walk in the door and you can tell they're happy already."

While waiting in line, you can admire the eclectic memorabilia hung on the walls: old campaign posters for Lindy Boggs (Cokie Roberts' mom), ads for the dearly departed Pontchartrain Beach Amusement Park, T-shirts of past city football champs from the 1950s. You can also strike up a conversation with others in line. As Justin notes, "You've got your crooks, you got your artists, your judges, your big businessmen, your sewage and water guys, and your carpenters. They all come here.

We feed a thousand people a day. It's amazing, a whole mix of people. If you want to see New Orleans, just come in here and watch people come through."

Rosedale 801 Rosedale Dr.

Tucked away in a blue-collar residential neighborhood behind Holt Cemetery and Delgado College, Rosedale is fairly hard to find. But the new-ish restaurant, opened October 2016, is totally worth your wrong turns and outbursts at your GPS. It is the newest Susan Spicer restaurant, serving what she calls "West Bank food." By that, she means more local fare and more casual than her other restaurants, Mondo in Lakeview and the brilliant Bayona, a French Quarter institution. Rosedale is housed in a former jail. She has smartly preserved an old cell as the restroom. Graffiti from its former incarcerated occupants remains scratched into the walls. She's kept the old steel sink. A part of me wishes she'd maintained the old metal toilet without any seat, but I get why she updated.

I was there on the second day they were open. I know you're supposed to give a new restaurant a month or two to settle in and hit their stride, but it was Susan Spicer. I couldn't wait. My wife and I shared the warm mushroom salad with Manchego cheese and turtle soup with spinach dumplings, which were both exceptional. But her barbecued shrimp was the best I've ever had. In this city, with Mr. B's and Pascale Manale's, that's saying something. I went again the fourth week they were open.

Toups' Meatery 845 N. Carrollton Ave.

Don't ask for vegetarian or gluten-free specials. Remember, Chef Isaac Toups is carrying a meat cleaver and he knows how to use it. It's all meat, meat, and meat, from the small-plate Meatery Board to the à la carte cracklins, rillons, and boudin balls, and on to the entrees: tri tip steak, massive double cut pork chop, and the in-your-face challenge of the lamb neck. Ordering the lamb neck will require picking through many small vertebrae to dig out shreds of marrow-laden meat strips. Just think of it as a meat version of eating pistachios or edamame.

Isaac and Amanda Toups opened their restaurant in 2012. Isaac had spent a decade with Emeril's restaurants, starting out as a cook at Delmonico's. He'd been named *The Times-Picayune* "Chef to Watch 2010." Amanda's background is in wine and wine education. She managed W.I.N.O. (Wine Institute of New Orleans) for the enterprise's first 4 years. The manager, Larry Nguyen, also comes with a pedigree. He was named maître'd of the year by *New Orleans* magazine in 2010.

If you're a meat lover looking for more sophistication than is found in a meat-lover's pizza, Toups' is a nearly perfect restaurant. The "nearly" has to do with the decor, and this is just my fuddy-duddy opinion. Some may like the minimalist design. It's a bit too *Dwell* magazine and nouveau for my taste.

Isaac opened a second restaurant, Toups South, in late 2016 inside the Southern Museum of Food & Beverage (1504 Oretha Castle Haley Blvd).

Venezia 134 N. Carrollton Ave.

Venezia is my neighborhood joint where, on most Friday nights, I'll pick up eggplant parmesan or spaghetti to go home and carb out in front on the TV. I also feel their al dente pasta is simply much better than Vincent's or Irene's or other New Orleans Italian restaurants.

They opened in 1957, when pizza was just catching on across America. Venezia was one of New Orleans's first pizza places. Their vintage neon sign, "Venezia/Pizza Pie/Italian Food," reveals not much has changed there since 1957. When's the last time you saw a restaurant advertise pizza *pie*?

It has been described as a "red gravy" kind of place, or a neighborhood joint where people bring mama and all the *bambinos*. On weekend nights, there's usually a family outside on the bench or huddled up at the bar, waiting for a table to open up.

The restaurant is reputed to have been Mafia kingpin Carlos Marcello's closer-to-home substitute for Mosca's, the legendary roadhouse hangout.

The Central Business District and Warehouse District

Cochon 930 Tchoupitoulas St.

Cochon, whose name is French for "pig," boasts not one, but two James Beard Award-winning chefs. Donald Link is the star and face of Cochon and his mini restaurant empire. Stephen Stryjewski joined Link's James Beard awards as the 2011 winner. When Cochon opened in 2007, much of the Cajun food being served in New Orleans (with the notable exception of K-Paul's) could be characterized, as Chef Link put it, as "a fried shrimp plate, a fried oyster plate, a fried catfish plate, and a fried combination plate—with fried shrimp, fried oysters, and fried catfish."

Cochon's only combination plate is their boucherie, which includes paper-thin slices of house-made salami, spicy tasso, and pork belly, served with homemade bread-and-butter pickles, pickled jalapeños, and house-made mustard. Other small-plate pork-atizers include their best-in-the-city fried boudin, smoked pork ribs with watermelon pickle, and pork cheeks with baby limas, mushrooms, and peach relish.

Back in 2007, my wife and I lived in Ohio, a state whose culinary contributions were the creation of the popcorn ball (Euclid Beach Park) and the fried baloney sandwich (Waldo). On a trip to New Orleans, we ate at Cochon. Marnie seemed suddenly overcome with emotion. When I asked, "What's up?" she replied, "I'd forgotten what food's supposed to taste like."

Cochon's entrees include smothered pork loin with apples, caramelized onions, and cheddar; smoked ham hock with farro, cucumbers, and English peas; and namesake Louisiana cochon with turnips, cabbage, pickled peaches, and cracklins.

The year the restaurant opened, Link won the James Beard Award for Best Chef South, and Cochon was nominated for Best New Restaurant.

Cochon Butcher 930 Tchoupitoulas St.

The Butcher is found around the side of Cochon's building on Andrew Higgins Boulevard. Same building, same chefs, they share the bathroom, and you can get some of the same dishes—for less. It has a meat counter where they sell boudin, andouille, Kurobuta bacon, sopressata, guanciale, pâtés, and rillettes, plus packaged foie gras-enriched butter, house-made pickles, mustards, and hot sauces to take home.

For a mere $6 to $12, the Butcher serves best-value-in-New-Orleans sammitches: a buckboard bacon melt, duck pastrami sliders, pork belly on white bread with mint and cucumber, and the house-smoked turkey, watercress, grilled onion, and lemon thyme on pecan bread. Their boudin and pickle appetizer went from $3 to $6 this past year, but remains a steal—and I think it's the best boudin in the city.

I dip into the Butcher about every other month to grab and go with a quick and near perfect brisket slider for a mere $7.

Domenica 123 Baronne St., inside The Roosevelt Hotel

Located inside the stunning and historic Roosevelt Hotel, John Besh's Domenica is an Italian restaurant with a Jewish executive chef, Alon Shaya. Shaya has won the James Beard Award as Best Chef in the South, quite the odd honor for a boy born in Israel who developed his trade in Philadelphia. While the restaurant serves many rustic Italian dishes, including a salumi tray and a noteworthy whole-roasted cauliflower, they are known for their pizza. *New Orleans Magazine* chose it as Best Pizza in the city. Eaternola.com chose it as the Best Restaurant, pizza or otherwise, in New Orleans. On my first visit, I had the Calabrese Pizza. It was a little too spicy for me (and I like spicy), but I knew from the practically perfect crust that a second try was needed. I went back two days later and ordered the Cotechino (pork sausage, scallions, and tomatoes) and the Bolzano (roast pork shoulder, fennel, bacon, and sweet onions). Chef Shaya claims what makes their pizza better is they have the only Pavesi wood-fired oven with a rotating stone deck in America. I have no idea what that means, but I do know good pizza. Domenica is good pizza.

Drago's 2 Poydras St., inside The Hilton-Riverside

The original Drago's was opened in 1969 out in Fat City by Lake Pontchartrain. Drago and Klara Cvitanovich opened a second location inside the Hilton Riverside Hotel, a stone's throw from the Mississippi River. Their Charbroiled Oysters, topped with Parmesan, butter, parsley, and garlic, have been called "The Single Best Bite of Food in New Orleans." Drago's also serves creative dishes like Shuckee Duckee, two blackened and lean duck breasts surrounded by creamy linguine and oysters; and Cajun Surf & Turf, blackened medallions of rare filet mignon, with oysters and shrimp.

Emeril's 800 Tchoupitoulas St.

When Emeril Lagasse opened Emeril's as his first restaurant in 1990, it was chosen as Best New Restaurant in America by *Esquire*. He has since received two James Beard Awards, been inducted into the IACP Culinary Hall of Fame, and has become possibly the most famous chef nationwide.

The restaurant does seafood particularly well, whether it's sizzling sea scallops, crusted drum, char-grilled salmon, or shrimp and mussel fettuccine. But then, they do great pork chops, glazed chicken, and quail too.

Herbsaint 701 St. Charles Ave.

Born in Crowley, Louisiana, chef and owner, Donald Link, is a "real" Cajun, which is also the name of his James Beard Award winning book, *Real Cajun*. Chef Link was named a James Beard Best Chef in the South in 2007, and has several nominations for what's called "The Big One": the James Beard Award for Outstanding Chef in America.

Herbsaint's menu can lean a little French (Muscovy duck leg confit with dirty rice and citrus gastrique) or lean a little Italian (gnocchi with pancetta and Parmesan), but is always squarely Southern-style (fried catfish with green rice and chilies). The restaurant's setting is part of the appeal. The intimate bistro has an outdoor patio and large interior windows through which diners can watch the St. Charles streetcar, a.k.a. the Green Bullet, s-l-o-w-l-y roll by.

Gourmet magazine listed Herbsaint as one of the Top 50 Restaurants in America. It was also inducted into *The Nation*'s Restaurant News Hall of Fame and was listed in the *New York Times* as "one of the top 3 restaurants that count."

Little Gem 445 S. Rampart St.

The Little Gem first opened roughly 100 years ago. It was an intimate jazz club and restaurant where Louis Armstrong often performed. After it sat vacant for decades, local physician Nicolas Bazan bought the property and quickly completed a stunning renovation in the historic jazz neighborhood, well on its way to a full revitalization. I don't know who sold the idea or books the musical acts for Little Gem, but they've done an amazing job bringing in superstars like Kermit Ruffins and Delfeayo Marsalis and street stars David and Roselyn, the latter singing on Royal Street since 1975 with six recorded albums.

The restaurant's first chef, Robert Bruce, built the launch menu around vintage Creole flavors. He'd worked in kitchens all over New Orleans, including Upperline, Commander's Palace, Ruth's Chris, and Emeril's. He's also been at the helm of Smith & Wollensky and the Palace Cafe. But his menu at the Little Gem drifted from promising to pedestrian. They started serving Caesar salads, grilled salmon, and the frighteningly named Little Gem Burger. Bruce is a fine cook, but it's hard to draw in a stylish nightclub crowd peddling Little Gem Burgers.

Bazan's son Nicolas Jr. was brought in to run Little Gem. He brought with him Miles Prescott, his chef and partner at RioMar, to take over the kitchen. Prescott, a Georgia native, has given the menu a decidedly Southern identity. You got charmarked, crisp-crusted rabbit tenderloin laid on top of a mix of cheese, cauliflower, and a little mo' rabbit, piled with cabbage and apples. You got yer fried frogs' legs with a tomato concoction they call "jam." You got yer sides like Hoppin' John and cane-syrup sweet potatoes. Then, because you're in New Orleans not Georgia, you got yer oysters (served five different ways). For dessert, you got yer foie gras mousse slathered in salty caramel sauce.

Mother's 401 Poydras St.

Cab drivers will all tell you Mother's is a "must." The perpetually long lines waiting on Poydras Street may convince you it's a "must." There are generalist guides like *Fodor's* and *Frommer's* that praise Mother's as a "must." Let me be at least one voice to say: maybe not. I sense there was a time when Mother's was the perfect response when visitors wanted to find a hole-in-the-wall serving "authentic" New Orleans food where the locals go. But it's been a long time since the original owners, Simon and Mary (Mother) Landry, first served po'boys to longshoremen and laborers in 1938.

Mother's of today has evolved into a densely packed (almost exclusively by tourists), cafeteria-style joint with minimal service. Their perhaps too-broad menu is a smorgasbord of "local" dishes. The whole experience feels about as "must" as going to Vegas to hear Wayne Newton sing "Danke Schoen" one more time.

Pêche 800 Magazine St.

I consider Pêche the best seafood restaurant in New Orleans. The James Beard Awards considered it the best new restaurant in the entire country with their award in 2014. Donald Link and his co-chefs and partners, Stephen Stryjewski and Ryan Prewitt, betray their Cajun roots with every meal. You don't get your fish reduced to a fillet nor rounded into a cake. You get the whole fat fish on your plate. If you have any "I don't eat seafood" whiners in your group, they serve a skirt steak and chicken diablo. A word of warning to more genteel seafood eaters: the chefs are Cajun. When you order a fish, you get the fish—head, tail, eyeballs, and all. Pick around them.

Restaurant August 301 Tchoupitoulas St.

August is housed in an 1800s French-Creole building with high ceilings, wood paneling, large windows, twinkling chandeliers, and brocade-draped dining rooms. The food ranges from the deceptively simple, like heirloom beets or gnocchi with crabmeat, to the "don't try this at home" Amuse-Bouche, which is seafood sabayon, fish fumet, egg custard with a hint of truffle, topped with bowfin caviar and served in an eggshell.

John Besh's other restaurants are Domenica (profiled earlier in this chapter); Besh Steak House (228 Poydras St., inside Harrah's Casino); Lüke (333 St Charles St., inside the Hilton), inspired by bistros in the Alsace region in France; Johnny Sánchez (930 Poydras St.), which combines Johnny Besh's talents with Aaron Sanchez's, and where they serve not-your-typical Mexican foods such as pickled cactus and spicy grasshoppers; and Borgne (601 Loyola, inside the Hyatt Regency).

Borgne is the only restaurant I know with culinary tributes to Isleños. The Islenos are descendants of Spanish settlers in the Canary Islands who made their way into Louisiana in the 1770s. They now live largely in St. Bernard Parish, just southeast of New Orleans, and have maintained their own culture and distinctive cuisine. If you are ever here in March during the Isleño Fiestas, a celebration of Canary Island food and music, Borgne offers crawfish croquettes with chipotle rémoulade (only 50 cents during Happy Hour), a ten-clove garlic white shrimp, and a creamy broth of oysters over spaghetti with grated bottarga. Bottarga is the pressed dried eggs of tuna or gray mullet. Yummy.

Root 200 Julia St.

Root opened at the tail end of 2011 and has been racking up awards and accolades ever since. The restaurant was named one of *Bon Appétit*'s 50 Best New Restaurants; it was awarded Best New Restaurant 2012 by *New Orleans* magazine;

received the "So Hot Right Now" Eater Award for New Orleans; and earned a rare four-bean review from *The Times-Picayune*. Root has been featured in *Southern Living, Fodor's Travel Intelligence*, and *Forbes* magazine. Owner and executive chef Phillip Lopez was honored at the 2012 Eater Awards as New Orleans' "Chef of the Year," Star Chefs named him one of its "Rising Star Chefs" in 2012, and *Louisiana Cookin'* magazine named him a "Chef to Watch."

Chef Lopez has said, "To me, cooking is a form of communication, and I want to talk to my guests through each bite they take." For some diners, Root is the most inventive and outstanding restaurant in New Orleans. For others, each bite will communicate, "WTF?" Root is most definitely not like any other restaurant in New Orleans (except their newer location, Square Root, in the Lower Garden District at 1800 Magazine St.). They famously serve scallops in cigar boxes. You can order marrow baked in the bone and served with toast points infused with squid ink. My "WTF?" moment came with my Ménage à Foie appetizer. I love foie gras. But I was less enthused when one of the three varieties started snapping in my mouth as though it had been stuffed with Pop Rocks candy. Just the mention of the last three dishes should resolve the question of whether Root's culinary creativity is spot-on perfect for you or meant for more adventurous eaters.

Ruby Slipper 200 Magazine St. and 1005 Canal St.

There are five Ruby Slippers in New Orleans. The original is in Mid-City (139 S. Cortez St.). There's a fourth location at 2001 Burgundy Street in the Marigny and a new fifth location in the Garden District at 200 Magazine Street. I choose to highlight their Canal Street and Warehouse District locations because they're much more convenient for most visitors. There is usually a line of people waiting to grab a table or counter stool, but not as long a line as Mother's, which sits between the two, and the wait here is so much more worth it. Their offerings lean toward the eclectic, with signature dishes like Bananas Foster Pain Perdu (French-bread based French toast topped with rum-flambéed bananas and raisins, served with applewood-smoked bacon), Eggs Cochon (poached eggs over apple-braised pork debris and an open-faced buttermilk biscuit, finished with hollandaise), and their most popular dish, BBQ shrimp and grits (sautéed Gulf shrimp with an amber beer and rosemary reduction, over Falls Mill creamy stone-ground grits, served with a buttermilk biscuit). While I'm an Elizabeth's Restaurant guy, many others think Ruby Slipper is the #1 best breakfast spot in New Orleans.

Garden District and Uptown

Atchafalaya 901 Louisiana Ave.

Atchafalaya is a Choctaw word meaning "long river" and is also the name of the Louisiana-situated largest swamp in America. The restaurant has had a swampy succession of owners, with each having a different idea of what the restaurant should be. For most of the 1920s, the building housed Petrossi's, a casual seafood house. In the early 1990s, it became a contemporary Creole bistro called Cafe Atchafalaya. The cafe had a series of owners, some trying to be down-home Southern, others trying to go upscale, all rushing toward being out of business, until it was acquired by Tony Tocco and Rachel Jaffe in 2009. Tony might be the last person you'd see as the savior of Atchafalaya. He started the Oak Street's diviest of dive bars, Snake & Jake's. The bar has a specialty cocktail called the Possum, named after the time a possum fell through Snake & Jake's waterlogged ceiling and into a man's drink. But Tony and Rachel pulled off a *Restaurant:* Impossible-type makeover, and then went out to market it.

They knocked on doors, asking neighbors to give the place another chance. They set up a food booth at the Wednesday concert series in Lafayette Square. They started hosting wine dinners to bring back a skeptical fine-dining crowd. Atchafalaya brought in musicians for live music at Sunday brunch and at dinner on Sundays and Mondays. Weekend brunches include a make-your-own Bloody Mary buffet.

Above all, they improved the food. Atchafalaya does great versions of New Orleans classics like fried green tomatoes with crab rémoulade; BBQ shrimp; and the New Orleans by way of Carrboro, North Carolina shrimp and grits. They also serve their own bacon-wrapped, boudin-stuffed quail, and fried oysters in tasso cream. The waiters ride with the theme and serve you with energy (sometimes raucous) and a little banter.

Casamento's 4330 Magazine St.

In a town where we will argue (intensely) about where to get the best gumbo or po'boy, Casamento's is routinely considered the best oyster house, period. Acme, with its location in the French Quarter, is more popular, particularly with tourists, but Acme can't touch the ambiance or the food of Casamento's with a 10-foot shucking knife.

Started in 1919 by Italian immigrant Joseph Casamento and then run for 50 years by his son, also named Joseph, the restaurant is now in the hands of great-nephew C. J. Gerdes and his wife Linda. A sleeveless C. J. is always cooking in the kitchen, which you get to walk through if you use their toilets. Linda is always waiting on tables or working the cash register.

Casamento's may be the least romantic restaurant in the city. The decor is floor-to-ceiling white tile shown off in harsh fluorescent lighting. Calvin Trillin described it as "having lunch in a drained swimming pool."

During the hard-to-remember hours they are open, you will undoubtedly have to stand in line before getting a table in one of their two small dining rooms, with a total seating capacity of only thirty-three. If you make it to Casamento's after a Saints loss, hold out for the back dining room. Front-room waitress Angela is a passionate Saints fan and will be severely depressed. Be advised to do one of two things while you're waiting for a table: (1) You can practice the art of conversation with others waiting in line (and it is an art in New Orleans), or, (2) you can belly up to the oyster bar, where your shucker can quickly pop open a dozen raw oysters to suck down while you wait.

When you do get a table, you'll discover a short menu. Casamento's only offers a few dishes, like oyster loaf, shrimp loaf, and soft-shell crab. But everything they do is simple and excellent (well, maybe the spaghetti is merely passable). Their seafood is fresh, bought locally, and fried immediately before serving. Somehow even their pan bread is great. Pan bread is nothing more than uncut loaves of Bunny Bread, cut into Texas toast-sized hunks, and sent through the grill. The result of this simple process is perfect for sopping up the last of their exceptional oyster stew or the soupy but superb gumbo. I'm convinced Casamento's gumbo has healing powers.

If you're in New Orleans during the summer, be forewarned that Casamento's subscribes to the credo, "raw oysters should only be eaten in months ending in an R." Since 1919, Casamento's has been closed May through August.

Commander's Palace 1403 Washington Ave.

Chef Tory McPhail won the 2013 James Beard Award, joining Emeril Lagasse, Frank Brigtsen, Paul Prudhomme, and other legendary chefs who have passed through the kitchen of this stately Garden District mansion. Winning a James Beard is almost expected at Commander's, the same way national football championships are expected at Alabama or snagging a rich husband is expected at Williams College.

Commander's Palace is actually named after a guy named Commander. Emile Commander set up a small saloon in 1880, and within a few years expanded it to a fine restaurant patronized by the wealthy families of the Garden District. Frank Giarratano became the second owner in the 1920s. He lived upstairs with his wife

Rose and two sons. Rumor has it that the Giarratanos shared the upstairs with small rented rooms where riverboat captains would take a wench and bottles of illegal libations (this was during Prohibition) while New Orleans's most upstanding citizens ate directly below. When the Brennans bought Commander's in the 1960s, it had since passed through ownership by Frank and Elinor Moran. The upstairs had ceased operating basically as a de facto bordello, but downstairs, the restaurant had lost some of its heat as well.

After the Brennan family tiff in 1973, when Ella and Dickie lost control over the original restaurant in the Quarter, they finally focused more intently on their acquisition of Commander's Palace. They redesigned the interior, putting up large windows and adding on custom-built trellises and commissioned paintings to dress up the walls. The biggest change came when they hired seriously innovative chefs like Paul Prudhomme, Gerard Maras, and Emeril Lagasse. Decades ahead of the curve, these chefs introduced the idea of an ever-changing menu based on seasonality of local, farm-to-table foodstuffs. This was nothing shy of a revolution in the New Orleans restaurant scene.

The height of Commander's national and international acclaim came during Chef Jamie Shannon's tenure. He had replaced Emeril Lagasse as executive chef. In 1995, *Food & Wine* named Commander's the # 1 restaurant in America. The following year, the restaurant won the coveted James Beard Foundation Outstanding Restaurant Award. In 1999, the James Beard foundation named Shannon the Best Chef in the South, while the Robb Report claimed him as the #2 chef in the entire world. A cloud overtook the restaurant in 2003 when Chef Shannon contracted cancer and died a year later. He was 40 years old.

The hiring of Tory McPhail and the need to put the restaurant back together after Katrina (it took over a year) refocused the spirit of Commander's. The restaurant today still serves long-term classics like its third-generation sherry-spiked turtle soup, shrimp rémoulade, and the command-performance bread pudding soufflé. But the menu is intertwined with new dishes like a dome-shaped pastry filled with oysters poached in absinthe, artichokes, bacon, and cream or their foie gras "du Monde" (seared duck liver, foie gras-infused café au lait, blackberry beignets). Then there's the Chef's Playground, with a new menu every night where the chefs experiment with new ideas.

Commander's offers weekend brunches with live music. They were the first restaurant in the world to host Jazz Brunches. Dickie Brennan stood in the lobby of a London hotel, witnessing a jazz quartet on one side of the massive lobby and guests eating breakfast on the other wide of the lobby, much too distant to hear the music. His lightbulb moment was to put the music and the food together. Creating the Jazz Brunch made Commander's for years the most profitable restaurant in America. You were paying over $20 for basically eggs to accompany the music. On weekdays (lunch only), you make your own music with their 25-cent martinis. They limit you to three, though two would put me under the table. You will never have better service. Anywhere. And a final bonus is calling for a reservation. Jimmy Boudreaux, the effervescent voice on the other end of the line, has his own fan club.

Coquette 2800 Magazine St.

On my first visit to Coquette, I had a very simple red and green tomato sandwich with garlic mayonnaise on house-made toast. That no-frills sandwich made me a lifelong champion of Coquette. It was practically perfect.

In 2008, Chef Michael Stoltzfus and Lillian Hubbard opened the restaurant on a busy (for New Orleans) corner of Magazine and Washington where there'd previously been a grocery store, an auto parts store—and a chef's graveyard, as a stream of restaurants opened and closed. With great reviews six feet deep, a growing entourage of regular patrons, and now a second James Beard nomination for Chef Michael, Coquette seems destined to buck the trend.

Two weeks before he was to go to college, Michael's mother decided to open a bakery/breakfast spot in Maryland and enlisted his help. Previously, he knew little more about cooking other than how to scramble an egg, but while working at his mom's place, he discovered his passion. Michael got his big break when hired by Restaurant August in New Orleans, where he was promoted to sous chef within the first half-year.

Since opening his own place, Chef Michael still enjoys experimenting and playing around with personalized tasting menus and five-course blind tastings. He's served grilled beef heart at least two ways: with chanterelle mushrooms and pickled peaches, or with giardiniera horseradish and satsuma. But if grilled beef heart doesn't cause yours to flutter, he's working on a first smoked and then fried chicken.

Gautreau's 1728 Soniat St.

Gautreau's is hidden away in an otherwise residential area in Uptown. If you hit the St. Vincent's Cemetery, you just went too far. For a while, Chef Sue Zemanick looked like she was headed toward being a culinary version of Alfred Hitchcock. She was nominated six times for the James Beard Award before she finally won hers in 2015. Sadly, the owner of the restaurant still does not give her her due. The website is sure to mention "Proprietors, Rebecca & Patrick Singley, welcome you to experience Gautreau's," but merely states that *Food & Wine* claimed their nameless chef as tops in America. (It's Sue Zemanick.) Sue Zemanick creates outrageously creative and elegant dishes. Her versionn of Surf 'n' Turf is Sauteed Shrimp and Crispy Pork Belly with hominy, poblano peppers, Vidalia onions, and green chili broth. Did I mention their award-winning chef is Sue Zemanick?

Lilly's Cafe 1813 Magazine St.

Most visitors to New Orleans aren't aware of the richness of our Vietnamese food, and instead choose to focus on Cajun and Creole restaurants. Lilly's can and should change your mind. They serve the best pho I've ever had, period.

Lilly Vuong previously worked in a nail salon. Every time she brought food from her kitchen into work, everyone repeated the refrain, "You should open a restaurant!" Finally, she did.

The small space has relatively few tables. You'll often see them filled by owners and top chefs from other restaurants. I have, more than once, seen JoAnn Clevenger, owner of Upperline and a finalist for the James Beard Award, eating there. Celebrity chef Tom Colicchio repeatedly brought his *Top Chef* cohorts to Lilly's when filming in New Orleans.

Lilly and her staff are always, without fail, gracious and welcoming.

Shaya 4213 Magazine St.

In a city where chefs are revered as rock stars or All-Pro athletes, Alon Shaya may be the hottest player on the current stage or roster. He recently won the 2015 James Beard Award for Best Chef in the South, this after being a finalist in 2012, 2013, and 2014. *Esquire* magazine named Shaya one of four Chefs to Watch back in 2010, and he has been named "Chef of the Year" by both Eater New Orleans and *New Orleans Magazine*. Then he opened Shaya, which was crowned Best New Restaurant in America 2016 by both *Esquire* and the coveted James Beard Awards.

Born in Tel Aviv, Israel before moving to Philadelphia, he'd tested the waters of serving Israeli cuisine in New Orleans with his Passover menu at Domenica. Israeli food is having something of a resurgence, nationally, so it seemed like an ideal time to open Shaya, an Israeli restaurant totally unique to New Orleans.

Israeli food is not just one thing, as people from many countries immigrated there. The national cuisine is a mixture of these many culinary cultures. The Curried Cauliflower has a Yemenite spice blend. The Kibbeh Nayah is beef and lamb tartare with Baharat, a Lebanese mixture of allspice, black pepper, and clove. Shakshouka, a warming dish of tomatoes with a runny egg, comes from Turkey. Lutenitsa, a puree of peppers and eggplants, is a Bulgarian dish.

In the back of the dining area is a wood oven for roasting dishes, but more for constantly churning out freshly baked and near perfect pita bread, served with every meal.

Shaya's menu has one section built around his hummus, which is pretty incredible hummus. I've had two expertly seared scallops and crushed pistachios over hummus. The small plate portions are sized just right, modest yet filling.

The whole place is modest yet rich. The brick walls, painted white, and the floor, streaked with a blond paint, aged and polished (and which somehow makes sliding your chair completely effortless . . . I actually looked down to see how I was moving with such ease and grace) captured my attention only thanks to the clear intent of not grabbing attention. The forks and knives are pleasingly slightly heavier than normal. The waiters seemed cast rather than hired. All of them, dressed in charcoal shirts with black pants, were attractive, but in subtle ways that likewise didn't call for attention.

Throughout my meals there, I am constantly struck that someone or ones had thought through *everything* in putting together this restaurant.

Square Root 1800 Magazine St.

Earlier in this chapter, I mentioned the wildly creative Chef Phillip Lopez in talking about his other New Orleans restaurant, Root. Square Root literally does multiply upon itself, taking the artfulness of Root and advancing it all the way to avant-garde.

Upstairs is for drinking at the bar or dining on a series of small plates. The downstairs dining area is only sixteen stools hovering over the open kitchen where Chef Lopez and his staff do their magic. Food writer Brett Anderson wrote, "Chef Phillip Lopez's calling cards are the cooking equivalents of back-flips, the bits of technical wizardry that take food into the realm of pure chemistry and ideally carry even familiar dishes to previously unexplored frontiers of vividness." It's a Broadway play camouflaged as a restaurant. As Chef Lopez says, "Cooking is an art form and it's very important for the guests to experience that." He cooks up surprise dishes right in front of diners. These do, however, come with Broadway play-like prices. The meal is a fifteen—yes, fifteen—course tasting menu, served on a parade of unusual plates from Barcelona that look like white porcelain volcanoes. Unlike most restaurants, the chef is up front and center, not buried in a behind-the-scenes kitchen. As he serves each dish he narrates its creation, sometimes adding in a bit of history. It's all rather like a culinary theater in the round.

What you'll get any evening is anyone's guess. Their website states, "We do not divulge specific details about our menu in order to preserve the element of surprise."

If you're not into surprises, or $150 prix fixe, you can order something less exotic from the menu, like their pig's head with caramelized squid, boiled peanuts, and seaweed.

As was the case with Root, Square Root is either a spot-on, one-of-a-kind restaurant for the adventurous foodie or an expensive "WTF?" for others.

Upperline 1413 Upperline St.

You have two reasons to go to Upperline. One is, of course, the food, which explodes with flavor, starting with the jalapeño cornbread. The second is the owner, JoAnn Clevenger, who explodes with personality. She's just two steps away from the circus, and she'll regale you with stories as she works the room. With her trademark hairdo, called "a sinuous approximation of a meringue knotted into a bun the size of a beignet," she elevates the role of hostess to theater. JoAnn Clevenger also has a philosophy of what makes a good restaurant: "Restaurants were originally more than just a place to find a meal; restaurants existed to soothe and bolster the weary soul with comfort and indulgence. Like the earliest restaurants, my goal for the Upperline is to be a haven for our guests, restoring their serenity after the daily hassles of the world with great Louisiana food, serious wine, and Creole hospitality."

The menu has signature dishes like duck and andouille étouffée with corn cakes, drum piquant with hot-and-hot shrimp, and a legendary deep brown gumbo. Upperline invented one of New Orleans' best appetizers (I think *the* best), which you can now get all over town: shrimp rémoulade over fried green tomato.

As *Southern Living* wrote, "If you can eat at only one fine restaurant in New Orleans, make it the Upperline."

Central City

Casa Borrega 1719 Oretha Castle Haley Blvd.

Hugo Montero, a local artist and first-time restaurateur, and his wife Linda Stone, co-founder of the Green Project and director of the New Orleans office of Global Green, have totally refurbished a nineteenth-century house into a dreamland. For Linda's green dream, everything in the interior is salvaged, recycled, and repurposed, including the handmade tables, the stained glass, the iron chandeliers from Mexico, the LP album covers decorating the walls, the collection of ceramic skulls, and the most beautiful ceiling fan I have ever seen. Hugo told me he spotted the fan in a hotel lobby in Cuba. Hugo said the restaurant is his art installation, a labor of love that he's worked on for four years. It is, in my mind, the most beautiful restaurant setting in New Orleans. You could spend the entire meal just taking in the rotary phones used as decorative accents, the fanged two-headed piñata riding in an antique child's car, and the little altars everywhere.

The menu springs from what Hugo remembers of his mother's kitchen and street food in Mexico City, his hometown before he moved here 25 years ago. The food is "real" Mexican food, very unlike what you may be used to. Hugo states, "I

Casa Borrega, open for business

adore Tex-Mex, but it's not Mexican." Don't ask for burritos. "No one ever ate burritos where I'm from," says Hugo. Casa Borrega's menu features antijitos, Mexican appetizers such as tostadas, gorditos, panuchos, and griddled masa cakes called sopes. The traditional entrees include the namesake Borrega, slow-braised lamb with a slight buzz, cooked in tequila and mescal. And for God's sake, get anything with the not-too-sweet mole sauce. Side bowls made from (recycled) hollowed-out gourds are filled with black beans and guacamole several times better than anything served at Don Pablo's or Chi-Chi's.

But the showstopper was the first thing served, the Coctel de Camarones, a shrimp cocktail appetizer served in a large rococo blue Mexican margarita glass. With at least six or seven large shrimp served with avocado, cilantro, onions, celery, garlic, and crushed tomatoes in what could pass for the best tomato soup ever, it tempted me to skip the meal and tell the waitress, "Bring me another and leave the bottle on the table."

Latin jazz or Afro-Caribbean bands perform on Friday and Saturday nights, completing what Hugo and Linda call their *peña. Peña* is a Mexican word meaning a community meeting place where artistic expressions, accompanied by food and drink, are showcased.

Kin 4600 Washington Ave.

Owner Hieu Than and chef Nate Nguyen seem to want to run a restaurant by putting as many obstacles in the way of their superior cooking as possible. First, they chose to open Kin in an easy-to-miss location inside an isolated building on a concrete island, shoved between a drainage canal and residential homes that seem ready for foreclosure or demolition. Atop the building are two large billboards, one for a pro-life organization, the other for McDonald's. There's almost no chance of walk-in traffic. Inside, you'll be faced with just one long communal table and a few stools shoved up to a bar. They can accommodate no more than twenty-five people, and none can be under 10 years old, for reasons only known to Nguyen and Than. It's surprisingly loud for so few diners, and you will be subjected to the thoughts and opinions of others sharing your table, no matter how boorish. Kin does no advertising. Their menu constantly changes, and the game hen and rice is the only ongoing dish.

When you go, you *might* be able to order their sugarcane-skewered lamb with mint and pine nut pesto, covered with a second layer of coconut and galangal sauce, or lightly battered and fried oysters with crawfish tails and pan-fried gnocchi placed on top of fennel-orange puree, or braised short ribs and polenta garnished with charred sweet red peppers, wilted greens, balsamic-glazed cipollini onions and bright green chimichurri. We were offered none of these, but instead ordered and then inhaled a small plate of duck leg, citrus-cured, with Corn Maque Choux and something they called a blini (but which we considered a crepe), a bowl of steamed mussels, spiced lime tomato broth, Chinese sausage gnocchi, allocacia, Chinese celery, culantro, preserved lime creme fraiche, and chicken-fried pork cheeks, grilled romaine, lemon cucumbers, cabbage slaw, bourbon tamarind reduction, and lotus stems. I don't think I'd ever before eaten lotus stems.

No matter what's on the menu of the day, they are all affordable (appetizers run around $10, and the most expensive entree will be about $25) and they are all exceptional.

Leidenheimer Baking Company
1501 Simon Bolivar Ave.

Leidenheimer Baking Company is not a restaurant, serves no food on the premises, and unless you're a local grade school kid on a field trip, you aren't welcomed inside. I profile the bread bakery here because they are hugely important to our culinary history and current food scene. As Julia Child said, "How can a nation be called great if its bread tastes like kleenex?"

New Orleans' bread heritage dates back to 1722, when Bellegarde Bakery opened their doors as the first commercial bakery in town. Bellegarde was an alias used by Francois Lemesle. Why a baker would need an alias remains a riddle, wrapped in a mystery, inside an enigma drizzled with conundrum. It was a terrible time to be a baker here. Wheat was not yet widely grown in the United States Bread bakers depended on ships from France and Spain to bring flour among their cargo, and it often arrived having turned rancid during the voyage, or riddled with mold or insects. Local bakers substituted available grains like corn, rice, amarinth, millet, and sorghum. In addition, the high humidity here made producing the hard crust preferred by the French nearly impossible.

The Germans immigrated to New Orleans in the 1800s and brought new bread techniques, including adding milk to the dough to make a lighter, airy texture, a style that became the basis of the city's signature po'boy bread, much lighter than the French baguette. At the peak, there were over 250 bakeries in the city producing a huge variety of breads; Bavarian rye, anise brioche, Acadian miche, pira, Vienna, and the ever-present croissants. But then came the introduction of preservatives, and grocery store chains almost overnight replaced craft or artisan breads with tasteless pre-cut loaves of Wonder and Bunny Bread. This was a national failing, not just in New Orleans.

At least here there remained a local demand for po'boy bread not shared by the rest of the country, so bakeries like Leidenheimer remained in business.

Today, the bread used in most every Parkway, Mahony's, Johnny's, and every other po'boy establishment comes from Leidenheimer's. George Leidenheimer came to New Orleans from Germany and set up shop in 1896. At first he baked the dense, dark breads of his native land, and he would have gone out of business before the twentieth century had he not adapted to the tastes of the predominantly French city. He perfected the crispy crust and airy interior of the best French breads and has dominated the New Orleans market ever since. Leidenheimer Bread has been baked in the same brick building on Simon Bolivar Avenue since 1904. Their signature trucks, with Bunny Matthews' Vic & Nat'ly cartoons painted on the side, can be seen each morning, dropping off bread at po'boy shops all over town.

Riverbend and Carrollton

Brigtsen's 723 Dante St.

Frank Brigtsen learned at the apron strings of chef/icon Paul Prudhomme. In 1979, he responded to a help wanted ad when he was young, broke, and just got dumped by his girlfriend. He apprenticed at Commander's Palace and then followed Chef Prudhomme for the opening of K-Paul's Louisiana Kitchen. There, Frank advanced from Night Chef to Paul's Executive Chef before opening his own restaurant in 1986. Housed in a quaint cottage, the menu at Brigtsen's restaurant changes daily to make use of the freshest ingredients. You might have the Braised Two Run Farm Free-Range Lamb Shank with Lentil Cake, Rosemary Mint Jus & Asiago Cheese Grits, or you could have to settle for BBQ Seasoned Redfish with Chipotle Grits Cake and Shrimp and Corn Macque Choux.

Camellia Grill 626 S. Carrollton Ave.

After Katrina, Camellia Grill took longer to reopen than many other nearby restaurants and businesses. The reason wasn't as much damage from the storm as it was getting back their staff, which had scattered to Houston, Atlanta, and other distant cities. The waiters at Camellia are as much a reason to go as their burgers and breakfast-anytime menu. In their white shirts with black bow ties, they greet diners with quick wits and easy familiarity. And their skills presenting drinking straws rival anything Michael Jordan ever did with a basketball. Many of the waiters are long-standing fixtures, none more so than Harry Tervalon, Sr., who was the first waiter hired in 1946, and who, even after his retirement in '96, remained a part of the restaurant (including cutting the ribbon when Camellia Grill finally reopened after Katrina) until his death in August 2007.

During the months the restaurant remained closed, loyal patrons began posting notes on the locked front door. A note signed "Ashleigh" said, "I came here for law school just so I could have my Camellia Grill fix regularly. Please come back." Eventually there were hundreds of notes with messages such as, "I miss coming here after every baseball game," or "We came from Florida. I'm hungry. I need a handshake. And a milkshake," and another: "I can't bear the thought of you not being here. My parents dated here. I dated here or came with friends in the late '60s and early '70s . . . Now I've been bringing my kids here," signed "Janet."

A second Camellia Grill location opened in the French Quarter (540 Chartres St.) in December 2010 with the same serpentine Formica counter, where all patrons "belly up." A sign outside the new establishment says, "Since 1946." It's two years old.

Jacques-Imo's 8324 Oak St.

Outside the restaurant hangs a sign: "Warm Beer. Lousy Food. Poor Service." Like so much about Jacques-Imo's, they're just playing with you. When I visited New Orleans, but did not yet live here, Jacques-Imo's was my favorite restaurant in the city. But when I visited here and did not yet live here, Austin Leslie manned the kitchen. With his passing, Jacques-Imo's is now among my favorite restaurants in

LUMINS OF NEW ORLEANS:
Mr. Okra

Arthur Robinson, m.k.a. (mostly known as) Mr. Okra, has been peddling his fruits and vegetables for over 30 years from the back of a battered, chugging Ford pickup truck. The truck is decorated with his name and folk art painted by Dr. "Be Nice or Leave" Bob.

CHERYL GERBER

Seven days a week, Mr. Okra roves the streets of Bywater, Treme, and Mid-City—unless he doesn't feel well or his truck has one of its frequent breakdowns. His calling card is his deep, bullfrog voice, bellowing what he has to sell each day.

Years ago he was known as "Li'l Okra" when he worked with his dad, the original Okra Man. He sold produce and random meats at first from a wheelbarrow, then from a horse and buggy. For awhile, Mr. Okra ran his own tire shop, servicing eighteen-wheelers. But eventually he settled into his dad's business, his colorful truck replacing the wheelbarrow and buggy.

Back in the day, New Orleans had many vendors working the city streets, like the ice man, the coffee man, and the charcoal man, who brought their goods or services directly to customers' doors. The calls of itinerant hawkers and bootstrap entrepreneurs used to echo through the air. Now there's just Mr. Okra.

He has since become a mobile civic icon. Residents passing by his truck in their cars or on bicycles will mimic Mr. Okra's "I got orrrr-angesss. I got banaaa-nasss." His banter has been featured on numerous albums by local bands, plus "Squirm," a song by Dave Matthews Band. He was the subject of the 2009 documentary *Mr. Okra*. Said the film's director, T. G. Herrington, "He's so iconic and such a part of the fabric of my community. After the first screening in New York, people walked up to us and said, 'This makes me want to move to New Orleans. I want to know people like Mr. Okra.'"

The Mayor's Office bestowed upon Mr. Okra an honorary "Ambassador to New Orleans" commendation. Of all of this attention, Mr. Okra says, "I'm a celebrity, but I'm a broke celebrity."

the city. Jacques Leonardi, the irrepressible owner and chef, is still very visibly on the premises as he works the room, generally two—but not three—sheets to the wind.

Jacques is another in the long and forever ongoing line of expat Yats. Raised on a farm in upstate New York by a French mother and an Italian father, he came to New Orleans as part of his tour of duty with the Coast Guard. Like so many, Jacques fell in love with New Orleans and all it had to offer . . . and stayed. His restaurant career began with working for minimum wage in the bowels of Chef Paul Prudhomme's K-Paul's Louisiana Kitchen. In 1996, he purchased the building on Oak Street. With considerable help from legendary Chef Austin Leslie, combined with his own wild creativity, he established one of the most popular New Orleans restaurants. They only take reservations for parties of five or more. Parties of four or fewer can wait up to two hours for a table. Or you could, if you choose, be seated and served in the flatbed of a decorated truck parked in the front of the restaurant. My wife, daughter, and I have done this. The food's just as good in the truck, and you'll have lively conversations with people waiting to get in or just passing by on the street.

Where I've just listed seventy-five of our 1,420 restaurants (or about the number you can get to in a week), you can also get not just good, but great meals all over town standing alongside food trucks (La Cocinita is my far-and-away favorite) and convenience stores.

Old neighborhoods used to be, and many still are, dotted with brightly colored corner markets. One might be painted bright yellow, with nearby marts bright purple or red. The story is that back in the day, many people were illiterate, so that rather than sending a family member to pick up food at the Cajun Market or Quicky's, they'd say to go to the Yellow Store or Red Store. Plus, your tab might be running high at the Yellow Store, so you'd hang out at the Purple Store for a bit.

A number of people here think New Orleans best shrimp po'boy comes from Rampart Food Store (1700 N. Rampart St.). Few people here actually call it the Rampart Food Store. We know it as the Orange Store.

CHAPTER 2

Listening

From Bamboulas to Brass Band to Bounce—and, of course, Jazz

I'm not sure, but I'm almost positive, that all music comes from
New Orleans.
—Ernie K-Doe

Admit it, you still tear up when watching Renée Zellweger, for the twenty-fifth time, say "You had me at hello" in the movie *Jerry Maguire*. And this is even after you've come to realize that both Renée and Tom Cruise in real life are complete lunatics. I've come to find out that we here in New Orleans feel that level of emotion whenever we hear Anders Osborne sing "Summertime in New Orleans."

At a reading and signing for my book, *Hear Dat*, drummer Stanton Moore, who joined me, talked about getting choked up the first time he heard it. I immediately recalled my first time. I was standing at a listening station at the old Louisiana Music Factory on Decatur Street. I had to compose myself and wipe away my tears before turning back to face other customers and store clerks. Even Anders Osborne himself has admitted, "I choked up singing 'Summertime.' It was weird to be so emotional about your own stuff, but it meant so much."

If you want to go bring it up on YouTube right now, we'll wait for you.

Music is a profound part of our lives, not just in the way teenagers play a song over and over and over again (in my day it was "Stairway to Heaven" and "Rosalita"), but here music is everywhere and it is essential. It practically bubbles up from the streets, as famously claimed by Ellis Marsalis, jazz pianist and patriarch of the musical royal family in New Orleans.

From the time you wake up to a jazz brunch (and hear street musicians on the way there) until the last club closes along Frenchmen Street past 3:00 in the morning, live music will be as much a part of your day as eating, drinking, and buying things you don't need.

Live music will accompany your meals at restaurants like Palm Court Jazz Cafe, Little Gem Saloon, The Bombay Club, and Bacchanal, among many others. It will be played in your hotel lobby if you stay at The Columns Hotel, Hotel Monteleone, Irvin Mayfield's Jazz Playhouse inside the Royal Sonesta, and the Davenport Lounge inside the Ritz-Carlton. At least four, sometimes five nights a week, you can go bowling while listening to some of the city's best musicians at the Rock 'n' Bowl. The Grammy-nominated Dukes of Dixieland play nightly for the dinner cruise aboard the Steamboat Natchez.

Street musicians line Royal Street and Jackson Square, playing for loose change and wrinkled bills. They are a cut above the buskers you'll find in any other city. Each day the section of Royal Street between St. Ann and St. Louis streets in the French Quarter is closed off from automobile traffic, essentially making it a pedestrian mall. During these hours, Royal Street will be lined with mimes, magicians, and people who pretend to be statues and get paid for literally doing nothing. The top draw, however, is always the street musicians. It's a tradition that goes back hundreds of years and is an integral part of the city's culture. Said longtime civil rights lawyer and defender of public performers, Mary Howell, "Apparently people have been playing music in the streets as long as there has been a city here. You go to other places and they try to create what we already have here—some cities pay people to create this cultural life!"

A number of New Orleans' most noted musicians got their start on the street, including Troy "Trombone Shorty" Andrews, The Rebirth Brass Band, Dirty Dozen Brass Band, the lesser known but beautifully named Emile "Stale Bread" Lacoume and his Razzy Dazzy Spasm Band. Before Meschiya Lake became four-time Best Female Vocalist and before Professor Longhair became the legendary heart and soul of New Orleans music, you could have heard them out playing for tips on the streets of the French Quarter.

Some current street bands like the Slick Skillet Serenaders and Grandpa Elliot have regular followers camp out in "their" section of the street. The bluesy-country husband-and-wife team known as David and Roselyn have been playing on the streets of the Quarter since 1975. They've recorded six albums and do performance tours on the West Coast and overseas. The couple has four grown children who they've put through school, paid for by performance tips earned on French Quarter streets.

Whenever you visit New Orleans, there will probably be a music festival going on, or at least a food festival or street fair that includes a heaping dose of live music. The Jazz & Heritage Festival, the French Quarter Festival, the Voodoo Music + Arts Experience, Crescent City Blues & BBQ Festival, Mid-City Bayou Boogaloo, and the Essence Festival are signature events each year. They draw as many as half a million visitors (per event) to New Orleans.

Our most common nickname, The Big Easy, originated as a musical term. Some assume it derives from the slow and easy way New Orleanians choose to live their lives. A New Orleans astrologer, Lynn Wilson, said of the city, "New Orleans value to the world lies in its charming dysfunctionality. The world doesn't need more Atlantas. We need a place where 'slow' is accepted as the treasure that it is."

However, the most consistent and reliable derivation seems to come from "back in the day," when musicians used to ride the rails looking for paying gigs in New York, Chicago, Memphis, St. Louis, and elsewhere. Musicians shared the sentiment that New Orleans was the #1 place to go. They tabbed the city the Big Easy because there were so many bars, clubs, dance halls, and juke joints that any halfway decent musician would always have an easy time finding work.

Next you should know that most New Orleanians like being called "the Big Easy" as much as San Francisco residents like the term "'Frisco."

I fretted greatly, and apologized at least three or four times in *Hear Dat*, because I was afraid of leaving out worthy musicians. And I most definitely did overlook many. There's even one, James Black, about whom I'd never read nor heard until after the book's publication, whose biography I am now considering writing. Obviously, since I couldn't fit everyone into a 200-page book, I certainly can't do it in this lone chapter.

Jazz

Louis Armstrong said, "If you have to ask what jazz is, you'll never know." So, I won't waste too much time trying to define it, but will trace its ancestry. Jazz was born in New Orleans. Jazz *had* to be born in New Orleans. Owned by France, New Orleans was the one place in America where slaves had Sundays off from work under the French Code Noir. In New England, slaves were sometimes given a pound of salted cod on Sundays, but they still worked.

Here, they were free to practice their religion (voodoo) from West Africa and Haiti and play their musical traditions (bamboula). Elsewhere in America, those freedom-seeking Brits took away the music, religion, and all culture of the enslaved Africans, trying to convert them to Christianity, unsavory food, and lusterless clothes. Originating in Africa, the bamboula refers both to the instrument, a drum where animal skin is stretch across a bamboo frame, and a dance syncopation performed to the rhythm of the drum during festivals and ceremonies.

Under Code Noir, slaves gathered all over the city each Sunday. Then in 1817, Mayor Macarty issued an ordinance that restricted slave gatherings to one single location placed in the less desirable back part of town, Place des Nègres, informally known as Congo Square. The most positive aspect of Macarty's restrictions is that we now know exactly where jazz was born. Congo Square also became a boon for New Orleans tourism, drawing numerous visitors and their dollars to hear the unique bamboulas and banzas playing on the square.

The actual word jazz is, in one story, said to have come from the brothels of

Storyville and the jasmine perfume that most of the prostitutes wore. Musicians of this hot new style, not yet called jazz, were hired to play in the lobbies in order to lure in customers. After a gentleman partook of the sexual services offered in Storyville, their friends or business chums would often say, "Man, you smell like you just got jassed." Though, there's also another story that the word jass was first used in 1916 to describe a baseball pitcher in San Francisco who put jass on the ball when he hurled his zigzag pitches.

Buddy Bolden, born 1877, is credited by many as the Father of Jazz. He played the cornet strictly by ear and in a music style that merged marching band music, black spirituals, and rural blues. Jazz also fuses French quadrilles, beguine, and other styles. Buddy was known for his improvised, wide open, and intensely loud playing. Before performing, Buddy would blast his signature "call his children home" riff so folks across town could hear he was about to unleash a raucous set. Most importantly, he is said to have invented the so-called "Big Four." As contemporary jazz great Wynton Marsalis describes it, "The Big Four was the first syncopated bass drum pattern to deviate from the standard on-the-beat march. The second half of the Big Four is a pattern commonly known as the habanera rhythm, one of the most basic rhythmic cells in Afro-Latin music traditions."

More than using new technique, Buddy Bolden captured a young audience with his revolutionary raunchy lyrics, delivered in Buddy's reportedly guttural moan. Consider Buddy's band the 2 Live Crew or NWA of their day.

The band would squeeze overflowing crowds into funky, rough roadhouse places like the Union Sons Hall on Perdido Street, and they'd often play on until 5:00 a.m.

Bolden, always a heavy drinker, also used a ton of medicinal drugs that in those times contained cocaine. He suffered episodes of acute alcoholic psychosis and was given a diagnosis of dementia at the young age of 30. He spent the last 24 years of his life in the Louisiana State Insane Asylum. He was buried in Holt Cemetery, a potter's field, at the edge of New Orleans. There are two plaques inside Holt honoring the Father of Jazz, but no definitive gravesite. There are likewise no known recordings of Buddy Bolden's band. Trombonist Willy Cornish, recalls that the band made a phonograph cylinder in the late 1890s, but none have ever been found.

As jazz spread from New Orleans, it evolved different regional and local musical styles. By the 1930s, Kansas City-style jazz was heavily arranged dance-oriented swing band music. Gypsy jazz, a style that emphasized musette waltzes, had become popular up North. Bebop emerged in the 1940s and shifted jazz from dance music toward a challenging "musician's music," which was played at faster tempos and used more chord-based improvisation. Cool jazz introduced smoother sounds and long, linear melodic lines that you'd associate with clubs teeming with black turtlenecks, cigarette smoke, and earnest poetry. Jazz today is . . . well . . . jazz.

The one constant and key element of jazz is improvisation. As saxophonist J. J. Johnson said, "Jazz is restless. It won't stay put and it never will."

In addition to Buddy, Joseph Nathan "King" Oliver, "Jelly Roll" Morton, Edward "Kid" Ory, Willie Gary "Bunk" Johnson, and, most famously, Louis Armstrong, nicknamed both Satchmo and Pops (and, once in a while, Dipper), were all the George Washingtons and Thomas Jeffersons of jazz.

King Oliver may not have been the Father of Jazz, but as written by one of his disciples, Louis Armstrong, "I still think that if it had not been for Joe Oliver, jazz would not be what it is today." Unlike Buddy Bolden, Oliver's band crossed racial lines. His music was popular in both black dance halls in Storyville as well as at white society debutante balls. Sadly, like Bolden, at the end of his life Oliver also experienced many misfortunes. He ended up working odd jobs at a fruit stand and as a janitor. He died at age 57, unable to afford treatment for arteriosclerosis.

Jelly Roll Morton grew up in New Orleans and started to learn piano at the age of 10. Morton uniquely fused a variety of black musical styles—ragtime, vocal and instrumental blues, minstrel show tunes, field and levee hollers, religious hymns, spirituals, plus hints of Caribbean music. Like so many of the early jazz musicians, hard times hit Jelly Roll hard. His brand of music went out of style, replaced by the swing and big band era. He ended up managing and only occasionally playing at a dive bar in Washington, D.C. In 1938, Jelly Roll was "re-discovered" by Alan Lomax, who recorded him in a series of interviews about early jazz for the Library of Congress. In this invaluable oral history, Morton recalled in words and performances his early days in New Orleans. The Library of Congress recordings rekindled public interest in Morton's career and helped lead to a New Orleans music revival.

Willie Gary "Bunk" Johnson was born either 1879 or 1889. An uncovered census shows his birth as the latter. He claimed the former to back up his assertion that he played in Buddy Bolden's band, which would have meant he was wearing diapers at the time. He also claimed to have taught a young Louis Armstrong everything he knows. Armstrong himself refuted that boast and said King Oliver was his mentor. These statements, plus many others, show how he got his nickname, Bunk. He became critically important in the revitalization of jazz, not just for his playing or for his spreading the gospel through long stints in San Francisco and New York with visits to Los Angeles, Boston, Chicago, and around the world, but also for his recorded interviews where he talked about New Orleans, his life, Buddy Bolden, funeral parades, and early jazz music. Bunk, in effect, laid down a permanent history of jazz. Bunk's influence and popularity were especially strong with European and Asian fans. Some say, and certainly Bunk would have agreed, that his legacy for New Orleans jazz overseas surpasses even that of Louis Armstrong.

Born 1897, **Sidney Bechet**, a contemporary of Louis Armstrong and the undisputed king of the soprano saxophone, sadly has no nickname. We can make one up and call him "Shooter" for the incident in Paris when a woman was wounded during an exchange of gunfire that resulted in Bechet being jailed for nearly a year. The shootout started when another musician told Bechet that he was playing the wrong chord. Bechet challenged the man to a duel, saying, "Sidney Bechet never plays the wrong chord." His influence can be heard in countless musicians, including John Coltrane, Wayne Shorter, and Branford Marsalis.

Danny Barker was not one of the founding fathers of jazz, but a key member of the next generation. He was a jazz banjoist, singer, guitarist, songwriter, and ukulele player. He played with Louis Armstrong, Fess Williams, Billy Fowler, the White Brothers, Buddy Harris, Albert Nicholas, Lucky Millinder, Benny Carter, Bunk Johnson, Dexter Gordon, Charlie Parker, Jelly Roll Morton, Baby Dodds, James P. Johnson, Sidney Bechet, Mezz Mezzrow, Red Allen, Ethel Waters, and Cab Calloway—in other words, everybody. After leaving Calloway, he started his own group that featured his wife Blue Lu Barker and the Fairview Baptist Church Brass Band. The band, renamed the Dirty Dozen Brass Band in later years, was pivotal in New Orleans jazz history, launching the careers of brothers Wynton Marsalis and Branford Marsalis, Shannon Powell a.k.a. "The King of Treme," Lucien Barbarin, Dr. Michael White, Leroy Jones, and others. Joe Torregano, another Fairview band alumnus, said this: "That group saved jazz for a generation in New Orleans."

Getting the last word on historical jazz is an honor that simply has to go to **Louis Armstrong**. Louis Armstrong's importance cannot be overstated. He was an innovator of epic proportions. Armstrong's sense of rhythm and timing took jazz from a formal $^2/_4$ beat to a languid, more sophisticated $^4/_4$ feel. He completely redefined the context in which the trumpet was played, launching the instrument from a backup role to center stage. His talent as a singer, trumpeter, composer, and showmanship brought worldwide attention to New Orleans jazz. Pops' recordings in Chicago with the Hot Five, a group of first-rate musicians (most from New Orleans), are among the most important recordings in jazz history. Emerging as the hanky-waving entertainer, he went on to become the official ambassador of music and goodwill, performing jazz throughout the world under sponsorship of the U.S. Department of State.

Even with my total lack of music sophistication (despite a third-grade flutophone education), I always liked Louis Armstrong's music. But it wasn't until I saw a film clip of jazz scholar Gary Giddins that I fully appreciated Satchmo's genius. Playing the opening cadenza of the song "West End Blues," Giddins explained what we hear basically cannot be done by a human being. Now, every time I hear it, I get all choked up.

If you want to go take another YouTube break, we'll wait for you.

Where you can hear live jazz tonight has to start with Preservation Hall (726 St. Peter St.). It is located in the heart of the French Quarter, a block behind Jackson Square, right next to Pat O'Brien's and directly across the street from Reverend Zombie's House of Voodoo. I give all these landmarks because Preservation Hall's sign, hung much too high and lettered in much too discreet old gold letters on black backing, is easy to miss. This intimate venue has been playing three shows a night, at 8:15, 9:15, and 10:15, 350 days a year, since 1961. Preservation Hall easily draws in more listeners than any music club in New Orleans.

Inside, they serve no food, offer nothing to drink, provide no air-conditioning, and have no bathrooms (and no seats for late arrivals). Patrons, however, are welcome to sit on the floor or stand. It's been this way since the beginning, when Allan and Sandra Jaffe were passing through the city on the way back from their honeymoon. The space was previously an art gallery where the owner, Larry Borenstein, had the bright idea to have noted jazz musicians practice and perform inside his art space. His goals were to draw in more customers but also to allow himself to hear the music he loved.

During their (intended to be) short visit, the Jaffes heard about "Mr. Larry's Gallery." Going there, they were seduced—to the point of tearing up their roots in Pennsylvania, moving to New Orleans, buying the gallery space, and converting it into the now-famous jazz hall. In his passion to preserve the old-time music, Allan Jaffe organized the Preservation Hall Jazz Band for performances both in his space and in a series of performances in the Midwest he set up to spread the gospel. Fifty-five years later, now under the leadership of the Jaffe's son, Ben, the performances remain today as they ever were. As you sit and some nights sweat for the 45-minute session, it's just you and musicians, playing at arm's length in an intimate and moving experience of live acoustic jazz performed by masters. The band actually has many members, making it possible to have nightly performances in New Orleans as well as over 100 tour dates worldwide. They are now spreading the gospel as far as Japan.

Another classic jazz spot, the Palm Court Jazz Cafe (1204 Decatur St.) doesn't have quite the history and reputation of Preservation Hall, but a venerable jazz orchestra along with their Creole cuisine is served up every Wednesday through Sunday since 1989. Unfortunately, their headliner, trumpeter Lionel Ferbos, passed away in 2014. Up until a few weeks before his death, Mister Lionel sat in with the band every Friday night. He was 103 years old, at the time the world's oldest living jazz musician. When I spoke with a staff person at Palm Court, they reassured me: "We still have two 90-year-olds."

Jazz can be heard in a great many other clubs. Stanton Moore's Jazz Trio plays most Tuesdays at Snug Harbor. Kermit Ruffins can be heard most Saturdays at Little Gem, Thursdays at Bullets Sports Bar, and sometimes twice a week at his own Kermit's Mother-in-Law Lounge. But these clubs all play a variety of music in addition to jazz.

Kermit Ruffins at Little Gem

Kermit Ruffins is New Orleans jazz royalty. He began his professional career as a founding member in the Rebirth Brass Band back when he was still in high school. In 1992, Ruffins set off on a career that dropped brass band and focused on his passion for classic New Orleans jazz. His new quintet was named the Barbecue Swingers because of Kermit's practice of firing up the grill in the bed of his pickup truck before the band played. By the end of the first set, the barbecue was ready.

Beyond his virtuoso trumpet playing (or cooking) skills, Kermit in many ways embodies the spirit of New Orleans music. Like his hero, Louis Armstrong, he's free-spirited, swinging, and always with a ready smile. When I saw him one year at French Quarter Festival, Kermit closed his set with the comment, "This was the first time I've played straight in I don't know how many years." He also delivered the far and away best line from the HBO series *Treme*. Asked if he wanted to waste his whole life getting high and eating barbecue in New Orleans, Kermit responded, "That'll work." Like Louis Armstrong, Kermit's importance to New Orleans jazz cannot be overstated, as he helped keep it alive by bringing jazz to younger and hipper audiences.

The Marsalis Family is the unofficial first family of jazz. Patriarch Ellis Marsalis, the great pianist and teacher, helped to raise four noted musician sons: the saxophonist Branford, trumpeter and composer Wynton, trombonist Delfeayo, and drummer Jason.

Ellis was a cofounder of AFO (All For One) Records, one of America's first independent, black-owned record companies. He was, at that time, one of the few New Orleans musicians just not that into New Orleans Dixieland or rhythm and blues. Instead, he played the more sophisticated hard bop and modernist jazz. The Ellis Marsalis Quartet play most Friday nights at Snug Harbor on Frenchmen Street. The entire Marsalis family of musicians won the 2011 Jazz Master Fellowship Awards from the National Endowment for the Arts. It is the highest honor that the United States bestows upon jazz musicians.

In this city, there are just too many other jazz greats like Shannon Powell, Shammer Allen, Terence Blanchard, Tim Laughlin, Dr. Michael White, Leroy Jones, etc., etc. to appropriately portray in a mere chapter. You're just going to have to get your wiggle on and get into the music clubs.

Blues

In the post-Emancipation era, which is roughly between 1870 and 1900, juke joints opened up all over the South. These were ramshackle places where blacks went after a backbreaking day's work to listen to music, dance, and drink. Because blues was the first nonwhite music to take hold in the larger popular culture, it predates rock 'n' roll and rap as being the "devil's music." White folks considered it disreputable and said that it incited violence, and maybe even provoked those much-feared sexual activities.

W. C. Handy, a deeply religious man from Alabama who always looked dapper in a suit, tie, and pocket square, has been called the "Father of the Blues" even though he came along a good 20 to 30 years after the birth of the blues. He was, however, the first to make the music popular with non-black audiences, even playing at Carnegie Hall in 1928.

The New Orleans style of blues is a variation that developed in the 1940s and '50s in and around the city. The style is strongly influenced by the strut of Dixieland jazz and the Caribbean sounds so prevalent in the area. The music is dominated here by piano and horn, rather than the Robert Johnson guitar style heard everywhere else. New Orleans blues has the cheerful and lazy feel of good-time music, no matter how somber the lyrics may be.

The earliest star of New Orleans blues was **Guitar Slim**, much less known as Eddie Jones, best known for his classic, million-copy-selling song, "The Things That I Used to Do." It's listed on the Rock and Roll Hall of Fame's "500 Songs That Shaped Rock 'n' Roll." With his experiments and distorted overtones on the electric guitar, Guitar Slim also greatly influenced many future guitarists, including Jimi Hendrix.

Slim Harpo, a.k.a. James Moore, was a leading exponent of the swamp blues style and one of the most commercially successful blues artists of his day. His hit songs include "I'm a King Bee," "Rainin' In My Heart," and "Baby Scratch My Back" that reached #1 on the R&B chart and #16 on the U.S. pop chart. A master of the blues harmonica, his stage name was derived from the popular nickname for that instrument, the "harp."

Never able to be a full-time musician, Harpo had his own trucking business to make ends meet when he wasn't on tour and playing in the studio for other musicians. His harmonica can be heard on albums by The Rolling Stones, The Yardbirds, The Kinks, and Pink Floyd. The Moody Blues took their name from an instrumental track of Slim's called "Moody Blues."

Champion Jack Dupree was orphaned at the age of 2 and sent to the New Orleans Colored Waifs Home, the same place as Louis Armstrong. Dupree's piano playing was all straight blues and boogie-woogie. He was not a sophisticated musician or singer; he sang about his life, mostly jail, drinking, and drug addiction. His song "Big Leg Emma's" is said to be one of the precursors of rap music. Some of his saucier lyrics include lines like, "Mama, move your false teeth, papa wanna scratch your gums."

Blind Snooks Eaglin had a vocal style compared to Ray Charles. Like Ray Charles, he lost his eyesight as a very young man. He was completely self-taught as a musician, and he did this by listening to and playing along with the radio. His range was legendary. Snooks could play blues, rock and roll, jazz, country, and Latin music. He claimed in interviews that his musical repertoire included some 2,500 songs, earning him the nickname The Human Jukebox.

One of my regrets in life is that time and again I meant to go hear Snooks Eaglin at the Mid-City Rock 'n' Bowl while visiting New Orleans. But I always got distracted, as New Orleans can distract you. I figured I could catch him "next time," because he played there regularly. By the time we actually moved to New Orleans, Snooks had passed away.

Of the current blues scene and musicians you might actually see, **Little Freddie King** is probably playing somewhere tonight. He's a regular at BJ's Lounge, d.b.a., and the Old Arabi Bar, occasionally playing at Le Bon Temps Roule or Ruby's Roadhouse. And if there's a blues festival anywhere, he's no doubt part of the lineup. He's played the Jazz & Heritage Festival forty-two times and counting.

Little Freddie has been dubbed "one of the last great country-blues players." Local music writer Robert Fontenot perfectly captured his music: "It ain't pretty . . . you can practically smell the Chinese food and chicken coming from Chun King . . . the slop bucket wheeze put out on his cover of Kinurtis's "Soul Twist" is potent enough to turn George W. Bush into the Godfather of Soul. It's THAT country and THAT ghetto."

When he was 14 years old, Little Freddie King began to land gigs, but not in the swankiest of clubs. The Busy Bee on Perdido Street he later immortalized in his song "Bucket of Blood," so named because of the frequency of patrons being shot or stabbed there. He worked his way into the legendary Dew Drop Inn, where he played backup to the female impersonator Patsy Vidalia. Little Freddie has survived rough rooms, alcoholism, and a wife who shot him five times. King immortalized her in his song "Mean Little Woman."

Walter "Wolfman" Washington blends in funk and R&B to create his own unique blues sound. He's a masterful guitar player with a great, nickname-producing howl of a voice. Wolfman has been performing since the 1960s. It wasn't until after 20 years on stage that Washington released his first solo album, *Rainin' In My Life*. He plays around town each week, most frequently every Wednesday at the music club d.b.a, and often at the Maple Leaf Bar.

Originally from New York, **Washboard Chaz** lived in Boulder some 22 years, and didn't show up in New Orleans until 2000. He has since become an integral part of our music scene, and is counted among the best acoustic blues performers in New Orleans. He's played with The Iguanas, New Orleans Jazz Vipers, The Palmetto Bug Stompers, New Orleans Nightcrawlers, Tuba Fats, Royal Fingerbowl, Washboard Rodeo, and his two main bands, The Tin Men and The Washboard Chaz Blues Trio.

He's just as indiscriminate with his settings. In a one-week stretch, Chaz can be heard at d.b.a., The Spotted Cat, Blue Nile, Three Muses, 21st Amendment, and The Columns Hotel. He's accomplished all this as a musician whose only instrument is his tricked-out washboard and finger thimbles.

Tab Benoit's playing combines a number of blues styles, primarily Delta blues. He's won the B.B. King Entertainer of the Year award, the Best Contemporary Male Performer at the Blues Music Awards (formerly the W. C. Handy Awards), and received a Grammy nomination for Best Traditional Blues Album. When not on tour, Tab Benoit can be heard regularly at Rock 'n' Bowl.

The first time I heard **John Mooney** on the radio, I thought I was listening to John Hiatt. The slide guitar, the voice—there is a strong similarity. But after learning I was really hearing a New Orleans-based artist, I dug around YouTube and spent some time at the listening stations at Louisiana Music Factory. I realized this was something even better: a John Hiatt sound enhanced by combining Delta blues and New Orleans funk.

Mooney is actually from East Orange, New Jersey. He left home when he was 15 and within the year had the good fortune to meet Mississippi blues legend Son House.

Mooney moved to New Orleans in 1976 and began playing with a host of A-level musicians that included Earl King, The Meters, Snooks Eaglin, and Professor Longhair. He released his first album, *Comin' Your Way*, on Blind Pig Records in 1979. Two years later he formed his own band, Bluesiana. He has been recording and touring with them ever since.

The most concentrated and best place to hear live blues (and jazz, and funk, and brass band, and maybe a little reggae) is Frenchmen Street in the Marigny neighborhood. It has replaced Bourbon Street as the live music street of New Orleans. It's our version of Beale Street in Memphis or 6th Street in Austin (only much, much better).

Places to "do" on Frenchmen Street

30°/90° 520 Frenchmen St.

30°/90° is the latitude and longitude of New Orleans, the name of an all-female blues band, and also this cozy club with cocktails, decent pizza, and live music.

Apple Barrel 609 Frenchmen St.

A tiny bar below the restaurant hosts nightly music in a funky setting. The place is decorated with dollar bills taped to the walls behind the bar, and a mural of Louis Armstrong hangs where the musicians play. Originally it was the setting where the late Coco Robicheaux replaced the jukebox and dartboard as the entertainment. Coco actually died seated at the bar.

Bamboula's 516 Frenchmen St.

Opened in 2013, Bamboula's is the newest kid on the block. This is a regular stop for Smoky Greenwell, The Messy Cookers Jazz Band, John Lisi, Troy Turner, and the place's own Bamboula's Hot Trio.

Blue Nile 532 Frenchmen St.

The Blue Nile is the most eclectic, or at least the most wide-ranging, of the clubs that line Frenchmen. On its two stages you can hear most any kind of music from blues to New Orleans's top line jazz performers like Kermit Ruffins. You can also expect plenty of brass band, hip hop, and an occasional taste of indie rock music. The club also hosts weekly reggae dance parties with DJ T-Roy.

Twelve clubs are packed together door-to-door in two and a half blocks. The performers are drastically better than the current Bourbon Street cover bands. I might be tempted to suggest you go see Meschiya Lake at The Spotted Cat, or John Boutté at d.b.a., or the venerable Ellis Marsalis at Snug Harbor. But in truth, the best way to "do" Frenchmen is not to have a specific club or act as your destination. Instead, just go and let your ears be your guide.

Cafe Negril 606 Frenchmen St.

Their Mexican food, which I've never tried, garners a range of comments online, from "Best Tacos" to "Burrito Bust." The music is more consistently thumbs up. John Lisi & Delta Funk, a blues band with a little funk, plays on Tuesdays and Saturdays. Dana Abbott, singer, songwriter, and HBO *Treme* star, performs Fridays and Sundays. The Higher Heights Reggae Band seems the most suited for this stage, which has a huge Bob Marley mural covering the wall. Unlike most clubs on Frenchmen, Cafe Negril has a sizable dance floor.

d.b.a. 618 Frenchmen St.

As one of the gems of Frenchmen Street, d.b.a. is an attractive club with high ceilings, paneled walls, and a lineup of New Orleans' finest musicians performing two times each night at 6:00 or 7:00, and a second show at 10:00. The music offerings span a full range, from jazz (Glen David Andrews), jazz vocalist (John Boutté), blues (Walter Wolfman Washington), brass band (Treme Brass Band), funk and R&B (Jon Cleary), Mardi Gras Indians (Big Chief Monk Boudreaux), swamp pop (Palmetto Bug Stompers), and even flamenco (Ven Pa' Ca).

Dragon's Den 435 Esplanade Ave.

The bright red Dragon's Den is technically not on Frenchmen Street. It's just around the corner, and so fits in with a nighttime of Frenchmen club-hopping. The front room is the setting for live bands like the Bayou Saints, Up Up We Go (a jazz ensemble), and Loose Marbles. The venue is also used for DJ-themed nights. The upstairs room hosts the burlesque show "Talk Nerdy to Me" on Saturday nights and features electronic dance parties on others.

Maison 508 Frenchmen St.

Maison is the largest venue on Frenchmen. The three-story building has a front room stage, a backroom used for big shows (most weekends), and an upstairs room with a balcony that is used for private parties. They also serve better-than-passable Creole food.

Snug Harbor Jazz Bistro 626 Frenchmen St.

You eat in one room and then slide over to the music room, where each night's performer plays two sets, one at 8:00 and a second at 10:00. Charmaine Neville on Monday nights has been their mainstay for years. She is a part of the famous Neville clan, and daughter of saxophonist Charles Neville. The Marsalis clan practically fills up the rest of the week, with Delfeayo playing on Wednesdays, father Ellis on Fridays, and Wynton and Jason making guest appearances. More recently, the Stanton Moore Trio has become the draw on Tuesday nights.

The Spotted Cat Music Club 623 Frenchmen St.

Their website says they're known by locals as "The CAT." I've only lived in New Orleans for 6 years (and have been visiting at least once a year for 32 years), and I've never heard them called that even once. They are, however, assuming the mantle as one of New Orleans top music spots. With no cover charge (they do require a one-drink minimum) and among the best musicians each night (most often three performers each night), if you don't come early, it's very likely you'll stand, or rather sway and shimmy the entire night in a lively elbow to ass cheek crowd.

The SPOT, as now called by me alone, starts live performances earlier than the other Frenchmen clubs, sometimes as early as 2:00 p.m. Regulars Andy J. Forest (Tuesdays and Fridays) and Sarah McCoy (Mondays and Thursdays) go on at 4:00 p.m. Washboard Chaz (Fridays), Meschiya Lake (Tuesdays), and the Panorama Jazz Band (Saturdays) are the 6:00 p.m. slot. The late sets (10:00 p.m.) are occupied by jazz troupes, the New Orleans Jazz Vipers (Mondays), the Cottonmouth Kings (Fridays), and Smoking Time Jazz Club (Tuesdays).

There's no reservations, no food in the bar, and, as proclaimed by the hand-painted sign by locally renowned artist, Simon, there's to be "No Drinks or Drunks on the Pianee."

Three Muses 536 Frenchmen St.

The three muses intended here are food, spirits (the alcoholic kind), and music. The featured musicians include Luke Winslow King, a unique slide guitarist who mixes Delta blues with ragtime and small sips of rock 'n' roll. Glen David Andrews is recognized as among our best trombone players, along with Trombone Shorty. The Shotgun Jazz Band recalls the hot, bluesy, no-frills jazz melodies that poured from the New Orleans's dance halls. And the Hot Club of New Orleans has an almost missionary zeal to champion the swing-era music of Duke Ellington, Django Reinhardt, and Stéphane Grappelli, though they infuse this classic sound with their own modern sensibilities.

Vaso 500 Frenchmen St.

This lounge lizard setting hosts brass bands, DJs, and decent food.

Yuki Izakaya 525 Frenchmen St.

This new-ish Japanese tavern serves homestyle tapas and many small plates with a wide selection of sake and shochu, as well as Japanese beers. Yuki doubles as a dimly lit late-night haunt with live music each night. The performers tend toward the peculiar like the cabaret-style goth band, Morella & the Wheels of If.

R&B and Funk

Rhythm and blues was originally coined by record companies to describe recordings marketed predominantly to urban African-Americans. It replaced the term "race music," after that term was deemed offensive. Go figure. R&B song lyrics usually focus on the ups and downs in relationships, finances, and, well . . . sex. New Orleans R&B is characterized by extensive use of piano and horn sections, and our complex syncopated "second line" rhythms.

The term "funk" goes all the way back to the beginning of jazz and Buddy Bolden's signature song, "Funky Butt." This music is rhythmically based on a two-celled onbeat/offbeat structure, which originated in sub-Saharan African music traditions. The New Orleans style appropriated the bifurcated structure from the Afro-Cuban mambo and conga. Now, in plain English, that simply means that funk music is slow, loose, "sexy," riff-oriented.

The most renowned local hero of R&B and funk, sometimes revered, other times flabbergasted, is, was, and always will be **Ernie K-Doe**. Even in New Orleans, where eccentrics are cherished more than merely accepted, K-Doe is in a class by himself. He loved to talk, mostly about himself in a manically, self-aggrandizing way. When he labeled himself "The Emperor of the Universe" no tongue was shoved into his cheek.

Ernie began recording when he was 15 years old. Ten years later, his song "Mother-in-Law" was the first #1 Billboard hit recorded in New Orleans. The song was a tribute to his real life mother-in-law. He said, "Her name was Lucy. Should have been Lucifer." He'd tell anybody listening that there are only two songs to stand the test of time: "One of them is 'The Star-Spangled Banner.' The other one is 'Mother-in-Law.'" Again, no tongue was planted in any cheek.

K-Doe made a comeback of sorts in the 1980s, thanks to the efforts of David Freedman, the station manager of WWOZ radio. Freedman gave K-Doe his own rambling and offbeat radio show, which was broadcast from a low-wattage studio located in the beer storage room upstairs over Tipitina's. Some DJs would drop a microphone through a hole in the floor to transmit live performances on Tipitina's stage. Fueled by an abundance of ego and alcohol, K-Doe would assault the airwaves with rants about anything that popped into his head.

K-Doe's often-repeated on-air signature lines included, "I'm so slick, grease gotta come ask me how to be greasy!" Or: "I'm so bad I got to pinch myself in the morning to see if I'm still alive!"

And there was also: "There have only been five great singers of rhythm and blues—Ernie K-Doe, James Brown, and Ernie K-Doe!"

When the financially strapped Nora Blatch Educational Foundation had to sell WWOZ to the Jazz Heritage Foundation, new management was less enamored by Ernie K-Doe's on-air stream of semi-consciousness. He was again on the streets.

This time he was quickly swept up by old friend Antoinette Dorsey Fox, who would later become his second wife. Antoinette clearly had visions for how K-Doe would create his next act. She made him flashy, attention-grabbing outfits and opened the Mother-in-Law Lounge mere yards from where he used to camp out as a homeless person.

Ernie K-Doe died in 2001 at the age of 65 of liver and kidney failure. Antoinette commissioned a life-sized mannequin made of K-Doe by artist Jason Poirier. Antoinette often planted the statue on stage in the club so that people could take pictures with the plaster rendition of the late singer. But she would sometimes take the statue out on the town where it might join her at a table inside Galatoire's, ride in parades, and even make a rare appearance at church. The K-Doe mannequin also rode along in a mule-drawn hearse with the procession at Antoinette's funeral when she died in 2009, in a sense making K-Doe the first man ever to attend his own widow's funeral.

Shirley Goodman and Leonard Lee (**Shirley & Lee**) were branded Sweethearts of the Blues, even though they weren't sweethearts and their music wasn't the blues. However, their #1 biggest hit is not in doubt. They recorded "Let the Good Times Roll" in 1956. The song has been covered by Sonny & Cher, Bunny Sigler, The Righteous Brothers, Delbert McClinton, Barbra Streisand, The Searchers, Whiskey Howl, Joe Strummer of The Clash, Harry Nilsson, Roy Orbison, The Youngbloods, Conway Twitty, Slade, Freddy Fender, Buckwheat Zydeco, The Animals, Fishbone, The Kingsmen, and The Sonics. The funkiest rendition is by George Clinton, featuring the Red Hot Chili Peppers and Kim Manning.

Their other massive hits were "Feel So Good" and "I'm Gone," the latter of which was covered by The Rolling Stones, Barbra Streisand, the Righteous Brothers, and Roy Orbison. Their songs created a fictionalized soap opera story of Shirley & Lee's made-up relationship. Fans would buy the singles simply to keep up with the continuing saga of the two (not really) sweethearts. Their heartbreaker song "Shirley Come Back to Me" was, for example, followed up by "Shirley's Back."

Sisters Barbara and Rosa Hawkins and their cousin Joan Johnson had been casually singing together since grade school. When a local talent competition had a cancellation, the girls were asked to step in just to fill the time slot. This led to them being "discovered." They were whisked to New York where they recorded a few songs, and they came back to New Orleans with no real expectations. As Rosa Hawkins told NPR, "The first time I heard 'Chapel of Love' on the radio, it was on a Saturday morning and I was doing my chores. This record came on and it was like, 'Oh, that record sounds familiar. Oh, I know that song.' And then I realized, 'Hey! That's my voice there!'"

"Chapel of Love" would knock The Beatles out of the #1 spot, and it would stay at #1 for three weeks. The reverse side of the 45 came about when the three girls were fooling around in the recording studio while everyone else was taking a break. They started singing an old Mardi Gras Indian chant, and the New York control room guys were blown away, having never heard anything like it. That song, "Iko Iko," would become a Top 20 hit and a New Orleans standard.

The name **Dixie Cups** was foisted on them, thank God, just before their first record release. They had been calling themselves Little Miss and the Muffets.

The funkiest of the funk, without a doubt, is **Professor Longhair**. Born Henry Roeland "Roy" Byrd, he began playing music as a boy on the streets of New Orleans after he discovered an abandoned piano in an alley. Some believe his idiosyncratic and completely original style was the result of learning to play on a busted piano that was missing some keys and strings.

There's a current phrase printed on T-shirts and bumper stickers from Dirty Coast Press that states, "Listen to Your City." This phrase was a reality for Professor Longhair. He taught himself to play by soaking up influences from everything he heard on the streets of New Orleans and outside the clubs he was too young to enter. Barrelhouse boogie-woogie, Caribbean rhythms, and second line parade were all used in his unprecedented and thereafter quintessentially New Orleans mix.

In 1949 he formed his group, Professor Longhair and His Shuffling Hungarians. The group was given the name by Mike Tessitore, owner of the Caldonia Club, because all the band members had long hair, which was uncharacteristic at the time. The following year, he was signed by Mercury Records and his "Baldhead" reached #5 on Billboard's R&B chart. Longhair later recorded on more than a dozen labels, but never caught on as a star because of a combination of poor health and mismanagement.

Probably the primary reason why Professor Longhair never took off commercially had to do with this unique style. Tony Russell, in his classic book *The Blues*, writes: "The vivacious rhumba-rhythmed piano blues and choked singing typical of Fess [another of Professor Longhair's monikers] were too weird to sell millions of records."

He abandoned music altogether in 1964 to work odd jobs. Allen Toussaint was shocked one day when he visited a record store on Rampart Street and discovered that his musical hero was working the back room as a stock clerk. After languishing in total obscurity, Professor Longhair was rediscovered by talent scouts for the New Orleans Jazz and Heritage Festival. They asked him to play at the second-ever festival in 1971. He performed at every New Orleans Festival thereafter until his death in 1980.

Professor Longhair is now hailed as "the Picasso of keyboard funk" and "the Bach of rock." His style profoundly influenced many of New Orleans's best known musicians, including Mac Rebennack (a.k.a. Dr. John), Fats Domino, Huey "Piano" Smith, James Booker, The Meters, the Neville Brothers, and Allen Toussaint. Many of his songs like "Tipitina" and "Big Chief" have become essential lexicons of New Orleans music. "Tipitina," the song, is supposedly about a French Quarter woman with no toes who was, quite literally, Tippy Tina. His "Mardi Gras in New Orleans" serves as the soundtrack to Carnival season every year.

The iconic club Tipitina's (501 Napoleon Ave.) was created in 1977 by young Fess fans. The Fabulous Fo'teen wanted to insure that Professor Longhair always had a place to play his weird rumba-boogie. Not only was his style too out there at the time to be appreciated in clubs or on air, but Fess had burned too many bridges in the French Quarter.

Tipitina's has a large single room that can easily accommodate over 1,000 people. As you enter the front door, you'll meet a bust of Professor Longhair right in front of you. I guess you could rub it for good mojo. I've never seen anyone do it. I've never done it. You can be the first.

It is one of the premier hangouts of New Orleans's live music scene. The venue helped launch the careers of the Neville Brothers, Harry Connick Jr., Dr. John, and many others. An all-star cast has played and continues to play Tipitina's. The acts include The Meters, Cowboy Mouth, the Radiators, Galactic, Better Than Ezra, and Trombone Shorty. National artists that have played there include Wilco, Nine Inch Nails, Pearl Jam, Lenny Kravitz, Bonnie Raitt, James Brown, Widespread Panic, Stevie Ray Vaughan, Tim McGraw, Goo Goo Dolls, Parliament Funkadelic, Robert Cray, Patti Smith, Willie Nelson, Buddy Guy, Dresden Dolls, and Medeski Martin & Wood.

Probably the best-known disciple of Professor Longhair is **Dr. John**, more properly Mac Rebbenack. Dr. John does still play, but rarely. I went to hear him at a French Quarter Festival, but the crowd was so massive, I couldn't see him and could barely hear him. His personal story reads like an episodic nineteenth-century novel or the script for a Coen Brothers movie. It's filled with twists and turns, good and evil, highs and lows, but always with a twinkle in the eye. He wrote a memoir himself, *Under a Hoodoo Moon*, which is superb reading. His music education is sort of a street hustler's guide to success. Dr. John had next to no formal education. As a kid he joined a choir, but got kicked out. Mac used to accompany his father on one of his side jobs, supplying records to second-rate hotels. His dad would drop off blues, jazz, and what was then called race records, and pick up overly used ones. Mac got to keep all the ones considered too scratchy, and he started mimicking the style he heard on the records he played. The Professor taught Mac about technique. In Dr. John's own unique style of talking, revealed in a *BOMB Magazine* interview, he described his interactions with Professor Longhair: "He and his vibe were so hip that I was just magnetized to the cat, you know? I asked him, 'Wow, what are you doin' when you're doin' all the stuff like that?' And he said, 'That's double-note crossovers.' And I said, 'Well, what is that stuff when I see your hands going all over?' And he says, 'Over and unders.' He had names for everything. He'd say things to his band guys, like, this oola-mala-walla stuff, and I thought, Wow, this guy's speakin' in tongues." Longhair also taught him respect for the music. "If you played music for the money, you wasn't gonna be a good musician. But if you played music for lovin' the music, at least you cared about that. It was a major thing, because it connected with my livelihood, you know?"

In the late 1960s, Rebennack gained fame as a solo artist after creating the persona of Dr. John, The Night Tripper. Dr. John's act combined New Orleans-style rhythm and blues with psychedelic rock and elaborate stage shows that came off like Screamin' Jay Hawkins's act with voodoo religious ceremonies, complete with elaborate costumes and headdress.

A decade later, he'd had enough of what he called "the mighty-coo-de-fiyo hoodoo show" and so dumped the routine in favor of New Orleans standards. He is now worshipped by R&B lovers and is respected by the jazz and rock crowds. Dr. John has six Grammy Awards and many hit songs that will forever be a part of New Orleans musical heritage: "Right Place Wrong Time," "Gris-Gris Gumbo Ya Ya," "Mama Roux," "I Walk on Guilded Splinters," and "Goin' Back to New Orleans."

Professor Longhair and Dr. John are absolute icons of New Orleans music. There are countless other merely great musicians. This entire book could be filled front to back by listing their names, from Alvin Alcorn to Linnzi Zaorski.

Allen Toussaint, who passed away in November 2015, had been a key figure in every major development in New Orleans music over the past 50-plus years, from R&B to Soul and Funk. He worked with major performers from Lee Dorsey to Dr. John, The Meters, The Pointer Sisters, Aaron Neville, Solomon Burke, Patti LaBelle, even Paul McCartney, and more recently Elvis Costello and Eric Clapton.

His songs have been covered by The Rolling Stones ("Fortune Teller"), The Doors ("Get Out of My Life Woman"), Devo ("Working In a Coal Mine"), Boz Scaggs, Robert Palmer, and hip-hop stars O.D.B., Biz Markie, KRS-One, and Outkast. Glenn Campbell took his song "Southern Nights" to the top of the charts.

In 2013, he was awarded the National Medal of Arts. As President Obama said in presenting the honor, "Mr. Toussaint has built a legendary career alongside America's finest musicians, sustaining his city's rich tradition of rhythm and blues and lifting it to the national stage."

Fats Domino now lives on the West Bank and no longer performs in public. His pianos, though, are all over town. His all-white piano is in the Jazz Museum, along with Louis Armstrong's first trumpet, located inside the U.S. Mint just past the French Market. A water-logged piano, recovered from his Ninth Ward house and

Allen Toussaint

recording studio after Hurricane Katrina, is on display at The Cabildo museum at the back of Jackson Square.

Fats sold more than 65 million records over his career. He had thirty-seven top-40 hits. Only Elvis sold more records over the same time period. His Billboard hits include "Blue Monday," "Blueberry Hill," "I'm Ready," "Ain't That a Shame," and "Walking to New Orleans." He was awarded the Grammy Lifetime Achievement Award and was part of the Rock and Roll Hall of Fame's inaugural class in 1986.

Many consider Fats the father of R&B, and some feel that his single "The Fat Man" is the earliest rock 'n' roll song. That spirited single hit the Billboard chart on April Fool's Day in 1950.

Fats stopped performing after his 2007 farewell concert in Tipitina's. He neither tours nor travels. When he was awarded the National Medal of Arts, he turned down President Clinton's invitation to accept it at the White House, commenting, "I traveled so much, I don't have anywhere left to go."

For me, the late **James Booker** is the father of the musical style I term "*WTF is That?*" Booker has been called "the Black Liberace" and "the Bayou Maharajah." Practically every other important piano man of New Orleans has waxed poetic while worshipping at the altar of James Booker.

Allen Toussaint had said, "Genius is a word that is thrown around so loosely, but let me say that if the word is applicable to anyone, the person who comes to mind is James Booker. Total genius. Within all the romping and stomping in his music, there were complexities in it that were supported by some extreme technical acrobatics finger-wise that made his music extraordinary."

Josh Paxton elaborates: "It's Ray Charles on the level of Chopin. It's all the soul, all the groove, and all the technique in the universe packed into one unbelievable player. It's like playing Liszt and Professor Longhair at the same time. I can now say with certainty that it's a pianistic experience unlike any other. He invented an entirely new way of playing blues and roots-based music on the piano, and it was mind-blowingly brilliant and beautiful." Harry Connick Jr. called him "a powerful genius of a unique and complex mind. I hear joy and struggle. I hear perfection and error. I hear confidence and hesitation—I hear James Booker, the greatest ever."

Dr. John playfully described Booker as "the best black, gay, one-eyed junkie piano genius New Orleans has ever produced."

In other words, no one has ever played the piano like Booker.

In spite of all his current adulation, Booker never gained huge fame in America while alive, but he did find it in France and Germany. Some feel it was Europe's lesser degrees of racism and homophobia that opened doors. Returning to New Orleans, Booker was devastated by the reduced notoriety he received. He took to playing house piano at the Maple Leaf and other small bars.

He died at the age of 43 while waiting to receive medical attention at New Orleans's Charity Hospital. Lily Keber's 2013 much-awarded documentary film, *Bayou Maharajah*, I consider a must-see. As far as a must-hear, pretty much anything Booker ever recorded has his unmistakable stamp, from "True" to the song recorded by everybody from Count Basie to Doris Day, "On the Sunny Side of the Street." For me, Booker's blow-away song is his perfect and funked up cover of Chopin's "One Minute Waltz," a song he named "Black Minute Waltz."

If you want to go bring it up on YouTube, we'll wait for you.

Joining Booker on the shortlist as the funkiest of the funk would be **The Meters**. James Brown, the Godfather of Soul, brought funk to the masses. But James Brown, when he was just a young man in knickers and conk, schooled off The Meters. They never themselves broke into the mainstream, but they were an extraordinary live band, packing houses in New Orleans and having a below-the-radar reputation as being the hottest thing going.

The four original members were Art Neville on keyboards, George Porter, Jr. on bass, Leo Nocentelli on guitar, Zigaboo Modeliste on drums. Cyril Neville joined The Meters as a vocalist and percussionist in the 1970s. They performed and recorded their own unique music from the late 1960s until 1977. They developed a fanatical following, among them Paul McCartney and Mick Jagger. Rickey Vincent, in his book *Funk*, wrote, "In and outside of New Orleans, people came to understand that they were the core of a revolution in rhythm."

After eight highly acclaimed albums, The Meters became frustrated by their lack of commercial success and broke up. Their songs "Cissy Strut" and "Look-Ka Py Py" are considered funk classics today. Their sound is unquestionably the basis for much of the hip-hop of the '80s and '90s.

Where the Marsalis clan is the first family of jazz, the Batiste family could be said to be their equal in funk (plus R&B, blues, and yes, jazz, too). They are the largest musical family in the South, and at one time there could be as many as twenty-three Batistes on a single stage.

Estella and Jean Batiste, the matriarch and patriarch of the clan, met in New York City and settled in New Orleans. They had seven boys, guided them towards music, and assembled the **Batiste Brothers Band**. At least one Batiste has played with most every major New Orleans musical group, from Professor Longhair's group, to the Olympia Brass and Treme Brass Bands and Dirty Dozen Brass Band, to The Funky Meters, which is a reincarnation of the original band, The Meters.

The brood includes Harold Batiste, a record label founder, composer, and saxophonist, who predates Jon as a TV show bandleader. (Harold was the band director for the *Sonny and Cher Show*.) Percussionist Damon Batiste has performed with other prominent bands, recording with Dirty Dozen Brass Band and George Clinton and P-Funk All-Stars. Damon also played a vital role in the development of Frenchmen Street as New Orleans's music hub. Trumpeter and educator Milton Batiste used to lead Olympia Brass Band. David Russell Batiste has been playing the drums since he was 4. He still plays regularly around the city in a trio with Joe Krown and Walter "Wolfman" Washington. The late and beloved Treme Brass Band leader Lionel Batiste was more than a musician. He was an ambassador for the city, often seen around town dressed (for no particular reason) in his finest suits, bowler hat, two-tone shoes, a sash like he was the grand marshal in a parade, and his signature watch, draped across his fingers rather than on his wrist, because he said he "always wanted to have time on my hands." Kermit Ruffins said of Uncle Lionel: "He taught me how to act, how to dress, how to feel about life."

Perhaps the best-known member of the clan right now is **Jon Batiste**. The

31-year-old has already performed in over 40 countries, in Carnegie Hall, at Lincoln Center, and at the Kennedy Center. His high-profile collaborators include Lenny Kravitz, Jimmy Buffett, Harry Connick Jr., and Wynton Marsalis. Jon is best known as the leader of Stephen Colbert's Late Show Band.

If you're looking to play that funky music tonight boy, you should check wwoz .org, where they display nightly venues. Live performances will also be printed on the back pages of *Offbeat*, a free monthly magazine devoted to New Orleans music that will be stacked up at your hotel's concierge desk and in many coffee shops, tour kiosks, and food markets.

King James & the Special Men call themselves R&B&D, Rhythm and Blues and Drunk. They used to be called one of New Orleans's best-kept secrets. However, the cats are well out of the bag. They play at Sidney's Saloon (1200 St. Bernard Ave.) every Monday night. Frontman Jimmy Horn brings the red beans and rice.

Flow Tribe, founded in 2004 by six high school friends, represents one of the hotter next-generation New Orleans bands. They play a classic style of funk, their horns and pop sensibility recounting early-'90s ska. Their guitar work, featuring the Cuban-born Mario Palmisano, displays a Caribbean and reggae influence. Their polyrhythmic percussion is pure New Orleans. Like the Beastie Boys, their music makes you want to dance and rage at the same time.

A Long Island boy, **Joe Krown** was drawn to New Orleans in 1992 to join Clarence "Gatemouth" Brown's band. He was the band's keyboard player for 22 years, until Gatemouth's death. From 1996 to 2001, he held the honor of being the Monday performer for the Traditional Piano Night slot at the Maple Leaf Bar. The spot was formerly held by Professor Longhair, and later James Booker.

Krown plays in several different styles. When he plays the piano as a solo artist, he typically plays in the traditional New Orleans jazz style. When he plays with his band, the Joe Krown Organ Combo, the sound is funk. And then there's his trio with Johnny Sansone and John Folse that plays an early dinner set at Ralph's On the Park, and then an after-dinner set (9:00 p.m. to midnight) at the Public Belt inside the Hilton Riverside Hotel. In the spring of 2007, Joe started playing again every Sunday night at the Maple Leaf with Walter "Wolfman" Washington (guitar and vocals) and Russell Batiste Jr. (drums).

Growing up in St. Louis, **Tom McDermott** drank in the ragtime blues there, earned a master's degree in music, and then was sucked into New Orleans by his love for our piano greats, Professor Longhair, James Booker, and Dr. John.

For most of the '90s, he played for the Dukes of Dixieland. He then ventured off on his own to form The Nightcrawlers. He is one of the more educated and eclectic players in New Orleans. He is perhaps the only piano man in town who even knows of Louis Moreau Gottschalk, let alone includes his numbers from the 1800s in his sets. He also loves (and will play) Brazilian choro music, French musette, The Beatles, and early Duke Ellington. When you go to a Tom McDermott show, you sort of have to be ready for anything.

Tom plays Wednesday nights with Meschiya Lake from 7:00 to 9:00 p.m. at Chickie Wah Wah's, and on Thursdays he plays an early set (5:00 to 7:00 p.m.) at Three Muses and a later set at Buffa's on Esplanade. The first Friday of each month, Tom joins Aurora Nealand at The Bombay Club.

Singers

In addition to great piano men, jazz, and funk musicians, New Orleans, like any musical hot spot, has its share of great singers. Historically, we are the home of **Mahalia Jackson**, the Queen of Gospel, and **Louie "Just a Gigolo" Prima**. Undoubtedly, the best known currently is **Harry Connick, Jr.**, but good luck finding him in a local venue. These days, he mostly seems to split his time between the TV screen, where he had a stint as a judge on *American Idol*, followed by a gig hosting his own sadly insipid daytime show, *Harry*, and the big screen, playing a wife-beating husband, a savior of the world as a fighter pilot, and a savior of a dolphin without a tail. I hope he's making a ton of money because it all seems (to me) like distraction and clutter for one of the greatest living musical arrangers.

Irma Thomas started to acquire some local notoriety on the job as "The Singing Waitress." She was eventually fired from her restaurant gig because customers kept asking for the singing waitress rather than an omelet with a side of grits. With more time on her hands, she started sitting in with Tommy Ridgley and the Untouchables band at the Pimlico Club in Central City. Tommy introduced her to Ron Records, where she cut her first single in 1959 for what would become the classic, "(You Can Have My Husband) But Don't Mess with My Man."

Irma was soon snatched up by Minit Records, where she began recording a series of hit songs written and produced by Allen Toussaint. "Cry On," "I Done Got Over It," "It's Raining," and "Ruler of My Heart" made her a local celebrity. For whatever reason (and a lack of talent was not the reason), Irma Thomas never managed to cross over into mainstream popular success like her contemporaries Aretha Franklin, Gladys Knight, and Dionne Warwick.

Irma abandoned her pursuit of a career in singing and took a day job at a Montgomery Ward department store while she raised her four children as a single mother. In the same way the New Orleans Jazz & Heritage Festival saved Professor Longhair's career, it saved Thomas' as well. Organizers invited her to perform, which led to the revival of her career. Producer Scott Billington brought Irma to Rounder Records in the mid-'80s and they produced a string of great albums: *The New Rules*, *The Way I Feel*, *Simply the Best*, *True Believer*, *Walk Around Heaven*, *The Story of My Life*, and *Sing It! Simply the Best* and *Sing It!* both received Grammy nomina-

Irma Thomas

tions. In 2007, she won a Grammy Award for *After the Rain*. The one-time "singing waitress" is now known as the "Soul Queen of New Orleans."

Where Irma is the Queen, New Orleans has many singers who rate at least a princess.

As the daughter of two opera singers, **Debbie Davis** seemed destined to have a career as a singer. She made her first professional singing appearance at age two. She had a budding reputation as a rock singer in her home state of New Jersey when she moved to New Orleans in 1997. Here, she did a hard-left turn into jazz and the Great American Songbook (though she does, now and again, sing covers of songs by Led Zeppelin and The Velvet Underground). Debbie has become one of the city's better singers, and is sometimes compared to Miss Peggy Lee for her hand-on-hip style. She is also New Orleans's absolute best ukulele player (I can't really name another).

She has performed with a wide range of performers, from New Orleans staples like John Boutté and Tom McDermott to a couldn't-be-more-different Soul Asylum and The Misfits. And yes, she is one of the current Pfister Sisters. Debbie plays a variety of clubs, but she can most reliably be found at Three Muses most Saturday nights.

Banu Gibson cut her singing teeth in sunny-happy places, working for Jackie Gleason at his Joe the Bartender room in Miami and at Disneyland in California. Then, her husband accepted a job with Tulane University in New Orleans. New Orleans blew its own version of pixie dust over her, and she's been singing the city's praises ever since.

Banu told MyNewOrleans.com, "What I realized is that every place else in the United States is white bread and mayonnaise, and everything here is not—it's spicy and the architecture is so different. You can't control where you were born, but you have a choice where you live!"

Her music choices remain Great American Songbook standards from the '20s to the '40s. She's one of the few, perhaps the only, New Orleans singers absolutely and exclusively devoted to the classic songs of Gershwin, Duke Ellington, Irving Berlin, Hoagy Carmichael, Cole Porter, and Rodgers and Hart.

If your desire is to hear great renditions of songs like "Top Hat" or "Isn't it Romantic," you need to see which of her venues she's playing tonight. Her band plays regularly at Snug Harbor Jazz Bistro, The Bombay Club, Three Muses, and the Museum of Art.

Aurora Nealand's regular spots are many: the Blue Nile, The Spotted Cat, and Snug Harbor Jazz Bistro (all on Frenchmen Street), and Siberia and Cafe Istanbul on St. Claude. She arrived in New Orleans in 2005 with a degree in music composition from the Oberlin Conservatory of Music and another from Jacques Lecoq's school of physical theatre in Paris. I have a handle on a conservatory of music, but a physical theatre in Paris offers up visions of Marcel Marceau and Jacques Tati doing orchestrated pie fights. She does at times perform with a gas mask and an accordion.

Aurora, however, also has a more serious side, most notably when she plays soprano sax and clarinet at Preservation Hall with her traditional jazz band, The Royal Roses. Aurora sometimes performs with the Panorama Jazz Band, and she is also the singer in the rockabilly band, Rory Danger and the Danger Dangers. In addition, she is a member in Why Are We Building Such a Big Ship?, an amorphous group that consists of anywhere from six to ten members who play what's been called "half brass-band dirge and half indie-rock sea shanty." She is definitely one of the more interesting singers in New Orleans, but there's always this Yma Sumac sort of disconnect in her performances. Aurora clearly has loads of talent, but at times you'll wonder if she's just putting you on.

Ingrid Lucia moved to New Orleans when she was one year old. Her father, going by the moniker Poppa Neutrino and his family, The Flying Neutrinos, spent 20 years as gypsies touring the world, living and traveling the United States and Europe in buses, tents, and amazing homemade rafts. The family became a band when Ingrid was 11, and they played their self-taught Dixieland jazz on street corners, small halls, and anywhere anyone would listen. Her father was either a master showman or a first-class eccentric, depending on your orientation. When in New Orleans, he'd stand on Jackson Square, megaphone in one hand and a mannequin's leg in high heels as his musical instrument in the other.

When I first heard her sing, I told my wife, "Close your eyes and you'll swear it's Billie Holiday." Since then, I've read this comparison by others seemingly a hundred times. It has been Ingrid's self-expressed desire to show a younger generation the power of traditional jazz and how it was the original rock and roll.

Meschiya Lake is the little girl who ran off to join the circus, literally. Born in Oregon, she moved to South Dakota when she was eight and literally joined the

Meschiya Lake at French Quarter Fest

circus as a sideshow fire dancer and glass eater for the Know Nothing Family Zirkus Zideshow and The Circus at the End of the World. When the troupe took their off-season hiatus in New Orleans, Meschiya joined the long list of Ex-Pat-Y'at's who come to New Orleans for the first time, are immediately seduced, and decide that they have to live here. As Meschiya said in answering one of her twenty questions for Gondola.com, "I knew immediately that this was where I belonged. I am just so happy to live in a place where, if a guy rides by on a bike in full red body paint at 2:00 p.m. on a Monday, he isn't considered weird."

At first, Lake performed as a street musician on Royal Street. In 2009, she formed The Little Bighorns jazz band. They started out also playing in the streets, but then slowly started getting gigs in clubs. They are now one of the essential acts to see in New Orleans. I try to take all my out-of-town visitors to one of their performances, and I get to watch their jaws drop as they take in her sultry voice and the band's casual but completely tight jazz mastery. There is a reason why she has been awarded Best Female Vocalist for the last 4 years and counting.

I've described Meschiya as looking like she belongs painted on the front of a B-52 Bomber. She resembles a 1940s pin-up queen, except for her many, many, many tattoos. The band plays regularly at d.b.a. and once or twice a week at The Spotted Cat. They have frequented Little Gem Saloon, and Meschiya performs without the band (but with premier pianist, Tom McDermott) on Wednesdays at Chickie Wah Wah.

For male crooners, **John Boutté** is, for my money, our best current club singer. He performs most often at d.b.a. on Saturday nights. He has the mixed blessing of being renown as the singer for the HBO *Treme* series buck jumping theme song. If you see him, please do not shout it out as a request. Boutté concedes, "I know I need to sing it, even when I might feel like singing something else."

Bobby Lounge is not from New Orleans, but comes from McComb, Mississippi. He did not start singing until after his daddy died (Daddy would not have approved), and he had to quit singing for a spell for health reasons. He doesn't play often in New Orleans, but does perform at most every Jazz Fest and has sung at Tipitina's, House of Blues, and the makeshift stage at the Louisiana Music Factory. I include him here because if Bobby Lounge is in town, you need you some Bobby Lounge. *The Times-Picayune.* newspaper asserted he is best experienced "by the open mind or at least a mind half-clouded with drink."

He takes the stage in an iron lung (don't worry, it's just a prop), accompanied by Nursie (not a real nurse, but a voluptuous model in nurse's wear). Bobby then starts banging on the piano like it insulted his momma. Of his two-fisted playing, he has said that, "I weed out the inferior instruments." The delight of his performance comes from his spewing wildly eccentric lyrics, like a deep-fried version of Tom Waits.

The Lost Bayou Ramblers

Bobby is aware of his limitations, saying, "I hear wrong notes and I wish my voice sounded better. I am pretty limited. I play everything in C." But his outrageous enthusiasm and his gift for storytelling will win you over.

Cajun and Zydeco

A large number of visitors come to New Orleans each year wanting to hear live Cajun music and high-energy Zydeco. Hearing recorded Zydeco or Cajun is no problem at all. It'll be blaring from every T-shirt, Mardi Gras bead, and dried alligator head tourist shop on Decatur Street. Live music, however, is a different story. You're basically in the wrong place at the wrong time. You'll need to travel a good hour or two outside the city, to Mamou or Opelousas in the heart of Cajun Country.

If you do a road trip out into Cajun Country, then a stop at Fred's Lounge in Mamou is a must. Fred's has been airing live radio broadcasts every Saturday morning since 1962. The music will be loud, raucous, and sung 100 percent in French. If you don't arrive before 8:30 a.m., there won't be any place to sit. An hour later, there won't be any place to stand. And there's a rule at Fred's: Once you enter you don't get to leave until you dance.

Cajun music is rooted in French ballads. It's a waltzin' and a dancin' music, and it uses only a few instruments, like the Cajun accordion, fiddle, and triangle. Zydeco is the Creole-influenced cousin of Cajun music, with some blues and R&B mixed in, and uses the accordion (squeeze box) and frottoir (washboard). These styles share common musical origins and influences, and an oversimplification would be to say that Cajun is the music of the white Acadians of South Louisiana, and zydeco is the music of the black Creoles of the same region.

Now, I don't mean to make it sound like finding this music is impossible. David Doucet, former member of the multi-Grammy Award-winning BeauSoleil, performs every Monday night at The Columns Hotel. For the last 25 years, Tipitina's has hosted a weekly Fais Do Do every Sunday, where Bruce Daigrepont and his button accordion have played more than 1,000 shows.

A Fais Do Do is the traditional name for a home dance party in Cajun Country. The term comes from Cajun mothers (or *maman*, pronounced "muh-mawn") who would take their young children to a separate "Cry Room" and gently encourage them to go to sleep (Do Do) so they could get back to dance floor.

The restaurant Mulate's plays Cajun music right across the street from the Convention Center every night after 7:00 p.m. The original Mulate's was located in the town of Beaux Bridge (two hours from New Orleans) and featured the great Zachary Richard as their opening night performer. Mulate's has become a bit of a tourist trap with Cajun food and resident bands that are fine—except when it comes to music and food, "fine" is far from high praise in this city.

Amanda Shaw is the darling of the current New Orleans Cajun music scene. She's been playing the Cajun fiddle and singing since she was eight years old. *The Rosie O'Donnell Show* gave Amanda her first national exposure when she was in grade school. Now in her mid-20s, Amanda is probably still carded in most clubs where she plays. I once witnessed two not-so-young clerks at Louisiana Music Factory get all silly-flustered like high school freshmen when she came in and actually spoke to them.

Amanda and her band, the Cute Guys, perform at state fairs, Andouille Festivals (andouille is a type of smoked sausage that originated in France), appear with some frequency at the Rock 'n' Bowl, and perform every year at Jazz & Heritage Festival. They've cut four albums, which are a mix of traditional Cajun dancehall standards with Cajun'd-up covers of songs like "Should I Stay or Should I Go," by The Clash, and "I Wanna Be Your Boyfriend," by The Ramones.

The commonly held explanation for the term zydeco is that it comes from the Creole saying, "Les haricots song pas salés," which means, "The beans aren't salty." Haricots (string beans) is pronounced "zah ree' co." Maybe the music had been played during the bean harvesting season. Regardless, little by little, "zah ree' co" evolved into zydeco.

There's a rather small group of really good musicians who play zydeco in the city, usually once a week (Thursday nights) at the Rock 'n' Bowl. That is an adventure worth your time. Rock 'n' Bowl (3016 S. Carrollton Ave.) is the spot whose calendar is most filled with zydeco, cajun, and swamp pop. It is a bar, bowling alley, and music hall all rolled into one. When it's zydeco night at the Rock 'n' Bowl, all the country boys come into the Big City to dance. And by "boys" I mean 70-year-old men with more moves than teeth. There is nothing creepy nor salacious about the boys, but they will line up in front of the purdy ladies and, one after another after another, wait for the last feller to finish his spin and then respectfully ask, "May I dance with you, Ma'am?"

The undisputed king of zydeco is **Clifton Chenier**. He ain't New Orleans. Clifton was born in Opelousas, died in Lafayette, and took with him a Grammy Award and a National Heritage Fellowship. He was inducted into the Blues Hall of Fame and the Louisiana Music Hall of Fame, and in 2014 he was a posthumous recipient of the Grammy Lifetime Achievement Award.

Zydeco musicians you can actually find while visiting include **Chubby Carrier**, a third-generation zydeco artist with famous Louisiana relatives. **Roy Carrier** (father), **Warren Carrier** (grandfather), and cousins **Bebe and Calvin Carrier** are all considered legends in zydeco. Chubby began his musical career at the age of 12 by playing drums with his father's band. He began playing the accordion at the age of 15, formed his own band in 1989, has recorded ten CDs, and picked up a Grammy Award for the 2011 album, *Zydeco Junkie.*

John Delafose's son **Geno** played rubboard with his dad's band, switching to accordion after his father's death. His music has been classified "nouveau zydeco" because he mixes in a little country and western.

Also following in his father's footsteps is **Rockin' Dopsie Jr.** When the original Rockin' Dopsie, called the James Brown of zydeco, unexpectedly passed away in 1993, the son vowed to keep his memory alive with his incarnation of the band, Rockin' Dopsie Jr. & The Zydeco Twisters. The Zydeco Twisters are the only band fronted (flamboyantly) by a washboard player in place of the accordionist or guitarist.

Nate Williams Jr. doesn't follow in his father's footsteps, but right alongside them. Both his band, Lil' Nathan & the Zydeco Big Timers, and his dad's band, Nathan & the Zydeco Cha-Cha's, alternate gigs at the Rock 'n' Bowl. Both bands play regularly on the road.

The music of **Sunpie Barnes & the Louisiana Sunspots** is not pure zydeco. Their music, termed "Bouje Bouje" has its own twists and turns, stirring zydeco with heavier doses of Caribbean and West African music. Sunpie's personal history has as many twists and turns. He's been a park ranger, an actor, former high school biology teacher, former college football All-American, and former NFL player (Kansas City Chiefs). He is Second Chief of the North Side Skull and Bone Gang, one of the oldest existing carnival groups in New Orleans, and a member of the Black Men of Labor Social Aid and Pleasure Club. Musically, Sunpie Barnes plays the piano, percussion, harmonica, and accordion. Sunpie & the Louisiana Sunspots play regularly way uptown at Dos Jefes (5535 Tchoupitoulas St.), a cigar bar with fine wine and spirits and live music.

Brass Bands and Mardi Gras

In addition to jazz and blues and, to a lesser extent Cajun and zydeco, the other distinctive New Orleans sounds include brass band, bounce, and Mardi Gras Indian music.

Brass bands go all the way back before there was a New Orleans, actually all the way back before there was brass, and the military bands were just drum and fife. Beginning in the sixteenth century, armies adapted and trained drummers and fifers to provide signals to direct troops, give them the hour of the day, and sound alarms, as well as to play popular music as entertainment while on the march. Adolphe Sax, a Frenchman and namesake of the saxophone, was the most noted of several inventors who developed a family of chromatic-valved bugles. In America, horns overtook woodwinds as the principal instruments for bands. By 1835, the first all-brass bands were established.

French military records identified over 100 French men in this city who per-

formed in fife and drum bands prior to 1763. In 1838, the *New Orleans Picayune* reported that "a passion for horns and trumpets has reached a real mania." The two most popular brass bands in New Orleans in the 1850s were the Bothe's Brass Band and Charley Jaeger's Brass Band. Both bandleaders were European immigrants who came to New Orleans during the 1840s. Jaeger was from Alsace-Lorraine, France, and Bothe was from Hanover, Germany. Their bands played for parades, dances, and general entertainment.

Patrick Sarsfield Gilmore was born in Ireland, immigrated to this country, and became the father of brass band music in America. Gilmore became the leader of the prestigious Boston Brass Band. Then, during the Civil War, he was put in charge of organizing bands for the Union Army. He organized over 300 bands for Union forces.

One of the brass bands, comprising thirty-two African-Americans, Gilmore brought from Boston to the then-occupied New Orleans in 1864. For two months, this band, identified in the press as Gilmore's Famous Band, performed almost on a daily basis. They marched down St. Charles Avenue and played in Jackson Square, Congo Square, and Lafayette Square. Not surprisingly, a tight, well-drilled, all African-American band made quite the impression on the Creoles and blacks then living in New Orleans.

Gilmore's Famous Band helped create the New Orleans style of brass bands. He did so by taking his European-styled military band music and stirring it (thoroughly) with the local sound, which itself was infused with African musical traditions. The earliest New Orleans-based bands include the Eureka Brass Band, the Onward Brass Band, the Excelsior Brass Band, the Tuxedo Brass Band, the Young Tuxedo Brass Band, and the Olympia Brass Band. The sound and style of these bands was worlds apart from the John Philip Sousa stilted type of songs such as "You're a Grand Old Flag" that were being played in other parts of the country. Brass band here developed at the same time as the beginnings of jazz. Many jazz founders, including Kid Ory, Buddy Bolden, Sidney Bechet, and Louis Armstrong played in brass bands as well as their jazz bands.

Bunk Johnson was the first to record New Orleans style brass band music (no, seriously) with his 1945 album, *New Orleans Parade*. His album was followed with records by the Eureka Brass Band in 1951 and the Young Tuxedo Brass Band in 1957.

The 1960s almost wiped out brass band music. Young musicians were getting into funk, and viewed brass band, as they put it, as "moldy figs." Pretty much one man, Danny Barker, saved brass band from fading into the dusty archives of history. He formed the Fairview Baptist Church Christian Marching Band. This decidedly uncool-sounding group kicked up the older brass band sound by making the "back row" (drums and tuba) much more prominent and integrating some hipper bebop stylings. The music was funkier and faster, and it led to a whole new renaissance that continues to this day. If you want to instantly hear the difference, bring up Eureka's classic "Didn't He Ramble" and sample it next to Rebirth Brass Band's contemporary classic "Do Whatcha Wanna."

There is no doubt you can hear live brass band this very evening. The To Be Continued Brass Band (that's their name) will probably be at their usual spot on Bourbon Street at Canal. The Young Fellaz Brass Band may be playing out on Frenchmen Street.

Rebirth Brass Band, which won a Grammy Award in 2012, is quite simply New Orleans's best. I hope the Hot 8, the Dirty Dozen, or the Soul Rebels are no more offended than Bill Russell, Oscar Robertson, or Magic Johnson would be hearing Michael Jordan being called the best basketball player. They're all great.

Rebirth formed in 1983 by local legends the Frazier brothers, Keith and Phil, and Kermit Ruffins when they all still attended Clark High School in Treme. Glen David Andrews and Corey Henry joined later.

They rejuvenated brass band by adding a little funk (and soul and hip-hop and some Michael Jackson for good measure) to traditional arrangements. They've been changing and evolving the brass band sound ever since. There are those who feel their 2001 album release *Hot Venom* represents a turning point in brass band that is as dramatic as The Beatles's *Sgt. Pepper's Lonely Hearts Club Band* was to rock in 1967 or Miles Davis' *Kind of Blue* was to jazz in 1959. On the tracks of *Hot Venom*, the band collaborated with rappers Soulja Slim on "You Don't Want to Go to War" and Cheeky Blakk on "Pop That Pussy." They also incorporated hip hop with the streetwise song "Rockin' On Your Stinkin' Ass."

I have seen Rebirth going on ten to fifteen times, and each time I listen in awe as their songs pretend to weave in and out of focus. Musicians seemingly cut loose from the band on high-energy improv and then, wham, they turn on a note and the group becomes the most unified and precise band you've ever heard.

Rebirth plays every Tuesday night at the Maple Leaf Bar (on Oak Street, not Maple Street). It is an iconic weekly event. The dented tin walls of the shotgun-shack shaped rooms are hung with old photographs of Mardi Gras Queens from the '30s and '40s. The band is billed to take the stage at 10:30 p.m. True to New Orleans style, where streetcars come when they come, I have never been there on a Tuesday night when the band started any earlier than 11:15 to 11:30. The place is dark. It will be packed crowded, hot, and sweaty. Your feet stick to the floor. Your ear will still be ringing an hour after the show has ended. In other words, it's perfect.

The Dirty Dozen Brass Band, established in 1977, or four years before Rebirth, is largely credited with being the first to infuse brass band with bebop, R&B, and other more contemporary styles. Their efforts injected the music with an energy that attracted a younger audience. Using their freewheeling style, one of their songs even played off the TV theme song for *The Flintstones*. Trumpet player Gregory Davis, who, along with Roger Lewis on the baritone sax, has been with the band since the beginning, and explained, "It's impossible to think that you can be exposed to the harmonies of Duke Ellington, the rhythms coming from Dizzy Gillespie, or the funk being done by James Brown, and then ignore it when you're playing New Orleans music."

In their current sets, you'll get a taste of old standards like "When the Saints Go Marching In" as well as brassy versions of today's hits like Rihanna's "Don't Stop the Music."

The Hot 8 Brass Band holds court every Sunday night at Howlin' Wolf in the same way that Rebirth does its thing at the Maple Leaf on Tuesdays. Compared to Rebirth and the Dirty Dozen, Hot 8 came late to the party. Bennie Pete, Jerome Jones, and Harry Cook formed the band in 1995, merging two earlier bands: the Looney Tunes Brass Band and the High Steppers Brass Band. Their music equally blends hip hop, jazz, and funk styles with traditional New Orleans brass sounds.

If Sunday with the Hot 8 at Howlin' Wolf and Tuesday at the Maple Leaf with Rebirth have you hankering for another helping, then you need to check out the Soul Rebels, who play every Thursday at Le Bon Temps Roule in Uptown. Currently, they may be the most-traveled brass band. They are now playing over 200 concerts a year all over the United States, Great Britain, South Africa, Brazil, and New Zealand. The Soul Rebels also have played with "everyone," from Green Day, Metallica, Drive-By Truckers, Arcade Fire, Marilyn Manson, Maceo Parker, Suzanne Vega, and Juvenile.

The Village Voice website described them as "the missing link between Louis Armstrong and Public Enemy," though for me, I think there's more than one link between those particular artists.

The Treme Brass Band is the most traditional of the current brass bands. They are less interested in integrating funk, R&B, or Rihanna songs into their mix and are more focused upon what band leader Benny Jones believes is essential. On NPR, he asserted that we "still need somebody to do the traditional music so we can pass that to the younger generation. Adding, "Somebody got to hold that spot down."

Their commitment to the old ways even includes a dress code. "Sound good, look good," says Jones. "My band always had the black pants, white shirts, ties, coats. That's a New Orleans tradition. What the older bands did years ago."

You can see them every Tuesday night at d.b.a., and Wednesdays at Candlelight Lounge.

The Brass-A-Holics (actual full name is the Brass-A-Holics Go-Go Brass Funk Band) formed in 2010 with the goal to merge the New Orleans brass sound with Washington, D.C.'s go-go groove. They cover songs by Miles Davis, Nirvana, John Coltrane, Wham, Cyndi Lauper, Kanye West, and Louis Armstrong . . . all in one set.

The Original Pinettes is New Orleans's only all-female brass band. It took them years to be accepted as a first-rate band rather than a novelty act.

The band was created in 1991 by St. Mary's Academy school's band teacher Jeffrey Herbert. He chose sixteen girls to create an all-female brass band. Percussionist Christie Jourdain, a sophomore at the time, was one of the sixteen girls. More than two decades later, she is the only Original Pinettes Brass Band member remaining and is now the band's leader.

Equal in stature to the New Orleans brass bands is the most beautiful way New Orleanians take it to the streets: the Mardi Gras Indians.

Historically, blacks were not welcomed to participate in Mardi Gras. So the black neighborhoods in New Orleans developed their own style of celebrating. Rather than Rex, Bacchus, and Proteus, their krewes took on names of imaginary Indian tribes like Wild Magnolias, the Golden Star Hunters, Black Eagles, Wild Tchoupitoulas Wild Squatoolies, and Fi Yi Yi.

On Mardi Gras each year, "tribes" of black Indians parade through their own neighborhoods singing and dancing to traditional chants. Music has always been a vital part of the Mardi Gras Indian experience. The tradition of their music is a distinctive call-and-response vocal that is heavy with drums and tambourine. Songs like "Iko Iko," "Hey Pocky A-Way," and "Indian Red" have been used as standards by all tribes and covered by various artists such as The Meters, the Neville Brothers, Professor Longhair, Dr. John, the Dixie Cups, and yes, The Grateful Dead.

In the mid-1950s, folklorist Samuel Charters collected field recordings of Indians in New Orleans and released them on the Smithsonian Folkways label. Since then, The Wild Magnolias, Golden Eagles, Wild Tchoupitoulas, Bayou Renegades, Flaming Arrows, Guardians of the Flame, Wild Mohicans, and others have left the streets long enough to be recorded in the studio.

If somehow you've reached this point in your life without knowing Mardi Gras Indian music, I suggest you bring up "Handa Wanda" on a device of your choice. We'll wait for you.

All the undecipherable phrases in the songs have meaning. "Cha Wa" is a slang phrase used by every Mardi Gras Indian tribe, meaning "We're comin' for ya." "Jock-A-Mo" was a chant called when the Indians went into battle. "Iko Iko" was a victory chant the Indians would shout. New Orleans tour guide and tribe member Milton "Boo" Carr, said "We didn't always know the meaning of the phrase, but we knew what action the call meant us to do."

The Wild Magnolias were among the very first tribes to perform their music publicly. In 1970, they recorded the revolutionary single, "Handa Wanda," and in 1974 they cut a full album. Since then they have been the highest-profile group. For many years they were headed by Big Chief Bo Dollis, who passed away in January 2014. Their beyond-funky tunes feature an eclectic range of instruments that include beer bottles, cans, snare drums, cymbals, and Big Chief's stunning vocals.

Today, **Big Chief Monk Boudreaux** is one of the most well-known Mardi Gras Indians playing on an international stage. He remains committed to keeping the 200-year-old tradition alive. When an accompanying musician once asked him, "Hey Monk, what key is this song in?" he replied, "Boy, this goes back to before they even had keys!"

When not on the road, Big Chief Monk Boudreaux appears at the Maple Leaf and d.b.a.

Rap, Bounce, and Hip-Hop

While not a musical style created in New Orleans, the city played an important role in the development of hip-hop and rap, and provided the foundation of bounce music. However, locally, these styles are still relegated to just one act (usually Juvenile or Lil Wayne) of the hundreds on the stages at the Jazz & Heritage Festival, and maybe one or two articles a year in local print, including *OffBeat*, a monthly magazine completely devoted to local music. After Hurricane Katrina, there were many concerts performed and CD collections released as tributes to honor and preserve the essential music of New Orleans: jazz, blues, second line, and our rumba-boogie-funk. There were no such concerts or collections to celebrate our rich rap or bounce scene.

Unfortunately, I do not have the room to detail the work of Henry "Palomino" Alexander, Ice Mike, DJ Captain Charles, Raj Smooth (called the greatest DJ in the world), Bust Down, Kilo, Mobo Joe, Devious, Gregory D, nor tens if not hundreds of others who form a core part of this music scene.

Southern rap or hip-hop, also called Dirty South, emerged in the 1980s as a reaction against the belief that New York City and Los Angeles are the only legitimate homes for the music. Just by virtue of not being from LA or New York, many artists were marginalized, and so had a hard time getting record contracts.

By the '90s, Southern rap started to emerge. Noteworthy artists and new and significant labels earned a place of prominence. We can look to three cities in particular: Miami, with 2 Live Crew and "booty rap"; Atlanta, with its bass-heavy party rap performers Arrested Development and OutKast; and New Orleans with its commercial enterprises, most notably the labels No Limit Records and Cash Money.

Master P built a rap empire with No Limit Records. Originally, it was a San Francisco-based label that was pumping out a series of chart-hitting records. But the label always had deep connections in New Orleans. Master P was born in New Orleans's 3rd Ward, as he called out in his own song, "I'm Bout It." He produced the

New Orleans-based act Kane & Abel (then known as Double Vision), Mystikal, and TRU. TRU's album, *True*, reached gold status.

In 1995, Master P officially relocated No Limit to New Orleans, adding more New Orleans rappers to the lineup: Mia X, Fiend, Tre-8, and Mr. Serv-On. No Limit could have had its super star in Soulja Slim, had the rapper not been shot and killed in 2003. His first album, *Give It 2 'Em Raw*, debuted at #13 on the Billboard charts, having sold 82,000 in the first week. Soul Slim was then convicted of armed robbery and incarcerated for three years. Released from prison, he recorded the album *The Streets Made Me* and hit the big time when his song "Slow Motion," recorded with Juvenile, became a #1 hit. "Slow Motion" has since grown to become a de facto stripper's anthem.

Cash Money Records was founded in 1991 by brothers Bryan "Birdman" Williams and Ronald "Slim" Williams. The brothers had the great insight or fortune to hire DJ Mannie Fresh as their in-house producer. Mannie had a distinctive approach to the Southern bass and mixed in a New Orleans sound: brass bands in the synthesizers, drum lines in the rattling beats, and Mardi Gras Indians in the call and response lyrics. Under Mannie's direction, Cash Money became an instant player with a succession of breakout hits. The music video for Juvenile's "Ha" featured a revolutionary look at the sometimes-harsh life in New Orleans's Magnolia projects. His album *400 Degreez* sold 4.7 million copies. The Hot Boys, where Juvenile is partnered with Lil Wayne, B. G., and Turk became the label's big ticket. Their initial success with "Get it How U Live" set up a huge and lucrative distribution deal between Cash Money and Universal Records. It also inspired B. G., when describing the deal, to coin the phrase "bling bling"—a term that instantaneously permeated the culture.

Dwayne Michael Carter Jr. would be the Cash Money superstar. Known by his stage name **Lil Wayne**, he was the youngest artist on the label, starting as a nine-year-old and joining the Hot Boys at 15. His debut solo album, "Tha Block Is Hot," was released when he was 17 and debuted at ≠3 on Billboard, going on to platinum. After a career of thirteen best-selling albums, eight lawsuits (including a $51-million suit he filed against Cash Money), and three arrests, Lil Wayne announced he was exiting the music scene to spend more time with his four children.

Master P and No Limit Records did not exit the New Orleans scene in any better style. One of his top artists, Mystikal, was sentenced to 6 years in prison for sexual battery and extortion, and while incarcerated was charged with two counts of failing to file tax returns. Even worse, Master P did a stint on *Dancing with the Stars*.

Bounce, a style that grew out of rap and hip hop, is the hot new music . . . that's been around for 25 years. The earliest bounce song can be traced back to a local duo, **MC T. Tucker and DJ Irv**, who were called the "Fathers of Bounce." The two changed the course of New Orleans music with their 1991 local hit, "Where Dey At." MC T. Tucker and DJ Irv perfected and popularized the new music while working local clubs and selling tapes "out-the-trunk."

Bounce was characterized by a call and response delivery and the use of several fast-paced sample tracks known as the "Triggerman beat" (also called "dat beat"). Bounce took over local clubs, bars, and school dances as quickly as Who Dat T-shirts. Its signature move occurs when a bounce artist yells, "hands on the floor" and the willing dancers collapse into an all-four position and start shaking their butts. You can think of it as a more choreographed version of twerking.

When the infectious, booty-shaking beat was picked up by Beyoncé, Katy Perry, and Adele, bounce became an international phenomenon. Bounce music had been around New Orleans since the late 1980s. In 2010, it got a burst of sudden attention when bounce rappers Big Freedia and Katey Red were profiled in the *New York Times* and *Vanity Fair*.

The New Orleans bounce artist Robert Maize, a.k.a. **Mr. Ghetto**, made a name for himself when his YouTube video "Walmart" went viral. Filmed with a handheld camera, it featured a couple of dancers popping (i.e., butt-shaking) in a Walmart parking lot and in store aisles.

By the time Miley Cyrus lit up the Internet with her twerking performance on the MTV Awards, it was old news in New Orleans. Said Big Freedia, "I am excited about Miley twerking on the VMAs. She didn't twerk properly, but she opened the door for New Orleans and bounce music and myself." Locally, Big Freedia had issued "Azz Everywhere," his genre-shaping bounce classic a decade earlier.

On the worldwide scale, **Big Freedia** has become the face of bounce music, thanks mostly to his musical talent, his larger-than-life personality, and now a best-selling book and his reality TV show, *Big Freedia: Queen of Bounce*.

You would be mistaken to think that bounce is male-dominated and misogynistic, like a lot of rap. There are in fact a number of female stars in the New Orleans scene. Of note is **Mia X** (should be XXX) who proves the point with the song "Funk You Up." Mia X has scripted some romantic lyrics like "Make the coochie scream for a 6-inch stick? I pushed an 8-pound baby out, so that's bullshit." Her words, not mine.

The queen of the rap scene in New Orleans has to be **Cheeky Blakk**. By day, she's Angela Woods, a nurse working in a retirement home. By night, she's Cheeky Blakk, songsmith of tunes like "Bitch Get Off Me," "Ride Fa My Nigga," and her massive hit "Twerk Something." She got into performing after an argument with the father of her child, Pimp Daddy Jenkins. He brought his anger to the stage, rapping a song with the line, "Here's another ho by the name of Cheeky Blakk." Livid, she wrote her own song with the line, "Well, Pimp Daddy, it's about that time / Cheeky Blakk tell you 'bout your funny, fake-ass rhyme." Their airing of domestic issues became first-class entertainment in the clubs. Pimp Daddy was later shot and killed. Her career, however, has continued to spiral upward. When asked by *OffBeat Magazine* why she's so successful, Cheeky Blakk answered, "Maybe it's because I touch people's penises when I go on stage."

For visitors looking to delve into the local bounce music scene, there are large-scale popping events at the Republic or the House of Blues, and at smaller venues, such as the Siberia lounge. There are also drop-in bounce fitness classes, held at the Dancing Grounds community center in the Bywater neighborhood.

Rock, Punk, and Discordant

Obviously, rock 'n' roll is not a distinctive New Orleans sound. Fred LeBlanc of Cowboy Mouth has said of the New Orleans music scene, "Rock is sort of treated like the red-headed stepchild." In a city renowned for jazz, blues, R&B, and funk, rock 'n' roll does take second fiddle. There's been no noteworthy movement like grunge rock in Seattle or glam rock in New York.

Well, there was a brief New Orleans movement called sludge metal in the early '90s, but I sense this is the first you've heard of it. Groups like Crowbar, Acid Bath, and Eyehategod created a dark and gloomy sound. If you YouTube Crowbar's "hit" song, "Existence Is Punishment," you'll get a sense of sludge from this four-minute video (unless you decide to kill yourself halfway through). Guitarist, lead vocalist, and founder Kirk Windstein continually reassembles members of Crowbar to keep the band going. They released their tenth album, *Symmetry in Black*, in 2014.

Cowboy Mouth, along with Better Than Ezra, are the two current bands most known to people not from New Orleans, and most revered by rock fans who live in New Orleans. Cowboy Mouth has been around since the early '90s, has released a dozen records, and has been featured on TV and radio stations nationwide. They are best known as a high-volume, powerhouse live act. Their performances have been likened to "a religious experience." Said frontman Fred LeBlanc, "If The Neville Brothers and The Clash had a baby, it would be Cowboy Mouth." They've cut back from being constantly on the road and now do about fifty live performances a year. In the New Orleans area, they can fill the Smoothie King Center, the same venue where the NBA Pelicans play. If you're lucky you might catch them for free during the Lafayette Square series. They play festivals, and were Tulane University's 2015 Homecoming dance band, which makes them seem less cool than they are.

Better Than Ezra recorded a lot of indie releases on their own label, Swell Records, before being signed by Elektra. Their very first demo cassette tape, circulated in 1988, is supposedly worth bejillions (well . . . a lot). Their single "Good" from their first Elektra release reached #1 on the Hot Modern Rock Tracks chart and the album went platinum. Band member Tom Drummond commented on CNN: "It took us seven years to get signed, and then seven weeks to get to number one."

Anders Osborne's music is sometimes considered blues. He's also written country hits for Tim McGraw, and has toured with a band featuring the Mardi Gras Indians' Big Chief Monk Boudreaux. But to me, he is mostly a classic rock 'n' roll singer strapped with a guitar and a New Orleans take on Neil Young or Jackson Browne.

He's also the embodiment of the great Miles Davis quote, "It takes a long time be able to play like yourself." Anders left his homeland of Sweden when he was 16, then experienced a lifetime and a half in America battling bipolar disorder and various addictions to anything you can drink, shoot, or snort. He describes those years in a *Gambit Weekly* newspaper interview, "All the terrible stories that come with addiction, I have them. Blacking out, waking up not knowing where my guitar is, and I've been running around with no pants on for two days."

Anders finally settled down both figuratively and literally in his adopted hometown of New Orleans. "New Orleans clicked for me. It's not something I have to reach for or touch. I am this city. I am becoming it, making it, shaping it. You have to constantly work on New Orleans, be a part of it. Carry on traditions while you make new ones."

His output (thirteen albums) and his range (from acoustic singer-songwriter to ferocious electric guitar-hero) is impressive. He's won *OffBeat Magazine*'s "Best Songwriter" the past two years, and he has been "Best Guitarist" three years and counting. If Anders had only written just the one song "Summertime in New Orleans" and then quit, he'd still have a locked-up place on my Forever list.

Another group worth your time and attention is **Generationals**, a two-person band consisting of Ted Joyner and Grant Widmer. They were previously a five-member band, The Eames Era, possibly best known for the song "Could Be Anything," which was featured on the TV show *Grey's Anatomy*. When three of the five quit, Ted and Grant became a New Orleans version of two-person bands like The White Stripes or The Black Keys.

Grant Widmer says of their New Orleans roots: "My reality of being from New Orleans was growing up and watching MTV. I grew up in Lakeview and there wasn't a second line going down the street. Beavis and Butthead was probably the most formative thing."

Wilco bills themselves as alternative rock. Lucinda Williams has been called American rock, folk, blues, and country. New Orleans band **Hurray for the Riff Raff** mines a similar vein. The band's fiddler, Yosi Perlstein, describes their music: "I think our sound is pretty unique. The band is influenced by a lot of different styles. You can hear influences from Appalachian old time, old R&B and gospel to '60s rock and roll with some New Orleans and Cajun sounds. You just have to listen to it for it to make sense."

It's not really a traditional New Orleans sound, though the songs are layered with New Orleanian lyrics. Singer-songwriter and banjo-guitar player Alynda Lee Segarra is the face of Riff Raff. She grew up in the Bronx, where she was a regular at the hardcore punk shows. At age 17, she pulled a Woody Guthrie, left home, and crossed America hopping freight trains. Like so many artists, writers, and musicians, when she arrived in New Orleans, the city gave her that vortex feeling of "Home." She told *OffBeat*, "Living here, it's really great because a lot of musicians are not playing to become famous or succeed in a monetary way, but because they love to play."

Since settling in New Orleans, Segarra and her band have already made six albums, and have been chosen Emerging Artist of the Year. Their 2014 album, *Small Town Heroes*, was named as one of the best albums of the year by *Rolling Stone*, *Spin*, and NPR.

Hurray for the Riff Raff is in the "intense road trips" stage of their career. But when they're in town they can be heard at One Eyed Jacks, House of Blues, and at every Jazz Fest.

Phil Anselmo is sort of the New Orleans renaissance man of punk rock. He is best known as the former lead singer of Pantera, but he has had many start-up and side project bands such as Eibon, a very short-lived supergroup; Southern Isolation, which recorded just four songs before breaking up; Superjoint Ritual; Philip H. Anselmo & the Illegals; and Christ Inversion, a short-lived metal project where Anselmo played guitar under the name "Anton Crowley" and their lyrics were based on horror films and Satanism. The group Down has been Anselmo's main recording and touring band since 2006.

Anselmo also started his own record label in 2001, Housecore Records, and is involved in a YouTube comedy series called Metal Grasshopper, with comedian Dave Hill. In addition, he was the founder of one of the country's most highly regarded Halloween attractions, House of Shock. Anselmo owns an extensive collection of several thousand horror films and possesses a world-class knowledge of horror films that would rival the late great Forrest J. Ackerman.

I could go on and annotate any number of bands from Bipolaroid, Clockwork Elvis, Sick Like Sinatra, and Buck Biloxi and the Fucks if only for the joy of typing their names, but we have a whole book to write and then read. I will, however, mention **Rik Slave** here primarily because he's a friend, and he works by day at one of my favorite food stops, Cochon Butcher. But I'm also mentioning him here because he's been called "one of rock's best kept secrets, and one of its great performers" by the online music guide *AllMusic*.

Rail-thin, with a greased-back receding hairline and a John Waters mustache, I have more than once said that Rik looks like a late-night TV horror host. As a singer since 1986, Rik has fronted a wide range of bands from sludge rock or punk bands like Swamp Goblin and the Cretinous to a brief fling with a hard-edged punk band, Man Scouts of America, to a truly bent country band, Rik Slave & the Phantoms, to his newer, benter country band, Rik Slave's Country Persuasion. Rik has said, "Every punk rocker goes through a Hank Williams phase." It took Rik 20 years of performing before he recorded his first album. He admitted, "We don't like to rush into things."

Many of the absolute best musicians you can hear tonight I define as discordant music. Discordant can mean good things like "at variance" or "divergent" as well as less complimentary like "harsh" or "jarring." Here, I intend the good kind of discordant.

My personal and unjustifiable taste places **Helen Gillet** as the number-#1 favorite Queen of Discordant Music in New Orleans. She plays the cello. She plays the cello in ways you've never heard it played, or even imagined it could be played.

She joined the New Orleans music scene in 2002 by way of Wisconsin, Chicago,

Singapore, and the French-speaking section of Belgium (Wallonia) where she was born. She has a master's degree in classical music, but her training as an improvisor began with North Indian Hindustani vocal ragas, which are your basic old run-of-the-mill, Vedic ritual chants.

A session with Gillet will include French chansons, a sort of traditional French folk music from the 1930s to '50s, jazz, funk, rock, what she playfully calls Hungarian rock opera, and, my favorite, the songs she performs with live tape looping. Her masterful skill with looping is no mere gimmick, but is absolutely mesmerizing and trance-inducing. For me, it's also a tear-jerking experience: It moves me to watch a real artist who is not the least bit focused on becoming a brand or concerned with performing in a style for mainstream radio.

Her wide range of talent has allowed her to play with Smokey Robinson, Nikki Glaspie (who's played with Beyoncé, Dumpstafunk, and the Neville Brothers), John Popper (Blues Traveler), members of Morphine, Ani DiFranco, The New Orleans Klezmer All-Stars, The Mardi Gras Indian Orchestra, and European avant-garde jazz musicians like Georg Graewe, Kresten Osgood, Tobias Delius, Frank Gratkowski, Almut Kuehne, and Wilbert de Joode. If you see a pattern here, please give me a call.

In New Orleans, Helen can be heard at the Antieau Gallery and the Blue Nile (upstairs). She plays every Monday night at Bacchanal, although the times I've seen her there have frustrated me—the other backyard diners clink glasses, rattle plates, and talk too loudly as they hardly notice that a true artist is performing right in front of their pairing of Jade Jagger wine and bacon-wrapped dates.

The New Orleans Bingo! Show is also my #1 favorite. (There is a burger joint in New Orleans, Dis n Dem. They have on their menu "The Only Omelette" and just below list "The Only Other Omelette." So, I can have two #1 favorites.) The Bingo! Show is hard to define even after you've seen it. I have described it as sort of a slightly deviant version of Cirque du Soleil. Sideshows of original short films, comedic skits, and burlesque, featuring Miss Trixie Minx, serve as the framing device for the uber-talented Clint Maedgen (who also plays with the Preservation Hall Band) and his randy, eccentric, and costumed band.

The Bingo! Show started in 2002 when Clint found bingo game boards in a thrift store and was inspired to create the first version of the group that merged theater, rock, and a game of bingo. They at first played in the back room of Fiorella's Cafe, but have progressed to become a semi-every-so-often performance at One Eyed Jacks. They've also played at the Kennedy Center.

I can't recommend strongly enough viewing Clint's YouTube video, "Complicated Life." For me, it captures the essence of New Orleans in 5 minutes and 7 seconds.

Until he recently retired, the diminutive Ron Rona, in face paint, bowler hat, and megaphone, served as the emcee. After seeing The Bingo! Show a few times,

The Bingo! Show

I knew my then-10-year-old daughter would be captivated. I texted Ron to see if there were venues or occasions where the show was less packed with megaphone-amplified expletives. There were. I took her to The Bingo! Show's outdoor performance during the French Quarter Festival. She was, indeed, captivated.

Their music runs the gambit, from a Nick Cave & The Bad Seeds sound all the way to the work of Kurt Weill. Warning: The Bingo! Show stops in the middle of the performance to play bingo. If you win, for God's sake don't tell them . . . unless you want to be brought up on stage to experience the hilarity of utter humiliation.

If I had a #1B favorite discordant musician or group, it would be **Sweet Crude**. I "discovered" Sweet Crude after they'd been around two years, when they were the opening band for the group I went to see one night, The Wild Magnolias.

Sweet Crude, a seven-piece ensemble Cajun indie-rock group, could be called rock 'n' roll or Cajun and zydeco music. Sweet Crude is neither fish nor foul. They're not really a Cajun band, because they play with a percussion-heavy rock sensibility. And they're a pretty weird rock band because of their insistence on lyrics that are mostly Cajun French and their assembly of instruments, which is random and weird and quite wonderful. Most notably, they perform without any lead guitars.

Percussionist Marion Tortorich described the process of how they put the band together in an *OffBeat Magazine* article, saying that members were chosen for the kind of energy they brought and "then we figured out what instruments they could play on different songs." What Sweet Crude ultimately put together was Alexis Marceaux and Sam Craft as vocalists (both of whom also play the drums—and Sam also plays violin), Tortorich and John Arceneaux as percussionists, keyboardists Skyler Stroup (who also plays trumpet) and Sam's brother Jack Craft, plus Stephen MacDonald on bass.

They also look different from what you might expect. While I'm certain the band members are in their 20s, they look more like high school Mathletes or members of the camera club.

Debauche, like Sweet Crude, could be considered rock 'n' roll. However, the fact that they sing in Russian and call themselves a "Russian Mafia Band" slides them over to my idea of discordant. The group got its start as a one-man whacking crew in 2008. Ukrainian-born Yegor Romantsov sang what he called Russian hooligan songs at Kahve Royale coffee shop on Royal Street every Friday from 10 p.m. until midnight. He drank his homemade honey pepper vodka while singing. Gradually, like-minded performers found Yegor and wild Russian jam sessions soon began breaking out. (I sense that only in New Orleans would there have been like-minded performers.) Eve Venema and Christian Kuffner of the former Zydepunks joined in. Then violinist Jesse Stoltzfus broke his hand and couldn't play, so he started with the band as a drummer. Now he's mastered both instruments and can play drums and violin simultaneously. He can also ride a unicycle and juggle at the same time. More ex-Zydepunks, bass player Scott Potts and drummer Joseph McGinty joined in. Vincent Schmidt, an accordion player from an Oregon Russian band, Chervona, was game. Kerry Lynn, a belly dancing percussionist, is the latest addition. Their sound is similar to Gogol Bordello and the Leningrad band style, which were made popular by the 2005 movie *Everything Is Illuminated*.

Tarriona "Tank" Ball sounds like she's campaigning for her band, **Tank & the Bangas**, to be considered discordant when she stated that, "They (New Orleanians) have never experienced anything like this before. And vice versa." Named "Tank" by her father (gee, thanks, Dad), Bell began her career as a spoken word poet. And she pretty much still is, though now she's backed up by singers Angelika Joseph and Kayla Jasmine, and a first-rate seven-piece band. In her sweet pixie voice, she creates and delivers some of the most oddly wonderful lyrics about the most wonderfully odd subject matter.

In one song, she compares shopping at Whole Foods versus Winn-Dixie to weave a metaphor of lost love. Walmart figures in another song as a place to shop for the perfect mate, where you can check the tag on their collar to see if they had

Quintron

any issues you might have to deal with later. Leaving her retail store comfort zone, one of the Bangas "hits?" is a song called "Bradys." It's about her longing for the comfortingly plastic lifestyle of Florence Henderson on the famed '60s TV show *The Brady Bunch*.

To many in New Orleans, **Quintron** is the unquestionable #1 discordant hero. It's hard to imagine a performer more at odds with every other musician or musical style. Since 1994, he's been cutting records—fourteen albums in all—inventing strange musical contraptions, and entertaining audiences with a combination of psychedelic soul live music performances and inflatable puppet theater put on by his wife, Miss Pussycat. I'm just getting started. But underneath all the weird electronics and puppetry, Quintron does manage to pull off a very danceable B-52's-esque sound.

Quintron has released strange soundscape recordings based on taping inner-city frogs and neighborhood ambience. He has also holed himself up in the New Orleans Museum of Art (for three months) to create the epic album, *Sucre Du Sauvage*.

His inventions include the Spit Machine, a hand organ that uses saliva as a tuning conductor, and the Disco Light Machine, a device attached to a drum kit that lights up to accompany the beat. With the latter, the harder you play the drums, the brighter the light and the louder the electronic sounds. His most significant invention, however, is the Drum Buddy. It is a light-activated analog synthesizer that creates murky, low-fidelity, rhythmic patterns. The Drum Buddy has been used by Wilco and Laurie Anderson.

Quintron used to play regular shows at Spellcasters Lodge (which he owned) in the Bywater neighborhood. Their own Facebook page currently states that Spellcasters "may be permanently closed." As of this writing, Quintron has upcoming shows confirmed at One Eyed Jacks and Gasa Gasa.

Brooklyn-bred **Cole Williams** moved to New Orleans in January 2015 and has rapidly become one of the new "wow" performers. She's a composer, producer, entrepreneur, WWOZ radio host, grade-school music teacher with her own jewelry line, and above all else, a powerful singer.

Cole performs at the Maple Leaf and Chickie Wah Wah with her band, That's Our Cole. Her gender-bending music has been termed "African rock meets Jamaican soul," but perhaps it is best described by the title of her album: *Out of the Basement, Out of the Box.*

DJs, Bars, and Clubs

DJ Soul Sister is not a live musician, but a revered DJ who puts on an intensely lively mix of Motown, old R&B, and techno-pop every Saturday night at The Hi-Ho Lounge. The show runs 11:00 p.m. to 3:00 a.m.

Known as the "queen of rare groove," DJ Soul Sister has hosted her "Soul Power" show on WWOZ radio for nearly two decades. Soul Sister has created her seamlessly blended, vinyl-only sets everywhere from New York to Los Angeles to London. Here in New Orleans, DJ Soul Sister's dance parties are well-respected and attended as much as any live jazz, blues, rock, R&B, or funk show.

There's a stretch of bars and clubs along St. Claude Avenue from the Marigny to Bywater that is much less frequented than Frenchmen Street. But it offers far more eclectic music, burlesque, and some performances that must be experienced because they can't be described.

You never know what you'll find at the AllWays Lounge (2240 St. Claude Ave.) until you open the door. (Well, I guess you *could* look at their calendar online.) When Nancy, my favorite cousin, was visiting New Orleans, our barhopping included the AllWays. That night it was amateur striptease night. Trust me, you don't want to see amateur striptease. We quickly left and went across the street to The Hi-Ho Lounge. There, it was bounce night. A significantly overweight white guy was doing some pretty amazing things with his gelatinous buttocks where each cheek gyrated independently, as if responding to completely different neurons.

On other nights, however, the AllWays is exactly where you want to be. The club has weekly readings. They also host the Freaksheaux to Geaux, a professional burlesque variety act, and regular shows by Bella Blue ("Pussy Magic" and Dirty Dime Peep Show). Thursdays are drag bingo with Vinsantos. Musically, the AllWays (not surprisingly) leans toward alternative music, head banging rock, and the unclassifiable weirdness of acts like Ratty Scurvics.

Directly across the street is The Hi-Ho Lounge (2239 St. Claude Ave.) with live music ranging among everything from hip-hop and funk to indie rock. One night I was there, the Detroit Party Marching Band (sort of Detroit's version of the Hungry March Band) chose to have half their band jump up on the bar itself to play. No one objected.

In addition to live music, the Hi-Ho hosts premier burlesque groups like Rev. Spooky LeStrange and Her Billion Dollar Baby Dolls, Storyville Starlets, and Slow Burn Burlesque.

What you'll hear at Kajun's (2256 St. Claude Ave.) may not fit your definition of music. It is the top karaoke bar in town, every night starting at 9:00 p.m. A wide range of songs for you to mangle are offered, including tunes from Pee-wee Herman films. During the football season, Kajun's gives out free jello shots every time the Saints score a touchdown. Lately, that's not been often enough.

Siberia (2227 St. Claude Ave.) books punk, metal, bounce, and . . . it may be the only place in town where you can hear Slavic music. Plus, there's weekly burlesque and some of the worst comics you'll ever hear. At the back of the bar, past the taxidermied deer and turkeys, is a pop-up restaurant, Kukhnya ("kitchen" in Russian), that serves Slavic soul food: pierogies, blini, and kielbasa. This bar recently edged out the legendary Tipitina's as the people's choice award for number one live music club.

Sweet Lorraine's Jazz Club (1931 St. Claude Ave.), unlike most of the others, never has burlesque nor cringe-inducing comedians. Sweet Lorraine's is instead focused solely on outstanding blues and jazz, with the occasional spoken word and jazz poetry session. The live jazz Sunday brunch is more locals/less touristy than the more famous Commander's Palace or Court of Two Sisters.

Where Frenchmen Street is New Orleans' main hub for music and St. Claude the epicenter of alternative music, there yet remain a slew of other places to go to hear live music. Some, but of course not all, are listed by neighborhood in the following pages.

Bywater and The Marigny

Bacchanal Wine 600 Poland Ave.

Bacchanal Wine has been profiled elsewhere. They opened as a neighborhood corner wine shop, right aside the Industrial Canal and the Mississippi River. Bacchanal is included here because you sit outdoors under string lights and tiki torches and listen to live music by noted New Orleans musicians. The brilliant Helen Gillet, also profiled elsewhere, performs most Monday nights. Thursday nights is usually The Courtyard Kings, a group that merges bebop, gypsy jazz, Brazilian jazz, and New Orleans traditional jazz.

BJ's Lounge 4301 Burgundy St.

BJ's Lounge is a bit frayed at the edges, with yard sale chairs shoved against the wall next to an old upright piano I can only assume hasn't been tuned in decades, a wall of snapshots of former patrons, and torn-out pages from old *Playboy* magazines taped to the bathroom walls. The bar is and always will be cash-only.

It's a perfect setting for the dirty blues of one of its regular performers, Little Freddie King. Every Monday night used to be King James & the Special Men, who brought their own red beans and rice. Now Mondays belong to one of the more unusually named bands in New Orleans—Lumpy Black Problem Variety Show: An Orgy of Remorse.

Cafe Istanbul 2372 St. Claude Ave.

Cafe Istanbul is the brainchild of poet Chuck Perkins, who aims to foster and promote performance art in New Orleans. The nearly 4,000-square-foot theater with balcony space shows locally made movies premiers, comedy shows (most notably the Goodnight Show with John Calhoun, which is basically a New Orleans take on A Prairie Home Companion), dance troupes, and live music. The cafe (without food) has hosted the Bad Boyz of R&B, the 10th Anniversary Mantra Music Concert, and NOLA Jam Session.

Checkpoint Charlie 501 Esplanade Ave.

This is actually named Igor's Checkpoint Charlie, but no one calls it that. Alongside the French Quarter, at the mouth of Frenchmen Street, Checkpoint Charlie is a hangout that can meet almost all your needs with its bar, pool table, pinball machines, wash and dry machines, passable half-pound Charlie burgers, jalapeño poppers, mini-pizzas, chicken nuggets, or cheese fries, and a small stage where you can hear rock, metal, or punk, depending on the night. Just don't use the bathrooms. A Yelp text commented that they "would be considered a disgrace in most 3rd world countries."

Regular bands include Bible Belt Sinners, Bad Moon Lander, and The Olivia de Havilland Mosquitoes, all bands you're not likely to see anywhere else. Tuesday evenings are the well-attended open mic blues jam.

Vaughan's Lounge 4229 Dauphine St.

Vaughan's Lounge had been, for over 20 years, Kermit Ruffins's Thursday night sessions. An entire book, Jay Mazza's *Not Just Another Thursday Night*, was written about the weekly party at Vaughan's. But after opening his own club, Kermit felt it was time for a change. This beautifully dilapidated corner bar still draws crowds for other performers like The Heart Attacks, The Southern BarBitchurates, and the rising stars of Corey Henry and The Treme Funktet.

French Quarter

Balcony Music Club 1331 Decatur St.

More often called BMC, there's almost always a barker out front trying to siphon off the stream of nighthawks headed right across the street toward Frenchmen's gauntlet of music clubs. There's never a cover for the seven nights of music, which feature jazz and funk, but most often blues.

The Bombay Club 830 Conti St.

The Bombay Club has the look and feel of a British hunting club with deep leather chairs, bronze equestrian statues, and a grandfather clock. It is also appreciably different from any other place in New Orleans where you might take in live music. They are first and foremost an upscale restaurant that features noted chef Nathan Richard. An essential part of the meal is their lineup of musicians. They serve jazz: pianists like Kris Tokarski and Tom Hook, jazz guitarists like Matt Johnson, and singers like Linnzi Zaorski and Banu Gibson. Occasionally they step ever-so-slightly outside the pure jazz lineup with Latin jazz (Los Tres Amigos).

Chris Owens Club 500 Bourbon St.

The lone remaining remnant from Bourbon Street's glory days. The ageless Ms. Owens has been hitting the stage in sequins and feathers since the 1960s. Her high energy and higher kitsch-value shows are most often accompanied by her Latin Rhythms band, but she's integrated all types of music into her act, including bounce. An evening at Chris Owens is the equivalent of taking in a Vegas show with Wayne Newton or Tom Jones.

The Davenport Lounge 921 Canal St.

Named after its headliner, Jeremy Davenport, a jazz trumpeter and vocalist, the scene is appropriately elegant, maybe even swanky. Live jazz is offered on Wednesdays and Thursdays from 5:30 p.m. to 9:30 p.m., and Fridays and Saturdays from 9:00 p.m. to 1:00 a.m.

Fritzel's European Jazz Pub 733 Bourbon St.

A classic jazz club that's been in the heart of the Bourbon Street madness since the early 1960s. They claim to be the city's oldest operating jazz club. (There's a lot of claiming going on in New Orleans.) Dixieland jazz is served near the fireplace or on the patio, along with imported beers or cocktails doused with European schnapps.

Funky Pirate Blues Club 727 Bourbon St.

The Funky Pirate is practically next door to Fritzel's and serves as the long-time home for Big Al Carson and The Blues Masters. The 495-pound blues and funk musician with the velvety voice has been performing on their tiny stage every Thursday through Saturday night for over 20 years. On other nights, the Funky Pirate features long sets of raunchy blues.

House of Blues 225 Decatur St.

Both a solid restaurant and live music venue, House of Blues has hosted famous musicians from New Orleans (Fats Domino, Trombone Shorty, and Dr. John) and beyond (Ziggy Marley, Lady Gaga, and Eric Clapton). Every Sunday morning, House of Blues has a rousing Gospel Brunch.

Irvin Mayfield's Jazz Playhouse 300 Bourbon St., inside The Royal Sonesta Hotel

Irvin Mayfield's Jazz Playhouse is a place of premier music that I nonetheless have a hard time recommending. The music is just as good as ever. Regulars like jazz singer Germaine Bazzle and Gerald French and the Original Tuxedo Jazz Band remain "should-sees." Trixie Minx, our premier burlesque queen, I'd rate close to a "must-see" for her performances every Friday at midnight. My issue is with the club's namesake and Grammy Award-winning jazz trumpet player, and former Cultural Ambassador of the City of New Orleans, Irvin Mayfield. He deserves to be profiled in this book. You'll note he is not. Post-Katrina, he managed the New Orleans Public Library system and managed to pay himself a six-figure salary, and also managed to funnel over $850,000 from donations earmarked for the library's private fundraising to his own New Orleans Jazz Orchestra. Some of his most egregious expenditures with that money have been his $1,400 breakfast in New York and his overnight stays at luxury hotels—while in his home town of New Orleans.

One Eyed Jacks 615 Toulouse St.

One Eyed Jacks has a rich history. A former movie palace, it eventually became the epicenter for the rebirth of burlesque in New Orleans, was home of the Shim Shamettes, and is now an eclectic, bordello-feeling club that hosts a variety of musical pleasures.

Inside One Eyed Jacks, there are three completely different bars. What used to be the theater's lobby is now an elegant setting to get stiffed. Chandeliers hang overhead. The walls are covered in flocked crimson wallpaper with vintage nude paintings. It feels like a 1900s brothel or Russian Tea Room. Behind it, in the theater, is a horseshoe-shaped bar where you grab a drink while watching alt music or burlesque. You can also watch the performances from the second floor bar, which is an ode to kitsch, with black-light velvet paintings and matador lamps.

Warehouse District

Circle Bar 1032 St. Charles Ave.

Circle Bar is standing (barely ... with peeling walls and warped floors) in the shadow of Robert E. Lee's statue on Lee Circle. The bar was originally the office of Dr. Elizabeth Magnus Cohen. She was the first female licensed physician in Louisiana. She came to New Orleans in 1857 to work with patients who were suffering through epidemics of smallpox and yellow fever. The tiny music room inside can cure what ails you between the hours of 9:00 p.m. and 4:00 a.m.

The names of the constantly changing bands alone reveal the types of music played there: Gramps The Vamp, Barb Wire Dolls, The Quintessential Octopus, and Those Folks with the Hokum High Rollers, and the Friday night regulars, Rik Slave's Country Persuasion. Hint: None of the bands play Dixieland or Top 40 hits.

The Howlin' Wolf 907 S. Peters St.

The Howlin' Wolf opened in 1988 in an old cotton warehouse, outgrew the space, and moved into what was previously the New Orleans Music Hall. Outside is a mural masterpiece created by artist Michalopoulos that depicts our music history from Louis Armstrong to a second line with the Dirty Dozen Brass Band. Inside is a bar that comes from Al Capone's hotel in Chicago. It was dismantled there and reassembled here. The black curtains on stage were salvaged from the Orpheum Theatre.

Over the years, The Howlin' Wolf has hosted The Foo Fighters, The Meters, Wu-Tang Clan, Dr. John, and Death Cab For Cutie. It is the Sunday-night home for the Grammy-nominated Hot 8 Brass Band. They occasionally have burlesque, and twice a week they showcase comedians: there's the Comedy Beast show on Tuesdays, and Comedy Gumbeaux on Thursdays.

Little Gem Saloon 445 Rampart St.

The first and, currently, the only restoration in the neighborhood that experts consider vital for the development of jazz. In the early 1900s, the then-sketchy area, bordering Storyville's red light district, was booze, jazz, and brothels. It was called "Back o Town" and was the hub for African-American social life in New Orleans, with the restaurant menus and musical styles that catered to those tastes.

The Little Gem Saloon dinner jazz club opened in 1903 under kingpin Frank Doroux. He also owned the Eagle Saloon, practically next door. The Iroquois Theater was on the same block. Jazz greats Joseph "King" Oliver, Jelly Roll Morton, Sidney Bechet, Kid Ory, and Buddy Bolden got their starts playing at these clubs. As a young boy, Louis Armstrong won a talent contest at the Iroquois by covering his face in flour and doing a "white face" routine.

Beginning in the 1920s, major changes dried up the neighborhood. The U.S. government shutdown of legalized prostitution was a blow. The second death blow came with the explosion of movie houses on Canal Street, which siphoned off the customers from vaudeville and live jazz. The last of the clubs closed in 1927. Little

LUMINS OF NEW ORLEANS:
Stanton Moore

The same way visitors flock to New Orleans to eat our Cajun and Creole food, many people come here seeking out traditional jazz. However, to be a relevant food capital and not a culinary theme park nor museum, the city needs new and expansive chefs like Phillip Lopez, Ryan Prewitt, and Alon Shaya. For our music, I'll borrow (steal) a catchphrase from WWOZ radio. To serve as "Guardians of the Groove," New Orleans needs places like Preservation Jazz Hall, the Palm Court, and the decks of the Steamboat Natchez to keep the traditional New Orleans jazz sound alive. But to remain a musical hub, we need musicians like Stanton Moore. Without improvisation and expansion, New Orleans music might eventually be no sexier than a corseted 75-year-old Tom Jones singing "What's New, Pussycat?"

Stanton Moore, born and raised in the New Orleans area and educated at Loyola University on St. Charles Ave, is a key figure in the evolution of the city's music. "My mom took me to Mardi Gras parades starting when I was 8 months old," he recalled in an interview. "So, around the age of 3, 4, 5, I started really being impacted by the sound of the marching bands coming down the street. By the time I was 6 or 7, I was hitting on stuff in the house—pots and pans, really whatever I could get my hands on. And by the time I was 9 years old, I knew I wanted to be a professional drummer. Now I travel the world playing music that is heavily entrenched in the musical traditions of New Orleans. What's so exciting to me is that I come home eager to go out and see all of my favorite musicians here in town. Guys like Shannon Powell, Herlin Riley, Johnny Vidacovich, Russell Batiste. I draw inspiration from these guys and get excited in the same way I did when I was a kid. Everything I do and see in this city, all that I listen to and participate in, are sources of inspiration and influence, and I continue to incorporate those things into my drumming and my music and continue to take it back out to the world. The musical heritage runs so deep here I'll never get to the end of it. This city is a never ending well of inspiration."

Moore has played, composed, or collaborated on virtually every style of music, always with a New Orleans sensibility; funk, soul, R&B, hip hop, bounce, Mardi Gras carnival music, electronica, straight ahead jazz, even heavy metal—pretty much everything except Tuvan throat singing.

Stanton considers his various groups as his diversified portfolio. But his unquestionable blue chip stock is Galactic. For me personally, Galactic is way beyond blue chip. They have replaced the Talking Heads as my all-time #1 favorite band. Similar to the way in which Talking Head's frontman, David Byrne, has collaborated with "everyone" from Brian Eno, Richard Thompson, and Devo to create "every" manner of music from their being called post-punk or new wave to mambo, cha-cha, and operatic arias with string arrangements, Stanton Moore has fearlessly joined forces with a great variety of performers to pull, poke, and prod the New Orleans sound into fresh and inventive directions.

Galactic has been called "a hybrid of Jazz, funk, blues, R&B, rock, and a horn section to die for, and the band is a perfect representation of what New Orleans can do for a musical soul."

Their first album, *Coolin' Off*, released in 1996, was widely acclaimed and introduced the band onto an intense tour scene. They played more than 200 nights a year for the next 10 years. When I sat down to interview Stanton, he had just returned from Brazil the night before and was flying out to Seattle the next day.

The five official Galactic members—Stanton Moore, bassist Robert Mercurio, keyboardist Rich Vogel, guitarist Jeff Raines and saxophonist Ben Ellman—have been together for over two decades. The original vocalist, Theryl DeClouet, left the band in 2004; ever since they've been what Moore has called "an instrumental band in search of a singer."

Galactic's stable of guest singers includes an incredibly diverse array of artists who couldn't be more diverse. Among their contributors are several stars united only by the fact of being New Orleans locals: Cyril Neville, Maggie Koerner, David Shaw of the Revivalists, bounce superstar Big Freedia, and rap queen Cheeky Blakk, known for repeating a two-word phrase on the song *Do It Again* that I dare not write. Galactic has featured non-New Orleanians like British New Wave singer, Joe Jackson, who sometimes tosses a little reggae or old-style swing into his music; LA rapper Chali 2na of Jurassic 5; from the hard-driving former lead singer for Living Colour, Corey Glover; to the calming raspy voice of the Grammy-winning R&B, jazz and soul singer, Macy Gray. DeClouet also rejoins the band on rare occasions. Currently, the much-admired jazz and soul singer Erica Falls does most of the live shows.

Instrumentally, Galactic has merged their music with members of the Soul Rebels, the Neville Brothers, the Dirty Dozen Brass Band, George Porter Jr. of the Meters, and the legendary Allen Toussaint, whose session with the group Moore called "pretty mind-blowing."

Not many of us get to live the dreams of our childhood. I'm certainly not the middle linebacker for the Cleveland Browns. Since he was in kindergarten, Stanton Moore wanted to be a drummer and remains head over heels in love with the music of New Orleans. For the last 20 years, he has been much more than a drummer. *Rolling Stone* lists him as one of the 25 Greatest Drummers of All Time, alongside John Bonham (Led Zeppelin), Neill Peart (Rush), and Ginger Baker (Cream). For the last 20 years, Stanton Moore has traveled the globe, from all over the United States, (and I mean all over, including Victor, Idaho; Blackstock, South Carolina; and Thornville, Ohio). Galactic has also traveled the world, hopping from Italy to Brazil, France, Japan, Australia, the United Kingdom, Netherlands, and Germany, where he has spread the gospel and the groove of New Orleans music. More than a mere advocate, Stanton Moore is an apostle.

Gem Saloon became a loan office. And the final blow came after Katrina, when, in a rush to rebuild, city officials unwittingly approved the demolition of the childhood home of jazz great Sidney Bechet and the Iroquois Theater.

Dr. Nicolas Bazan, along with his son, daughter, and son-in-law, bought the Little Gem Saloon in 2012 and set out to restore the venue. The space had been boarded up for the previous 40 years. Finally, more than 100 years after Little Gem Saloon first opened, it again opened for business. Little Gem Saloon is today an intimate and relaxed dinner jazz club. Regular performers include Kermit Ruffins (most Saturdays), Nayo Jones (most Fridays), and the Messy Cookers Jazz Band (most Tuesdays).

Republic 828 S. Peters St.

Republic is housed in a 150-year-old building, once a coffee warehouse. It has been converted into a spacious (a 2,500 square foot mezzanine hovers over a 4,000 square foot dance floor) uber-hip setting with art deco murals, vintage brick walls, large slate bar, crystal chandeliers, and exposed wooden beams. It also comes with a New York/LA attitude befitting the space. If you aren't "somebody" or you aren't friends with the bouncers, you'll wait in line to get in. Unless, of course, you've bought their VIP package (generally $35–100, depending on who's playing) whereby you skip the line and get exclusive seating, bottle service, and your own personal cocktail server.

DJ-themed bounce nights and Throwback nights occur on weekends. The club also features live performances with nationally known artists like Juvenile and Naughty By Nature, or up-and-comers like Unknown Mortal Orchestra and Girlpool and Alex G.

Treme

Candlelight Lounge 925 N. Robertson St.

Candelight Lounge is an often-packed neighborhood dive that features live music, brass bands, bold drinks, and lively times. It's also a favorite endpoint for second line parades. The Treme Brass Band plays there every Wednesday night.

Mid-City

Banks Street Bar & Grill 4401 Banks St.

Banks Street Bar & Grill is a tiny little watering hole populated mostly by locals. The music is a rotation of regional funk, blues, and rock bands every night. Ron Hot-stream and The F-Holes are semi-regulars. There's no cover. Better than no cover, Banks Street serves free red beans and rice on Mondays and free oysters on Thursday nights after 10:00 p.m.

Chickie Wah Wah 2828 Canal St.

Chickie Wah Wah can be accessed by either the City Park or the Cemeteries streetcar lines on the Canal, both of which stop directly in front of Chickie Wah Wah. The problem would be if you happened not to like the musicians on stage, you'll be out of luck, because it's located in a nightlife no-man's land. Chickie Wah Wah is nestled between a Harley dealer and a blood donation clinic.

Fortunately, Chickie Wah Wah has secured a solid schedule of New Orleans's premier performers. For me, Meschiya Lake and Tom McDermott on Tuesday nights are the "must-see." But for others, John Rankin (Wednesdays) or Jon Cleary (when he's in town) could easily fulfill that role. "The Punk Empress of African Rock," Cole Williams, is new to New Orleans but is already wowing audiences with her music, described as African rock meets Jamaican soul. Chickie Wah Wah generously gives the performers 100 percent of the door each night.

Bullet's Sports Bar 2441 A P Tureaud Ave.

Bullet's Sports Bar was regularly used as a setting on the HBO series *Treme*. Prior to their newfound "fame," it was very much a neighborhood joint, off the beaten track, and inhabited exclusively by locals. They offer R&B (five different R&B bands play on Sundays, starting at 7:00 p.m.), brass band (the all-girl brass band Pinettes performs on Fridays), and Kermit Ruffins & the Barbecue Swingers on Tuesdays. Food trucks line up outside during live shows.

Uptown and Carrollton

Carrollton Station Bar & Music Club
8140 Willow St.

A neighborhood bar and music club that is a bit out of the way for most visitors. Located at the end of the St. Charles streetcar line, the bar has events like open mic comedy (Wednesdays), live trivia (Thursdays), and the occasional ping pong tournament, none of which will make the destination worth the journey. One-dollar taco night (Fridays) is a bit more inviting. They have ten beers on tap and a signature drink, the Electric Blueberry Moonshine Lemonade. But the reason to go is the music on Friday and Saturday nights. They've hosted some of our best, like Little Freddie King and Debauche: Russian Mafia Band.

Dos Jefes Uptown Cigar Bar 5535 Tchoupitoulas St.

This is not a typical cigar bar where guys desperate to be like Arnold Schwarzenegger or Sly Stallone sit around posing with stogies in ways they've clearly practiced at home in front of a mirror.

It's become known for one of the best assortments of fine liquor in NOLA, and features top-notch live music six nights a week. Regulars include Joe Krown, Sunpie Barnes, gypsy swing from the Courtyard Kings, and Latin jazz from Rick Trolsen's Gringo do Choro.

Gasa Gasa 4920 Freret St.

Gasa Gasa is a funky art house that hosts weekly art exhibits, film screenings, and live music shows.

Le Bon Temps Roule 4801 Magazine St.

Le Bon Temps Roule is both a New Orleans signature phrase (it means "Let the Good Times Roll") and a rowdy and revered neighborhood bar. The bar and pool tables are upfront. The music stage, called "House of Dues" (because it's where local bands pay their dues before being discovered) is in back. The music is everything from brass bands to klezmer. The night to go is Thursday when the Soul Rebels play each week, though free oysters are on Fridays and dollar beers are served during Saints games.

Off the Map (literally and figuratively)

Dew Drop Jazz Hall 430 Lamarque St., Mandeville, Louisiana

Dew Drop Jazz Hall offers an adventure that will require you to cross the Causeway Bridge over Lake Pontchartrain (the world's longest bridge over a body of water—24 miles). The trip is totally worth the effort. On the other side of the lake is the town of Old Mandeville, and the Dew Drop is the oldest jazz hall in America (established 1895). Back in the early 1900s, New Orleans jazz pioneers, after playing more traditional music for whites-only audiences, would rush across the lake where they'd cut loose for black audiences who were receptive to their newfangled sounds. The Dew Drop's performers represent a who's who of jazz greats: Kid Ory, Bunk Johnson, George Lewis, Buddie Petit, and, most notably, Louis Armstrong, who played there often.

Today, the Dew Drop hosts two to four performances a month (check their website for a schedule: www.dewdropjazzhall.com). If you go, be prepared to step back into time. Very little has changed since Bunk Johnson and Louis Armstrong played there. It looks like an old country church, has no air conditioning or heating, no insulation, no running water, and no restrooms (you can use the building next door). Electricity is provided by a single line that powers multi-colored bare bulbs to light the room. The room itself can seat 100 people uncomfortably on wooden benches without backs.

Admission is $10 and is sold only in person. Next door, you can pay $10 for fried chicken or catfish dinners with rice and beans, potato salad, and cornbread that is prepared by the ladies of the First Free Mission Baptist Church. Dinner is served in Styrofoam boxes meant for your lap. Everything is cash-only.

My wife and I were literally in tears as 70-something couples executed perfect Cajun waltzes down the aisle, while Helen Gillet played from a tiny stage upfront. As said about the Dew Drop by performer, Deacon John, "The best thing about playing at a historic venue like this is that you feel the spirits permeating the room. When I get in here, I feel like my ancestors are playing backup."

In this chapter, I have listed roughly fifty music venues. There are many more. However, if you are agoraphobic (possessing a fear of open spaces or of being in crowded, public places) or a cherophobic (fear of gaiety), you can avoid our clubs altogether and take in New Orleans music in the privacy of your hotel room or rented car by tuning into WWOZ 90.7 FM. The station's stated mission is to be the worldwide authentic voice, archive, and flag-bearer of New Orleans culture.

Brothers Walter and Jerry Brock came to New Orleans from Texas in the 1970s, toting a massive record collection of New Orleans musicians, from Jelly Roll Morton to Dr. John. When they got here, they were amazed (Allen Toussaint might have said they got stomped) by the richness of the music they heard in the local clubs and bars and on the street. It was way beyond their collection. At that time local music was barely heard on the radio, except maybe a few classic songs around Mardi Gras.

Also at that time radio stations across the country were being snapped up and turned into Casey Kasem insipidness. The Brock brothers wanted the music, and not the on-air personalities, to be the focus of their station. The call letters WWOZ were chosen as a reference to the Wizard of Oz, as in "Pay no attention to the man behind the curtain." What was important was New Orleans music.

The station started out small—one might say Spartan. In the earliest days, WWOZ operated out of the upstairs beer storage room at Tipitina's. Often the DJs would drop a microphone through a hole in the floor and broadcast the live music playing on the stage below. The upstairs studio had no air-conditioning and, for a time, the only running water was from a neighbor's garden hose that was run in through a window. Everyone who worked there did additional tasks as a volunteer, be it addressing envelopes, sweeping the floor, or doing whatever needed to be done.

WWOZ was not only not your father's radio station, it wasn't your dentist's, accountant's, or weird uncle's. It was a thing unto itself. Jason Berry, in his excellent book, *Up From the Cradle of Jazz,* called WWOZ "the most exciting broadcast development of the 1980s. It became a kaleidoscope of voices, rich in oral imagery—jazzmen, composers, Cajun fiddlers, parades, grand marshals, gospel artists and R&B bluesmen, writers, occasional filmmakers, historians, Mardi Gras Indians, fathers and sons and mothers and daughters of musical families. WWOZ provided intimacy between the musicians and listeners, immeasurably broadening the sense of place."

In 1984, WWOZ moved out of the cramped space above Tipitina's and into what must have felt like Shangri-La: a three-room office in Louis Armstrong Park. Three years later, the financially strapped Nora Blatch Educational Foundation turned the station's license over to the Friends of WWOZ, a not-for-profit established by the New Orleans Jazz & Heritage Festival Foundation.

The foundation and local support have made it possible for the station to grow from the Brock brothers' beautiful idea to what is now widely recognized as one of the best radio stations in the country. *Rolling Stone,* in their feature "The 125-Plus People, Places and Things Ruling the Rock and Roll Universe," named WWOZ one of the top radio stations in the country. *Esquire* honored them as the Internet Radio Station of the Year, saying that this "resilient miracle of FM radio plays funk, jazz, blues, roots, Latin, soul, zydeco, R&B, and everything in between."

As Ian Neville said of growing up here, "Being a child in New Orleans, you're naturally exposed to music in ways you aren't anywhere else. Parades, marching bands, second lines, the sounds of the streets, the chants of the Mardi Gras Indians. My great uncle was Big Chief Jolly of the Wild Tchoupitoulas. My father and all my uncles were musicians. I met Allan Toussaint and Earl King and Dr. John when I was a kid. All of it was inspiration, available for us to soak up."

Pete Fountain echoes, "If I had grown up in any place but New Orleans, I don't think my career would have taken off. I wouldn't have heard the music that was around this town. There was so much going on when I was a kid."

The essential, ESSENTIAL, difference between New Orleans music and that found in other places is that it comes straight from the heart. Everyone from ballad singer Anders Osborne to Rap Poet Tank and the Bangas are, in their very different styles, throwbacks to the era when Bob Dylan, Bob Marley, and John Lennon were trying to change the world, or when MC5 merely wanted to kick out the jams and express their Rust Belt rage. When you go to music clubs or just walk the streets, listening to New Orleans' contemporary musicians, whom we call Guardians of the Groove, you'll experience the polar opposite of the modern over-hyped, brand managed musical era where Iggy Azalea et al. package, promote, and pay up-front placement fees for their mediocre talent to be one of the six newly released CDs on the Best Buy endcap.

The vast majority of musicians in New Orleans are far from focused on fame or success as measured by record contracts or CD sales. New Orleans is a city that understands the ancient quotation by Plato: "Music and rhythm find their way into the secret places of the soul."

CHAPTER 3

Drinking

Buzzed in the Big Easy

"I drink to make other people more interesting."   —**Ernest Hemingway**

When any Tom, Dick, and Peach Fuzz Harry first visit New Orleans, they feel they *have to* go down Bourbon Street. When I hear visitors say this, I think (but do not say), I must have been to the dentist 200 times and I never *had to* have a root canal just for the experience. Bourbon Street is made for 18-year-old boys with fake IDs, or older boys who don't need fake IDs, but are forever locked inside their 18-year-old selves. Bourbon Street doubles as both our drinking hub as well as our puking-in-public hub. You'll be greeted by the smells of urine and vomit pretty much 24 hours a day. The music isn't much better except for the 700 block, which houses Fritzel's European Jazz Pub and the Funky Pirate. The other clubs offer the steady stream of bad cover bands doing Journey and Foreigner.

Local residents hang out on Bourbon Street about as often as native New Yorkers go to the top of the Empire State Building. (I lived in the New York area for 27 years. I did it once.)

Bourbon Street is also where most visitors exercise their right to Open Carry. Here, Open Carry is for booze, not bullets. In Las Vegas, you can walk around with a drink in hand only on The Strip. In the historic section (and nowhere else) of Savannah, you can carry and drink an alcoholic beverage, but it must be in an open plastic cup of not more than 16 ounces. The Power & Light District (and nowhere else) in Kansas City permits open containers on the street. Here in New Orleans, it's however much you want, any place you want, and at any time of the day or night, from a Bloody Mary instead of breakfast to when you wake up to your sixth beer in the Ninth Ward at 3:00 in the morning.

At one time, you could drink outdoors like New Orleanians in almost any city. The law of the land was "drunk and disorderly." If you were drunk but orderly, you could imbibe on the streets everywhere from Boston to Bakersfield. But with the subjective interpretation of what constitutes "disorderly," the not-shocking results

were that far more blacks were arrested as disorderly than whites. The laws were challenged, and revised ones focus on the less subjective fact of whether you have a drink in your hand or not. Drinking inside and off the streets became the law of the land . . . except in New Orleans. The to-go cup is as much part of our culture as gumbo or brass band. Cocktail & drinking historian Elizabeth Pearce says, "The city has burned twice, flooded, survived recession, depression. New Orleans has known who she is for a really long time and changed with the times. But I do think if they fuck around with the go cup, the people will revolt."

The one important point to note is that you can open carry your drink in a plastic to-go cup, a plastic container shaped like a hand grenade, a skull, a fish bowl, or a 40-ounce Huge Ass Beer. But, you cannot walk around with a glass bottle. You'll get ticketed for that.

The attraction of getting sloshed while you stumble around our pothole-filled streets began in earnest in 1967. Some unremembered Bourbon Street pub came up with the bright idea of window hawking. Rather than trying to lure you into their club, they started peddling their drinks to passersby through open windows and doorways right onto the street.

Long before open carry and window hawking, the cocktail was said to be invented in New Orleans. Antoine Amedie Peychaud escaped from the French colony of Saint-Domingue (now Haiti) during the slave uprising. He settled in New Orleans and re-established his pharmacy business. Peychaud would mix medicinal concoctions in small French eggcups known as *coquetiers*. He would mix brandy, absinthe, and a dash of his secret bitters. (Peychaud's bitters are still available today.) The resulting drink came to be known as the Sazerac.

When Americans got a taste for his Sazeracs, they fumbled around with the pronunciation of *coquetiers* and would simply say, "Give me one of them cock-tails." Nine tour guides out of ten will tell you the cocktail was invented at Peychaud's home at 437 Royal Street. Now, some killjoy stickler for details pointed out the term cocktail was used before Peychaud was even born, but we willfully ignore that fact.

New Orleans' alcoholic history is layered with signature drinks, some invented in New Orleans, like Hurricanes, and others merely perfected here. The Pimm's Cup is from London but took root here as one of the city's signature drinks. For me, the Pimm's Cup, the Sazerac, and the Ramos Gin Fizz are all sneaky little bastards, where the first few sips seem "refreshing" but if you down two drinks, you will have a hard time finding the exit.

The Pimm's Cup was first "crafted" in 1823 by James Pimm, a farmer's son from Kent who became the owner of an oyster bar in London. He offered the tonic (a gin-based drink containing a secret mixture of herbs and liqueurs) as an aid to digestion. The Napoleon House has taken his creation and re-engineered it to make it one of the city's most noted intoxicants. They jumpstarted Pimm's original recipe by adding lemonade, Sprite, and a cucumber garnish. But you don't have to go to Napoleon House to try this recipe; you can find Pimm's Cups in most any local bar. However, the Napoleon House website cautions: "Be warned, home concoctions of the Pimm's Cup, no matter how accurate, for some reason never taste as good as those at the Napoleon House."

The Ramos Gin Fizz was invented in 1888 by Henry C. Ramos at his bar, the Imperial Cabinet Saloon on Gravier Street. It was originally called a "New Orleans Fizz." Governor Huey Long so loved the drink, he brought a bartender named Sam Guarino from the Roosevelt Hotel to the New Yorker Hotel to teach its staff how to properly make the drink so he could have it whenever he visited New York.

Tujague's created the Grasshopper. The second owner of the historical French Quarter restaurant concocted this cocktail with equal parts crème de menthe, crème de cacao, and straight-up cream for a 1918 competition in New York. It took second place, but as local food historian Poppy Tooker points out, "No one can tell you who won first place that year."

Bourbon Milk Punch is a New Orleans way to start your day that serves as an alternative to the ubiquitous Bloody Mary. It consists of milk, Bourbon, sugar, and vanilla extract. It is served cold and usually has nutmeg sprinkled on top. While you should be able to order one at any decent Creole restaurants or bars in New Orleans, supposedly the best Bourbon Milk Punch is served at the Bourbon House.

A newer New Orleans signature is the Georgia O'Keefe, served at SoBou. This cocktail was created for Bryan Batt, a local actor known for his role in *Mad Men*. The bright pink hue comes from hibiscus.

The Hurricane, the #1 most consumed with irrational fervor cocktail, was created at Pat O'Brien's bar. But I find most of these drinks much too sweet for my taste. Though I did have one at the Victory Bar that didn't submerge the cocktail in simple syrup and grenadine, and instead used fresh passionfruit and lime, which made a quite different and considerably better drink.

O'Brien supposedly invented the Hurricane cocktail in the 1940s. The story of the drink's origin holds that, due to difficulties importing scotch during World War II, liquor salesmen forced bar owners to buy up to fifty cases of their much-more-plentiful rum before they could secure a single case of good whiskey or scotch. The barmen at Pat O'Brien's came up with a recipe for the Hurricane in order to cut into their burgeoning surplus of rum. When they decided to serve it in a glass shaped like a hurricane lamp, the Hurricane was born.

A newer drink that's increasingly popular is the Hand Grenade. It is billed as "New Orleans' Most Powerful Drink." Hand Grenade drinks are only served at Tropical Isle and the Funky Pirate locations on Bourbon Street. Pam Fortner and Earl Bernhardt, owners of the Tropical Isle Bar, created the melon-flavored Hand Grenade as their signature cocktail. They went so far as to register the trademark in 1987 for the name "Hand Grenade," as well as the unique green translucent plastic glass container in which it is served.

While they have legally secured the right to call the drink "Hand Grenade® New Orleans Most Powerful Drink," I think they'd be challenged as the "most powerful." "The Jester" is another sweet melon-flavored drink that masks enough Everclear to prep you for pickling or taxidermy.

Then there's the Cherry Bomb: thirteen cherries soaked in Everclear that you can inhale on your way to hangover hell at the Dungeon Bar. But at this point it seems less about drinking and more about testing your manhood (from a 16-year-old boy's perspective).

Where many come to New Orleans to eat at the restaurants of Emeril Lagasse or listen to Dr. John, the Nite Tripper, on one of the rare nights he plays, we also have our star bartenders. Please refrain from calling them "mixologists" rendering "artisan craft cocktails."

Murf Reeves is this chapter's Lumin of New Orleans. Other noted bartenders include Chris McMillian, a fourth-generation superstar bartender extraordinaire and resident historian. He and his wife, Laura, helped found the Museum of the

American Cocktail, inside the Southern Food and Beverage Museum (1504 Oretha Castle Haley Blvd.).

Chris' long career had placed him behind the bars at the now-gone Library Lounge inside the Ritz-Carlton Hotel, Bar UnCommon, and Kingfish. In 2016, he opened his first bar, where he is the owner as well as signature employee. Revel (133 N. Carrollton Ave.) also serves a beyond-bar-food menu, which includes brioche pretzel bites ($5), a Gulf shrimp, avocado and feta salad ($12), a cheeseburger on house-made buns ($12) and pulled pork on brioche with slaw and pickles ($10) in addition to his classic, complex or simple, or self-created drinks. McMillian is known for telling stories or reciting drink-themed poetry while making drinks. *Imbibe Magazine* chose him as one of the top 25 most influential cocktail personalities of the century.

Another Chris, Chris Hannah, is the bartender at the highly regarded Arnaud's French 75 (813 Bienville St.). French 75 is consistently rated one of the top bars in America on virtually everyone's list who rates top bars in America. While the bar is relatively new, dating to 2003, everything about it is absolute vintage. The bar and bar-back were custom-built in the late 1800s for a Gulf Coast restaurant and purchased from a local antique dealer. Chris Hannah is dedicated to classic and nearly forgotten cocktails from an Old Fashioned to complicated concoctions like a Tom & Jerry or an Aviation.

He seems to have personal passion for the lesser-known Brandy Crusta. "It's just as old as the Sazerac," says Chris, "and in my opinion, has just as much history with the city as well." Created in the 1850s by Joseph Santini at a bar called Jewel of the South in the French Quarter, this was arguably the first cocktail to use citrus, thereby being the father of all sours that would follow.

As gracious and hospitable as Chris Hannah is known to be, Paul Gustings is the perfect counterbalance if you desire your drinks served with Attitude. Paul has been profiled in the *New York Times* and *Garden & Gun*, and *Esquire* called him "crustiest bartender in America."

After moving to New Orleans in 1980, he has worked for various New Orleans landmark restaurants, including Olde N'awlins Cookery, Mr. B's, and Napoleon House, where he spent 20 years. Paul had been toiling away in their kitchens, making terrible money, while watching better-compensated bartenders, and thought, "I can do that."

After Katrina, he tended bar full-time at Tujague's, then took a short stint at the now defunct start-up restaurant, Serendipity, accompanying the brilliant chef, Chris DeBarr. He recently signed on and currently resides with Broussard's Empire Bar (819 Conti St.).

Paul loves his job, but does not view his role as the friendly neighborhood bartender like in *Cheers*. Paul says, "Sometimes I'm not the friendliest person. Just because you walk through the door, doesn't make you my best friend." He's likewise not a proponent of many new-wave bartenders making their own grenadine or orgeat (almond syrup) or bitters. "I don't do that. Why not? I can get it at the store!" And he's little interested in resurrecting century-old cocktails as Chris Hannah and others are. Says Gustings, "If they're extinct, they probably suck."

Martin Sawyer, bartender at the Rib Room and nicknamed "The Professor," has been making drinks for over five decades. He has old photographs of him with Louis Armstrong and serving champagne to Charles de Gaulle back when the French president visited New Orleans in 1969.

He got his first job as a bar-back at the infamous 500 Club, Leon and Louie Prima's burlesque club on Bourbon Street. A friend had recruited him for the job to help the illiterate bartender make out drink orders. Martin was one of the very few young men in his circle who could read.

Gertrude Mayfield, or Miss Gertie as she's known to regulars, was herself a regular at the Mayfair Lounge (1505 Amelia St.) for years before she and her husband bought the place in 1978. When Mr. Mayfield passed away, Miss Gertie jumped in, putting herself behind the bar, mixing drinks and greeting customers. In her days as a customer, the Mayfair was a low-rent neighborhood hangout for weary businessmen trying to avoid going home. As an owner, Miss Gertie began catering to the younger college crowd to drum up more active customers who, unlike the then regulars, didn't nurse a single gin & tonic for an hour. Miss Gertie would hold court, making speeches from behind the bar, knocking back a few Jagermeisters of her own, and dancing with students from Tulane in her signature leather pants. She's such a delightfully oversized personality, one gay patron wants to marry her son just so he can have Gertie as his mother-in-law. There are plenty of Miss Gertie stories to fill a book. A boyfriend once ended a spat by driving through the Mayfair's window and hurling their pet tarantula at her.

The Mayfair ain't craft cocktails. They have only one beer on tap: Budweiser. You have to buzz your way to get in using a well-concealed doorbell. Once inside, you are greeted by beat-up bar chairs, a very faded mural (I think it depicts the Mississippi River), and all manner of colorful beads, plastic gators eating plastic Barbie dolls, and other "weird shit" hanging from the ceiling. But, if you're hankering for a Charles Bukowski/Tom Waits kind of late-afternoon stupor, it may be New Orleans' finest venue.

Floria Woodard was one of the first female bartenders in New Orleans, and one of the first African-Americans to sling drinks as well. She might have tended bar at the Court of Two Sisters from 1967 until her death in 2010. When asked about her start date, Flo said 1967 "sounds about right. It's been a long time."

Flo was completely self-taught, intuitive and adept. Every year she entered the French Quarter Fest's bartending contest, she won. Her Hurricane beat out Pat

O'Brien's for first place one year—and Pat O'Brien invented the drink! Another year, she won with her own concoction, the Golden Coconut, which is amaretto, Malibu rum, orange curacao and milk. Her Sazerac, she says, will cure anything that ails you. Flo called it "The Potion."

After her death, The New Orleans Culinary and Cultural Preservation Society and Crescent City School of Bartending created the Flo Woodard Memorial Bartending Scholarship. It's a nice honorarium, but can never replace her constant greeting of, "What you need, baby?"

More than bartenders, the bars themselves are the real draw, from elegant hotel bars to sports bars, neighborhood joints, *Mad Men*-esque hip spots, to the deepest of dive bars. Here, you have a lot from which to choose. Jed Kolko, the chief economist for the San Francisco-based Trulia, examined data from the top 100 U.S. metro areas to determine the concentration of drinking and eating out across the country. New Orleans far outdistanced every other American city in bars per capita. I am at a loss to tell you the exact number. The study said we had a bar per capita ratio of 8.6. The way I am (clearly incorrectly) interpreting their data indicates we have over 39,000 bars. As much as we love to drink, and as much as our visitors come to drink, that number feels about 38,000 too many.

Even if there's only 1,000 bars in the city, obviously I can't annotate even a small fraction. Profiled below are but a surface scratch.

French Quarter

Bar Tonique 820 N. Rampart St.

Bar Tonique opened in 2008 as a drinking spot that rides the wave between a tony cocktail lounge and a neighborhood bar. It's a haunt for service industry workers, who get a hefty discount there, to unwind after a long shift of forced hospitality. Tasting Table, a noted eating and drinking website, named Bar Tonique one of the nation's top cocktail bars. Locally, NOLA.com and *The Times-Picayune.* have chosen it as one of New Orleans' five best cocktail bars.

The Black Penny 700 N. Rampart St.

Black Penny is a relative newbie, opened in February 13, 2015, just in time for Mardi Gras. They specialize in craft beers, over 75 brands, all served in cans. The beers have a regional bent, with Louisiana brands mixed with near-local brews like Southern Prohibition out of Hattiesburg, Mississippi. And Devil's Harvest Pale Ale. The bar works hard to maintain their shabby-chic ambience with exposed walls, vintage paintings, and old photographs.

The Bourbon Pub 801 Bourbon St.

The Bourbon Pub has two floors. Downstairs is a saloon; upstairs is a dance club with a balcony overlooking Bourbon Street. The club blasts what New Orleans would consider "alternative" music: jazz, blues, and bounce are replaced by disco and techno music. It is a wildly popular hangout with the "alternative" gay community. While straights are welcomed, they'll be greatly outnumbered. One presumed-to-be-straight woman is a frequent and more than welcomed guest: a ghost, called "Mam" by the bar's staff. The other ghost, Bastinado, is decidedly less sweet. He gets his name from an in-the-know form of S&M where the soles of the feet are struck with a wooden pole as a form of sexual arousal.

The Carousel Bar 214 Royal St.

Located inside the Hotel Monteleone, the Carousel Bar may be the most noted bar in New Orleans. The bar itself is a highly decorated and brightly lit carousel of sorts that slowly turns on its axis as the rest of the room and outer tables remain steadfast. Installed in 1949, the 25-seat circular bar turns on 2,000 large steel rollers, powered by a $\frac{1}{4}$-horsepower motor. The bar rotates at a rate of one revolution every 15 minutes. This way, if you're sitting at the bar and someone is hassling you from one of the tables, you only have to put up with them every 15 minutes.

Cat's Meow 701 Bourbon St.

Cat's Meow is what most visitors envision as a Bourbon Street bar. It will be teeming with bubbly bachelorette parties, has neon feline décor, offers karaoke as entertainment, and has the obligatory upstairs balcony from which to throw beads.

Empire Bar 819 Conti St.

The Empire Bar is for the exact opposite experience of a Bourbon Street joint. Here you sip a well-made cocktail by Paul Gustings (profiled earlier) from behind a marble bar while you sit beside a fountain in a French Quarter courtyard. In addition to all our traditional Sazeracs and Pimm's Cups, Empire also serves more exotic drinks like Nuremberg Punch and the Egyptian Campaign, made with Smith & Cross Jamaican rum and Batavia Arrack. Their website claims they cater to "Quarter residents and well-dressed refugees from Bourbon Street."

Latitude 29 321 N. Peters St.

Latitude 29 could have just as easily been listed under restaurants as bars. I choose to place it here because owner Jeff "Beachbum" Berry is a cocktail historian who's researched the original tiki drinks like the Zombie, Mai Tai, and the Suffering Bastard. He's also written six books on the topic. The bar/restaurant is a throwback to the 1950s and early '60s, when most major cities had a kitschy tiki- themed watering hole.

Pat O'Brien's 718 St. Peter St.

This may be the most noted bar in New Orleans. Opened in 1933, it's a relative newcomer. During Prohibition, patrons of an earlier bar, known as Mr. O'Brien's Club Tipperary, used the password "storm's brewin'" to gain entrance to the establishment. Not satisfied being known for just one thing, Pat O'Brien's is the famous inventor of the Hurricane cocktail, has the original flaming fountain (located in the courtyard), and boasts a piano bar, featuring twin "dueling" pianos where the entertainers take song requests. It is, unfortunately, the bar where you're most likely to hear people nearby say in their outside voices, "You from Ohio? Hey, I'm from Ohio! Go Bucks!"

Lafittes Blacksmith Bar 941 Bourbon St.

This may be the most noted bar in New Orleans. We have a lot of noted bars. It is casually and incorrectly said to be the oldest bar in America. The White Horse Tavern in Rhode Island, founded in 1673, is the oldest bar in the United States. Our back-up claim, that it is the bar set inside the oldest building to now house a bar (it used to be an actual blacksmith), may be every bit as false. And the tale of loyal patrons forming a bucket brigade from the Mississippi River to save the favorite pub from the great New Orleans fire is 100 percent absolutely not true. But it is old. There are still no electrical lights inside the bar, except for the ones on the ATM machine and the gaming devices. It is also said to be haunted by both cold spots and Jean Lafitte's flaming eyes, which peer at you from the center fireplace.

Cafe Lafitte in Exile Bar 901 Bourbon St.

This may be the most noted companion to the most noted bar in America. It is the oldest gay bar in the country. It was created when the owner of Lafitte Blacksmith Shop went out of his way to make his increasingly gay clientele uncomfortable and

Lafittes Blacksmith Bar

clearly not welcomed. So, regular patron Tom Caplinger upped and opened a gay-friendly bar a half-block away.

During their years in New Orleans, Tennessee Williams and Truman Capote used to frequent Lafitte in Exile. Tennessee's ghost is said to turn up quite often sitting at the end of the bar sipping a cocktail. Truman's ghost haunts the small stairwell leading to the second floor and very often has been captured on video and film. Some say he even strikes up little stair-side chats.

The Old Absinthe House 240 Bourbon St.

Some feel the Old Absinthe House should be the most noted bar in New Orleans. Built in 1807, this location was originally a local importing firm, then converted to a neighborhood grocery that imported fine foods, tobaccos, and wines from all over the world. As a bar, it became nationally famous when owned by Owen Brennan.

The gregarious patriarch of the many Brennan-owned restaurant empires, Owen had an infectious mix of hospitality and showmanship that made the bar a regular stop for visiting celebrities like Frank Sinatra, Clark Gable, and Liza Minelli. Earlier, it had been Teddy Roosevelt's must-go place in New Orleans, and had been patronized by Oscar Wilde, P.T. Barnum, Mark Twain, and opera stars Jenny Lind and Enrico Caruso.

Old Absinthe's ceiling is cluttered with old sports helmets and memorabilia, the walls are covered in pinned-up business cards, and, while they're no longer in use, they have the old spigot and paraphernalia used to make absinthe drinks—the kind no longer legal where you'd see green fairies.

One Eyed Jacks 615 Toulouse St.

The bar and music venue has a rich history, from its days as the Toulouse Theatre (when James Booker played piano in the cast of a musical) to its more recent incarnation as the burlesque revival hub, the Shim Sham Club, to today's role as the Quarter's primary venue for local and touring rock, punk and other alternative acts. The music offerings range the gambit from rock, including '80s large-haired glam rock, metal, national performers like The White Stripes, burlesque shows, and more. It is the ideal setting for The Bingo Show, which takes the stage every so often. The club's locally famous Fast Times '80s Dance Party happens every Thursday night and features live go-go dancers.

Voodoo Lounge 718 N. Rampart St.

Owner Cindi Richardson also runs French Quarter Phantoms, a ghost tour company. Most of their twice-nightly launches into our haunted streets start from the bar's side door. The lounge hosts a variety of monthly events from a show called "Chain Male," hosted by drag queen Vinsantos DeFonte, to Jennifer Jane's party, entitled "Glitter Tits." They also have periodic tarot card readings.

To the trained eye (which I definitely don't have), the bottles lined up behind the bar belie the dive atmosphere the Voodoo Lounge seeks to project. You'll spot Orphan Barrel Barterhouse, a 20-year-old Kentucky bourbon whiskey (retail: $72.99), and Orphan Barrel Rhetoric, a 21-year-old bourbon (retail: $129). As bartender Andy Overslaugh says, "Even lowlifes want to drink with some amount of sophistication from time to time."

Warehouse District and the CBD

The Sazerac Bar 123 Baronne St.

The Sazerac Bar inside the Roosevelt Hotel is where you want to meet and impress business clients, interviewees, or potential in-laws. It's beyond classy. It reminds me of the King Cole Bar inside the St. Regis on 57th Street in Manhattan. Replace the Maxfield Parrish mural in New York with one by Paul Ninas, keep the walnut bar, etched mirrors, elegant seating, and white-jacketed bartenders, and they both speak of century-old luxury. As the Sazerac's the polar opposite of New Orleans' many dive bars, maybe we should call it an ascent bar instead.

Victory 339 Baronne St.

Victory is another ascent bar, a classy after-work spot with rich red walls, appropriately low lighting, and the obligatory large flat-screen TV—only Victory shows old black and white movies rather than sporting events. Right next door, you can take an elevator to the second floor, which houses Drink Lab, where master bartenders teach the fundamentals of making the perfect cocktail.

Daniel Victory is the much-awarded proprietor of both the bar and the bartending school. He learned his trade at the upscale Roosevelt Hotel. After absorbing the "science of cocktail making," as he puts it, Victory had the blessing of working for Chris McMillian at the Ritz Carlton, where he got a first-class re-education. "If bartending was a science, then every martini would be exactly the same—at least if everyone was using the same brand," Victory says. "Exact measurements of all the ingredients would yield exactly the same drink. It's simple science—a system of repeatable experiments that yield the same results." To Victory, bartending has instead become an art form.

His art has earned him the Bombay Sapphire Gin & GQ Magazine's Most Imaginative Bartender competition in 2008 and 2009, then named Bartender of the Year by *New Orleans Magazine*. He both serves and teaches the New Orleans cocktail classics, like the Sazerac, Ramos Gin Fizz, and the Hurricane. But he also concocts wildly imaginative drinks like the city's only amuse bouche cocktail, which combines bourbon, blackberry, citrus, and egg white shaken into a frothy concoction; the "Beetin' the Lime," which combines beet juice and brown sugar to complement dark rum and lime; and the "Bare Necessities," which is anything but basic: Bärenjäger, basil, blackberries, ginger ale, and who all knows what else.

Drink Lab, a cocktail-making class, is so obviously fitting for a place like New Orleans, it's almost shocking that it seems to be the only one in business, whereas there are slews of cooking classes and culinary tours. Victory teamed up with partner and former news anchor Camille Whitworth. The pair gutted a former law office to create a space that feels like a cross between a speakeasy and a brothel. The setting is modeled after Lulu White's Mahogany Bar from back-in-the-glory days of Storyville.

"I wanted to do kind of the same thing, for the tourists and locals to come in and learn how to make cocktails, specializing in the craft cocktails of New Orleans classics," Victory says. "We're supposed to be the birthplace of the cocktail, so cocktail classes definitely have a place here." His "playground for cocktail enthusiasts" provides interactive drink classes Wednesdays through Saturdays.

Bywater and The Marigny

If you have an edgier or more adventurous sensibility and want to skip the popular French Quarter bars, head out to St. Claude Avenue in the Marigny and Bywater neighborhoods. Lining a 15-block stretch are some of the dingiest (in a good way) and fringiest watering holes in the city.

AllWays Lounge 2240 St. Claude Ave

Directly across the street from The Hi-Ho Lounge, you never know what you'll experience until you open the door. The club's stage hosts a variety of acts, from jazz and alternative to swing (they host swing dance lessons on Sundays), poetry readings like the twice-monthly Esoterotica (original erotic readings by local writers), and burlesque performances, including Bella Blue's Dirty Dime Peep Show, Drag Bingo with Vinsantos, and, as I experienced on my more recent visit with my cousin Nancy, amateur striptease night. (We stayed for about 30 seconds.)

The Hi-Ho Lounge 2239 St. Claude Ave.

The Hi-Ho Lounge has live music ranging from hip-hop and funk to indie rock. Their best night is Saturday, when DJ Soul Sister hosts her Hustle Dance Party from 11:00 p.m. to 3:00 a.m. with a lively mix of R & B classics, Motown, and techno-pop.

Igor's Checkpoint Charlie's 501 Esplanade Ave.

Away from St. Claude, standing on a corner of Esplanade Avenue, at the mouth of Frenchmen Street, is Igor's Checkpoint Charlie's. Checkpoint Charlie's is a bar, a game room, a live music venue, and a laundromat, all rolled into one. While you're waiting for your socks and sweaters to dry, there's much more to do here than read year-old magazines. The small stage delivers—depending on the night—a mix of rock, metal, and punk, and some performers who aren't welcome anywhere else. Regular bands include Bible Belt Sinners, Bad Moon Lander, and the Olivia de Havilland Mosquitoes. Tuesday evenings offer a popular weekly open-mic blues jam.

Kajun's Pub 2256 St. Claude Ave.

Kajun's Pub has karaoke every night starting at 9:00 p.m. They have over 50,000 catalogued songs, including some Pee Wee Herman hits. The bar serves locally sourced food at the on-the-premises Restaurant Borracho and, during football season, doles out free Jell-O shots every time the Saints score a touchdown. Even though the Saints have been hard-pressed to win games in recent years, as long as Drew Brees is around, at least you can still down a lot of Jell-O shots at Kajun's.

Saturn Bar 3067 St. Claude Ave.

Saturn Bar was voted best dive bar in America five times (yes, there is such an award). From the outside, the graffiti-covered planks covering the windows make it look like a place best avoided. Open the door and it's like when Dorothy opens her front door after crashing into Munchkin Land. You'll be greeted by bizarre paintings all over (including some on the ceiling), small-game taxidermy, ratty booths, and six jukeboxes (none of them work). Once a month, the Saturn hosts Mod Nite, where regulars drag out their go-go boots from the back of the closet to dance the night (and early morning) away to funky hits from the 1960s and '70s.

Siberia 2227 St. Claude Ave.

Siberia features punk, metal, bounce, and Slavic bands, plus burlesque and some of the worst comics you'll ever hear. At the back of the bar, past the taxidermied deer and turkeys, is a pop-up restaurant, Kukhnya, which serves Slavic soul food: pierogies, blini, and kielbasa. The bar edged out legendary Tipitina's as the people's choice award for number one live music club.

Sweet Lorraine's 1931 St. Claude Ave.

A revered bar and music club, known as one of our better jazz bars as opposed to the alt music and burlesque performed on the rest of St. Claude. Its nickname is the "club with a silver lining." On weekends, you're likely to hear top drawer performers like Michael Ward, Nicholas Payton, or Clarence Johnson, III.

Garden District and Uptown

I list Verret's Bar and Lounge here without any address because my basic message is "Don't go there!" It is a great neighborhood bar with a folksy history. The bar once served as the headquarters for the Fabulous Ladies Social Aid and Pleasure Club, along with the Uptown Swingers SAPC. They still fill the air with old R&B and blues. It's one of the few current bars that's preserved the old "set up" tradition. The tradition goes back to when a staple of black-owned bars catered to customers who would come in and bulk-purchase pints of hard liquor and a mixer with a bucket of ice to set up for the entire evening.

In 2013, Powell Miller took over the old Turning Point, a black-owned bar known for its motto, "Where the mature crowd comes." He and manager Marc House did a major makeover during which they uncovered an old sign reading "Verret's Lounge." They decided to give the bar its old name back, and then attempted to pull off a difficult balancing act of running a bar that draws heavily from their Central City African-American neighbors while appealing to a new mix of customers. The problem is too many new customers (like you) start to tip the balance and destroy the very reason to go.

Cure 4905 Freret St.

Cure is close to the opposite of Tracey's. Cure is widely credited for both sparking NOLA's cocktail bar craze and revitalizing a formerly tired neighborhood. Oddly, Cure is known for having the best large, crystal-clear ice cubes as much as for their drinks.

Half Moon 1125 St. Mary St.

Half Moon is a perfect corner joint with a beat-up neon sign, well worn pool tables, sofas with barely any springs left unsprung, passable food, and cheap drinks. I don't know what Half Moon was before it was a bar, but the space is odd, maybe even a little disconcerting as you enter the front door and then have to walk across a good 20 to 30 feet of bare cement to get to the bar.

Pal's Lounge 949 N. Rendon St.

Pal's is a classic neighborhood joint in a classy blue-collar neighborhood, just two blocks from where you can sit by the water or kayak on Bayou St. John. The bar has rotating pop-up food services, with Cajun-style Hot Fried Chicken on Monday, Flights of Fancy tacos on Tuesday, Crackburger on Wednesday and Thursday, Stickball Meatball on Friday, and Everything's Better with Beer on Saturdays. The bar

LUMINS OF NEW ORLEANS:
Murf Reeves

Like so many of New Orleans' most passionate, Murf Reeves is a Come Here and not a From Here. Back in his hometown of Boston, Murf was a bouncer in a club where the clientele was a volatile mix of blacks and skinheads. He notes, "They all liked playing pool and they all liked Toots and the Maytals—they just didn't like each other."

He moved to New Orleans and got a job at Maximo's and at Bistro Maison de Ville. He also worked in the kitchen at Stella, where he quickly realized he didn't want to be in fine dining because he didn't love being yelled at. So he took a job at Preservation Hall sweeping floors, and got yelled at for sweeping floors the wrong way. When he returned to restaurants, Murf knew he didn't want to cook anymore. He started waiting tables, first at Bourbon House, where they had sixty-five bourbons. Having been unaware that so many different types of bourbon existed, he vowed to try every single one, and did. He started reading about classic drinks. At first, "I was like, cocktails—vodka cranberry, sour mix—I didn't like any of it," Reeves says. "The Cape Codder, the Cuba Libre . . . Blech. Now I love making cocktails. I love coming up with names, trying to take weird ingredients and make them work together."

After Hurricane Katrina, he found himself back in his hometown of Boston, where he learned how to make drinks through intensive research. He discovered the sophistication of the classics: Manhattans, Old-Fashioneds, and the original Martini.

Back in New Orleans, Murf created his first cocktail list while managing at Elizabeth's. There, he met Ann Tuennerman, Founder and Executive Director of Tales of the Cocktail. She looked at his cocktail menu and saw his Ghetto Fabulous Mimosa. She asked: "Why is it ghetto fabulous?" Murf told her that's because it comes in a plastic cup.

Then Sylvain came and asked him to run their bar program. He was both the general manager and the bar manager. It was intense. Then, with Sainte Marie, it was the same thing. He's more recently been the bar manager at Square Root. Like most in the service industry, Murf gets around.

Now he happily tends bar at the Erin Rose, a cluttered dive bar at 811 Conti, two doors from the riff-raff on Bourbon Street. "I don't care if I'm cracking open a Bud Light or making a Manhattan. I like making people happy. They call us professional socializers; that's what we do."

Beyond creating and serving drinks, he's also taught the making of craft cocktails to local bartenders. He's hosted visiting distillers and worked with local distributors to organize tastings open to anyone who works behind a New Orleans bar counter.

As is the case with other Lumins of New Orleans—Bunny Mathews, Ryan S. Ballard, Chris Trew—as well as many of us here, Murf Reeves is no one thing. In addition to bartending, he is a drummer and may be best known as a DJ. His radio show on WWOZ 90.7 airs Mondays at 11:00 a.m.

Murf has yoked his various lives together by creating pairings of alcoholic spirits and spirited local songs. As soon as I heard his concept, it made total sense. Tony Bennett goes great with a Singapore Sling. Tom Waits pairs well with straight shots of *anything* over 110 proof.

was also competing for "Best Bathroom." Their facilities have naked pictures of Burt Reynolds in the women's room and vintage porn in the men's.

The Saint Bar & Lounge 961 St. Mary St.

When your night of partying has crossed over into ruminating on where your life went wrong or how much you miss your last dog, the Saint is your place, a fitting end-of-night watering hole. They're open late (5:00 a.m. late). They don't really hit their stride until about 2:00 in the AM. The drinks are cheap and you can dance all night to some exceptional DJs.

Snake and Jake's 7612 Oak St.

One online reviewer contends that it is a misnomer to call Snake and Jake's a "dive bar." More properly, it "is a straight-up shit hole." The dark interior is illuminated by red Christmas lights such that you can barely see your hands, your date, nor (thankfully) the stained walls and low ceiling. The bar itself used to be a trailer. I have never used the men's room there. I've heard that is something you should never ever do. Bukowski-like stories abound. One specialty cocktail is called The Possum Drop, named for the time a possum fell through the waterlogged ceiling into a customer's drink. That customer got off easy; another one was shot inside Snake and Jake's and now gets free drinks at the bar for the rest of his life.

Tracey's 2604 Magazine St.

Instead of Verret's, you might consider Tracey's, which welcomes you to jam into their already-filled bar. For many locals, this is their favorite place in New Orleans to watch sports on large-screen HD TVs. Tracey's was the original Irish Channel bar, established in 1949, made popular by their frozen glasses for cold beer and variety of po'boys. They also have an oyster shucker on the premises.

Where to Risk a DWI

If visiting, you'll need to rent a car to enjoy a local institution: the Drive-Thru Daiquiris stand. The state may have declared the Sazerac the official state drink and tourists may stumble around the Quarter holding on to Hurricanes and Hand Grenades, but frozen daiquiris are local Louisiana's unofficial drink of choice. They are a staple at JazzFest, in Mardi Gras crowds, backyard barbecues, movie theaters, and the aquarium and the Audubon Zoo sell daiquiris in animal-themed souvenir cups.

Daiquiris are of Cuban origin, a blended frozen drink that starts with the basics of rum, lime juice, and sweetener, which can then be launched into a variety of technicolor fruity directions. The brightly colored (some might say 'shocking') drinks have names like Shockwave, Jagerburn, Kitchen Sink, the 190 Orange Anti-freeze, and one simply called Abuse. They are served in cups sized from small to family size, to "The Monster," a gallon-sized portion. Prices run in the $5 to $6 range ($22 for the gallon-sized). For a slight increase, you can order extra shots.

David Briggs introduced the frozen drink to America when he opened the first New Orleans Original Daiquiris stand in 1983. A chain in Texas, Eskimo Hut, tries to claim they were first, just like Texas makes the bogus assertion that the Cowboys are "America's Team." However, the Texas Alcoholic Beverage Commission mandates that "to-go" drinks cannot contain distilled spirits. So Eskimo Hut was selling fruity wine coolers at best—hardly daiquiris.

If you wonder how selling alcoholic drinks at drive-thru windows is the least bit legal, the Open Container Law that allows New Orleanians to walk city streets with drink in hand has been adapted. As long as the drink is contained in a sealed cup, the drive-thru is in accordance with the law. Therefore, the straw is presented by itself, still wrapped and laid across the lid, so technically the cup with the drink remains sealed. Some daiquiri shops even stick a piece of tape over the straw hole on the lid. Clearly, with the tiny piece of tape and the sealed straw barriers, there is just no way a driver can possibly imbibe before getting home.

For whatever reason, DBC (1001 Veterans Memorial Blvd, Metairie) has been chosen as the one that news crews and TV shows, like Anthony Bourdain's *No Reservations*, visit and film. Perhaps it's their menu, which offers a variety of greasy comfort foods; burgers, nachos, tamales, a ribeye steak on Wednesdays, and crawfish in season on Sundays. DBC, which stands for Daiquiri Bay Cafe, has 40 brands of beer, but you go for the daiquiris. If you can't decide among the flavors, DBC offers "The Kitchen Sink," which is a scary concoction of all flavors mixed together.

CHAPTER 4

Creeping Around

The city that takes Halloween seriously and Death playfully

Everyone who's chosen this place to live knows how seductive it is; the city has almost a vortex feeling about it—it just sucks you in. There's definitely something cosmic going on here. **—Richard Ford**

While food and music are the top reasons New Orleans gets 9 to 10 million visitors a year, our dark muses of voodoo, vampires, ghosts, and aboveground cemeteries are right behind them in our list of attractions.

Gina Lanier, dubbed the Ghost Hunter's Ghost Hunter, is a well-established and nationally recognized paranormal investigator. When asked where the most haunted city in America is, she says: "New Orleans, Louisiana, by far. I have traveled the United States and it seems that Southern Ghosts are more apt to come out and show themselves more readily. Southern Haunted Hospitality, I guess."

Maria Shaw Lawson moved to New Orleans from Detroit because she and her husband, Joe, a paranormal investigator, were drawn in by the psychic energy of the place. She's now an internationally renowned psychic, founder of the annual Psychic Fair, and has ongoing gigs as the psychic scribe for *Soap Opera Digest* and the *National Enquirer*. In other words, hers is the only piece in the *Enquirer* that's not completely fabricated. Maria has said, "There's a spirit to this city. This city has a soul. If you can sense it, you don't want to go anywhere else."

But, more than psychic endorsements, just think about the tourists who come to New Orleans. In what other city (anywhere) can they stay at a four-star hotel that's haunted (Hotel Monteleone) or dine at a haunted four-star restaurant (Muriel's)? In what other city do tourists line up ten deep to pay $20 to traipse through cemeteries or cluster in groups for ghost tours as though they're waiting to see the Mona Lisa or climb to the top of the Statue of Liberty?

I offer the following opinion based on my personal experience: If you don't believe in ghosts, live here a year and you will. I'm about as "normal" as they come. I grew up in Ohio, where Gosh Darn and Oh Nuts were curse words. I was captain of the football team. In junior high, I would rush home from school, not to watch *Dark Shadows* like everyone else, but to turn on *The Rifleman* with Chuck Connors. I am not prone to believe in events that seem to be best classified as ghosts. What I have experienced here in New Orleans could logically be explained as a series of very isolated and repeated tectonic plate shifts. But the presence of ghosts is actually more plausible.

Why is New Orleans such a hotbed for hauntings and havoc?

Some feel it is our long history of death and disaster, including two fires that nearly destroyed the city (1788 and 1794), three outbreaks of yellow fever (1853, 1878, and 1905), and countless hurricanes and floods. Seasoned with an ample dose of voodoo and hoodoo, and simmered over our many aboveground cemeteries, and you have a recipe for a tasty woo-woo gumbo.

If you have even the slightest intuitive sense, you'll feel the seductive pull of psychic energy here. New Orleans has a vortex feeling that sucks in a certain type of person, the same way Hilton Head draws in men who like to wear offensively loud golf pants.

Voodoo

The city is unquestionably the Voodoo Capital of America. The first thing you should know about voodoo is that it is probably not what you think it is. You've most likely fallen under the spell of the 1930s Hollywood version. Victor Halperin's cheaply made *White Zombie* (1932), followed by the even worse sequel *Revolt of the Zombies* (1936) created an impression of voodoo that's about as accurate as director Oliver Stone's historical docudramas or Michael Moore's docu-completely-mental-ries. (Notice I didn't bash Fox Noise . . . this time.)

Voodoo was recognized as a legitimate faith by the Catholic church in Rome in 1960. Pope John Paul II, in a speech he gave in 1983, apologized for how Catholics had treated practitioners of voodoo all these hundreds of years. Voodoo is at its heart an ancestor-based faith where you call upon your deceased relatives or other spirits to help you in this life. It has some similarities to Catholicism; each faith has one god (the voodoo god is Bon Dieu); just swap out your intermediary saints for loa. Voodoo also has strong parallels to Shinto, for you scholars of Japanese religion.

Now, while the Vatican has accepted the legitimacy of the voodoo faith, the Archdiocese of New Orleans is not yet on board. The plaque affixed to Marie Laveau's tomb states that she practiced "the cult" of voodoo, not the religion. When writing *Fear Dat*, I contacted the Archdiocese to request they connect me to a gravedigger. In their response, they wrote that they would never get involved with a book that also presents voodoo. They then offered the suggestion that I contact the Presbyterian cemeteries, as though they're godless enough to work with me.

Voodoo was first brought here from Africa. Slaves in Louisiana began arriving in 1719. The majority of enslaved Africans came directly from what is now Benin, West Africa, bringing with them their language and religious beliefs rooted in spirit and ancestor worship. In Benin's Fon language, Vodun means "spirit," an invisible, mysterious force that can intervene in human affairs.

Countless tourists will fly home from New Orleans with a packet of Love Potion Number 9 or a voodoo doll keychain in their luggage. But in New Orleans, voodoo is more than cute souvenirs. In New Orleans, Voodoo is the Real Thing.

One reason voodoo developed here and much less so in the rest of America is largely because the French, then Spanish, then French again owned Louisiana. They were far more tolerant of the practices and faith of the slave population than all those Brits who came to America for their own religious freedom, but suppressed all others.

Another reason was sheer numbers. According to a census of 1731–1732, the ratio of enslaved African to European settlers in New Orleans was over two to one. The white minority would have been hard-pressed to suppress the voodoo faith.

New Orleans-style voodoo evolved like New Orleans-style Creole cuisine as a blend of different cultures. One of the main different cultures was Catholicism. Some feel the people who practiced voodoo started using Catholic saints, holy water, and the Lord's Prayer in their ceremonies as a mask to hide voodoo in plain sight. Others feel it was a conscious decision by the enslaved to integrate some Catholicism into voodoo because the white man's magic seemed to have more power; the white man certainly had the much better deal, as slave owner rather than slave. For many, the blending of voodoo with Catholicism was simply a matter of natural evolution. Over many years away from their homeland, slaves slowly lost the thread of their native beliefs, and the predominant Catholicism of New Orleans bled into their language and practices.

Marie Laveau herself was a lifetime Catholic. Jerry Gandolfo, owner of The Historic Voodoo Museum, says that "voodoo is the black sister of the Catholic church." Brandi Kelley, owner of Voodoo Authentica, describes her own integrated Catholic-voodoo lifestyle: "On Sundays, I light candles and make offerings to Catholic Saints. On other days, I light candles and make offerings to voodoo Loas."

Voodoo here grew to be quite a bit different from Haitian Vodou. The evolution of a local style created many new and first-time practices we now associate as the basic tenets of voodoo, including Gris-Gris, voodoo dolls, and, most importantly, Voodoo Queens. In Africa, voodoo is male-dominated. The opposite grew to be true in New Orleans. The slaves gave credit to a female spirit, Aida Wedo, for allowing them to survive the ocean crossing. Women achieved central importance in New Orleans-style voodoo.

Marie Laveau is far and away the most famous Voodoo Queen, but she was not the first. Sanite Dede was an earlier practitioner of voodoo in the city. She was a young woman from Santo Domingo who would hold rituals in her courtyard on Dumaine and Chartres Streets, just blocks away from the St. Louis Cathedral. *The Times-Picayune.* printed sensationalized articles about these rituals, telling of "wild and uncontrolled orgies" and "serpent worship."

Annoyed by the drumbeats playing during their Masses and outraged by supposed orgies, the church pushed through an ordinance in 1817 that Catholicism was the only recognized faith in New Orleans, and it became illegal to practice others. Shortly thereafter, the police arrested 400 women for allegedly dancing naked in Queen Sanite's courtyard. The unsubstantiated charges were later dropped for lack of evidence. Some Catholics felt voodoo spells had either erased the evidence or at least befuddled the minds of prosecutors and judges. But the message was clear: Voodoo was not welcomed in New Orleans. Spanish Governor Galvez went so far as to place an embargo on importing any slaves from the Caribbean because he worried they were more likely to bring their scary (misunderstood) voodoo practices into his city.

Plus, whites worried about too many slaves having the power to stage a revolt, as had occurred in Saint-Domingue. There, 100,000 natives drove out Napoleon's army, abolished slavery, and established the new country of Haiti. To avoid further harassment in New Orleans, voodoo practitioners moved outside the city limits to swampland on Bayou St. John, near what is now City Park.

The next head of New Orleans voodoo after Sanite Dede was John Montenet, a heavily tattooed voodoo doctor better known as Dr. John. He was a well-respected freeman of color who alternatively said he'd been a prince in Senegal or an African priest. Dr. John had a number of beautiful wives and mistresses, with whom he had over 50 children. Beyond spreading the gospel of his Dr. Johnson, he was famous for predicting the future, casting spells, making gris-gris, and reading minds.

Dr. John was the first in New Orleans to use voodoo for personal profit. He'd charge fees to whip together potions and gris-gris. He reportedly confessed to friends that his magic was faked. "He had been known to laugh," writes Robert Tallant in *Voodoo in New Orleans*, "when he told of selling a gullible white woman a small jar of starch and water for five dollars." Dr John was later the mentor, instructor, and, some even say, the power behind Marie Laveau herself. She eventually decided to break away from Dr. John and set up what could be considered her own practice.

Marie Laveau became for voodoo what Louis Armstrong is for jazz. By that, I mean there are several who claim to have invented jazz. "Jelly Roll" Morton said, "It is known, beyond contradiction, that New Orleans is the cradle of jazz, and I myself happen to be the inventor." Most music scholars attribute the invention to Buddy Bolden. But it was Louis Armstrong who made jazz internationally famous. Marie Laveau may have followed Sanite Dede and Dr. John, but it was she who made voodoo notorious and everlasting. After Elvis, hers is the second-most visited grave in America.

Born in New Orleans, maybe in 1794, Marie was the illegitimate daughter of a rich Creole plantation owner, Charles Laveau, and his Haitian slave mistress. She married Jacques Paris who, like her, was a free person of color, but she was soon abandoned or maybe widowed. (Dates and facts about people who were not emperors nor decorated generals are not always well-documented.) About 1825, she entered a second, common-law marriage to Christophe de Glapion, another free person of color, with whom she would have fifteen children. Yes, fifteen. I'm surprised she had any time left for readings and conjuring, let alone hairdressing.

Marie was a hairdresser for the affluent ladies of New Orleans and used her position doing do's to gather gossip. Some of her clients would talk to her during hair appointments about anything and everything. They would divulge their most personal secrets, just like today where you'll reveal your Facebook friends the most intimate details of your life that you'd never tell anyone else. Marie Laveau gathered additional information using cooks, maids, and domestics as a network of household informants that could rival any FBI sting operation.

Thereby, her "cold readings," where she appeared to "just know" all the little secrets like, "So, your son got in trouble at school last week," were far from her psychic or intuitive gifts alone. Her informants had fed her information about the family before she'd ever met them. To visit Marie for a reading (at 1022 St. Ann St.) became fashionable throughout New Orleans, even among the city's most well-heeled residents. Politicians would pay her as much as $1,000 for her help in winning elections. Uptowners paid $10 (a lot back then) for a simple love potion. Rather than straight-up cash payments, judges would often make rulings in ways she desired in order to keep her from revealing the things she "just knew" about them.

Above and beyond being a great networker, Marie Laveau had P. T. Barnum-level showmanship. She knew how to pull in the white man's dollars to see her staged rituals. "Simulated orgies" gets 'em every time. Men and women danced in abandonment after drinking rum and seeming to become possessed by various loas. Seated on her throne, Marie directed the action. She kept a large snake called Le Grand Zombi that she would dance with in veneration of Damballah. She would shake a gourd rattle to summon the snake deity, repeating over and over, "Damballah, ye-ye-ye!"

Once a year, Marie presided over the ritual of St. John's Eve. It begins at dusk on June 23 and ends at dawn on the next day. St. John's is still the most sacred of Holy Days in the voodoo faith. Hundreds attended her ritual, including white reporters and curious white onlookers, each of whom was charged a sizable fee. Drum beating, bonfires, animal sacrifice, and nude women dancing seductively were all included in the marathon ritual.

St John's Eve at the Magnolia Bridge

Except for the nude dancing and the animal sacrifice and the bonfires (basically just the drum beating remains), this St.John's Eve ritual still takes place today. You can join Sallie Ann Glassman and La Source Ancient Ounfo to celebrate St. John's Eve with the annual head-washing ceremony, a form of voodoo baptism. To do so, go to the Magnolia pedestrian bridge crossing Bayou St. John, near Cabrini High. You are asked to wear all white and bring a white scarf or rag for your head. Though, as one spiritualist pointed out to me, "It looks a little suspect when it's all white people dressed in all white that come to participate in a ritual based on an Afro-Caribbean faith."

During the 1930s, true voodoo went underground again. Tourism had become the foundation of New Orleans economy. City leaders didn't want to frighten off tourists with the completely sensationalized image of voodoo as depicted in Hollywood movies like 1932's *White Zombie* and *I Walked with a Zombie*, or in bestselling books like *Magic Island* by W. B. Seabrook. The Roman Catholic Church continued their decades-old campaign to present Catholicism as the legitimate religion and voodoo as pagan heresy.

It was during this time Fred Staten was born in New Orleans. Frank reinvented himself as "Prince Keeyama," a voodoo man. Keeyama would tell outlandish tales. He claimed to be a native of Port-au-Prince, Haiti. He claimed his brother was the Haitian Prime Minister, and that they were both raised by Papa Doc Duvalier. Keeyama told these stories without the slightest hint of a Haitian accent, mon. He bragged of his expertise with snakes, yet couldn't answer the most basic questions about the different types of snakes. He took credit for training two lions at the zoo, although the zoo had no such knowledge of his activities.

Rather than a genuine voodoo man, most considered him a genuine voodoo nightclub act. His performances consisted of eating fire, handling snakes, and sticking needles through his throat. But it was the finale that made Prince Keeyama a local legend. He would pretend to place a chicken in a trance, then bite off its head and drink the blood. He then ripped open the breast and ate raw chicken meat. That he never got Salmonella poisoning may attest to his powers.

Known to everyone as "Chicken Man," Keeyama was entertaining, in an over-the-top Marilyn Manson kind of way. He was generally beloved as a French Quarter character, but few took him seriously as a voodooist. He was deliberately not invited to participate in a Tulane University panel discussion on voodoo. As years went on, Prince Keeyama was often found wandering the French Quarter in his voodoo attire, selling voodoo dolls and gris-gris bags, but he had abandoned his signature act. Chicken Man admitted, "I got tired bitin' chicken heads. It got kinda funky." He briefly had a shop called "Chicken Man's House of Voodoo" located on Bourbon Street. Fred Staten died in December 1998. His ashes were donated to the Voodoo Spiritual Temple.

Voodoo today is making something of a comeback in two, practically opposite, directions. On the hokey side, there's the touristy voodoo re-birth; voodoo shops selling made-in-China gris gris bags and pin dolls are nearly as common as snowball stands. You can even pick up your voodoo candles at Zuppardo's Grocery the next aisle over from your instant grits and frozen burritos. You can buy Go Away Evil air freshener and Shut Your Mouth mouthwash. You can have your picture taken with The Voodoo Couple or The Voodoo Man, people who wander the French Quarter on sunny days, hoping to get cash tips for posing in front of tourists' cameras. You can even pay a for-hire voodoo doctor or queen to attend your next party or function.

If you want to experience real voodoo while in New Orleans, I would suggest walking right by the Marie Laveau House of Voodoo on Bourbon Street and Rev. Zombie's House of Voodoo. They and most other French Quarter shops are stocked to the gills with made-in-China stuff to suck up your tourist's dollars. You need to question the authenticity of voodoo shops that also sell T-shirts, coffee mugs, and Zippo lighters emblazoned with their store's logo. Although you might consider buying one of their raccoon penis bones for only $12.95. Penis bones are claimed to be used in love spells or to provide luck for gamblers, depending on which fabricated story you want to adhere to.

In addition to Erzulie's Authentic Voodoo, Esoterica Occult Goods, Voodoo Authentica, House of Voodoo, and others, the French Quarter does have a Voodoo Museum (724 Dumaine St.). At least here they try to give you a little history before

Priestess Miriam

taking more of your money (the museum itself costs $7) for farce-i-facts (made up artifacts). For a mere $1, you can get a bag of snake scales.

The Voodoo Museum is run by Jerry Gandolfo, a former insurance company manager. There is some voodoo history embedded in his family's past. But it was his older brother Charles, an artist and hairdresser, who created the museum because he wanted a more stable career. "Voodoo Charlie," as he was later known, set about gathering a hodgepodge of artifacts of questionable authenticity: horse jaw rattles, strings of garlic, statues of the Virgin Mary, yards of Mardi Gras beads, alligator heads, a clay "govi" jar for storing souls, and the wooden kneeling board allegedly used by Marie Laveau.

Priestess Miriam's Voodoo Spiritual Temple burned down on the 800 block of Rampart in February 2016 and recently re-opened on the 1400 block. Priestess Miriam is rated one of the top "real" voodoo priests in New Orleans, but she is not infallible. She oversaw the wedding of Nicolas Cage and Lisa Marie Presley, a marriage that lasted only three months. She performed a ceremony outside the Super Dome to guarantee the Saints a victory when they played the Cleveland Browns on Halloween 1999. Browns quarterback and overall #1 NFL draft pick Tim Couch had his one and only shining moment in an otherwise total bust of a career: His 55-yard TD pass on the last play of the game beat our Saints and his Hail Mary beat our voodoo.

You'll need to leave the bright lights and noxious smells of the Quarter to get to more of the real stuff.

My personal #1 spot is F & F Botanica Spiritual Supply (801 N. Broad St. in Mid-City). Walk in the front door of F & F, and you'll be overwhelmed by the largest collection of voodoo candles you've ever seen. There are candles to help you get a job, to help win your court case, to attract money or love; there are candles to keep the law away, to cause a breakup; and, perhaps best of all, there's the all-encompassing candle I've bought several times. It's simply marked DO WHAT I SAY.

Like po'boys, candles can come "fully dressed." Dressed candles have been anointed with appropriate oils and herbs. They are twice as pricey, but if you really want people to Do What You Say, it's worth the extra expense.

F & F was originally named The Kingdom of the Yoruba Religion by the shop's founder, the reverend Enrique Cortéz, author of *Secretos del Oriaté de la Religión Yoruba*. "New" owner (for the last 30-plus years) Felix Figueroa had already been selling spiritual candles and goods around New Orleans for some time when he bought the place in 1981. With more than 6,000 items on display in the store today, F & F has become the Walmart or Costco of voodoo supplies, or sometimes called a Ritual-Aid Charmacy. In addition to candles, they have essential oils, fragrance oils, roots and herbs, books, artisan jewelry, photographs, statues of saints and demons, prayer cards, and, for some reason, Mardi Gras beads. They also have those hard-to-find items like a white hair plucked from the second-born fawn of a blessed doe from the North Shore. What the white hair is supposed to do is unclear, but it's probably good to have one around "just in case."

The other "real" voodoo shop is Island of Salvation Botanica, home of Sallie Ann Glassman, a nice Jewish girl from Maine who spent years in Haiti and really is ordained as a voodoo priest. She is our current voodoo star attraction. Sallie has been featured in numerous publications such as *The New York Times, The Los Angeles Times, The Wall Street Journal* and *The New Yorker*. She has appeared on CNN, National Public Radio, CBS News, The Discovery Channel, and *ABC World News Tonight*, all with more cred than the Danh-Gbwe *Daily*.

Vampires

If you're still a skeptic and you view voodoo as silly or made-up, New Orleans may have to suck you in with our long history and deep association with vampires.

New Orleans definitely embraces this most alternative of alternative lifestyles. I assume every single reader of this book already knows Bram Stoker based his *Dracula* on Romanian prince Vlad Tepes, or Vlad the Impaler. Vlad was murdered in 1476 and his tomb is, predictably, reported as empty. But vampire mythology seems to go all the way back to ancient Sumerian and Babylonian myths about *ekimmu*, or one who is not buried properly and returns as a vengeful spirit to suck the life out of the living. In the text of the Egyptian Book of the Dead, Pert em Hru, if not all five parts of the soul receive specified offerings, the unattended piece will wander out of the tomb as a *kha* to find nourishment, often by drinking the blood of the living.

New Orleans vampire lore began in the late 1800s, when young French girls arrived at the Old Ursuline Convent, getting off the boat with their entire belongings in a single coffin-shaped suitcase. They'd been sent over to provide proper wives for the male French settlers. Previously, young French men, deprived of young women, risked life and scalp when they went out into the wilds to cruise for Choctaw chicks. Collectively, the girls from France were called *fille à la cassette* (girl with a cassette), shortened to "casket girls."

The little coffin-shaped suitcases were stored in the convent's attic on the third floor. When some of the suitcases were found to be empty, rather than thinking the girls' possessions had been stolen, hyper-imaginative residents began circulating stories that the casket girls had smuggled vampires into New Orleans.

Adding to the Ursuline story, the third-floor shutters, where the caskets were stored, are to this day bolted and permanently shut. The shutters were forever closed using studs consecrated by Catholic priests to keep the vampires inside.

In addition to introducing vampires to New Orleans, Ursuline was also the first school in America to teach girls, and later the first to teach Native Americans and African-Americans. Nuns from France were sent to America to serve as instructors for girls, either at the request of Thomas Jefferson or by the decree of King Louis XV, depending on which Google entry you choose to believe.

It wasn't just New Orleanians grown hyper-sensitive about vampires. Much of Europe was, at the time, obsessed with vampires almost to the point of mass hysteria. The vampire myth seems to have really taken hold in Slavic countries back in the 1700s. During the eighteenth century, a.k.a. The Age of Enlightenment, there was a frenzy of vampire sightings in Eastern Europe. Spot checks for vampires, where folks dug up graves and drove stakes into the hearts of the dead bodies (just in case).

From our distant, more enlightened twenty-first century perspective (when nearly half of current Americans believe in Creationism and 25 percent believe the Sun orbits the Earth), we can see that symptoms from then-common diseases were misinterpreted as signs of vampirism. The Black Plague had given way to tuberculosis, or as it was called back then, consumption. Common tuberculosis symptoms include red, swollen, light-sensitive eyes, pale skin, a weakened heartbeat, and coughing up blood, all lining up perfectly with commonly reported characteristics of vampires.

One of the most famous "real" vampires is Le Comte de Saint Germain. Le Comte de Saint Germain, or Comty as he was known to absolutely no one, was an alchemist who claimed to have the "elixir of life." He was said to be more than 6,000 years old, with vast knowledge in the sciences and history, and was well-spoken in many languages, including French, German, Dutch, Spanish, Portuguese, Russian, and English, along with a passing familiarity in Chinese, Latin, Arabic, ancient Greek, and Sanskrit. As a great storyteller, Compty became a darling at the court of Louis XV of France.

He was invited to many banquets in the finest homes of Paris, but reportedly, he never ate at a thing. The first record of his suspected immortality was at a party at the manor of Madame de Pompadour. The year was 1760, and a confused guest approached the man she thought was the look-alike son of the Compty she knew back in 1710. She discovered it actually WAS Compty, who hadn't aged a day in 50 years.

Years later, in 1902, a man going by the name Jacques St. Germain moved to New Orleans, into the prestigious building at the corner of Ursulines and Royal. He claimed to have immigrated from the south of France and was a descendent of the Count Saint-Germain. Upon arriving, Jacques threw elaborate parties. He fed his guests from an elaborate menu on the finest china and silverware, yet didn't himself eat a bite. Family tradition.

He was described as charming, highly intelligent and a master of languages and art, but he was also an abrasive party boy, hanging out on Bourbon Street with gangs that would today be the equivalent of Roll Tide or Buckeye fans whoopin' it up on Sugar Bowl weekend.

Out in public, Jacques seemed to have a different young woman on his arm each night. On one cold December evening, he picked up one woman at a local pub and brought her back to his home. Later that night, she flung herself from the second story window. As bystanders rushed to her aid, she told them how Saint Germain had attacked her. She said he came at her with alarming speed and strength and began biting her viciously on her neck.

When New Orleans police kicked in the door of Saint Germain's home to arrest him, he had already escaped. Inside they discovered large bloodstains in the wooden floor and wine bottles filled with human blood.

As the most vampire-friendly city in America, New Orleans has many resources for the adventurous undead. The New Orleans Vampire Association (NOVA) describes itself as a "non-profit organization comprised of self-identifying vampires representing an alliance between Houses within the Community in the Greater New Orleans Area. Founded in 2005, NOVA was established to provide support and structure for the vampire and other-kin subcultures and to provide educational and charitable outreach to those in need."

NOVA has been behind the creation of a web series, *Vampires: The Show*, and core members founded Vampsta Vixens in 2011. The Vampsta Vixens are a dance/performance group of models, tabbed "Beauty with Bite." Founder Lady Dark Adora (somehow that feels like a made-up name), describes the Vixens evolution: "We began to entertain at the Bad Things monthly parties. It is a fun way to relax, have fun, and meet new people. The Bad Things party became popular, and White Wolf of CCP Games used the Bad Things crew, including the Vixens, to perform for an amazing event pre-party. Later we performed at the House of Blues in New Orleans for a crowd of over 850 people at the Endless Night Vampire Ball."

Belfazaar Ashantison, or Zaar, (somehow that also feels like a made-up name) is a Spiritual Consultant at Voodoo Authentica and does Tarot card readings in

Jackson Square, but is probably best known as the most visible Elder in The New Orleans Vampires Association.

Maven Lore (somehow that feels . . .) is another elder and locally renowned as New Orleans' premier fangsmith. A fangsmith is someone who specializes in the art of making custom fangs for members of the Vampire community, as well as others who may want them. Maven's business, Dark Awakenings Custom Fangs, was founded in 1998, and she has made fangs for everyone from UFC fighters and exotic dancers to once-a-year fang wearers on Halloween.

Anne Rice is our Louis Armstrong or Marie Laveau of the vampire world. Her first novel, *Interview with the Vampire*, was published in 1976 and was written, in large part, as a way for her to deal with the raw feelings surrounding the death of her six-year-old daughter, Michele. Anne has written, "I got to the point where the whole thing just exploded! Suddenly, in the guise of Louis, a fantasy figure, I was able to touch the reality that was mine. It had something to do with growing up in New Orleans, this strange, decadent city full of antebellum houses. It had something to do with my old-guard Catholic background. It had something to do with the tragic loss of my daughter and with the death of my mother when I was 14. Through Louis' eyes, everything became accessible. But I didn't ask when I was writing what it meant; I only asked if it felt authentic. There was an intensity—an intensity that's still there when I write about those characters. As long as it is there, I will go on with them. In some way they are a perfect metaphor for me."

By her second and third vampire novels, *The Vampire Lestat* and *Queen of the Damned*, Anne had become a fixture on top of bestseller lists and had awakened book publishers to the cash cow opportunities offered by vampire novels. *Interview* had been rejected five times before being sold to Knopf (actually not so bad considering Stephenie Meyer's *Twilight* was rejected fourteen times), and even then, Anne received a rather lukewarm advance of $12,000. But in just a few short years, she had become as big a celebrity as any writer. Fans, many made up as vampires, would camp out and line up for her book signings in numbers that were the book versions of queues waiting for Bruce Springsteen or Rolling Stones concert tickets. Anne thrilled her fans by sometimes showing up for book signings lying inside a quilted coffin in a horse-drawn hearse. At the events, she would sign as may as 6,000 books. My record book signing is sixty-four copies, and this was for an all-day street fair with the additional draw of live music and peanut butter & bacon crepes.

Then the film rights to *Interview* were sold, and the resulting production served as the beachhead for an onslaught of vampire movies filmed here. While the movies have greatly helped the local economy, other than *Interview with the Vampire*, they have not been heaped with great praise nor great success.

Critics were luke-cool (38 percent on Rotten Tomatoes) in their praise of *Cirque du Freak*, but it did make money for Universal Pictures. The film, based on graphic novels by Darren Shan, yielded $14 million domestically and nearly $40 million worldwide. It was the #1 movie in the Ukraine and #2 in in the United Arab Emirates. And it's always a pleasure to see John C. Reilly in anything. A sequel has been threatened.

Dracula 2000 has spawned a three-film series, though the two sequels were direct-to-video releases. The premise of the first was that Dracula was resurrected in 2000 and went to New Orleans, not because of the tax incentives Louisiana gives to movie makers, but because of some telepathic connection to Van Helsing's daughter. Don't ask.

In the movie, Dracula reveals he is none other than Judas Iscariot, who betrayed Jesus for thirty pieces of silver. As he tried to hang himself in guilt and shame, the rope snapped, and as punishment he was cursed to live two thousand years as a vampire. Again, don't ask.

The New York Times called *Dracula 2000* "a grating new cliché carelessly tossed into a picture to give it a hip kinetic gloss." It got a desperate-for-blood-infusion 17 percent on Rotten Tomatoes.

Dracula II: Ascension was routinely dismissed as "a tired collection of cliches" (*Entertainment Weekly*) where *Dracula III: Legacy* fared slightly better. For one, it starred the Anne Rice-approved Rutger Hauer as Dracula/Judas. One reviewer wrote, "At least (it's) somewhere just north of mediocre."

I actually liked watching *Abraham Lincoln: Vampire Hunter*. I've seen this robustly terrible movie three times. My pleasure mostly comes from recognizing local spots used as the movie sets: "Hey, that's the Pharmacy Museum! Isn't that the Jonathan Ferrara Gallery?" The acting and the plot, such as they were, provide decidedly less pleasure.

Ghosts

Now, if you're just an old fuddy-duddy and you refuse to believe in voodoo or vampires, let's try ghosts. The International Society for Paranormal Research (ISPR), sort of the FCC of psychic foundations, has documented at least twenty-seven areas of paranormal activity (i.e. ghosts) in New Orleans. If you believe the hundreds of ghost tour guides who haunt the Quarter each night from 6:00 p.m. to 10:00 p.m., you can easily triple or quadruple that number.

I'm choosing not to fill the next 100 pages with ghost stories, even though I easily could. If you crave more, you can (1) buy my other book, *Fear Dat*, or (2) take one of countless ghost tours. Some are the kind of boring ones where the guide seems most intent on letting you know they don't believe any word of what they're telling you; one bills itself like a snotty contrarian teenager, as their web copy claims they "provide researched information to debunk the most fantastic of Big Easy ghost legends." Seriously, what withered soul would want to waste money on a ghost tour whose purpose is to convince you everything they're saying is hogwash? On the more earnest side, there's Bloody Mary, which goes inside a cemetery at night, Lord Chaz's wildly over-the-top "vampire theater," to Peter Venkman and Egon Spengler wannabes traipsing through graveyards and haunted buildings with their Echovox System 2.5 and K2 EMF Meters.

Echovox, in case you're not up on the latest in ghost hunting equipment, is a mobile monetization company focused on monetizing web and traditional media audiences with transaction-enabled mobile services. In English, that means the machine creates a sort of white noise that spirits are able to use to enable them to form words and communicate with the living.

Our most famous haunted house is, without question, The Lalaurie Mansion (1140 Royal St. in the French Quarter). Madame Delphine Lalaurie, a New Orleans socialite, and her husband, Dr. Lou, both had colossal sadistic streaks. In public, they were a well-respected couple. But behind the closed doors of their home, they exercised whatever wretched impulse popped into their sick little minds. Madame Lalaurie is said to have killed over seventy slaves in the most horrific ways. Her first known victim was a 12-year-old girl who fell to her death from a balcony while trying to run away from a bullwhip-wielding Madame. They tried to secretly bury her body in an old well in the rear courtyard. However, once discovered, charges of abuse were brought upon Delphine Lalaurie. The court issued a fine of only $300, which even by 1800s standards was a mere slap on the wrist. Her slaves, however, were taken away and sold at public auction. But the couple got a friend to buy all the slaves and then give them back to the Lalauries.

Then, the Lalauries, as Emeril might say, kicked it up a notch. They chained slaves to the wall to perform experiments. Then the house cook purposefully set a fire on April 10, 1834, so firemen would enter the mansion and discover the Lalauries' horrendous hobbies. According to Jeanne deLavigne's book, *Ghost Stories of Old New Orleans* (written in 1946), the responding firemen found "male slaves, stark naked, chained to the wall, their eyes gouged out, their fingernails pulled off by the roots; others had their joints skinned and festering, great holes in their buttocks where the flesh had been sliced away, their ears hanging by shreds, their lips sewn together . . . Intestines were pulled out and knotted around naked waists. There were holes in skulls, where a rough stick had been inserted to stir the brains." *Journey Into Darkness: Ghosts and Vampires of New Orleans* (written 52 years later in 1998) by Kalila Katherina Smith, added more explicit details, including a "victim [who] obviously had her arms amputated and her skin peeled off in a circular pattern, making her look like a human caterpillar," and another who had had her limbs broken and reset "at odd angles so she resembled a human crab."

The story gets more embellished and deeply disgusting with each retelling and it gets retold about twenty times a night by a continuous parade of ghost tour guides. It's kind of like how the older I get, my high school football exploits become more and more filled with last-second heroics. Give me another year or two and my football career and Peyton Manning's will be indistinguishable.

One night, one of the tour guides was retelling the nasty tales at the front of the mansion. When the guide told the gathered tourists that current owner, Nicolas Cage, has never dared to spend the night there, the formerly hidden actor leaned over from the upstairs balcony and yelled down to the crowd, "Oh yeah? Well, I'm here tonight and I ain't leaving!"

Cage did eventually have to leave, thanks to $12 million in back taxes he owed—I guess he forgot some movies he was in. The IRS seized the mansion and auctioned it off, eventually selling to Michael Whalen, a wealthy Texas real estate developer. Whalen hired interior decorator Katie Stassi-Scott to redo the inside. Even though she grew up in New Orleans, the interior designer had never heard the horrible tales of Madame Lalaurie. Learning the stories, she adopted the position, "Every time I went to Lalaurie, I would say my prayers and put on the holy water. It was my perfume."

The IRS auction includes one sad detail. The under-bidder to Michael Whalen was Johnny Depp. That boy is made for New Orleans. It was rumored that Depp intended to turn the Lalaurie home into a museum. Woulda, coulda, shoulda.

After the Lalaurie mansion, the Le Pretre house (716 Dauphine St.) is probably our second most haunted place of murder, mayhem—and lingering ghosts. On the outside, it's pretty typical: wrought-iron-laced balcony, courtyard out back, stunningly beautiful French Quarter Mansion. Nothing on the outside betrays the grisly things that took place inside.

Jean Baptiste Le Pretre wanted to rent out his home for the long stretches when he was not in town, and chose the younger brother of the Turkish Sultan, Prince Suleyman, as his tenant. The prince moved in with a complete entourage, including harem girls and his loyal eunuch. I guess in those days, would-be tenants didn't have to fill out forms stating how many would occupy the apartment. An answer of "forty-eight and a eunuch" might have raised a few questions.

Once inside the house, the not-quite-a-Sultan held lavish all-night absinthe and opium parties. Some say what happened next came about because the sultan's brother had come to New Orleans with stolen money and jewels. Others say it was a hired execution by the Sultan to safeguard his own rule and to prevent the wild younger brother from assuming the throne.

One morning, a neighbor was strolling down the sidewalk and noticed a large amount of blood running out of the house onto the street. When the police went inside they discovered what was left of everyone from last night's bacchanalia. It was a Manson Family-esque scene times six. All forty-eight members of the entourage had been so thoroughly chopped up and dismembered that police couldn't identify what piece went with whom. The prince had not been hacked to pieces like his retinue. He was found to have been buried alive out back in the courtyard.

The Le Pretre House is now one of the most haunted places in New Orleans. Witnesses say they have seen the ghosts, heard screams and music, and smelled incense coming from the house.

La Pharmacie Francaise (514 Chartres St.) is the largest and most diverse pharmaceutical collection in the United States. For $5, you can see display cases containing artifacts of historical medicinal practices: pills and powders with their original packaging, early and massively cringe-worthy hypodermic needles, and tools for therapeutic bloodletting, including a jar labeled "Leeches."

The medical museum is the former establishment of Louis J. Dufilho, Jr., the first licensed pharmacist in America. Upon his retirement, Dr. Dufilho gave his practice and the pharmacy to his longtime assistant, Dr. Dugas. Dr. Dugas kept losing his patients. He claimed they were all moving back to France. After he died from syphilis in 1867, workers found multiple bodies, all believed to be his missing patients, buried in the back courtyard. In addition to murdering his paying customers, Dr. Dugas was revealed to have conducted horrific medical experiments on pregnant slaves.

The brochure for the Pharmacy Museum glosses over these atrocities, scripting, "Visitors are encouraged to walk through the newly renovated courtyard, which contains a garden of herbs used for medicinal purposes in earlier years. The courtyard provides a pastoral, characteristically French Quarter setting for private parties and receptions and is available for rental to large and small groups."

Your private party or reception might have an uninvited guest. Dr. Dugas' apparition has been seen after hours wearing his brown suit or lab coat. He has been known to throw books and move items in the display cases, and he occasionally sets off the security system.

Another site of restless spirits is the block-long federal building at 400 Royal Street. The facility was a courthouse from 1909 to 1964, then headquarters for the Wildlife & Fisheries Museum, then returned to its role as the Supreme Court of Louisiana in 2004. While undergoing extensive interior renovations to turn a wildlife museum back into a courthouse, the ever-busy International Society of Paranormal Research (ISPR) entered the property and discovered several entities.

There's the specter of an African-American man who is dressed in a white shirt and pants. There's a white woman, described as young and dressed in a brown suit and skirt. Researchers discovered these two were witnesses in a Mafia murder trial in the 1930s. Prior to giving their testimonies, both were shot and killed inside the courtroom. Workers renovating the building and visitors to the courthouse building have also documented observations of the two witnesses. While filming *JFK* inside the building, Oliver Stone is rumored to have shot several scenes over and over again, as unwanted (and no longer living) extras kept showing up in the dailies.

Back in the 1800s, a young German couple opened a sausage factory in New Orleans. OK, you can probably guess the rest of the story on that sentence alone. He'd married her for better or worse, but not for deboning and filleting.

If you are just now planning your trip, New Orleans has many haunted hotels where you might stay.

The Hotel Monteleone 214 Royal St.

The Hotel Monteleone is one of the last, great family-owned hotels in America, having been operated by four generations of the Monteleone family since it was founded in 1886. Tennessee Williams, William Faulkner, and Truman Capote have all lived at the hotel. Truman told people he was born in the hotel, while the facts may be otherwise. Eudora Welty was a frequent guest. These residents prompted the Friends of Libraries organization to designate the Monteleone a Literary Landmark. The Hotel Monteleone is also home to more than a dozen ghosts that have chosen not to check out.

For years, still-living employees and guests of the hotel have reported sightings, ghosts opening doors, moving soap, and running up honor bar charges at check out. OK, I made up that last part, but not the rest. In March 2003, the International Society of Paranormal Research spent several days investigating Hotel Monteleone. While at the hotel, the team made contact with enough entities to fill out the cast for a David Simon series. Among them was a man named William Wildemere, who died inside the hotel of natural causes; the ghost of a jazz singer; a boy who was much older when he died, but who enjoys returning to Hotel Monteleone as a 10-year-old to play hide-and-seek with another young spirit; and a naked man in a feathered Mardi Gras mask (there's always one in every crowd).

The Cornstalk Hotel 915 Royal St.

A charmer of an old French Quarter hotel with the namesake corn-shaped wrought-iron fence, I stayed at The Cornstalk Hotel several times before moving to New Orleans. The bedrooms have chandeliers. There's a great second-floor balcony from which you can look down on people strolling down Royal Street, and listen to boats on the Mississippi. It was built in the early 1800s and was the home of Judge Francois Xavier-Martin, first Chief Justice of the Louisiana Supreme Court. The hotel also housed Harriet Beecher Stowe, during which time she was inspired by the sights at the nearby slave markets to write *Uncle Tom's Cabin*. But it's listed here because it's also haunted as shit.

Reported activity includes the sounds of children running, playing, and laughing, and light footsteps in the halls when no one is there. But the best and one of the creepiest things I've ever heard are tales of guests staying alone in a room and waking up the next day to discover photos of themselves on their cameras or cell phones, taken while they slept in the room's bed and taken from . . . the . . . ceiling. There are debates, depending on which verbal hash-slinging ghost tour guide you choose to believe, as to whether it's the Cornstalk or the Andrew Jackson Hotel next door that is inhabited by Polterazzies.

Le Pavillon Hotel 833 Poydras St.

Le Pavillon Hotel is a luxury hotel, nicknamed "The Belle of New Orleans." It has old style charm with crystal chandeliers from Czechoslovakia and French marble floors and marble railings, imported from the lobby of the Parisian Grand Hotel. Spectacular Italian columns and statues were bought to add drama to the front entrance.

If you can expense your stay on the company, you should request Palace Suite 730—not for the ghosts, but for the single-piece marble bathtub given as a gift by Napoleon Bonaparte. It's one of only three in the world. One sits in the Louvre. One is in a private collection. And the third is ready to receive you and your travel-size rubber ducky.

What was not imported, but just happened to show up anyway, are the many ghosts. Paranormal investigation groups line up to conduct research in the hotel. One group got documentation of over 100 entities and various "haunted hot-spots." Another investigation group found so much activity inside Le Pavilion they concluded the hotel is a portal to the other side.

The most regularly spotted ghost is Adda. The teenaged girl was reportedly set to board a ship with her family when she was killed by a runaway carriage. The hotel staff sees her ghost frequently shuffling around the lobby, dressed in a long, flowing-to-the-ankle skirt, a black long shawl, and a broad black hat, often crying.

One New Orleans taxi cab driver tells a story of Adda over and over again. He swears she got into his cab one cold, rainy night, and asked to be taken to the ship passenger terminal. After the cab got only a few blocks from the hotel down Poydras Street, she simply disappeared.

Says the driver, "I thought she was a real person, I saw her face to face and in my rearview mirror. The doorman actually opened the door for her. I drove straight back and told him what happened. The doorman shrugged, and said to me, 'Well, this has happened a lot to other cab drivers.'"

Aside from the ghosts, Le Pavillon is also noted for their peanut butter and jelly sandwiches. A guest checked in late one evening, went to the bar and ordered a glass of milk. When the bartender asked him, "Why milk?," the guest told of his family tradition where he shares a glass of milk and peanut butter & jelly sandwiches each night with his kids before they go to bed. When on the road and away from his family, he has a glass of milk to keep the shared moment alive. The bartender that night was the hotel's manager, filling in for the staff. He went back to the kitchen, made the man a sandwich, and established the hotel's ongoing tradition of complimentary peanut butter & jelly sandwiches in the lobby each and every evening.

Bourbon Orleans Hotel 717 Orleans St.

Bourbon Orleans Hotel was one of New Orleans' grand ballrooms, where gentlemen met young Creole women to take them on as well-cared-for mistresses. In the 1800s, the space went a completely different direction and became a convent for girls. Both figure into the hotel's present status as as one of New Orleans' top haunted spots.

Chip Coffey, internationally acclaimed psychic and host of A&E's *Psychic Kids*, performed a reading at the historic Orleans ballroom, where he detected and communicated with several spirits. From the convent days, "spirited" laughter and voices are heard from the little girls that roam the halls. The most frequently told tale is of a little girl rolling her ball and chasing it down the sixth-floor corridors. You also might want to watch your language inside the hotel. Guests have received a slap on the wrist after cursing, presumably from the ghosts of convent nuns.

The most famous ghost at the hotel is the Lady in Red. For well over a hundred years, she's been seen frequently dancing, alone, inside the second-floor ballroom.

St. Peter House 1005 Saint Peter St.

St. Peter House has a wait-list to check into a hotel room because it was the death scene of Johnny Thunders, guitarist in the punk rock band The New York Dolls. His style was described as "raunchy, nasty, rough, raw, and untamed. It was truly inspired." He either died or was murdered in room 37. The room had been ransacked and most of his possessions were missing. Friends and acquaintances stated he had not been using heroin for some time, but usually did have massive doses of methadone when he traveled, none of which was found. True to their "Not Our Problem Darlin'" moniker, the NOPD did not open a criminal investigation.

Myrtles Plantation 7747 U.S. 61, St. Francisville

Myrtles Plantation is located closer to Baton Rouge than New Orleans (about 85 miles from the city). It's worth the trip. You can take in the 120-foot veranda, exquisite ornamental ironwork, hand-painted stained glass, open-pierced frieze work crown molding, Aubusson tapestry, Baccarat crystal chandelier, Carrara marble mantels, gold-leafed French furnishings, and dine at the Carriage House Restaurant on the premises. You can also spend the night . . . if you dare. The plantation bills itself as "One of America's Most Haunted Homes."

There's a complete cast of ghosts. Chloe is a former slave who was hung on the premises for serving poisoned cake to the two little girls who lived there. The ghosts of the two murdered children have been seen playing on the veranda. William Drew Winter, an attorney who lived at Myrtles from 1860 to 1871, was shot on the side porch of the house by a stranger. Winter staggered into the house and began to climb the stairs to the second floor. He collapsed and died on the seventeenth step. His last dying footsteps can still be heard on the staircase to this day. The ghosts of other slaves occasionally show up to ask if they can do any chores. The grand piano has often been heard to play by itself, repeating a single chord—either haunting or annoying depending on your perspective.

Cemeteries

OK, let's say you are one of those nutty climate change deniers and you also still don't believe in anything I've written thus far in this chapter. I hope and trust that you do at least accept people do die, almost without exception, and are most often buried in cemeteries.

There are thirty-eight aboveground cemeteries in New Orleans. If you are visiting the city, you just have to accept the fact that you aren't going to get to them all in one trip—unless you approach vacations like my dad. My dad, and I think all dads of that era, measured the success of a vacation by how many miles you packed into each day.

Each cemetery has its own unique charms. All are free access except St. Louis #1, our oldest aboveground cemetery and where Voodoo Queen Marie Laveau is buried. What happened here is that someone jumped the cemetery wall at night and painted Laveau's tomb bright pink. They used latex paint, which does not breathe and would have destroyed it. So the Archdiocese dropped $10,000 to repair the vault and established new rules on March 1, 2015. All visitors must be with a tour guide, which means you have to pay to play, generally $20 per person. I wrote to the mayor and the head of the Archdiocese, complaining that the cemetery is our history. I did not write to the Pope. Probably I should have; he seems like a cool guy. I personally feel banning free entry is as though San Antonio restricted access to the Alamo. I would not want to be whoever painted Marie Laveau's tomb. You don't mess with our Voodoo Queen. After it was painted, a Florida man, Edward Archbold, died choking to death in a cockroach-eating contest. I thought, "Maybe that's the guy." But then I read about Friedrich Riesfeldt, a zookeeper, who died the worst way I can imagine: An elephant had diarrhea and buried him alive under 200 pounds of elephant shit.

The first public cemetery in New Orleans was erected on St. Peter Street in 1721. All burials there were in the ground, not above. Everything changed in 1788, but not because residents got tired of burying and re-burying Grammy and Papaw over and over again each time it rained. 1788 was the year of the Great Fire.

It started when Vincente Nunez lit his candle for a Good Friday altar. The candle fell over and quickly lit up his home. Back then, most buildings were made from

the plentiful cypress wood. Cypress is very dense. It keeps mosquitoes out. But it is also oil-infused and highly flammable. Vincente ran down the half block to the St. Louis Cathedral to have them ring the bells. There was a certain bell pattern which would have told the volunteer firemen, "Come out. We have a fire." But because it was Good Friday, the bells were wrapped in burlap, and the clerics refused to uncover them—ringing bells on Good Friday would be a sacrilege. So instead the fire burned down 80 percent of the city and killed over 1,200 people. The Saint Peter Street Cemetery couldn't handle the overflow of bodies, so they were taken outside the city walls and buried in the cypress swamp in what is now Basin Street between Conti Street and St. Louis Street.

The original Saint Louis Cemetery was twice as big as it is today. Many resident dead in the original cemetery were dug up and relocated elsewhere when workers began digging the New Basin Canal right through the cemetery. The canal project was intended to connect Lake Pontchartrain and the Mississippi River to form a more convenient shipping lane and trade route. Slaves were considered too valuable a commodity to risk working in the snake-filled, mosquito-laden marshes, but Irish immigrants flowing into America during the Potato Famine were a renewable resource. They worked for a dollar a day. If they keeled over, their bodies were simply tossed in the recently turned over muck as roadway fill.

Finally, someone with a little engineering savvy realized the river was higher then the lake. Had they finished digging Canal Street and all the way to the river, New Orleans would have been washed away. The project was abandoned and the canal filled back in. An estimated 8,000 to 10,000 Irish immigrant workers died digging the immediately discarded canal.

The commonly held belief is that we bury the bodies aboveground because New Orleans is below sea level; therefore, if you bury your loved ones below ground, during a large storm with any flooding, the bodies will rise to the surface. This is only partly true. There are tales of early settlers burying their neighbors and loved ones in the earthen levees and then, during heavy rains or floods, the decaying bodies of the dead would come rushing through the city streets, swimming backstroke (or femur-stroke). But for the first 70 years of New Orleans history all burials were underground, six feet under being the standard.

Why six feet under? Most historians believe the practice of burying the dead six feet under started during London's Great Plague of 1665. As the disease spread, the mayor of London laid down the law, literally, about how to handle dead bodies infected with black plague to avoid more infections and death. He created "Orders Conceived and Published by the Lord Major and Aldermen of the City of London, Concerning the Infection of the Plague," containing the phrase "all the graves shall be at least six feet deep." The belief was this was the proper depth to keep the plague-cooties away from the living.

The reason the St. Louis Cemetery is aboveground seems to be a jambalaya of reasons involving economics, effective land use, the Catholic Church, and, as much as anything, a fashion statement. If you go to Paris or Barcelona, you'll find most of the cemeteries are likewise aboveground.

Toward the end of the 1700s, Paris experienced serious land shortages for burials. Bodies were shoved into the spaces in the sewers, and corpses did burst through walls at times of heavy rain. City planner Nicholas Frochot, a.k.a. The Father of Aboveground Cemeteries (though I may well be the only person in history to call him that) came up with the creative plan to deal with too many dead. I have told far too many tour takers and readers of my book, *Fear Dat*, that the first aboveground cemetery was Père Lachaise in Paris. Her famous residents include Oscar Wilde, Colette, Isadora Duncan, Edith Piaf, Gertrude Stein, Marcel Proust, Marcel Marceau (but let's not talk about him), and the occupant of the most visited gravesite in Père Lachaise, Jim Morrison of The Doors. Problem is, Père Lachaise was built in 1804, or 15 years after St. Louis #1. While giving a French couple a tour, I learned that the real first aboveground cemetery was the Cimetière des Innocents, described as a "bulging, festering sore that could be seen blighting the face of Paris in the 1730s." It was finally closed in 1780 because there were just too many bodies jammed in and it smelled wretched."

As trendy as Parisian fashion or perfume, aboveground cemeteries became the "in" thing in internment throughout France, then spread to Spain and Portugal and became a cultural tradition in areas colonized by those countries—New Orleans among them.

So, the #1 reason New Orleans has aboveground cemeteries is that we are merely copying burial practices in France and Spain.

Then there's the Catholic Church, those fun folks who brought you the Inquisition and the Crusades. There are those who believe the whole story of dead loved ones popping up from New Orleans underground cemeteries was concocted, or at least greatly exaggerated, by the Catholic Church as a sales pitch. It is a lot more expensive to bury folks in an aboveground vault than tossing them underground. The church peddled their higher-priced internments by pushing fear and guilt. ("You don't want to bury your mother underground. She's going to pop up like a whack-a-mole during the first good rain.")

Now, coffins or bodies do pop up now and again. During the summer of 2016, the central part of Louisiana got deluged with 31 inches of rain in 24 hours. A few coffins were unearthed. So, it can happen, just like you can be eaten by a great white shark. But being below sea level is far from the #1 reason we bury aboveground.

The aboveground cemeteries had their own set of house rules. Each family vault was large enough to hold more than a single body. But by law, you got cut off after burying two fresh ones. Once occupied, the burial houses were sealed, and had to remain sealed, for 366 days. It is believed 366 days, or a year and a day, was decreed when New Orleans was hit with outbreaks of Yellow Fever. The living (incorrectly) worried they could catch the disease from the dead bodies, as though they were contagious like the bubonic plague.

The year and a day rule means the body would pass through a New Orleans summer inside the vault. The Catholic Church did not allow cremation until 1960. When it's 110 degrees outside on an oppressively hot August day in New Orleans, it'll be well above 300 degrees inside the tomb. The body would be cooked and naturally cremated whether you wanted it or not. At the end of the 366 days, the vault could be opened, the ashes and what's left of bone could be scooped and bagged, then placed at the base of the tomb, called the caveau, to make space for the next body. It was a wonderful recycling system.

If a third member of your family died during the 366 days, they were out of luck. They weren't getting in with the rest of the family until the decreed time had passed. Each cemetery is lined with thick exterior oven walls. They look very much like brick pizza ovens—and took on the name oven vaults. These walls received some regular internments, but were largely used as rental properties. A family can store a dearly departed there for whatever was needed until the 366 days are up, and the body could slide over into the family tomb.

If you failed to pay the rent, you were evicted. A cemetery employee would use a long pole to push the body to the back of the wall, where an opening in the floor would allow the remains to drop through a shaft to the bottom of the vault and mix with other non-paying dead-beats. This is where the phrases "getting the shaft" or being "shafted" come from. Use of the long shaft may also be the origin of the phrase not touching something "with a 10-foot pole."

The first outbreak of yellow fever in 1853 claimed 7,849 residents of New Orleans. The press and the medical profession did not alert residents of the outbreak until more than 1,000 people died, because the New Orleans business community pressured silence. They feared any word of an epidemic would cause a quarantine to be placed on the city, and their business would suffer. However, in a city of only 154,000 people, when nearly 8,000 residents drop dead with yellow skin, vomiting black gruel, and bleeding from the nose, mouth, and eyes, people eventually started noticing something is up.

One of the symptoms, considerably less gruesome than vomiting black gruel, was that your metabolism shut down. It was often hard to detect a pulse. Many people were buried alive. Realizing that someone not quite dead might be tossed inside a tomb, people started to tie a bell to fingers so that one could start ringing to signal, "Hey! I'm not quite dead yet!" The common phrase that comes from this practice is "dead ringer."

I'm not sure if "saved by the bell" originated here or with boxing, but they're free to claim it because we also are the origin of another phrase: "graveyard shift." Knowing a recently buried person might not be dead, someone associated with the family, usually a maid, would sit at the base of the grave all night long. If you came to inside the tomb at 3:00 a.m., someone had to be there to hear the bell. Hopefully, the person on post would not be someone you'd insulted, or they might come off their nighttime shift, "Nope, didn't hear a thing."

In addition to family vaults, most of our cemeteries will include jumbo-sized grave sites where a large number of residents will be thematically grouped. Many poor immigrants could not afford funeral expenses nor a personal tomb. Benevolent societies were formed in New Orleans allowing members to pool their financial resources, almost like an insurance policy, so you could be buried inside a society's vaults.

In St. Louis #1 Cemetery, Marie Laveau shares the grounds with the tallest monument in the cemetery, The Italian Mutual Benevolent Society tomb. The cemetery also has a Portuguese tomb, a French monument, and others. Lafayette #1 has a society tomb for volunteer firemen and another for orphans, etched on the tomb as "Destitute Boys." Greenwood also has a volunteer fireman tomb along with a Police Mutual Benevolent Association, a Confederate monument, and the Benevolent and Protective Order of Elks, Lodge 30.

The next few pages will serve as what I call a Bonewatcher's Guide to New Orleans, or Who's Buried Where.

St. Louis Cemetery #1 425 Basin St.

This is the oldest and most visited aboveground cemetery in New Orleans. Residents include Marie Laveau, our Voodoo Queen, and it is the future home of Nicolas Cage, our Scenery Chewing King. Among the over 700 vaults, there are a number of society tombs: Societe Francaise, the Benevolent Society of France, a Portuguese Benevolent Association, one for the Orleans Battalion of Artillery dedicated to anonymous soldiers killed at the Battle of New Orleans and that uses once-active cannons as a hedge around the monument.

Some think Marie Laveau's grave actually holds her daughter, also named Marie Laveau. Others think they're both buried there. Still others think the Glapion family vault, of her husband's family, is a ruse and Marie and her daughter are hidden elsewhere. There are stories that her bones were removed by voodoo practitioners to be used as high octane gris gris, or that her body was tossed into Lake Pontchartrain for reasons unclear. You can stroll through the cemetery and find two other tombs covered in the three-X voodoo pattern and offerings left for Marie.

People love conspiracy theories: Elvis lives in Kalamazoo. The moon landing was a hoax. Donald Trump is really Andy Kaufman in bloated disguise. The Glapion vault, which WAS Marie's final resting place, is the second-most visited gravesite in America. Elvis in Memphis is number one. The vault is covered in three Xs, which represent "spirit, unity and power" in the voodoo tradition. The theory is if you scribble three X's, knock three times, turn around three times, or spit spirits from your mouth (the alcoholic kind) onto the grave three times, your wish will be granted. The Archdiocese frowns upon spitting or drawing X's. In fact, if you now spit or draw on the tomb you'll be evicted and your tour guide's license revoked.

After you're (still permitted) knocking or spinning, you are also supposed to say aloud whatever you wish for. I once followed another tour group and witnessed a woman do all the ritual, but then she started to just walk away. I beckoned her back. "Whoa. Whatever you just wished for, you're supposed to say it aloud." Horrified, she looked at me, "Really?!" I assured her if she wanted her wish to come true, she had to ask for it . . . aloud. Finally girding her strength, the woman belted out, "I want a rich husband!"

You might also still notice a variety of offerings at the base of the grave: fake flowers, loose change, Mardi Gras beads, a pen out of ink, a number of lipstick tubes, rosary medals, an unused condom pack—pretty much anything to symbolize an area you need help. The point is, when you visit Marie Laveau's grave, you should honor the sacred spot and leave her "something." I used to tell tour takers, "You don't have to leave her anything. But, if you don't and you go home and your teeth start falling out, don't blame me." Here, too, the grumpy Archdiocese no longer allows anything to be left at her gravesite.

Right next to Marie was New Orleans's first black mayor, civil rights activist Ernest "Dutch" Morial. He was also the first African-American to graduate from LSU, the first African-American assistant to the U.S. Attorney's Office, and the first black person elected to the Louisiana Legislature since Reconstruction. The Morials are sort of the Kennedys or Roosevelts of New Orleans. Ernest and Sybil had five children. His son Marc Morial served 8 years as New Orleans' second black mayor, and then served as President of the National Urban League. His daughter Monique was elected a City Court judge. Cheri became the chairwoman of the Baton Rouge Downtown Development District. Jacques became a political consultant, and Julie became a doctor. Dutch was a combative and combustible politician, called everything from "feisty" to "uppity" depending on who was doing the calling. Noted a close friend, "Dutch wouldn't bend his knee to anyone." UNO professor Arnold Hirsch said of Morial, "He had his signature on almost every case that began to dismantle the edifice of Jim Crow here, brick by brick." He's also the namesake for New Orleans's Convention Center, which conventioneers seem unable to pronounce. (It's "MORE-ee-ALL.") He vigorously pushed for building the convention center, overriding a city council that didn't want to pay for it. The 11-block, 3-million-square-foot center is today the third highest volume in America, bringing the city around 770,000 convention attendees each year. Visitors to New Orleans are estimated to spend $249 per day. So, if my calculations are correct, the Morial Convention Center each year brings New Orleans *a shit load* of income.

A few years ago, Dutch was removed from St. Louis #1 and reburied in St. Louis #3. I figure either Marie Laveau was just too noisy as a neighbor, or the Morials had insider information that St. Louis #1 was about to be cut off from free and public access.

A hop, skip, and no jump needed from Marie's grave is Paul Morphy. He was the greatest chess player who ever lived. Morphy won 83 percent of the games he ever played. Bobby Fischer won 71 percent of his games. Morphy's first big win occurred when the U.S. champion was doing a barnstorming tour and wanted to play the best player in each city. When the champion rolled into New Orleans, the city brought out Paul, then 9 years old. The champion was insulted, thinking he was being poked fun at. Morphy beat him in a handful of moves. He went on to become the international chess champion at age 19, but grew bored traveling Europe and Russia and easily winning every match. He returned to New Orleans in 1859 and officially retired from chess at age 23. Paul's plans were to become a lawyer, but instead he lounged for years, alone in idle wealth inside his family's home at 417 Royal Street, or what would become the location for Brennan's famous (pink) restaurant. Morphy was found dead in his bathtub at age 43. The official cause of death was cardiac arrest, presumably from jumping into a cold bath on a particularly hot day. The "official" report made no mention of the collection of ladies' shoes that encircled his tub o' death.

You can't miss a very large, very bright, very garish pyramid-shaped tomb. There's no name on the tomb, just the words Omnia Ab Uno, which translated is "All from one." When the cemetery was open to the public, there also would have been lipstick kisses all over the edifice just like the three X's used to be on Marie Laveau's. The kisses were not left to grant wishes, but to honor the owner and eventual resident, Nicolas Cage. His is one of several Egyptian pyramid tombstones in our cemeteries. All things Egyptian became popular in America during the first half of the twentieth century. The craze was sparked by the uncovering of Tutankhamun's tomb in 1922, and was spread everywhere in newsreel footage and magazine covers. Eventually it bled into newly popular architectural styles. The all-seeing eye above the pyramid was added to the dollar bill during this time. And a bunch of people wanted to be buried like an Egyptian pharaoh. The Angelus-Rosedale Cemetery in Los Angeles has a number of pyramids.

In seizing his homes in New Orleans, the IRS could not legally take Cage's final resting place. Someday he will be buried there. Right now—**there is nothing inside the tomb**. I emphasize that because some Internet wackos insist there's buried treasure inside, I guess based upon his movies *National Treasure* and *National Treasure Book of Secrets*. I'm tempted to quote ET: "This is reality, Greg!"

Italian Mutual Benefit Association is the tallest monument in the cemetery—14 feet 6 inches high—and housed more than 2,400 remains. Many call it the Easy Rider tomb because in the movie starring Peter Fonda and Dennis Hopper, they pick up two prostitutes and bring them to the cemetery, where all four take LSD. Fonda then climbs up this tomb to have a chat with the statue. Hopper remains below with the prostitutes doing what one does with prostitutes. The Catholic Archdiocese was not tickled pink when they viewed the final film and since then have instituted very tight guidelines. To this day, tour takers can snap photographs inside the cemetery but are forbidden to take video. How they know what your cell phone is set to, I have no idea.

Homer Plessy was Rosa Parks more than fifty years before Rosa Parks. Homer was $\frac{1}{8}$ black, making him black in the eyes of the law, but he could easily pass for white. He purposefully sat in the whites-only car of the railroad with the full intention of being arrested. Plessy was a member of the Comité des Citoyens, or Citizens' Committee of New Orleans, formed to strike down segregation laws. Contrary to the rest of the country, blacks in New Orleans, even before the Civil War, were mostly already "free men of color" by being born Creole, being runaway "maroons," or having bought their freedom under "coartación." In New Orleans, former slaves lost rights rather than gained freedom after the Civil War. Plessy took his case all the way to the Supreme Court. On May 18, 1896, the court issued their infamous "separate-but-equal" ruling that basically legalized segregation anywhere in America, better known as Jim Crow.

Further back, near the back wall, Bernard Xavier Phillippe de Marigny de Mandeville is housed in my personal favorite spot in St. Louis #1. The tomb has rose bushes on either side. The one and only bench in the entire cemetery is here. Until about noon, the bench is even in the shade.

De Marigny's family was rich as Croesus. When the Duke of Orleans visited, his family threw them a dinner party and made special plates out of gold. After dinner, they threw the plates in the Mississippi River because no one else should ever eat from plates created for the Duke. The river here is 200 feet deep and the flow rate is 600,000 cubic feet per second with wicked currents. Michael Phelps could not swim across the river. Those plates have never been found.

Both parents died, leaving Bernard the richest teenager in the world. He was 15 years old and had seven million dollars. This was 1805 seven million dollars. Displaying all the reserve and self-control of most 15 year old boys, he blew his fortune traveling Europe and gambling (and losing) and playing (and losing) his new favorite dice game, Crapaud, which today we shorten to Craps. Other than flushing his $7 million inheritance, Bernie's greatest accomplishment was introducing the game of craps to America. In order to pay off his gambling debts, he sold much of his plantation to New Orleans in what is now the Marigny and Bywater neighborhoods. Again displaying his youth, Bernie christened the streets running through his property with all the solemn thoughtfulness of teenagers naming their garage bands. Desire Street, Peace Street, Frenchman, Piety, Humanity, and Pleasure Streets are all Bernard's work. Sadly, his Love Street became Rampart, and worse, a church petitioned the city because they didn't want to be known as The Church on Crap. Crap Street has been changed to Burgundy.

At the very back of the St. Louis #1, behind the back lot oven vaults, is a grassy area with some heaped bricks that looks like the cemetery ghetto. This is where we buried the Protestants.

After the Louisiana Purchase, Puritan-Americans flooded into the city to live and—eventually—die, requiring a place to be buried. Even this low-rent section wasn't the final resting place for many non-Catholics. As the city expanded outside the French Quarter and projects like the Basin Street Canal pressed at the borders of the cemetery, many bodily remains from Protestant graves were dug up and moved to First Protestant Cemetery on Girod Street in 1822; later on, they were pretty much moved all over town. When the Girod Street Cemetery was deconsecrated in 1957, most white corpses were move to the Holt Cemetery; most blacks were shipped to Providence Memorial Park. Today, the Super Dome stands atop these old Protestant burial grounds. Some long-suffering football fans felt those years of terrible "Aints" teams were caused by playing on burial grounds. Even today, if you dig a swimming pool in the French Quarter or the CBD sections of town, such as Vincent Marcello did in 2010, you're likely to find some buried bodies. Vincent found fifteen caskets.

Benjamin Latrobe was first buried in the Protestant section. He has been called "The Father of American Architecture." Latrobe is most famous for designing the Capitol Building in Washington, DC. In New Orleans, he lived long enough to complete the new St. Louis Cathedral and the U.S. Customs House before he succumbed to Yellow Fever. After being dug up at least once, maybe twice, we really don't know where The Father of American Architecture is. He does have a nice plaque in the back of St. Louis #1.

Years before Latrobe, the original designer of the original St.Louis Cathedral was French engineer Adrien de Pauger. De Pauger requested to be buried under the floorboards of the church, as this was considered an honor. One hundred thirty-some Popes are buried under the floor of St. Peter's Basilica. Unfortunately, he died in 1726, before the church was completed. To honor his wishes, workers tossed de Pauger's body in a wall and just kept going. When the church burned, we lost track of de Pauger's remains.

William Charles Cole Claiborne was the first American Governor of Louisiana. Yep, we don't know where he is either. Claiborne, who didn't speak a word of French, was wildly unpopular when he moved to New Orleans. He quickly followed up with the gaffe of placing a $500 bounty on the pirate Jean Lafitte. Lafitte was no swashbuckling Errol Flynn-type pirate, but more like Tony Soprano with 1,000 men. He knocked off ships on the Gulf and brought the goods back to New Orleans to offer residents Walmart prices on goods stolen off ships. The stolen goods were sold from inside the fenced-in courtyard behind the church. This is where the phrase "fencing the goods" comes from. Lafitte laughed off Claiborne's $500 bounty by posting his own $5,000 bounty for the Governor. They worked it out. No one was ever killed.

After Claiborne's first wife succumbed to Yellow Fever, he married Clarisse Duralde, a French Creole. He probably did this to soften his image with his constituency. It worked about as well as presidential candidate Michael "Tough Guy" Dukakis riding a tank or George Herbert Walker Bush trying to prove he's "just folks" like us, and not a Yalie blue blood patrician. (While trying to navigate a grocery store, Bush, who had never seen a supermarket scanner before, marveled at this crazy far-from-new thing, thus proving he WAS an out-of-touch Yalie blue blood patrician.)

There is a Claiborne family vault in the Metairie Cemetery. His remains might have been moved there, or they might be mixed in with the transient Protestants by the Super Dome, or he may still be hanging out someplace in St. Louis #1.

St. Louis #2 300 N. Claiborne Ave.

Walking distance from St. Louis #1, this is not a cemetery where I would choose to wander. It has become a human version of a cat colony. Feral people with "issues" like being homeless, addicted, or mentally unstable, like to be left alone here, and tend to be huddled here between the cracks or draped across slabs of concrete.

St. Louis Cemetery # 2 led to the creation of the Save Our Cemeteries organization. In 1974, the Archdiocese of New Orleans proposed to tear down the wall vaults and replace them with a chain link fence. Preservationists in the city were appalled, and SOC was founded in response. Over the next 10 years, working with the Archdiocese, the City, and other preservation organizations, SOC was able to restore the wall vaults rather than destroy them.

St. Louis #3 3421 Esplanade Ave.

When the city needed more space to bury the overflow of bodies from another outbreak of Yellow Fever in 1848, New Orleans bought a tract of land for $15,000 and created St. Louis #3. Previously, it had been a leper colony with a small makeshift burial ground known as Bayou Cemetery.

The original St. Louis #3 cemetery was expanded in 1865 and again in the 1980s. There are now approximately 10,000 burial sites, a figure that include 5,000 mausoleums, 3,000 wall vaults, 2,000 individual family tombs, and twelve society tombs. This cemetery is larger than both St. Louis #1 and 2 put together.

Because of its easy access (just pull over and park on Esplanade), St. Louis #3 is used by the majority of city tour companies. It is still an active cemetery, with a waitlist to buy space nearly as long as the one for wanna-be Saints season ticket holders.

Lafayette Cemetery #1 1416 Washington Ave.

The Garden District cemetery received its first body in 1833 after the land had been a section of a former sugar plantation. Madame Jacques Francois Livaudais had been awarded most of the land that today constitutes the Garden District and the Lafayette Cemetery as part of a divorce settlement. When she moved to Paris, Madame Livaudais sold the land for a sweet $490,000.

Lafayette is the oldest city-owned (i.e. non-Catholic) cemetery in New Orleans. It is sometimes called the "American" cemetery because it's not predominantly French or Spanish like other cemeteries. It holds the remains of citizens from twenty-five different countries. Also unlike most cemeteries in New Orleans, Lafayette was never segregated by race, ethnicity, nor religious denomination.

There are about 1,100 family tombs and more than 7,000 people buried in Lafayette, but fewer renowned residents than St. Louis #1. The most famous residents of Lafayette Cemetery are fictional ones. The tomb for the Mayfair witches, created by Anne Rice in *The Witching Hour*, was set here. Anne Rice also staged her own jazz funeral and mock burial here, when she rode in a glass coffin to launch her book *Memnoch the Devil*.

Many movies have been filmed in the cemetery, including *Skeleton Key*, *Double Jeopardy* (where Ashley Judd was shoved inside a vault) and *Dracula 2000* (filmed in 2000). *The Originals* TV series used the cemetery as well. LeAnn Rimes and the New Kids on the Block have filmed music videos here.

If you take the Canal Street Car line, aptly named "Cemeteries," to the end, there is a cluster of Cypress Grove Cemetery, Odd Fellows, Greenwood, St. Patrick's, and the Metairie Cemetery. Hidden behind a gas station and flower shop is the Katrina Memorial, built in 2007 on top of what used to be the Charity Hospital Cemetery (5050 Canal St.).

Lake Lawn Metarie Cemetery 5100 Pontchartrain Blvd.

While location keeps this from being as visited by tourists, Lake Lawn Metarie is New Orleans' most photo-friendly cemetery, with the largest collection of marble tombs, some with stained-glass windows, noted funeral statuary like the Weeping Angel. And unlike the congested and arbitrary design of St. Louis #1, Metairie is a drive-thru cemetery with wide and open vistas.

It also has a storied history. In the mid 1800s, it was the site of a country club and race track, a popular place with the wealthy and powerful elite. They refused to allow Charles T. Howard to become a member because he was nouveau riche, having recently gained his wealth from starting the Louisiana State Lottery. Worse, he was a Yankee. In response to his rebuke, Charles T. vowed that he would one day buy their privileged club and then besmirch its memory by turning it into a cemetery.

After the Civil War, Confederate money was worthless. Many club members fell on hard times, and soon enough the race track was put up for sale. Poetically, Charles T. Howard bought it and followed up on his promise to turn it into a graveyard.

The cemetery has become the final resting spot for many noted people who would have been more than welcomed into the country club. There are eleven Louisiana governors, nine New Orleans mayors, dozens of Confederate officers, and an area called Millionaire's Row, so named because it costs so much to be buried in this prime real estate section. Attorney Ray Brandt justified paying over $1 million for an eight-crypt mausoleum for his family, "Eventually everyone will end up somewhere. I guess it's the last house I'll buy."

By far the tallest monument on the property is the obelisk marked Moriarity. It's the first thing you'll see upfront at the corner nearest route 10. Daniel Moriarity immigrated from Ireland, and met and married Mary Farrell here. While he and his wife accumulated great wealth, they were never accepted into upper class society because they didn't have generational New Orleans bloodlines. When Mary died in 1887, Daniel erected a monument from which she could look down upon all the French and Creole society snobs buried near her tomb.

Louisiana Division-Army of Tennessee is a 30-foot-high tumulus (burial mound), topped by a bronze statue of General Albert Sidney Story in a pose described to the sculptor as the moments before Story died at the Battle of Shiloh. Story himself was buried here only briefly before his body was moved to the Texas State Cemetery.

General Pierre Gustave Toutant Beauregard is still buried here. The Little Creole, or The Little Napoleon as he was called at different times, was a native New Orleanian who singlehandedly started the Civil War when he ordered the first shots fired on Fort Sumter. Speaking only French in New Orleans, he didn't learn a word of English until he was a teenager and sent to New York for education. He graduated second in his class at West Point. Maybe 618,222 lives could have been saved had the little general never learned English and instead yelled "Feu à volonté!" to his befuddled rebel troops. After the war, Beauregard was active in campaigning for voting rights and education for freed slaves.

The most famous and most photographed statue in the cemeteries of New Orleans is The Weeping Angel, bowed inside the family vault constructed by Charles Hyams. He was a stockbroker, art collector, and philanthropist who helped create the city's Art Museum in 1911. The statue of the angel is a replica of a stylized tomb first used in Rome. There are now some forty weeping angels all over the world, found in Luxembourg, Costa Rica, Quebec—and nine in Texas alone.

Josie Arlington was an infamous madame from Storyville. Her brothel, which she named The Chateau Lobrano d'Arlington to class it up, was especially popular because she fired more common whores and brought in a wealth of educated foreign girls. Learning she intended to be buried in Metairie Cemetery, a cartel of society women were mortified that such a person would be buried near their husbands or fathers and sought to block her. Josie responded, "I wonder how many of these ladies know their husbands visit me weekly?"

Thanks to all her money, Arlington did get to rest among the upper crust—for a while. Near the front of the cemetery, Josie was interned in a beautiful red granite tomb with carved burning urns and a bronze statue of a woman reaching for the door. But under steady and heavy protests, the cemetery did finally agree to remove her remains. The mausoleum today is etched in the names of just one family, ironically the Morales, or Spanish for virtue and moral correctness.

Other notables include singer Louie Prima. Many leave pennies on his grave, commemorating his hit, *Pennies from Heaven.* Baseball great Mel Ott is buried there, along with Andrew Higgins, the man General Eisenhower credits for winning WWII. Ruth Fertel of Ruth's Chris' Steakhouse' musician Al Hirt; artist, writer, and husband of Anne Rice, Stan Rice; and notable at least to me and my daughter, Angelo Brocato, founder of New Orleans premier gelato and confections shop.

Jefferson Davis, the President of the Confederacy, was buried in the Metairie Cemetery for $3\frac{1}{2}$ years. He died in the home of friend Jacob Payne at First and Camp Streets. Virginia demanded his body be brought back. I'm guessing at that point, Mister Jeff's remains could have been transported to Virginia in a shoebox.

Greenwood Cemetery 5200 Canal Blvd.

This final resting place is owned by the Firemen's Charitable & Benevolent Association. They bill themselves as "still the best value in town." Personally, in my unjustifiable opinion, other than the large bronze elk that greets you, it's one of the more visually boring cemeteries here, as the landscape is laid out in rows on a grid pattern and all the mausoleums look pretty much alike. But it does hold two of New Orleans' more eccentric characters.

Ruth Grace Moulon, better known as Ruthie the Duck Girl, was a French Quarter icon. A tiny woman with a near constant grin (except when she was hurling profanities), she zoomed from bar to bar on roller skates, mooching drinks and cigarettes, wearing a ratty fur coat and long skirt or wedding gown and veil (she considered herself engaged to a sailor who passed through the Quarter in 1963). She was always trailed by a duck or two. Ruthie had legendary status in a city that treasures people far, far outside the mainstream, sort of an inadvertent tourist attraction.

The more famous Greenwood resident is John Kennedy Toole. He resides on Latanier Row between Magnolia and Hawthorne. The most prominent name on the grave is Ducoing, his mother's maiden name. John wrote *A Confederacy of Dunces*, considered THE quintessential New Orleans Novel. The work details the misadventures of protagonist Ignatius J. Reilly, a lazy, obese, misanthropic, self-styled scholar who lives at home with his mother. All of these descriptions applied quite well to Toole himself.

Odd Fellows Rest Cemetery 5055 Canal St.

I hesitate to write this next cemetery entry, but there's also a for-those-in-the-know cemetery gate (I know its name, but dare not write it down). It serves as a portal to the dead. They say just to talk about the accursed cemetery gates spells doom to those who speak of it openly.

However, if you're an Odd Fellow walking down the widest street in America, you just might find it. Speak the name of the deceased loved one five times (or two more than Beetlejuice) through the bars, and they will come and speak to you from the other side. One warning though: If the rusted shut gate creaks open, do not enter. You will be trapped in the world between the living and the dead forevermore. If you arrive and the gates are already open, immediately turn and walk away (quickly) crossing yourself three times, maybe toss in a few Hail Mary's, and for heaven's sake, don't look back.

Holt Cemetery 635 City Park Ave.

This is New Orleans most eccentric, anything-goes cemetery. Originally it was a Potter's Field, or indigent cemetery for those who couldn't afford otherwise. The graves are mostly underground with some Coping graves, which are slightly aboveground memorials with boxed frames made from stone, brick, or plaster (in one case plastic plumbing tubes), and filled with earth, covering the remains.

There are two tributes to Buddy Bolden here, but no known site of his actual grave. While you won't be finding Buddy's grave, you will find a bizarre landscape of stuffed animals; Home Depot-quality statues of Mary, St. Francis, and singing cherubs; plastic flowers; and carpet remnants. Miss Thelma Lowe has a coveted Zulu coconut on her grave. There's a sea of wonderful hand-carved headstones with hand-written names, some in magic marker, others in broken plate mosaics. Emily Lorraine's headstone details she died in 2004, and she was "BONE" June 20th, 1947.

St. Roch Cemetery 1725 St. Roch Ave.

In 1867, Father Peter Leonard Thevis arrived from Germany to minister to the neighborhood's largely German parish. This was the time of a Yellow Fever outbreak. There were over 3,000 deaths the year before. Father Pete gathered his congregation and announced that they would pray to St. Roch, the patron saint of dogs, plague and pestilence, in order to intercede on their behalf. When not one parishioner contracted the disease, he began raising money to build a shrine to St. Roch, completed in August 1876. The grotto to the right of the altar, called The Healing Room, has become one of the coolest, if lesser-known, spots in New Orleans. The small room is filled with tokens of thanks: plaques, abandoned leg braces, crutches, and plaster or cement statues of a previously afflicted body parts; hands, hearts, brains, ears, and eyeballs healed through prayer at St. Roch's. Bring your camera and, if you're suffering with a hangover, may I suggest a plaster cast of your brain?

Mount Olivet Cemetery 4000 Norman Mayer Ave.

Only visitors on a pilgrimage come to this cemetery, located in the Gently neighborhood. The cemetery will be surrounded by the fewest points of interest, though there is a McKenzie's Chicken in a Box nearby.

Still, many make the journey to honor Henry Roeland "Roy" Byrd, better known to the world as Professor Longhair. Cemetery employees say he gets three to five visitors every day. Mount Olivet is also the final resting place of musicians Shirley & Lee, former teen Doo Wop stars, and rapper Soulja Slim.

Funerals/Second Line

If you're lucky (and some other poor soul is unlucky), you will get to experience a "real" second line. Second line processions have been called the "quintessential New Orleans art form." As with many New Orleans customs, the origins are rooted in West Africa. During a traditional African circle dance, adults formed the inner circle and children assembled on the periphery. In the New Orleans style, the family of the deceased forms the first line. The second line are friends, more distant relatives, and plenty of room for people who didn't even know the deceased but want to join the party.

The first known funeral that featured an African-American second line in New Orleans was in 1863 for Captain Andre Cailloux, who was killed during the Battle of Port Hudson. Over 10,000 African-Americans turned out for his funeral.

Brass bands accompany funeral party from church to gravesite, playing traditional slow spiritual dirges and hymns like "Just a Closer Walk with Thee" and "Amazing Grace." Leaving the cemetery, however, becomes a completely different tune. Handkerchiefs carried for sobbing and grief become a sashaying flag. Umbrellas used as protection from intense sun or rain become a festively twirling joystick. The music kicks up to New Orleans style. "Some people call it funk," notes Big Chief Jake Millon in a 1976 documentary *Black Indians of New Orleans*, "but to us it's

St. Roch Cemetery

LUMINS OF NEW ORLEANS:
The Psychic & The Scream Queen

I once moderated a panel at the Words & Music Festival where I invited fellow speakers Chris Melancon, founder of the New Orleans Paranormal Society; Cari Roy, the #1 rated psychic in America; and Geretta Geretta, rated the #9 sexiest scream queen ever by *Playboy* magazine. One of my great delights has been to witness, via Facebook posts, how Cari Roy and Geretta Geretta have become inseparable BFFs since meeting for the first time that day. They have been invited to events where their presence makes it more eventful.

Physically, they couldn't be more different. Cari, a New Orleans native, is a petit, voluptuous blonde. Geretta, who was born and raised near Portland, Oregon, then passed through Los Angeles, New York, Ireland, South Africa, Switzerland, and Italy, is a tall, slender black woman.

Cari is sort of our Emeril Lagasse or Fats Domino of clairvoyants. To visit her, you enter The Exchange Centre, an innocuous twenty-one-story, 84,000-square-foot office building in the Central Business District. Her office feels about as mystical as visiting a financial planner or marriage counselor. Cari insists there's nothing unusual about her gifts, that everyone has them. She's just better plugged into the psychic realm, the way other people run faster or are better at math. Her readings are not intended as shock and awe experiences, but rather as opportunities to provide psychic and medium information and to give clarity, positive direction, and peace of mind. Her clients have referred to their readings as "a massage for the soul" and "better than a Valium."

Cari was always predisposed toward psychic work, as her grandfather had been a numerologist and astrologist and her mother was a psychic medium. Her first hints that she had psychic gifts came when she was 7 years old. She would catch glimpses of apparitions or spirits at the base of her bed. The same year, a man approached her when she and her mother were shopping at a department store. This was an era, now gone, when parents felt safe leaving their children alone as they browsed a different department. The man came up to Cari and asked if she wanted to see his watch. When she later described the man and his watch in detail, her mother knew exactly who had approached the young girl: a relative for whom his watch was his prized possession—and who died years earlier.

Once confirmed she had psychic gifts, Cari said the most important thing her mother taught her was how to turn it off. Not only would it be exhausting to receive a constant flow of messages and images from "the other side," but, in controlling her gifts, she can also turn it on and be more intensely present and focused when doing actual readings.

Cari does pure psychic readings, meaning she doesn't use Tarot cards, palmistry, nor crystal balls. It's not that she discredits these as props, but she does feel they give the reader an "out" or the ability to back away from full responsibility for their reading, saying, "Well, that's what the cards said." She feels that "ultimately the psychic buck stops with me and the accuracy or not of the reading is mine."

She's been featured in several documentaries filmed in New Orleans, appeared in A&E's *Haunted Houses—Tortured Souls and Restless Spirits,* The Travel Channel's *America's Most Terrifying Places*, ISPR's *New Orleans—Rich and Haunted*, on *The Today Show*, and in Creative Health & Spirit Film's *The Many Faces Of Psychic Ability.* TravelChannel.com named her "New Orleans most renowned psychic and New Orleans best psychic to see."

Her customer base is a wildly divergent mix, from investment bankers trying to supplement their market research, to a group of gangbangers who, quite frankly, scared the bejesus out of Cari. They showed up wanting her to contact a murdered fellow gang member so they could identify his shooter.

As a top psychic, Cari is consistently spot-on in her readings and predictions, but she does not claim infallibility. She says that if a psychic claims 100 percent accuracy, you should run like hell. Even New Orleans' best chefs like Susan Spicer have off nights. Drew Brees does, on rare occasion, throw three interceptions in a game.

Geretta Geretta, the Scream Queen, is an actress, director, screenwriter, and producer who has an MFA in screenwriting from the American Film Institute. She's the author of one book of poetry, *Pardon Me While I Eat My Young*, and is currently working on a memoir, tentatively titled *I Was Young and Needed the Money*.

She has starred in such classic Italian horror films as Lucio Fulci's *Murder Rock*, Bruno Mattei's *Rats: Night of Terror* and Lamberto Bava's *Dèmoni*. At horror and film cons, she is as mobbed by the horror movie cognoscenti as William Shatner would be at *Star Trek* conventions.

Beyond acting, Geretta has been awarded Best Female Director in the Melbourne Underground Film Festival and Action On Film Festival. When I last sat down with her, Geretta was in town as the host for the New Orleans Horror Film Festival and just about to embark on a ten-city circuit of other horror film fests. Best of all, she has been recreated as a collectible polyresin bobble head Demon Doll that spews green vomit, with a suggested retail of $40.

Geretta grew up in a town so white that if you were a black male, a stranger's first question might be, "What position do you play?" She'd visited New Orleans four or five times prior to living here, drawn in by both the city's rich black culture and the overwhelming gregariousness of the people who live here.

She came here on a permanent basis after a painful breakup. She brought only her French Bulldog, named Poupon, and a Louis Vuitton suitcase. She later had to sell the suitcase to make ends meet.

At the time of my writing, Geretta and Cari are filming and editing a pitch for a TV series. As Cari notes, "It's crazy there's never been a paranormal show based in New Orleans." This odd pairing is looking to launch *The Psychic & the Scream Queen*. It would be an eerie equivalent of tag-team TV shows like the old Siskel & Ebert, Regis & Kathie Lee, or ESPN's *First Take*, only their format would focus on other worldly experiences rather than movies, sports. or topical chit chat. With Geretta as the chit, usually dressed in her ever-present kitty-kat ears and tail, and Cari as the chat, who might suddenly spot a spirit jumping on screen as an extra without a SAG card, this will be no "normal" TV show.

strictly second line." Classic songs for the second line leaving the cemetery, include "Hey Pocky-a-Way," the 1960s Dixie Cups hit, "Jock-a-Mo," and the newish (1990s) but seemingly timeless anthem of Rebirth Brass Band, "Do Whatcha Wanna."

It's basically a frenzied celebration for the life that was and thank God you got to participate with them when they walked the earth. To me, that's the right way to go out.

Historically, second lines occurred in the predominantly African-American neighborhoods of Treme and Central City. But today, they can be pretty much seen all over the city, and not just for funerals. There are second lines staged for weddings, sometimes a store opening, and can be seen cutting through the Fairgrounds during Jazz Fest.

I am less a fan of second line parades that don't include a dead body. Many 'crafted' parades are hired out by event planners so conventioneers from Cleveland and Charlotte can stiffly shuffle from their hotel lobby out to Canal Street waving hankies like they're having a stroke and trying to hail an EMS vehicle. (I probably just lost 390,000 potential buyers from Cleveland.) There's a whiff of something very Vanilla Ice or Milli Vanilli about the whole concocted-for-tourists second line thing.

There is a more recent burial style in New Orleans where I am delighted by the weirdness of it but, I confess, I'm not quite "down with" the actual practice. New Orleans being New Orleans, and committed to the philosophy "anything worth doing is worth overdoing," now takes twenty-first-century preparation of dead bodies to the next level, pushing the envelope, literally, out of the box.

When beloved musician Uncle Lionel Batiste died in 2012, the hundreds of people attending his funeral received a surprise greeting. Said one attendee, "They've even got his watch on the mannequin's hand," referring to the life-like figure standing in the funeral home's chapel. But it wasn't a mannequin, noted another. "That's him."

Several of Mr. Batiste's children, in consultation with Louis Charbonnet, owner of Charbonnet-Labat-Glapion Funeral Home, concocted the idea of standing him up for his wake. During his fifty years in the funeral business, Charbonnet had never before embalmed a body in a lifelike pose. The deceased Mr. Batiste was presented standing up against a faux street lamp, decked out in his signature man-about-town finery. Uncle Lionel's body, in his habitual-in-life sunglasses, wore a cream-colored suit, tasseled loafers, an ornate necktie with matching pocket square, and bowler hat. His bass drum and his Treme Brass Band uniform were positioned nearby. His hands rested atop his omnipresent cane. The gold watch draped across his left palm rather than on his wrist was his trademark, representing his desire to always have "time on my hands." "That's something I've never seen before," said Charbonnet, "It's perfect. It's a wonderful, strange thing."

Not quite two years later, philanthropist, socialite, and legendary party hostess Mickey Easterling went out in the larger than life, or larger than death, fashion in which she lived. More than a thousand people attended her memorial service at the Saenger Theater. Mickey was presented casually perched on a wrought-iron garden bench. To her right sat a bottle of her favorite Champagne, Veuve Clicquot, and in her hand was a Waterford crystal champagne flute she used to carry around when restaurant glassware just wouldn't do. Mickey was dressed in her famous accouterments: a Leonardo outfit, large floral hat, feather boa, and cigarette holder. Her dead body wore her favorite diamond pin, spelling out "B-I-T-C-H."

In June 2014, diorama funerals crossed over from noted musicians and socialites to mainstream, when everyday people like Miriam "Mae-Mae" Burbanks were given the Charbonnet Funeral Home treatment. She was memorialized with a "last party," sitting at a fold-up table, wearing a Saints jersey, holding a menthol cigarette and a can of beer.

Not to say that New Orleans has the monopoly on bizarre practices with dead bodies. The Torajan people of the Sulawesi island in Indonesia proudly honor their dead relatives by digging them up every three years, dusting them off, dressing them in a new set of clothes, parading them around town, and then posing the bodies for portraits with living family members. As the grand kids get taller in each portrait, grammy's nose, ears, or fingers have fallen off. The ancient festival is known as Ma'nene.

For a boy grow'd up in Ohio and not named Jeffrey Dahmer, I find that just kind of creepy.

CHAPTER 5

Shopping

You Came to New Orleans,
and All You Got Was a Lousy T-Shirt?

We're rapidly approaching a world comprised entirely of jail and shopping.

—Douglas Coupland

A part of me wants to skip this chapter entirely because while many visitors do come to scarf up cheaply made Mardi Gras masks, dried-out alligator heads, and matching T-shirts printed "Drunk 1" and "Drunk 2," shopping for stuff seems antithetical to the spirit of New Orleans . . . with a few exceptions.

There is a shop on Roman Street in Central City with a hand painted sign reading "Undertaker, Grave Digger, & Mike's Auto Repair." That's quintessentially multi-purposed New Orleans, like a Turducken (a local dish that's a chicken inside a duck inside a turkey).

After you visit New Orleans, trust me, you will never, not once, wear that T-shirt printed "I Got Bourbon Faced on Shit Street." Those Mardi Gras beads will probably sit in your garage for a year or two until you throw them out. New Orleans is about collecting experiences, not things.

This chapter is the most likely to become outdated by the time the book hits bookstore shelves. Nothing turns faster than shops opening and closing. I find today's French Quarter almost unrecognizable from 10 years ago. Sadly, many of the buildings are being bought by outsiders and foreign investors who raise the rent over 100 percent. Shops selling nothing but Fabergé boxes or walking canes will forever be slow-turning inventory. The higher rents are driving out unique boutiques and replacing them with touristy shops stuffed with fast-selling but cheaply made collectibles.

To me, the French Quarter is a bit less interesting than when I first started haunting New Orleans. Fortunately, Uptown, Mid-City, and Bywater have developed such that in the end, I think the city is as inviting and magical as ever.

I highlight roughly fifty shops. Hopefully, most will still be in business if you seek them out.

We do have our shopping malls, but there are two in the entire city, and we have just one Walmart. There are Starbucks in New Orleans, just not one on every corner. The Shops on Canal Place is an upscale mall with stores like Saks Fifth Avenue, Anthropologie, and a movie theater where you sit in high backed plush leather motorized recliners, with a call button to ring for a glass of wine or a small plate from the in-lobby restaurant, Gusto. The highlight of Canal Place is the effervescent concierge, Tara Schroeder, who's also a licensed tour guide.

There is also The Outlet Collection at Riverwalk, the only outlet mall in America set inside a city. All other outlet malls tend to be an hour or so outside a city, sitting on paved-over former pumpkin patches and corn mazes. The Outlet Collection is a six-block corridor of Neiman Marcus, Coach Leather, Fossil, Forever 21, Tommy Bahama stores, all at bargain prices and all lined up like an endless airport concourse of shoppes.

On the following pages, I list some of our more unique shops, organized by neighborhood.

French Quarter

A Gallery for Fine Photography 241 Chartres St.

This is a two-story store filled with prints, books, and ongoing exhibits that definitely favor the artful and eclectic over collections of LIFE magazine's best shots or William Wegman's Weimaraner dogs. Here you can find the work of New Orleans greats like Fonville Winans to international aberrants like Joel-Peter Witkin. For years they had, and may still have, one of the only 10,000 copies printed of Helmut Newton's *SUMO*. It is the biggest (66 pounds) and most expensive ($15,000) book produced in the 20th century.

Bottom of the Cup 327 Chartres St.

This is the oldest (1929) and premier psychic reading shop in the city. It is presented in much greater detail in the Exploring chapter.

Boutique du Vampyre 709 ¹/₂ St Ann St.

New Orleans has a long history of vampires, and may in fact be the vampire capital of America. Therefore, it's hardly surprising New Orleans also has the only brick and mortar vampire shop in America, and only one of three in the world. Boutique du

Vampyre was created and is run by Marita Jaeger, another in a long line of visitors seduced by New Orleans. "When I first came here (from Munich, Germany), I fell in love with the city and never left."

Her shop is mostly filled with one of a kind treasures made by one of the 130 local artisans she uses. Here you can buy candles, pewter charms, handmade paper, leather journals, vampire perfume made by Hove, a 100-year-old perfumer on Chartres Street, hot sauce from Transylvania, Louisiana, Vamp N.R.G—the "energy drink for when the sun goes down"—and a decorated Vampire Lesson Box. A Lesson Box is $65 worth of wisdom from elders who have lived for centuries. Marita warns that Vampire Lesson Boxes cannot be re-gifted.

Noted fangsmith (one who makes fangs as their trade), Maven Lore will meet you in the shop by appointment and make you custom fangs using premium dental equipment, style, and color matching your teeth, and then bond them onto your teeth. Yes, I wrote "bond." The price range for fangs is from $100 to $800.

The Brass Monkey 407 Royal St.

The shop is sort of a catch-all of somewhat pricey curiosities. The shelves present an extensive group of French Limoges boxes, Halcyon days enamels, antique walking sticks all with elaborate and one-of-a-kind handles, medical instruments, and French and English antique reproductions.

Faulkner House Books 624 Pirates Alley

Unlike many cities, where Barnes & Noble or Amazon dominate book sales, New Orleans still has a number of quality independent bookstores. I choose to highlight Faulkner House Books over the excellent Octavia Books in Uptown, Garden District Book Shop, and Blue Cypress Books, because of its historic setting. This is where William Faulkner lived and wrote *Soldier's Pay* and *Mosquitos*. The store is tiny, no bigger than the Pets & Nature section in a chain store. But each book has been carefully curated by the charming owner, Joe DeSalvo.

Fifi Mahony's 934 Royal St.

Fifi Mahony's is a New Orleans take on the Ricky's mini-chain in New York City and Miami or Claire's in malls across country. Only rather than too-bright make-up and too-cheap jewelry, Fifi's has their own line of cosmetics accompanied by glittery mini top hats, feathers flowing everywhere, and what they're best known for: wigs. There are usually close to 100 styles on display, from ready-to-wear wigs to ones adorned with fake flowers or unicorn horns all the way to wigs with Christmas scenes embedded in the hair or plastic surfers riding the waves of seafoam blue-green hair.

Frank Relle Photography 910 Royal St.

Relle's own gallery opened relatively recently in April 2016. New Orleans has numerous outstanding photographers. Rick Olivier, Marc Pagani, and Ryan Hodgson-Rigsbee are excellent photographers who have brought my books to life. Cheryl Gerber and Richard Sexton did their own stunning books, *New Orleans: Life and Death in the Big Easy* and *Creole World* respectively.

Frank Relle's haunting images have been featured in the collections of the Smithsonian Museum of American History, the New Orleans Museum of Art and the Museum of Fine Arts Houston and in the private collections of Wynton Marsalis, Brad Pitt and Angelina Jolie, Ellen DeGeneres, Drew Brees, Sheryl Crow, and Kanye West. We'll forgive him that last one.

The French Market N. Peters St.

The market has been there since 1791. There are over 250 vendors in the two-block open air market. But, if you come anticipating the Paris Flea Market, you will be hugely disappointed. It's mostly T-shirts, sunglasses, and junk jewelry.

Greg's Antiques and Other Assorted Junk
1209 Decatur St.

The antique stores that used to line Chartres and Royal Streets have been greatly reduced in number. My favorite antique store in the city, Bush Antiques, closed their doors on Magazine Street years ago. Greg's Antiques is newer than most. Greg came to New Orleans to photograph the devastation after Hurricane Katrina. His shop is more eclectic than all other antique dealers. In addition to the European furniture for which they are known, Greg's Antiques sells wonderful junk: taxidermy animal heads, dented musical instruments, kimonos, and vintage product signs, all presented in a wonderfully haphazard way. Plus, Greg's also rents bikes.

Hové Parfumeur 434 Chartres St.

Mrs. Alvin Hovey-King spent much of her life traveling around the world and expanding her love of making her own perfume, a craft learned from her Creole French mother. Her hobby grew into a full-time retail shop in 1931. Hove's crafted perfumes are sold in their standard line and premier line of scents. Neither are priced to be impulse buys. The standard perfumes are $87 per ounce. The premier line is $112 per ounce.

James H. Cohen & Sons 437 Royal St.

Opened in 1898, Cohen & Sons is the oldest family-owned store in the United States. It started out as a vintage emporium that evolved to focus on weaponry and coins under the care of son Jimmie Cohen. Jimmie made his mark as a numismatic superstar when he obtained and sold a Confederate half-dollar, one of only four ever minted. Today, grandsons Jerry and Steve run the store and can give you a PhD thesis-level description of any coin, gun, or sword in the shop.

Krewe du Optic 809 Royal St.

Stirling Barrett founded his company in 2013. He is a New Orleans native and creative entrepreneur. The company's website states, "Our team passionately believes in spreading the culture of New Orleans and its celebration of individual style, one frame at a time." They make creative one-of-a-kind glasses—as in the objects that help you see, not glasses that help you get inebriated.

Nadine Blake 1036 Royal St.

Owners Nadine and Simon Blake were living in New York but making frequent trips to New Orleans. During one visit, while sitting at the Napoleon House and swooning over the vast collection of characters coming through the door, Simon said, "I want to live here one day." Their shop, born out of a love of decoration, travel, and collecting, offers a stylish mix of new and vintage furniture and home accessories, artwork, books, stationary, pajamas, jewelry, and a melange of urbane goods.

The New Orleans Historic Collection 533 Royal St.

Here is a museum, research center, and publisher dedicated to preserving the history and culture of New Orleans. The institution was founded in 1966 by General L. Kemper Williams and Leila Hardie Moore Williams. Both were collectors who wished to share their holdings with the public. You can take tours and view their rotating exhibits, but they are listed here because they have a very cool gift shop, selling all things New Orleans, including prints, maps, books, jewelry, ties, scarves, and Christmas ornaments. Another special treat is staff member Aine Branch. On her own time, Aine is an eclectic fashion designer and owner of/enthusiastic ambassador for Pug dogs.

Trashy Diva 537 Royal St.

Candice Gwinn moved to New Orleans in 1996, escaping from suburban Atlanta with a bag of vintage clothes and $5,000. She opened Trashy Diva with a partner in a shoebox-sized shop on Decatur Street. Today, there are five Trashy Diva stores located throughout New Orleans, including two dress stores, two lingerie stores (712 Royal St. in the French Quarter), and a shoe store (2050 Magazine St.). Candice has built Trashy Diva into a brand, selling jewelry and high-end styles from the 1940s and 50s, plus her own original designs.

Bywater and The Marigny

Antenna Gallery 3718 St. Claude

New Orleans art district has shifted from Royal Street in the French Quarter to Julia Street in the Warehouse District. There are additionally some very cool galleries in other parts of town. I list here two from Bywater and the Marigny area, collectively called SCAD (St Claude Arts District). Antenna was founded in 2008 by Press Street, a nonprofit dedicated to stimulating art and literature. They have hosted a variety of shows they've called "an array of risk-taking solo and group exhibitions that engage and interact with the New Orleans community." One collective was named *My Mom Says My Work Has Really Improved*, which displayed their grade school art next to their current work. Monu-MENTAL was another where artists created imaginative revisions to actual local statues and monuments. A personal favorite was where an artist had removed the engines from cars and made gizmos out of them, so that when you sat in the car, somehow shoehorned inside the gallery, and turned the wheel, the car would draw self-portraits. Not exactly something you'd bring back on the plane.

Barrister's Gallery, Inc. 2331 St Claude Ave.

Owner and rodelliur Andy Antippas says he specializes in ethnographic and contemporary Louisiana folk and fine artists. More to the point of his eccentric tastes, Andy has claimed to feature artists "so far removed from the mainstream that the term 'outsider art' doesn't even begin to describe their current location in space and time." Shows have carried names like *I Wish I Were Dead, Artists Who Wish They Were Dead II*, and *I'm Running Out of Coffee and It Smells Like Onions*.

The Bargain Center 3200 Dauphine St.

The store is a large (10,000 square feet large) fantasyland for thrift store aficionados. They have heaps of all manner of stuff: vintage clothing, costume jewelry, doll parts, vinyl records, old Mardi Gras outfits, and a massive collection of Mexican art (mostly relating to Day of the Dead), plus brightly colored Mexican oil cloth that you can buy by the yard.

Dr. Bob's Studio 3027 Chartres St.

Bob Shaffer, a.k.a. Dr. Bob, is a dumpster diving, self-taught artist/sign painter whose work may be the most seen all over New Orleans. His "Be Nice or Leave" paintings can be spotted in most restaurants, bars, and gift shops around town. His very first Be Nice sign was created to keep people passing by his sculpture studio from bothering him while he worked. He transformed a former mule barn into his disheveled open-air studio. Finished pieces and works-in-progress are stacked everywhere. Dr. Bob's now sells over 2,000 of his signed paintings every year. They have been shown in galleries across the country and inside the Smithsonian Museum.

Dynamo: A Romantic Boutique in the Deep South 2001 St. Claude Ave.

Dynamo is an independent, female-run, female-friendly romantic boutique (i.e. a sex shop not frequented by creepy old men in soiled trench coats). Their website claims, "We strive to promote happy, healthy sexuality through education, community outreach, and high-quality, body-safe products." In addition to a great variety of lubricants, vibrators, and dildos, they have things like Energie Kegel Bars and Luna Beads whose purpose is nothing I know nor can even imagine. Proprietor Hope Kodman is also a licensed and delightful tour guide for French Quarter Phantoms.

Euclid Records 3301 Chartres St.

Euclid is "the other" music store in New Orleans. Louisiana Music Factory (two entries from now) is our premier shop. But being #2 in a city as music-based as New Orleans is still a high honor. The original and flagship Euclid Records store has been operating in St. Louis, Missouri, for more than 30 years. Owner Joe Schwab said he chose to open his first satellite store in New Orleans because "there are four cities in America that really support local music; Austin, Seattle, Portland, and New Orleans. Austin has enough record stores, and Seattle and Portland are just a little too far away." Their newest location is directly next to New Orleans' best pizza parlor, Pizza Delicious. As said by store manager, James Weber, "Records are round. Pizzas are round. It's almost too perfect." Euclid Records is particularly revered for the extensive vinyl collection. They also sell music-related books and ultra cool old concert posters.

Frenchmen Art Market 619 Frenchmen St.

Thursday through Monday, in a large alley in the midst of the music clubs on Frenchmen, there is an art market from 7:00 p.m. to 1:00 a.m., lit by strung lights. The market sells jewelry, photographs, paintings, fabrics, and other arts, all by locals. Word of warning: don't take pictures. The artists will jump on you like you left dog poop in their front yard.

Louisiana Music Factory 421 Frenchmen St.

Barry Smith, one-time booking agent for Tipitina's with an MBA from Loyola, and Jerry Brock, a former petroleum engineer who co-founded WWOZ radio, met working as overqualified clerks at Record Ron's. Rather than talking about the latest Jim Jarmusch film or arguing the merits of Jeff Beck versus Jimmy Page, like most record store clerks, they instead concocted a plan to open their own store. The Louisiana Music Factory has become one of the most respected record stores in the country and one of the hubs in the New Orleans music scene. They have moved for a third time in 2014, and are now housed amidst the music clubs lining Frenchmen Street. The store has an extensive stock of indigenous music: jazz, blues, zydeco, cajun, swamp pop, brass band, on both CDs and vinyl. There are many listening stations in the store and exceptionally knowledgeable clerks, some of whom have worked there since the Earth cooled.

The Central Business District and Warehouse District

Julia Street Art Galleries

This has become the hub for art galleries the same way Frenchmen has become our live music street. It's been nicknamed "Gallery Row," and is a five-block stretch of renovated warehouses turned into sleek art galleries. There are nineteen, yes nineteen, galleries grouped along six blocks. You can make a night of it the first Saturday each month when the galleries are open 6:00 to 9:00 p.m. The event on the first Saturdays has been creatively named *First Saturday*.

Meyer the Hatter 120 St. Charles Ave.

One block outside the French Quarter in the CBD is Meyer's Hat Store. It opened in 1894, more than a century before hipsters started wearing fedoras and pork pie hats again. It is both the oldest and the largest hat store in the South.

Paul, the great-grandson of the original owner, runs the shop today. He took over the business when his dad, Mister Sam, retired at 90-something years old. Mister Sam still comes to work every day. "I wasn't brought up to chase balls on a golf course or putter in the garden," he explains. Paul's brother and two sons also work at the store. The result is a shop filled with family banter and congenial complaining.

Hats are everywhere: stacked three and four high on counters, dangling from random hooks, and tucked inside the many towers of shipping cartons that clog the long, narrow aisles. Straw hats from Ecuador are joined by berets from France, bowlers from England, an Italian straw boater if you want to look like a gondolier, or the yet-to-be-sold cherry-red beaver-fur homburg.

The Meyer clan will give you lessons in hat etiquette (never pinch a hat) and expert advice on what style best fits your face. With their reputation and vast inventory, it is not surprising that Meyer the Hatter is the go-to store in New Orleans for costume designers and in-town film companies in search of the perfect hat to complete a character's look. Notes Mister Sam, "You don't look at John Wayne's shoes."

Mid-City

F & F Botanica Spiritual Supply 801 N. Broad St.

Highlighted in the Creeping Around chapter, I will simply reiterate here that it is a legitimate voodoo store, very much unlike the made-in-China ones that litter the French Quarter.

Kitchen Witch Cookbooks 1452 N. Broad St.

The incredible Debbie Lindsey and Philipe LaMancusa are victims of rising rents in the French Quarter. While the new Mid-City location is not as convenient for visitors, it is totally worth the trip. There are vintage and first edition cookbooks, as well as more current ones, and they will forever have hardcover copies of *A Confederacy of Dunces* on hand. The eccentric layout of the store has little altars everywhere. If you leave with nothing, the conversations you'll have with Debbie and Philipe are worth your cab or Uber fare.

Le Sex Shoppe 4901 Canal St.

Le Sex Shoppe is a pop-up (careful now) sex shop located inside Vapors. The buoyant manager, J. J. Jenkins, says their best sellers are sexual stimulants, glycerin-based lubes, and bondage paraben-free devices such as the happy kitten rope, made of jute, hemp, and cotton and made by New Orleans-based businesses. Buy, bond, and lube local!

NOLA Til Ya Die 3536 Toulouse St.

Joining The Big Easy, The Crescent City, and The City That Care Forgot, the term NOLA has taken over as one of New Orleans' top nicknames. It simply means "New Orleans Louisiana."

Before Hurricane Katrina, there were 134 local businesses registered using the name NOLA. Today, there are over 1,750. NOLA Til Ya Die is located in a large warehouse nestled between the post office and the Mid-City Theater.

They sell mostly clothing: T-shirts, tank tops, hoodies, caps, scarves, bandanas, and pet ware using their distinctive logo, but they also have buttons, bags, tea cozies, stickers, decals, magnets, flags, glasses, candles, back packs, bottle openers, beach towels, temporary tattoos—pretty much every and any way you can show your fierce loyalty to New Orleans. My car has several NOLA Til Ya Die stickers. I bought NOLA Til Ya Die dog tags for my whole family. The back side of the tag reads, "If found, return to NOLA."

Ricca's Architectural Sales 511 N. Solomon St.

Peter Ricca could be considered Mr. Wreck-It of New Orleans. His company demolished more than fourteen blocks of commercial buildings to make way for the widening of Poydras Street in the 1960s. He also razed the former public library at Lee Circle, plus a few seen-better-days mansions along St. Charles Avenue, the Holy Family Convent on Orleans Street, the Soniat Memorial at the old Mercy Hospital on Annunciation Street, the New Orleans Home for Incurables on Henry Clay Avenue, and maybe most famously, the Higgins Industries plant on City Park Avenue, where the PT boats used at Normandy Beach on D-Day were designed and built.

But he wasn't just a wrecker. Ricca's company is, as their slogan states, "Working to Preserve New Orleans' Architectural Heritage." Since 1956, Ricca's has saved much of what they tore down in a small warehouse in the backstreets of Mid-City. On display and up for sale is a treasure trove of salvaged architectural goods. They have a huge selection of oversized doors, vintage lighting, antique wrought-iron fountains, garden benches, claw-foot tubs, old and intricately designed metal gates and fences, door knockers, glass and crystal doorknobs, plus the iron horse-head posts you'll see around the city. You can even find refurbished skeleton-key locks. If you've been looking "forever" for hard-to-find and no-longer-produced hinges or bolts, Ricca's probably has them.

Central City

Cleaver & Co. 3917 Baronne St.

Arguments can break out deciding the best place to eat meat in New Orleans. Cleaver & Co. wins hands down as the best place to buy it—at least if you can find it. Tucked on a less-traveled street in Central City, on blocks that look hungry for gentrification, the artisan butcher is a hidden treasure for carnivores.

Cleaver & Co. sells virtually every cut of meat you'd find in any grocery store, plus many you never would. More exotic meats include Nduja, a spicy Calabrian (Italian) version of Andouille (Nduja can be described as spreadable salami); Basterma, a spiced and dried beef from the Eastern Mediterranean, shaved or sliced thin; Linguiça, a Portuguese smoked pork sausage with paprika, garlic, and coriander; Matambre, an Argentinian preparation of beef filled and rolled with hard-boiled eggs, mushrooms, and vegetables; and Merguez, a spicy Moroccan sausage of lamb and/or goat mixed with Moscato, paprika, anise, and other spices.

Their selection changes each day, depending on what they can source freshest from local and sustainable farms. More often than not, Cleaver & Co. will have cracklin' and cracklin' butter, marrow butter, tubs of duck fat, and the best beef jerky you've ever tasted. We usually buy two bags of jerky because the first bag won't survive our 10-minute drive home.

The service by the bearded staff (are all butchers men with big beards?) is friendly, casual, and can be hugely informative if you're up for mini meat lectures.

Cleaver & Co. also teaches classes in butchering and sausage making. But, what puts them over the top is their piece de resistance, the WHOLE ANIMAL CARD. For a bargain price, you can buy a frequent shopper hole punch card that, by the time you've had all holes punched, you will have eaten an entire cow or pig, gland meats and all.

Garden District

Magazine Street

Magazine Street, running along the Riverside base of the Garden District (and beyond), stretches for 6 miles of shops, galleries, salons, and restaurants. The stretch is an utter hodgepodge, where an upscale jeweler will be next door to a shoe repair shop next to a four-star restaurant next to a vintage clothing store that's more threadbare than trendy.

Before my wife and I lived here, we spotted a Necromancy Shop on Magazine Street. Assuming that "it can't really be that," we went inside. It was. We left rather quickly. Other than that shop, which is no longer in business, Magazine Street is where "we" locals prefer to shop. Our reasons are less about Magazine prices versus the French Quarter shops (they're still not that cheap) than for the ability to park the car without dropping $20 to $30 as you will in the Quarter.

In a city steeped in tradition, the shops on Magazine seem to change every week. We lost my favorite antique store in all New Orleans when Alaine Bush decided to close Bush Antiques. Magazine Street also lost Sputnik Ranch, run by husband & wife Gary and Debra Parky. Their store was a little slice of Western & Rockabilly heaven.

Listed below alphabetically, are some that remain (as I write).

Antiques on Jackson 1028 Jackson Ave.

The store is not on Magazine, but "just" off it by mere yards. The antiques gallery is run by Maria Hardeveld, sometimes called "Miss Chippy Peely" for her taste for well-worn (loved-up) pieces. In addition to great antiques, the gallery is also the studio home for her husband, the wonderfully eccentric Simon (pronounced See-Moan).

Simon is one of two New Orleans' great sign painting folk artists (along with Dr. Bob). He was trained as a chef in France. But after arriving in New Orleans, he discovered he had more customers for his hand-painted signs saying things like "Hamburgers $3" than for his actual food. His distinctive "naive art" signs painted with squiggles, starbursts, and a predominant "SIMON" can be seen in shops and restaurants all over the city, from Lola's in Bayou St. John to Slim Goodies in Uptown.

As You Like It 3033 Magazine St.

The store has heirloom and collectible silver pieces and settings. Their special and exclusive offering is shop owner, Duncan Cox, who is unassumingly the most knowledgeable silver authority you'll ever encounter.

Bootsy's Funrock'n 3109 Magazine St.

Thousands of vintage and retro iron-ons to customize your clothing, plus new kitschy and rediscovered older toys you loved as a kid. Exclusive home of The Battle of New Orleans & New Orleans "You Gotta Be Tough" T-shirts. This is our version of Chicago's Uncle Fun, Seattle's Archie McPhee, LA's Wacko's, or New York's . . . well, with the loss of Little Ricky's and Love Saves the Day, New York doesn't really have a counterpart anymore. Bootsy's has also opened a new location in the French Quarter (1125 Decatur St.).

Buffalo Exchange 4119 Magazine St.

It has been voted Best Vintage Clothing store by *Gambit Weekly*, *Where Y'At*, and *Best of NOLA*.

Fleurty Girl 3117 Magazine St.

Fleurty Girl is a New Orleans-inspired line of T-shirts, accessories, and other locally-made goods springing from the creative vision of NOLA native Lauren Thom. Lauren launched the original Fleurty Girl line in May 2009, using the money from her income tax return. Her original T-shirt line was just four different designs. Today there are three stores. In addition to Magazine Street, Lauren has a new location in the French Quarter (632 St. Peters) and at Lakeside Plaza in Metarie. Lauren can be seen all over the TV and in video loops in tourism centers as a spokesperson for New Orleans.

Funky Monkey 3127 Magazine St.

This pretty small store is jammed with a large assortment of new, used, and vintage-inspired clothing, plus custom-made T-shirts, handmade costumes, and quirky accessories for people who want to look East Village on a Bowery budget.

Sucré 3025 Magazine St.

While I consider Angelo Brocato's our best confectioner, Sucré's three locations, including their Magazine Street and their French Quarter spots (602 Conti) make them far more convenient for the traveler. Sucré is a sweet lover's emporium of everything sugar: gelato, chocolate, and what they do best, macarons. The confection shop also boasts of their ultimate: the All Things NOLA Sundae. It starts with a base of classic bread pudding made with yesterday's croissants and brioche and topped with butter-pecan gelato. Then on goes Bananas Foster sauce, with crystallized pecans and a drizzle of Steen's as the finishing touches.

LUMINS OF NEW ORLEANS:
Elizabeth Werlein

This particular Lumins of New Orleans could just as well be called Forgotten Forebears. Elizabeth Werlein is rarely mentioned in other guidebooks or broad histories of the city. Yet she played an essential role in making the New Orleans of today.

Elizabeth Werlein came to New Orleans from Detroit in 1908. Like so many others, she was completely seduced by the city. Unlike others, she completely saved the city. I have said to more than a few tour takers, if not for Elizabeth Werlein, of whom they've never heard, they might not be standing in front of me.

Elizabeth was strolling down Royal Street one day when she spotted a stucco California-style bungalow at 813 Royal Street. You can walk by it today. It's now painted light blue and currently sells movie posters.

Werlein was mortified because the architectural style was glaringly aberrant from anything else in the French Quarter. She'd been a long-time advocate for preservation. In 1910, she published a booklet entitled *The Wrought Iron Railings of Le Vieux Carré in New Orleans*. In her mind, this bungalow was hideously unacceptable, so she rallied all her

Uptown and Riverbend

Dirty Coast 5631 Magazine St.

This store, yet another—in this case, brilliant—New Orleans-themed T-shirt purveyor, was opened in October 2004 but became an institution a year later. After the flood, Dirty Coast launched a battery of stickers and T-shirts that captured the post Katrina spirit, with the slogans "Be a New Orleanian, Wherever You Are" and "Listen to Your City." The store now sells over eighty shirts designed by local artists, with 100 percent of them made by local companies. They also sell prints, books (including mine), and enameled pins of archetypal wealthy friends to join the existing preservation society. They helped establish the Vieux Carré Commission and tried to give it more teeth. Frustrated by what she considered to be the VCC's indifference, Werlein became the founding president of another neighborhood group called the Vieux Carré Property Owners Residents Association, or VCPORA. In that role, she twisted the ear of Mayor Robert Maestri to strengthen VCC regulations and increase police enforcement of quality-of-life issues.

The new VCC has control and oversight of exterior surfaces of all buildings in the French Quarter, including roofs, facades, and courtyards. They pushed through an ordinance that still stands today whereby owners of buildings in the Quarter can make no alterations, not even changing the color of their shutters, without permission from the VCC.

Back in the '30s, the area was becoming a slum. Even area residents viewed it more as old and dilapidated, rather than historic and charming. Had she not championed this cause, there's a very good chance there would be no French Quarter today. It would have been razed and replaced by a sea of monotonous steel and glass buildings. New Orleans would be just another Southern city, a Birmingham or Atlanta, only with higher humidity and periodic threats of hurricanes. Conventions like The Benevolent & Protective Order of ELKS (14,000 attendees), The American Society of Plastic Surgeons (7,000), and The Ancient Egyptian Arabic Order Nobles Mystic Shrine (hey, don't laugh, they bring 6,000 visitors) would have all chosen somewhere else to land.

Elizabeth was quite the feisty and fearless firebrand. In addition to saving the city, she became a licensed pilot and an accomplished soprano singer, was one of the first women to fly in an air balloon, the first president of the Louisiana's League of Women Voters, and was public relations director of the Saenger Theatre movie chain—much of this before women had the right to vote.

According to fellow preservationist Martha Gilmore Robinson, Werlein "inspired many creative and influential people with her drive and spirit."

New Orleans things like po'boys, shotgun houses, and shrimping boots. Their other location is at 2121 Chartres.

Hazelnut 5525 Magazine St.

The store's subtitle is "Fine Gifts and Elegant Home Accessories." It was created by actor and New Orleanian Brian Batt (best known for *Mad Men*) and his partner, Tom Cianfichi, and named after his grandmother, Hazel Nuss. They carry upscale ceramics from Bellezza White, Incanto, Lastra, Forma and Natura, several pieces of Vietri barware, plus books, frames, stemware, and their exclusive toile fabric using New Orleans settings.

International Vintage Guitars 3342 Magazine St.

Not shockingly, the store offers vintage, used, and new guitars, amps, effects, and accessories. They are authorized dealers for Fender guitars and Fender parts and accessories, and also sell guitars by Martin, Gretsch, Guild, National Resophonic, Jerry Jones, and Rickenbacker.

For over 20 years, Steve Staples has been the proprietor. In the 1960s, Staples played with New Orleans teenage psych garage-rockers The Gaunga Dyns. The store was designed to be similar in spirit to the music stores of yesteryear, where both young and established musicians can hang out, trade licks, and talk shop. Visiting musical royalty like Bruno Mars, Billy Gibbons of ZZ Top, and Richie Havens frequent the store when they're in town.

JeanTherapy 5505 Magazine St.

Of the many contemporary clothing stores on Magazine, I choose to highlight this one. Let's call it preordained. The store opened when brother and sister Steven and Vicki Adjmi experienced a "sign." On the same day, Vicki received a call that a storefront was becoming available in New Orleans, her brother Steven was walking down a street in New York's East Village and spotted a vintage T-shirt with the logo for their father's old store on Canal Street in New Orleans, The Jean Scene. They decided these convergent messages were calling upon them to open their own jeans store. Seven years and four locations later, their JeanTherapy store is full of upscale casual clothing, jeans, tops, and the softest Saints & Hornets T-shirts known to man. I have no idea what they use. Feels like cotton and silk's love child.

Mignon Faget 3801 Magazine St., also The Shops at Canal Place at 333 Canal St.

Mignon is New Orleans best-known jewelry designer. "I was born here and I've lived here all of my life," she says. "What is so beautiful about Louisiana comes out through my work. It is a mysterious place." Mignon's is driven to design jewelry derived from natural and architectural forms found in her native New Orleans. She's been doing so since 1969.

Miss Claudia Vintage Clothing & Costumes
4204 Magazine St.

The small but well-composed store has vintage clothing with a theatrical twist perfect for adult dress-up parties, like Halloween in most cities and any day in New Orleans.

Mushroom New Orleans 1037 Broadway St.

The historic music/head shop has served the Tulane students and the wider New Orleans market since the 1970s. Walking by the psychedelic mural to take the stairs to the second story, the feeling is more '60s. My flashback, while being there, had me wonder what ever happened to my knee-high lace-up fringed boots and purple bell-bottom pants with the white pinstripes.

Uptown Costume & Dancewear 4326 Magazine St.

If your appetite has been whetted by Miss Claudia, Uptown Costume is the five-course meal just down the street. Wigs, fangs, outfits, incredible plumed headdresses, face paint, shackles, diamond-studded brassieres, cat eye contacts—it's got pretty much anything you need. Uptown Costumes will be jam packed elbow to elbow near Halloween or Mardi Gras and merely crowded the rest of the year.

Perlis Clothing 6055 Magazine St.

I would normally skip over a clothing store as white bread and preppy as this one, but they get a get out of jail card for being a New Orleans-centric white bread preppy clothing store. Perils has offered high-end men's, ladies, and boy's clothing since 1939. They are known for the red crawfish embroidered on their shirts where a Lacoste gator or Ralph Lauren polo player most often resides.

CHAPTER 6

Bonking

Sex, Jugs, and Out of Control

New Orleans, like any sexual offender, can leave permanent scars.
—**Tom Robbins**

Pretty much every city will have stories of sexual indiscretion or scandal, most often involving a priest or an elected official with a "working girl" or a young boy. Here, we have a rich and colorful sexual history.

Our tale begins with the *fille à la cassette*, or casket girls. Young women were shipped from France and began arriving in New Orleans in 1727, nine years after the founding of the city. Their mission was to mate with the rough and ragged male population of trappers, traders, and other men who rarely bathed and never flossed after meals.

Antoine de la Mothe Cadillac, founder of Detroit and overseer of Louisiana for six years, described New Orleans male residents much in the way that Donald Trump described Mexican immigrants. Said Cadillac: "They are the very scum and refuse of Canada: ruffians, vagabonds, graceless profligates."

Casket Girls were kind of a cross between an arranged marriage and prostitution. The purpose was to seed and grow a native population. They were at least a step up from France's initial practice of shipping prisoners, bonded servants, and the criminally insane across the Atlantic to serve as the original settlers in La Nouvelle-Orléans. There was briefly a law enacted in France that anyone who could not show gainful employment for four days in a row was classified as indigent and packed on a ship headed toward New Orleans.

In addition to the virginal casket girls were the correctional girls. Between 1720 and 1750, France additionally shipped over women straight out of prison. There are some historians who believe the casket girls and correctional girls were one and the same, and the idea of the virginal girls with their coffin-style luggage was just a misnomer.

Plaçage is probably our most unique sexual practice. Whenever I want to point out just how different we are, I skip over jambalaya and second line parades and go straight to plaçage. Plaçage was a practice started in 1769 where white gentlemen of means would attend organized social events called Quadroon Balls. There they would meet young Creole women, who were paraded in front of them as potential mistresses. Quadroon literally means the women were one quarter black, though, the term quadroon was erroneously used to cover all mixed-race women. One could be as little as $1/64$th black and still be called a quadroon.

Until July 5, 1983, there was the one drop rule. You could appear as white as Olivia Newton-John, but if you were $1/64$th black, in the eyes of the law you were black. Certain clubs and dance halls had what was called the brown paper bag test. If your skin was darker than a grocery store brown paper bag, you were denied entrance. This led to the formation of the Autocrat Social and Pleasure Club (still located at 1725 St. Bernard Ave. today) where blacks could congregate, play poker, or do most whatever they wanted without harassment.

Back in the days of plaçage, lighter skin was considered more desirable. The Duke of Saxe-Weimar-Eisenach, when visiting New Orleans, attended a ball and came away saying he saw "the most beautiful women in the world."

The admission charge was $2, which at the time was not cheap and more like the cost of attending the opera or a Broadway play. The Quadroon Ball season began in October and ran until Ash Wednesday, what you might consider hunting season for rich white dudes trolling to hook up with their own bought-for version of Beyoncé or Halle Berry.

Miscegenation laws made it illegal for blacks and whites to marry. Though there is the story of one gentleman, visiting from the North, who became so enamored with a woman he met at an Quadroon Ball that he cut his forearm, then her finger, to mix their blood. That way, he could now say "I'm black and I'm proud" and, as a mixed blood couple, legally marry. This story is probably completely fabricated, but the relationships struck up at the balls were real and took on all the formality of a marriage. Women attending the Quadroon Balls were accompanied by their mothers. The mothers were very involved in working through the deal. While not legally recognized as wives, the women would be known as placées. The term comes from the French *placer* meaning "to place with." The relationships were called *mariages de la main gauche* or "left-handed marriages."

The gentleman would often pay for his placées' education, sometimes in Europe. It was also customary for the man to buy her a small cottage, initially across Rue de Rampart at the edge of the French Quarter in what is now Treme. Later, a great many more Creole cottages were built in Faubourg Marigny, next to the French Quarter on the downriver side.

Until the cottage was completed, a proper gentleman would never visit her alone. Thereafter, once built, he would live three months a year with his placées in

Treme or the Marigny and the other nine months with his real and legal wife back in the Quarter. This was an above-board and totally accepted practice. Unlike those Bible-thumping Puritans in the rest of the country, for the men of New Orleans, abstinence and fidelity were no virtues. A mistress was part of your presentation of self, along with cool clothes and a rad carriage ride. A hot mistress was a mark of social distinction.

When giving tours, I sometimes jokingly say the French Quarter "real" wives probably looked forward to those three months without the stench of cigar smoke or finding used socks tossed just anywhere all over the house. In truth, there was a little friction and the "real" wives were prone to jealousy. In 1786, Governor Esteban Rodríguez Miró y Sabater passed an ordinance that made it an offense for these femmes de couleur to walk around in silk clothing, wear any jewelry, or plumes. To make them seemingly even less physically desirable, Creole women were required to cover their heads in a turban-like twisted kerchief, known as a tignons.

With the influx of Americans, Quadroon Balls ran their course and the practice of plaçage became a juicy but historical footnote. Emily Clark, an alleged historian, supposedly teaching at Tulane, calls into question the whole notion that plaçage and Quadroon Balls ever took place. But rather than denying the existence of Miro's 1786 ordinance, the Duke of Saxe-Weimar-Eisenach's account, and an actual court case where Eulalie de Mandeville (the plaçage partner of Victor-Eugene Macarty) sued Macarty's estate on September 19, 1846 for the assets she and Victor-Eugene had accumulated over their fifty-year relationship, I prefer to think of Emily Clark (IF that's her real name) as a conspiracy theorist like those who deny the Manhattan Project or the existence of the Mafia. I have never met Emily Clark. I'm sure that I'd find her a perfectly pleasant person (IF she really exists). But I am not giving up on such a rich story.

The exotic plaçage gave way to the more commonplace institution of prostitution. The Sumerian word for female prostitute, *kar.kid*, dates back in their writings to 2400 B.C. Chinese statesman Kuang Chung started commercial brothels in the seventh century B.C. as a means to increase the state's income. Becoming an authorized prostitute in ancient Rome was just as arduous as some modern employers, with required personal references, FBI background checks, and pee-in-a-cup drug tests. A potential prostitute had to meet with the aedile (an officer of the Roman Republic, responsible for maintenance of public buildings, regulation of public festivals, and enforcement of public order), provide their proper given name, her age, place of birth, and the pseudonym under which she intended to practice her calling. And then they had to pay taxes on their earnings.

As a port city, filled with sailors on leave and traveling businessmen looking for a good time, it was almost inevitable that New Orleans would become a hotbed for prostitution. Between 1841 and 1860, a half-million immigrants docked in New

Orleans. Many of them didn't make it any further than Gallatin Street, which back then was Whorehouse Central. A majority of prostitutes in and around the area were immigrant women simply looking to financially survive.

Gallatin Street was not just sketchy back then, it was seriously dangerous. Police were known to avoid the area without a back-up partner, especially at night. The street was frequented by the Live Oak Gang, a disreputable crew that got their name by carrying around oak clubs and breaking things: windows, chairs, faces.

One working woman, Mary Jane Jackson, a.k.a. Bricktop, was as threatening as any Live Oak gang member. She was eventually deemed as too rough to work at Archy Murphy's, easily the roughest dance house on Gallatin Street. Bricktop carried a personally designed knife with two five-inch blades on either end. In addition to four other men, her own husband was one of her victims.

The 300 block of Burgundy, between Bienville and Conti Streets, was another area of debauchery during the 1870s. The area was called Smoky Row as opposed to Skid Row. Smoky Row was mostly African-American sex workers, who were known for their rough edges, smoking, chewing tobacco, and drinking beer and rot-gut whiskey, all to excess.

At the time, brothels were pretty much everywhere; Gallatin, Smoky Row, Franklin Street, an area known as The Swamp, so named well over 100 years before the bar, The Swamp, opened on Bourbon Street, became known for their mechanical bull and second-story balcony views.

The prostitutes were not of the Julia Roberts (*Pretty Woman*) or Elisabeth Shue (*Leaving Las Vegas*) mold. They were a rough bunch, with colorful names like One-Eye Sal and Kidney-Foot Jenny, as likely to earn their living by beating and robbing customers as having sex with them. Some would unceremoniously throw down a rug on the sidewalk and have paid-for sex right out on public streets.

During the Yankee occupation in the Civil War, federal documents record the loss of 50,000 to 100,000 days of service by Union soldiers having contracted venereal disease. Clearly, prostitution in New Orleans had grown a bit out of hand.

There were some earlier rather minor attempts to bring it under control, such at the Lorette ordinance in 1857, which prohibited prostitution on the first floor of buildings—do what you will on upper floors. But the turning point was a plan created by Uptown alderman Sidney Story. Under the assumption that wanton sex was inevitable, he studied port cities in Europe and concluded the best way to control prostitution and associated crimes was to make it legal, but within a very confined and manageable area.

In 1897, the city passed ordinance #13032, created a single and relatively small (three square blocks) legal red-light district. They chose an area away from the proper Uptown and Garden District (i.e. white) residents, plopped it in the predominantly black neighborhood on the other side of Basin Street, what is now Treme. Brothels weren't officially opened for another year because local resident George L'Hote sued the city. He claimed that his home area was then and always had been respectable. He learned that he and his lower working class neighbors had no real power.

Councilman Story was flabbergasted when the new neighborhood of sex and vice took on his own name, Storyville. That wasn't part of his plan. He much preferred the more anonymous nickname, "The District."

Storyville quickly became a noted tourist attraction, nearly as enticing as our food and music. By 1900, Storyville was on its way to becoming New Orleans largest revenue center. The neighborhood even had their own version of a Frommer's or Fodor's guide, with the Blue Books. The Blue Book brochures described the best bordellos and listed professional names of the prostitutes, a price list and a description of any special services offered, plus placement ads for alcohol, a good lawyer, nearby sports bars, and quick cures for STDs a tourist might pick up in Storyville and want to leave behind before they returned home.

Just as early jazz had stars like Louis Armstrong, King Oliver, and Bunk Johnson, Storyville too had its star Madams. The over-6-foot-tall Amelia Williams billed herself as "The world's strongest whore."

The self-styled Lulu White was considered the most beautiful Octoroon ($\frac{1}{8}$th black) in New Orleans. She got her nickname, "Diamond Queen," for her practice of always wearing every diamond she owned, to offset her ever-present ratty red wig. Lulu often ran afoul of the law for selling liquor without a license and the occasional shooting, stabbing, and violent assault.

Emma Johnson was a huge woman and rather unattractive. She nonetheless flourished as a prostitute because of her willingness to engage in *any* sexual act. As a madam, she again showed a willingness to do anything, and would hold auctions for young prostitutes who were still virgins. Drawing near-homeless girls to her employ by using food and alcohol as bait, Emma's French House on Gasket Street used children as young as 10 years old.

The most expensive fee was charged by Madame Kate Townsend. After she had long ago retired from active whoring, she would still agree to see an important client if he was willing to pay her exorbitant fee of $50 an hour.

The most famous, however, was Josie Arlington. Where Emma Johnson was sort of the Bad News Bears of bordello madams, Josie was more like the New York Yankees. Her 'classy' whorehouse was named Chateau Lobrano d'Arlington. It was a four-story mansion at 225 N. Basin Street and staffed with women from Europe, trained in all the arts of fetish. The Blue Book characterized Madam Arlington's place of business as "absolutely and unquestionably the most decorative and costly fitted-out sporting palace ever placed before the American public." She usually employed ten to twenty working girls, but would double that number, taking on part-time holiday help during the hectic Mardi Gras season. Josie's house charged an outrageous fee of $5 per hour when the going rate was 22 cents. The Chateau had an event in a grand ballroom called the Sexual Circus, in which ten to twelve women would perform sexual acts in which patrons could join in or merely watch. Unlike Emma Johnson, Josie insisted no girl was ever defiled nor exploited in the running of her business.

When she died in 1914, it had been her intention to be buried in the upper-crust Lake Lawn Metairie Cemetery. Hearing this, a group of women rallied a protest because they didn't want an infamous madam buried anywhere near their fathers or husbands. Josie's response was "I wonder if they know how often their husbands came to visit me when they were alive." With her money, she did get in. Josie Arlington was buried in a red granite tomb with a bronze statue of a women reaching for the door. Overnight graveyard workers have claimed they've seen the statue get up and walk away. The gravesite has the family name of Morales etched in the stone. Morales is Spanish for "moral character."

Ongoing protests after her internment did eventually force the cemetery to move her remains to an undisclosed location. But, she's still in the Metairie Cemetery . . . somewhere.

After two servicemen were knifed in Storyville, the Secretary of the Navy, Josephus Daniels, insisted servicemen should not be exposed to such vice, and he spearheaded an effort which resulted in the closing of Storyville. Josephus was a mixed bag of causes, being a champion of public schools and women's right to vote, but he also supported prohibition and was an active advocate of white supremacy. Using his North Carolina newspapers as a bully pulpit, he sought to swing elections and block African-Americans from gaining political power. So, on the balance, I guess you'd have to say he was an asshole.

New Orleans mayor Martin Behrman said, when forced to close Storyville, "You can make it illegal, but you can't make it unpopular."

Norma Wallace and her house at 1026 Conti Street in the French Quarter became a testament to the mayor's statement. While prostitution was no longer legal, she became a hugely successful madam. Her upscale brothel catered to the wealthy and powerful. When gangster Alvin Karpis visited her house, she tipped off the NOPD. He was #1 on the FBI's Most Wanted List. The high profile credit for his arrest was lavished on the local police, who also got a commendation from President Herbert Hoover. Wallace, in turn, earned the police's complete and undivided inattention.

We say the NOPD's practice of not paying attention continues to this day. You might hear locals refer to the NOPD as "Not Our Problem, Darlin," as sometimes the police response time is no more reliable than our street cars.

As further insurance, Norma Wallace kept a black book of all her clients, where she listed their names, the dates they visited, and detailed descriptions of their physical 'assets.' This was nearly a century before Brett Favre and Congressman Weiner made dick pics 'a thing.' You can read her entire and pretty fabulous story in one of New Orleans' seminal books, *The Last Madam* by Chris Wiltz.

Prior to Norma Wallace, 1026 Conti Street had been the home of E. J. Bellocq. Bellocq had been a frumpish and boring little toad, working dull jobs as a clerk or accountant for local businesses. That is, until his mother died, which released his inner Ru Paul. He started sashaying around the Quarter wearing elaborate scarves and ostentatious monogrammed jewelry. Bellocq quit his dull jobs and became a photographer. He was mostly known for taking pictures of buildings and bridges. When he died of about everything one can be afflicted with—cerebral arteriosclerosis, diabetes, a concussion, obesity, senility, and the all-encompassing old age—his family entered his dusty old apartment. Among his hoarder's shrine of collapsed furniture, broken lamps, and scattered pieces of photography equipment, they found his private stash of photographs. Bellocq had taken image after image of the prostitutes of Storyville.

The odd part was that for most of the pictures, the prostitutes' faces had been scratched out. Breasts and vaginas remained on full display, but for reasons we'll never know, their identity had been removed. Maybe it was his aesthetic or maybe his perversion, or, just maybe his Jesuit priest brother was the first to find the photographs and he altered the images to make them more "proper."

The history of burlesque begins with a bellydancer named Little Egypt who performed at the Chicago World's Fair in 1893, though some would say that Salome's veil dance as recorded in the Bible was the actual first appearance of the artform. Little Egypt's gyrations caused a sensation that inspired many imitators. Because her smooth twists and turns were so difficult to replicate, other dancers were only able to pull off a more crude bump and grind, which became the foundation of burlesque. Burlesque was originally called the hootchie-cootchie dance. Newspapers coined the widespread cultural phenomenon "Salomania," sort of like Beatlemania or Lisztomania.

(Yes, there was a term, Lisztomania, used to describe the fan frenzy for Franz Liszt in the 1840s. It's hard to imagine today, but back in his time, Liszt playing the *Grand Galop Chromatique* would cause some women to faint.)

In the glory days of New Orleans burlesque, a 20-year run from the mid 1940s to the mid-'60s, Bourbon Street was the white-hot center of American "adult" entertainment. Bourbon Street is not named after a barrel-aged distilled spirits but the royal House of Bourbon, which ruled France in the sixteenth century. One member of the Bourbon clan seemed perfectly suited for New Orleans' Bourbon Street. Philippe II was a professed atheist who read the satirical and bawdy works of François Rabelais inside a Bible binding when he had to attend mass. He also took delight holding orgies on religious high holidays.

Along a five-block stretch of Bourbon Street, over fifty acts could be seen on any given night. The street was like a nightly circus or state fair with bright neon lights and barkers beckoning tourists and locals to step right up and come on into the clubs to see the exotic entertainments. The headline performers were pictured outside prominently like sideshow banners, huge photographs of dancers called cat girls, oyster girls, or heavenly bodies. While there are still large photos on display outside the clubs on Bourbon, today they display images of nameless "Barely Legal Teens" and "Live Sex Acts." In its heyday, Bourbon Street was lined with classier clubs like the Sho Bar, Casino Royale, the Poodle Patio, and the 500 Club. Each club featured well-regarded jazz musicians like Pete Fountain, Al Hirt, and jazz pianist Ronnie Kole. Noted jazz saxophonist Sam Butera got his start in Bourbon Street strip clubs when he was just a teenager. Louis Armstrong would, on occasion, play on Bourbon Street.

The New Orleans style of burlesque in the '50s took the more common bumping and grinding in back-alley strip clubs of Anytown, USA and added props and signature stunts. There was a certain level of class associated with the acts' imaginatively themed costumes, mood lighting, and especially the live music.

Burlesque is risqué not raunchy, coquettish not crude. It's hard to imagine today, when the street is now cluttered in people wearing cargo shorts and Roll Tide T-shirts, but you used to dress up to walk down Bourbon Street in the evening, as if strolling New York's Fifth Avenue or des Champs-Élysées in Paris. The great jazz combos of yesteryear's clubs have been replaced by today's second-rate cover bands.

Today, drunken tourists and conventioneers might stumble into Lipstixx or Rick's (formerly Big Daddy's, which famously advertised topless and bottomless dancers) to scan nameless girls willing to bare some flesh for blue-collar wages. No live bands. No creatively created props or scripts.

The performers in the '40s to the '60s were major celebrities who would draw patrons specifically to see *their* act, the way people buy tickets specifically for *Cats, A Chorus Line*, or *Phantom of the Opera*.

Evangeline the Oyster Girl starred at the Casino Royale. She was LIFE magazine famous, getting featured in a 1949 issue for an "impromptu" (quite possibly staged) catfight with Divena, the Aqua Tease. Back in the day, getting in LIFE magazine was the equal to hosting SNL or being the cover girl on *Sports Illustrated's* Swimsuit Issue. It was a big deal. For her act, she used to rise out of a giant oyster shell prop and then perform her dance, revealing her attributes from behind another prop made to look like a massive pearl. For a brief time, until scalp burns convinced her otherwise, Evangeline dyed her hair mossy green to make it look like seaweed. Her 'real' name was said to be Kitty West. Somehow that sounds even more made up than Evangeline. She was born in a poor Mississippi family, one of six children. Her father was a preacher, and her mother was a cousin of Elvis

Presley's father Vernon. That sounds like a Hollywood script about the making of a burlesque queen.

Rita Alexander the Champagne Girl had equally unique talents. She started dancing at 18 at the Silver Frolics, then she went to work at the Sho-Bar doing short bits during intermissions. After she got some coaching from veteran performer Tee Tee Red, Rita became a star. Her signature moves involved balancing full champagne glasses on her breasts and taking drinks from the glasses without using her hands. Rita also appeared in the movie *Hot Thrills and Warm Chills*. The storyline involves three lusty ladies who keep losing their clothes as they conspire to steal the King of Sex crown on Mardi Gras Day. The now very hard to find film is a masterpiece of schlock. In addition to terrible acting and nonexistent production values, the viewer is treated to numerous gratuitous sex scenes plus a shoot-out in the French Quarter. The story goes that the movie ended not at the close of the script, but when the director called out, "We're all out of film. That's a wrap!"

Tee Tee Red herself began performing at 17 after winning an amateur striptease contest. Tee Tee appeared briefly in the Jerry Lewis film *The Bellboy*. Her character was a stripper named Rock Candy. She spent years dancing on Bourbon Street at the 500 Club and Sho Bar. She called herself an acrobatic comedienne-contortionist. Tee Tee stopped shaking her tail feathers one week shy of her 50th birthday.

Lily Christine, the Cat Girl, was famous for her cat dance, voodoo dance, and her harem heat dance to jungle drums. Lily graced many girlie magazine covers, was featured in a number of B-films, and was the star of a short-lived Broadway play with Bert Lahr, a.k.a. The Cowardly Lion in The Wizard of Oz. Another Bourbon Street dancer, Kalantan the Heavenly Body, appeared in a higher-end movie, *Son of Sinbad*, which was produced by Howard Hughes. She performed exotic interpretations of Afro-Cuban dance at the 500 Club. *Night Spot Magazine* labeled her the "Most Photogenic Body of 1955." Kalantan abandoned the stage when she married TV and film actor John Bromfield. He had modest fame as the star of a TV series, *The Sheriff of Cochise*, and also appeared in several B-movies like *Return of the Creature* and *Curucu, Beast of the Amazon*.

Wild Cherry left her hometown, Tampa, Florida, based on her fascination with "The City That Never Sleeps," a radio show broadcast from New Orleans. She got her first dancing job at the Mardi Gras Lounge. The club owner gave her the stage name, "Torchy," but Wild Cherry earned her more lasting stage name thanks to her temperament and penchant for fighting and arguing.

Jezebel ran away from her North Carolina home to New Orleans at 16. She was a featured attraction, dancing under the name Wildcat Frenchie, and then under the moniker Jezebel at the club that would become the Poodle's Patio, named after her pet poodles, which she dyed different colors.

Linda Brigette, a.k.a. the Cupid Doll, was the last great Bourbon Street stripper from the glory days of burlesque. Born in backwater Louisiana, she wed at 13 and had a child at 14. After the death of Lilly the Cat Girl, Brigette took her spot as the featured attraction at the 500 Club. She was billed as "the Cupid Doll" and "America's Most Beautiful Exotic." Her act consisted of a striptease ending with seductive moves on a settee. At just under 5 feet tall, she was most noted for her huge breasts and even bigger platinum blonde hair. Brigette's other acts included dancing in an oversized champagne glass, fire-eating, and using live animals (a monkey and a python) as props. Brigette married her spotlight man in what was publicized as the first nude wedding ceremony.

But the unquestioned superstar of Bourbon Street, the burlesque version of Louis Armstrong, Tennessee Williams, or Marie Laveau, was the voluptuous Blaze Starr. She was also known as Miss Spontaneous Combustion. Blaze was born Fannie Belle Fleming. As a child, the eighth of eleven in her family, she washed laundry for $1 a day. As a teenager, she hopped a bus to Washington DC. While working at a doughnut shop to stay afloat, she met a promoter who persuaded her to become a stripper, telling Fannie the pay was much better.

Blaze had legendary creative shows with jungle drums, and once trained a panther to be on stage with her. When the panther was found dead, that night she played both roles—dancer and panther. As part of her act, Blaze would stretch out on a couch and wiggle seductively while removing her garments. When she got to the last threads of clothing, smoke would emerge from between her legs. Blaze wrote in her memoir, "If there is such a thing as getting nude with class, then I did it."

Blaze Starr famously had a tabloid affair with Governor Earl Long. There were also rumors that she had another with President John F. Kennedy. The governor's affair produced one of my all-time favorite banters. Long asked the burlesque queen, "If I wasn't the governor of the great state of Louisiana, would you still love me as much?" She replied, "If I had small tits and worked in a fish house, would you still love me?"

Their high profile affair was one of the things that led to the downfall of Bourbon Street. The overzealous District Attorney from 1962 to 1973 was Jim Garrison. One of his campaign promises was to clean up Bourbon Street when, if compared to Bourbon Street today, there was nothing to clean up. Garrison has his defenders. But, for me, he's right up there with Joe McCarthy, Karl Rove, and Dick Cheney as one of the most vile Americans of the twentieth century.

Garrison is most famously known for prosecuting (or screwing up) the evidence that Lee Harvey Oswald did not act alone in assassinating JFK. He wanted to challenge the Warren Commission's findings, largely because he saw it as an opportunity to make himself a national name.

He chose Clay Shaw as his lynchpin victim, hoping that the well-heeled New Orleans resident would break under pressure, maybe even kill himself, which Garrison would use as proof there was a conspiracy. To tie Shaw to crimes, the DA office bullied witnesses into giving false testimony and, behind the scenes, Garrison himself would leak concocted lies about Shaw's homosexuality and his theory that the assassination was a "gay thrill killing."

After dragging Clay Shaw through the mud, it took the jury less than an hour to acquit him, or as a defense attorney put it, "long enough for the jury to take a bathroom break."

Distortion, outright lies, and bullying was standard operating procedure for Jim Garrison. After a conflict with local judges over his budget, he accused them of racketeering and conspiring against him, with no evidence of course. The eight judges charged him with misdemeanor criminal defamation, and Garrison was convicted. Garrison indicted Judge Bernard Cocke with criminal malfeasance and, in two trials prosecuted by Garrison himself, Cocke was acquitted.

Garrison charged nine policemen with brutality, but dropped the charges two weeks later. At a press conference, he accused the state parole board of accepting bribes, but again, with no evidence, he could obtain no indictments. Garrison was eventually and unanimously censured by the state legislator it for "deliberately maligning all of the members."

His censorship came too late to preserve Bourbon Street. His championed vice raids, staged often on a nightly basis, which led to many arrests of club owners and the dancers for B-drinking and obscenity. B-drinking, for those of you who don't know (as I did not know before writing this book), is a scam where dancers on break would approach patrons to buy them a drink. Either a lonely man, in the club by himself, or a boastful man in a group, trying to impress his friends, would over-pay for watered down drinks. The club's dancer would get a commission or cut from drinks sold.

Most of the arrests made by Garrison's office did not result in convictions, implying that he was in the habit of making collars without evidence. But even without convictions, his harassment had its intended results, as the beaten-down clubs could no longer afford live musicians. The burlesque stars left for Las Vegas, Europe, or left the business flat out. The real, long-term results of Garrison's mission was to leave a void later filled up by the low-end and even more raunchy entertainment of the new Bourbon Street.

After several decades of virtually no burlesque in New Orleans, it made a comeback on several fronts. In 1999, in an old movie house on Toulouse Street, an unlikely trio of a retro visionary from Los Angeles, a punk band drummer from New York City, and a New Orleans-based dancer created the Shim Shamettes. Morgan Higby Night, bought the former movie palace. He was a Los Angeles DJ and film producer and director. I would say he was "known for" his films only if you consider a tiny circle of friends as being in the know. His barely seen films were *The Asylum Street*

Spankers and a music video, *Ragtime Man*, which got almost no airtime because stations had a problem with a film about a man who makes love to women during their menstruation cycle. Morgan was joined by Ronnie Magri as the club's musical director, bandleader, and drummer. Magri had played drums with Joey Ramone, Stiv Bators, and The Throbs (plus one session with Little Richard). He'd grown tired of an increasingly "too clean" New York and embraced the idea of coming to the forever funky New Orleans. Lorelei Fuller was the third and most essential partner in the launch of the Shim Shamettes. She was a local dancer, had appeared in the less-than-classic movie, *Zombie! vs. Mardi Gras*, and helped train dancers and recreate burlesque standards. She herself took the stage as a rekindled Oyster Girl.

The partners had a passion for retro-kitsch burlesque, but, other than Lorelei, not an ounce of knowledge. They rented old B-movies with scenes of dance routines to get a feel for historically accurate burlesque. When the Shim Shamettes took the stage in April '99 with Ronnie's band playing back up, banging out classic stripper numbers like "Stormy Weather" and "Mood Indigo," the Shim Sham Club became one of the first revival burlesque shows in the nation.

The club closed its doors in 2003 and Morgan returned to Los Angeles. There, his retro-cool passions are still being expressed through Devil's Night Radio, a station described as "The Best Dive Bar Juke Box You've Heard in Your Life"; Devil's Night Drive-In, a twice-a-month drive-in B-movie show with FM transmitters, car hops, and a concession stand right in downtown LA; and Hicksville Trailer Park, a motel and artists' retreat where you stay in vintage trailers. However, the Shim Sham Club inspired and spawned a great variety of burlesque venues throughout New Orleans and the country.

Local and legendary music writer Alison Fensterstock teamed with Artistic Director and Producer Baby Doe to create the first Tease-O-Rama in 2001. Two hundred performers from across the country gathered for a weekend in New Orleans to celebrate vintage striptease. A community was born. Tease-O-Rama has become a premier event and now takes place in various cities from New Orleans to San Francisco, Seattle, Portland, and Los Angeles.

Shortly after the Shim Sham Club closed, the flag to restore burlesque to New Orleans was seized by Rick Delaup. Delaup grew up on the West Bank (or Wank) of New Orleans. A profile described him as "looking for all the world like the kid you used to pay to do your math homework in junior high." Meeting him for lunch the first time, I thought there was more of a Peter Sellers quality that combines nerdishness with coolness. As he revealed, "I didn't know about the French Quarter or what Bourbon Street was like back in the '50s. One day, a friend of mine who grew up down there told me about it. His father was an emcee on Bourbon. The more he told me and the more photos I saw, the more interested I became. At the time, I was doing freelance video, commercials, documentaries, things like that. But then I got the idea to do a documentary about that era on Bourbon Street. I was contacting the former strippers and videotaping the interviews I was doing with them. But it was hard getting funding and trying to make a living at it. It was an ongoing project. It was tough, so I started the actual production of live stage shows."

Rick's resolve has been to restore traditional burlesque to the city where it once flourished. His own productions have grown to become burlesque institutions. The Burlesque Festival takes place each September, bringing international stars to New Orleans and has reached the size and scope to spill out from being set in the House of Blues to take up residence in the Civic Theater and Harrah's Casino as well.

Bustout Burlesque and Bad Girls of Burlesque are Delaup's two shows. Each take place at the House of Blues. Rick's shows cannot translate to the smaller venues as pop-ups or that line St. Claude Avenue because his productions include full jazz bands, elaborate costumes, and first-rate emcees. He needs to fill a large venue like the House of Blues just to show the barest of profit.

Bustout Burlesque has been rated the #1 burlesque show in America by *USA Today* and one of the Top 10 worldwide by *The Travel Channel*. The *Times-Picayune* theater critic David Cuthbert says, "'Bustout Burlesque has authenticity, electricity, and lubricity. It's a fun night out to savor the lost art of the striptease, lovingly re-created and performed by gloriously good-looking girls who are oh, so naughty, but oh, so nice." They perform two shows, at 8:00 and 10:30, most Saturday Nights at The House of Blues (225 Decatur St.).

Bad Girls of Burlesque, a monthly show, bills itself as a "rowdy celebration of the wicked, the wayward, and the wanton." Consider it the naughtier sister show to Bustout. There's usually lots of latex, live snakes, and straight jackets. And there's always the chance you may be brought on stage and spanked with a riding crop.

Both shows have featured star performers like Elle Dorado and Stormy Gayle, voted Queen of Burlesque 2015. You may also be treated to GoGo McGregor's terrifying bed of nails act or Nikki LeVillain belly dancing and snake show.

There are two basic styles of burlesque on stage in New Orleans. Rick Delaup's favored classic burlesque is a beautiful girl in a gown, jeweled lingerie, and gloves who does the slow unveil to traditional jazz music. If there's any theme to the performance, it's a thinly veiled excuse to remove articles of clothing. It is the art of tease and about sensuality and glamour.

In Neo-Burlesque, or new wave burlesque, the performer hits the stage with most of her assets already on display. The dancers are often not classic beauties, but can be rail-thin, or somewhat meaty. They can have crazy colored hair and many tattoos. Some come purposefully grotesque, streaming stage blood or fake black eyes and blacked out teeth. Usually set to contemporary music, it's more like performance art than classic tease. Some Neo-Burlesque artists are fire eaters, aerialists, and contortionists.

There is also a new wave of star performers, like in the days of Oyster Girls and Jewels of the Orient. Miss Trixie Minx is equally known for her comic talents as her buxom hourglass figure. She has toured with Comic Relief and one of her often repeated quotes (at least by me) is where she described herself as "just a Jewish housewife with no talent for cleaning nor cooking. But I can twirl tassels." You can buy sequined Trixie Minx tassels and T-shirts on her website, www.trixieminx.com.

Trixie and her husband moved from Nashville to New Orleans in 2001, after an injury to her foot ended her career as a ballet dancer and they were looking for a new beginning. The couple had fallen in love with the city when they visited a few months earlier for Jazz Fest.

Another Trixie-ism is her quote: "In other cities you reside, in New Orleans you live."

Much more than a dancer, Trixie has grown to both star in and produce three burlesque acts: Fleur De Tease, Burlesque Ballroom, and Creole Sweet Tease.

Fleur de Tease is more of a vaudeville variety revue. The shows tend to have actual story lines and themes, usually involving circus arts. A troupe of twelve performers—magicians, comedians, fire eaters, aerialists, burlesque dancers, and the mandatory stage kittens (also called panty wranglers—they gather up discarded costume pieces all over the stage after each dance) perform at One Eyed Jack's (615 Toulouse St.).

The Creole Sweet Tease Show is a smaller, some might say more elegant show. It's just one dancer, Trixie; a singer, Jayna Morgan; and a classic New Orleans style jazz band, The Creole Syncopators Jazz Band, with trumpeter Leon "Kid Chocolate" Brown and drummer Gerald French. They perform at the Burgundy Bar inside the Saint Hotel (931 Canal St.) with no cover charge.

Burlesque Ballroom is a show every Friday at midnight in Irvin Mayfield's Jazz Playhouse inside the Royal Sonesta Hotel (300 Bourbon St.). There's a rotating cast of singers, musicians, and dancers. Romy Kaye is most often the singer, the Mercy Buckets most often the band, and Trixie's most often the dancer. Though on any given night, the headline performer could be Charlotte Treuse, Bunny Love, Honey Tangerine, or Felix Roxx. The burlesque performers use the entire room as their stage and include the audience as part of the show. Writer Alison Fensterstock describes the experience: "Remember Jessica Rabbit's jaw-dropping crawl through the nightclub in *Who Framed Roger Rabbit?* It's kind of like that."

Bella Blue, profiled in this chapter, is on equal billing with Trixie as one of New Orleans' premier burlesque queens. Her style can be best described as anything goes. Bella has performed everything from classic fan dances and reverse stripteases to androgynous, blood soaked, and otherwise controversial pieces.

The New Orleans School of Burlesque, which she created 2008, offers weekly burlesque classes for both men and women. Her school is located in The Healing

Trixie Minx

Center (2372 St. Claude Ave.), a bright orange building on St. Claude that also houses a greengrocer, a two-guy barbershop, and a storefront for Sallie Ann Glassman, an ordained voodoo priestess.

The AllWays Lounge (2240 St. Claude Ave.) is something else. Regular burlesque performances include Bella Blue's "Dirty Dime Peep Show!," called "the most unpredictable and exciting burlesque in the city." Bella performs most Saturdays. Every Thursday, it's drag bingo with Vinsanto and a weekly surprise guest. Vinsanto is an assemblage artist/doll maker, music performer, and drag artist. Periodically The AllWays will put on "CLUE: A Burlesque Mystery," which is a vaudeville show with audience participation, based on the old board game. The "Look What I Can Do" variety show has a variety of performers, most often showcasing the aerial and hula hoop artistry of burlesque performer, Ooops the Clown. They sometimes spotlight touring shows like "Freaksheaux to Geaux," a mix of music, circus, sideshow and burlesque, with a Southern Gothic twist, and "Boobs and Goombas," a burlesque adaptation of the Super Mario Bros.

I've never seen their monthly show "Gag Reflex." The name alone kind of scares me away.

Slow Burn Burlesque is a popular troupe because they combine an anything goes attitude with heavy doses of grunge and goth. Roxie, Moxie, and Ruby are some of their dancers who perform monthly at The Howlin' Wolf (907 S. Peters St.), backed by the live band This Stunted Sextette. If I can interject my own snotty opinion, the one and only time I saw the show, I felt there was a strong need for a

LUMINS OF NEW ORLEANS:
Bella Blue

Bella Blue has been dancing since she was three years old. Obviously, back then, rather than the Shimmy, the Quiver, or Bump & Grind, it was ballet. She continued ballet and modern dance all the way through high school.

Upon graduating, she wanted to stay in New Orleans (who wouldn't?), but made barely livable wages teaching dance classes and struggled to find work as a performer. "New Orleans is a difficult place to make a living as a dancer," she explains. "It doesn't have a culture of supporting professional dancing outside of stripping. There are no dance companies here that you can audition for and make your living as a dancer."

Bella saw her first burlesque show when she was 16 years old. Underaged, she snuck into a bar to see a swing band she liked. Their set that night included burlesque performers dancing to their music. Bella was hooked. Then, to quote Paul Prudhomme, she was nudged toward the person she was meant to be. While scrolling MySpace, she brought up a screen for that swing band's page. There, she saw a profile of a dancer doing burlesque in New Orleans. It was Flour de Tease founder and premiere burlesque queen Trixie Minx. They started messaging one another and a month later, Bella did her first audition for burlesque. A month after that, she was on stage for her first show. This was back in 2007. "At the time, I wasn't trying to make this a career. I didn't have a plan."

Today, Bella Blue is easily the hardest-working woman in New Orleans burlesque. She is a creative director, artist, performer, and teacher. In addition to dancing with Fleur de Tease, she has gone on to cast, choreograph, and produce a considerable variety of her own shows.

Every Thursday night, her show, Whiskey and Rhinestones, may be experienced at 523 Gravier Street. Saturday night is her Blue Book Cabaret at the Bourbon Pub (801 Bourbon St.) followed mere hours later by a Sunday brunch, Legs & Eggs, inside SoBou restaurant (310 Chartres St.). Bella has two monthly shows (check their schedule) at the AllWays Lounge (2240 St. Claude Ave.). The Lounge puts on her signature show, The Dirty Dime Peepshow, and on other nights a playful Strip Roulette.

Strip Roulette is where two competing teams of burlesque performers have to make up improv strip routines, with themes chosen by DJ Ajent O to be especially awkward and hilarious. The teams will be given uncomfortably obscure props that they are required to incorporate into their striptease.

Another show, The Blue Book Cabaret, originally came together when the owner of Lucky Pierre's called Bella and said he wanted to bring burlesque back on Bourbon Street. Her show is an homage to traditional burlesque, but then breaks all the rules by incorporating male, drag, and transgender performers along with sideshow acts.

Then Bella caught unwanted national headlines, including *The New York Times,* when Lucky Pierre's undercut her by firing one of her troupe, Ruby Rage, for being too voluptuous and displaying more flesh than they felt their clientele wanted to see. After consideration, worried about cutting the performances and income for her other dancers, Bella chose to shut down the show and left the club in what was seen as a virtuous "girl power" moment. The Blue Book Cabaret has been restored in a new location, the Bourbon Pub (801 Bourbon St.).

The Dirty Dime Peep Show seems to be tenaciously pulling out (or off) all stops trying to shock the audience. Dirty Dime is equal parts comedy and raunchiness. As emcee Ben Wisdom says, "You can't put a premium on filth!" Others have called it "the most unpredictable and exciting burlesque in the city" (*New Orleans Advocate*); "this is burlesque that is literally in your face" (NOLA.com); and "some of the best burlesque that this country has to offer" (Yelp).

As if performing, preparing for shows, and keeping up with promotion weren't enough, Bella decided to open The New Orleans School of Burlesque (2372 St. Claude Ave.). The school was started in a small studio across the Mississippi River on the Westbank, or what locals call The Wank. What was conceived as possibly a one-time-only event has blossomed to be New Orleans'-only school to teach the art of burlesque. There are weekly one hour walk-in classes on Tuesdays and Thursdays that do not require registration and are open to anyone. Just shove your insecurities in a small (or massive) box and come on in. Yes, men are welcomed too. The cost is a mere $10 per session.

There are also private group or private individual class options. The private group sessions have been used as an energetic alternative to

Max Trombly

bachelorette parties, birthday parties, or any type of group get-together. If you're coming to New Orleans for a sales conference, try to convince your HR Director that burlesque lessons would be a hell of a lot more fun than any other of those boring "team building" activities they're considering.

Through the school, Bella sees herself as an advocate for burlesque as an art form and enjoyable pastime. "The school is so much bigger than me," she said. "It's about giving people the opportunity to get to know themselves, feel less self-conscious, and get some coaching in a new skill along the way."

I compare taking a burlesque class with Bella Blue to coming to New Orleans to be taught how to throw a football by Drew Brees or how to arrange a song by Harry Connick, Jr.

choreographer. Many of the performers just sort of eventually ran out of things to take off and slumped off the stage.

Siberia (2227 St. Claude Ave.) is more of a dive bar and alt music venue than a burlesque club. But, on most Monday nights they pair burlesque performers with some of the worst open-mic stand-up comedians I've ever experienced in their show called Bits and Jiggles. Sorry, there's just some reflex in me that can withstand a poor athletic performance, an out of tune band, or cheesy acting, but I get immediately angered when I have to endure a bad comedian.

The Hi-Ho Lounge (2239 St. Claude Ave.) has many reasons to go that have nothing to do with burlesque. They do not have a house burlesque troupe, but instead spotlight a rotating menu of acts like Rev. Spooky and her Billion Dollar Baby Dolls, Storyville Starlettes, and Slow Burn Burlesque on a monthly basis.

La Nuit Comedy Theater (5039 Freret St.) is in Uptown and is predominantly known as a comedy club. But usually once a month they will dip into burlesque with a comedic bent. The Society of Sin troupe puts on a burlesque parody of daytime television game shows called The Vice is Right. This group also produced Pulp Science Fiction: A Star Wars Burlesque Play and Talk Nerdy To Me.

The first and third Saturdays of each month, The Country Club (634 Louisa St.) hosts their off-kilter version of the traditional New Orleans brunch. Rather than a jazz quartet or guitar soloist, their eggs and bottomless mimosas are accompanied by a spectacular drag performance.

The Country Club used to be a place where I'd tell people to go eat but stay outside on the front veranda. Maryjane Rosas is a superb chef, but formerly they had a back courtyard with a clothing-optional swimming pool. Naked bathers would often come inside to the dining area to freshen their drinks. I would say the front veranda was a safe no-flying-genital zone. However, some killjoy city ordinances have outlawed nude bathing in a public setting.

The one feature that does not yet exist is Rick Delaup's dream to create a club that serves like a Preservation Hall for burlesque. Delaup is New Orleans' premiere advocate and historian, sort of our Stephen Ambrose (WWII historian, author, and the champion who brought the National World War II Museum to New Orleans) or Poppy Tooker (New Orleans food historian, author, radio host, an regular on the *Steppin Out* weekly TV show) for burlesque.

He's been the creator and producer of Bust Out Burlesque, as well as The Bad Girls of Burlesque, and The Annual New Orleans Burlesque Festival. He also produced the annual Burlesque Showcase (2012, 2013) and Miss Viva Las Vegas competition (2013) at the Viva Las Vegas Rockabilly Weekend, held at The Orleans Hotel & Casino in Las Vegas. Delaup has been researching the history of New Orleans burlesque for 15 years. He has spoken on the subject at festivals and events, including the New Orleans Jazz & Heritage Festival, The Tennessee Williams Festival, Tease-O-Rama, Tales of the Cocktail, the Burlesque Hall of Fame, and The Tour Guides Association of Greater New Orleans. Delaup worked behind the scenes to create the A&E documentary *It's Burlesque!* So he's kind of (overwhelmingly) The Guy when it comes to New Orleans burlesque.

Delaup yearns for a burlesque-only venue, preferably on Bourbon Street, where it all began. "I receive calls every day from visitors wanting to see a burlesque show," he said. "I feel like (if there could be) one place, where folks could come every night, just like Preservation Hall is for jazz, if there was a burlesque club that was open all the time, there would be huge lines."

Saints Super Bowl Victory Parade   EDGAR MATA

CHAPTER 7

Rooting

Whoopin' Up Some "Who Dat?"

I want to rush for 1,000 or 1,500 yards, whichever comes first.
—George Rogers, NFL Saints Runningback

If you're visiting New Orleans during football season, it's very unlikely you'll get into a Saints home game. Their waiting list of over 70,000 people is topped only by the New York Giants (there with a potential fan base of over 20 million) and the rabid fans of the Packers and Steelers. Still, you need to know about the Saints to fully "get" New Orleans.

I lived in New York City for two Giants Super Bowl championships and countless years when the Yankees won the World Series. While I didn't live there, I was in Chicago the night the Bulls won one of their six NBA titles. And I was there on December 27th, 1964, when the Browns beat the Colts 27–0 for the NFL Championship, which until the Cavs ended a 52-year drought, was the last time any sports team from Cleveland won anything. (My seat for that game, Section 6, Row V, Seat #19, probably now sits at the bottom of Lake Erie. When the city demolished the old stadium in 1997, they used the rubble to create underwater reefs.)

I have never experienced the way in which a city loves its sports team the way New Orleans loves their Saints. It's not a rah-rah go-team kind of love. It's not the haughty arrogance of Patriots fans or Kentucky basketball fans. It's not the ironic lovable losers fan worship you used to get with the Chicago Cubs or the Jamaican Olympic bobsled team. It's a romantic love. Win, lose, or draw, fans love the Saints fervently.

I'm sure you've seen the crazy outfits Saints fans wear at the home games in the Super Dome. The difference is that, unlike Raider Nation fans filling up the Black Hole in their Mad Max outfits or the dog mask wearing, big bone waving Browns' Dawg Pound fans, what you see decked out in the Dome as nuns, priests, voodoo kings, and whistle heads, is just New Orleanians in their everyday wear.

After they finally won a Super Bowl following the 2009 season, Drew Brees' house looked like a Buddhist shrine. He lives right in the city, a block from Audubon Park. His front gate had hundreds of notes tied to the railings. People had left him flowers and baked goods.

The victory parade drew 800,000 people—this from a city of only 340,000. I tried to explain to my friends back in New York that this would be like 22 million people coming out for a Giants Super Bowl parade. The 5 million people that turned out for the Cubs' victory parade is impressive, but Chicago would need to more than triple that number to be the mathematical equivalent of the Saints' parade.

Part of the massive turnout was a collective release for the first 43 years of near-record-setting ineptitude. Saints fans had been given false hope when John Gilliam returned the opening kickoff 94 yards for a touchdown on their very first play as a franchise in 1967. But they ended up losing the game to the Los Angeles Rams, 27–13. They continued to lose for 20 more years; the Saints first winning record didn't come until 1987.

Probably the "highlight" of the first 20 years occurred November 8, 1970. The Saints were losing to the visiting Detroit Lions 16–17, with two seconds left on the clock. They were a winless 0–8 at the time. Out trotted Tom Dempsey, the Saints' considerably overweight kicker who had been born without toes on his right foot and without four fingers on his right hand. Dempsey was about to attempt a 63-yard field goal, at the time 7 yards longer than anyone had ever made in the history of the NFL. Detroit Lion star Alex Karas recalled watching the chubby clubfooted kicker hobble onto the field: "We laughed our asses off . . . the first 62 yards." Forty-three years later, a Bronco kicker, in the rarified air of Denver, kicked a 64-yard field goal. While Tom Dempsey no longer holds the record for the "longest" field goal in NFL history, he still has the "greatest" one.

The Superdome, or as my wife calls it "Drew's House," opened five years after Dempsey's kick, in 1975. The stadium is 27 stories high, and the roof expands for 13 acres. The opening (week-long) celebrations included performances by Bob Hope, The Temptations, The Isley Brothers, Telly Savalas, Raquel Welch, The O'Jays, The Allman Brothers, and The Ringling Brothers and Barnum & Bailey Circus. Pope John Paul II used the Dome in 1987 to give the largest benediction ever. The Pope was outdrawn the same year by The Rolling Stones concert inside the Dome, as well as Wrestlemania.

The stadium was built where there was once the Girod Cemetery, where Protestant bodies were dumped. Some felt the year after year of losing seasons for the Saints was because they played atop cursed burial grounds.

The Super Bowl season for the Saints was an incredible time to be in New Orleans. I moved here December 23rd, 2009, or one month prior to the Saints beating the Vikings at the Dome in overtime to go to the Super Bowl. If you want to see a grown man cry in New Orleans, replay the audio of Jim Henderson's call of Garrett Hartley's winning field goal. "AND IT'S GOOD! IT'S GOOD! IT'S GUH-HUH-HOOD! Pigs have flown! Hell has frozen over! The Saints are on their way to the Super Bowl!"

The highlight from the Sean Payton-Drew Brees years, when they were actually good, could be that kick, or perhaps the onside kick to start the second half in the Super Bowl, but most black & gold fans would agree it was Steve Gleason's blocked punt in the Monday night game against the much-hated Atlanta Falcons.

Saints fans are different from most NFL fans in that our tourism-focused hospitality shines through. Come to New Orleans to cheer on your Bucs or Steelers or Texans playing the Saints and this city will throw its collective arms around you—unless you're rooting for the Falcons. We do not like those dirty birds. Come here wearing your Falcon jerseys and tees and we'll treat you like Eagles fans treat all visitors to Philadelphia.

Steve Gleason's momentous play came early in the game played on September 25, 2006. It marked the Saints' first game back in the Superdome after Hurricane Katrina turned the stadium into a netherworld of misery for those people trapped there in the flood. During the 2005 season, the Saints were forced to play their "home" games in Baton Rouge, San Antonio, and one in New York City.

Simply being back in their own stadium and playing in front of their hometown fans and a national TV audience on a Monday Night already made the game a hugely poignant one, representing a city getting back on its feet. Early in the first quarter, in a still scoreless game, the Falcons were forced to punt. Gleason crashed through and blocked the punt, which was recovered for a Saints touchdown.

The roar of the crowd was described as like "nothing anyone heard at the Superdome before or since." Longtime fan Christopher Bravender, practically enshrines it: "Gleason's play transcends football. Our city was crippled. We needed the Saints and we needed them desperately. We needed the distraction. We needed the inspiration. We needed to feel like we were a part of something. That blocked punt literally helped people rebuild their homes. It symbolized being back."

And what did Steve Gleason do that night after pulling off the greatest play in Saints' history? He went to the Maple Leaf and sweated with the crowd, dancing to the Rebirth Brass Band.

Gleason was an improbable hero. He was small-in-size, under 6 feet tall and barely 200 pounds. He'd been an undrafted free agent out of Washington State and was never a full-time starter during his NFL career. He wore his hair long, loved local music, particularly folk and roots, and rode around town on his bike. He was far more like everyone else in New Orleans than a sports star. Gleason's

Steve Gleason and family   Robert X Fogarty

interests ranged from reading the *Bhagavad Gita* to practicing yoga to surfing with his brother, Kyle, in Indonesia during the off-season. After he retired from football, Gleason backpacked around the world with his wife, Michel, and got a master's degree from Tulane.

Then he became much more than a football star or world traveler. In 2011, he was diagnosed with amyotrophic lateral sclerosis (more commonly known as ALS, or Lou Gehrig's disease). The disease has no cure. An ALS diagnosis is considered the beginning of the end. But Gleason decided the diagnosis was all the more reason "to get ready to live." He said, "Our being, our power and our potential, is not contained in our physical bodies but rather in our mind and our spirit."

He established the organization Team Gleason, with their slogan "No White Flags," and has worked to battle ALS. Team Gleason has been creating awareness and helping those similarly afflicted. They are actively collaborating with scientists to create new technologies, like a wheelchair that can be controlled with the eyes, to improve the lives of those suffering from neuromuscular diseases or other injuries.

In a symbolic but amazing odyssey, Team Gleason undertook a harrowing 11-hour trek on the Inca Trail up Peruvian mountains to reach Machu Picchu's ancient ruins, which are nearly 12,000 feet above sea level. Said former Saints teammate and now a member of Team Gleason, Scott Fujita, who literally carried Gleason in his wheelchair over some of the more treacherous patches on the journey, "Physically, that was the most exhausting and draining thing I've ever been through."

On the tenth anniversary of Hurricane Katrina, Steve wrote a love letter to New Orleans. I reprint it here in its entirety because (a) his words perfectly capture the city and (b) he more than deserves the space.

Dear New Orleans,

I was born amongst the mountains and cool, clear rivers of the Pacific Northwest, a place that is different from New Orleans in seemingly every single way. I first moved to New Orleans nearly 15 years ago to play for the Saints. At the time, I was fighting to find a home in the NFL. A decade and a half later, I can proudly say I am a New Orleanian.

New Orleans is a small city, which resonates of family, dysfunctional at times, but surely a family. It seems a normality now, but while exploring those first few years I was astonished by the closeness of the families I met. I love New Orleans, but I understand that this city is not for everyone. If you are a clean freak the city will likely give you hives. If you're intolerant of creative expression, the city will overwhelm you. Are you confined to a schedule, punctuality or structure? Good luck. If you're the reclusive, solitary type, the city will open you up like a can of sardines or maybe a lotus flower. If you're vaunting or spotless, the city will expose your humanity and promptly celebrate your stains. If you're the type of person who surrenders when adversity strikes, you won't last through hurricane or football season.

In 2011, I was diagnosed with a hurricane of a disease—ALS. Terminal. Death, two to five years. Like this city's levees in 2005, my invincible body has failed me. But like the residents of a city built 2 feet below sea level, I choose to be an idealist. We simply must be steadfast, maniacal idealists.

When the world sees tragedy, idealists see opportunity. When the world folds its hand, idealists double down. When the world retreats, idealists reinvent. Idealism isn't for the faint-hearted or weak-minded. ALS and the water surrounding New Orleans have shattered our hearts a thousand times over, but somehow, like the local banana tree, our enduring hearts piece themselves back together each and every time. Rebuild. Rebirth. Repeat.

Many people say the 2006 Saints gave hope to the people of New Orleans. I see it differently. When I blocked the punt on that Monday night with the world watching, I was buoyed by a stadium and a city full of preposterous, hair-brained, unyielding and passionate idealists. We call them Who Dats.

This city breeds and attracts unique, outrageous people. Bedraggled people who are honest enough to consecrate their shortcomings. Innovative people who see opportunity where others see chaos. Humble people who honor the mosquito and the cockroach. Transparent people who will share with you whether you like it or not. Persistent people who rebuild when their city or their lives fall apart. Fierce people who protect what they love, and love a great deal.

I helped win the first playoff game in Saints history. I have a Super Bowl ring and a 9-foot statue outside my old office, the Superdome. But what I enjoy most about New Orleans is the infatuated, idealist citizens and the pervasive wholly, nourishing culture of family.

Love y'all,

Steve, a New Orleanian

Gleason, the documentary of his ordeals and to make a record for his yet unborn son, opened July 29, 2016 to almost universal acclaim (and a 94 percent rating on Rotten Tomatoes). Said teammate Scott Fujita, "This whole thing was started with the intention of one man wanting to share himself with his child. A lot of these ideas were hatched in the back yard over beers and pizza."

The film was first screened in June for the Saints, and reportedly a room full of 250-pound men who run 4.6 40-yard dashes were in puddles of tears. Head coach Sean Payton, took the stage after the film to say a few words and became unable to finish his sentences. Gleason shared the stage in his wheelchair and, seeing his former coach overcome with emotion, typed into his Stephen Hawking's voice simulator, "p-u-s-s-y."

Super Bowl Sunday in 2010 was magical. My family went to mass at Our Lady Star of the Sea Church, in what might be considered a sketchy neighborhood. I'd heard their priest, Father Tony Ricard, was a huge Saints fan. He did not disappoint. In the middle of his sermon, Father Tony ripped off his clerical robes to reveal he was wearing a Saints jersey. Immediately, a sea of black & gold second line umbrellas popped open among the congregation, the choir broke into the Crunk Song, the Ying Yang Twins tune adopted as the Saints' theme song ("Here we come to get you"), and the whole team of Father Tony, a deacon, a crucifer, torch-bearers and the thurifer did a second line shuffle straight down the center aisle.

It was, without question, the best Catholic Mass I've ever attended. The most moving part was learning that Father Tony's church members had secretly collected funds and bought him a ticket to attend the game in Miami. He turned down the ticket because he noted his dad had waited 43 years for this moment and when the Saints finally won, he needed to be seated at home, on the couch, next to his dad.

The prognosticators, pundits, and on-air blowhards had pretty universally picked the Colts to win the game. Over and over again, we heard the "experts" say how Peyton Manning was just on a different level from any other NFL player. They asserted that if Manning had 2 weeks of prep time, he'd analyze and dissect game film and totally pick apart the Saints' defense.

Tracy Porter, a Saints defensive back, intercepted Manning with three minutes left in the game and returned it 74 yards for the game-sealing touchdown. In the locker room, after the game, Porter said, "I watch films too."

Tracy Porter has since left the Saints to play for the Denver Broncos, Oakland Raiders, Washington Redskins, and now the Chicago Bears. Many of the Saints best players have gone to other teams: Scott Fujita to the Browns, Reggie Bush to the Dolphins, then Lions, Jermon Bushrod to the Bears, Carl Nicks to the Bucs, Roman Harper to the Panthers, more recently the all-star running back Darren Sproles to the Eagles and tight end Jimmy Graham to the Seahawks.

The local joke is that the Saints long-time cheer, "Who Dat," now literally means, "Who ARE those guys playing with Drew?"

"Who Dat" and use of "Dat" in general has become ubiquitous in New Orleans. After the Saints finally won the Super Bowl, T-shirts and bumper stickers popped up saying "Repeat Dat" or "Two Dat." New Orleans anti-litter ads use the phrase "Don't Trash Dat." Dog runs and some front yards display the sign "Scoop Dat." And "Tru dat" is a commonly heard phrase, meaning "I agree" or "Yeah, you right."

There are many stories (fabrications) of where "who dat" originated. The most accepted is that the chant of "Who Dat?" originated in minstrel shows and vaudeville acts of the late nineteenth and early twentieth centuries, and was taken up by jazz and big band performers in the 1920s and 30s.

A common tagline in the days of Negro minstrel shows was "who dat?" Answered by "Who dat say who dat?" Many different blackfaced gags played off that opening. Vaudeville performer Mantan Moreland was known for the routine.

"Who Dat?" became a familiar joke with soldiers during World War II. Back in WWII, US fighter squadron pilots would often fly under radio silence. But things get lonely up there in the cockpit, so after a while there'd be a crackle of static as someone keyed his mike. Then a disembodied voice would reply, "Who dat?" An answer would come, "Who dat say who dat?" And another, "Who dat say who dat when ah say who dat?" After a few rounds of this, the squadron commander would grab his microphone and yell, "Cut it out, you guys!" A few moments of silence. Then . . . "Who dat?"

Roger Goodell, commissioner of the NFL and a man much despised in New Orleans, had the NFL send cease & desist letters to T-shirt companies displaying the WHO DAT phrase and the Saints' Fleur de Lis logo, claiming the NFL had intellectual property rights. After a large backlash, pointing out the use of "Who Dat?" pre-dates the NFL by 30 years, and the Fleur de Lis by 1,500 years, the NFL backed off. The behemoth league, which reaps over $7 billion a year in net profit, looked rather Scrooge-like trying to get every last penny from small local vendors in a city trying to recover from Hurricane Katrina. My favorite protest came from *Sesame*

Street, for which I will love them the rest of my life. Hearing about the brouhaha, their lawyers sent a cease & desist letter to the NFL, claiming they had the intellectual property rights for the letters N, F, and L.

Tru Dat.

After the most recent back-to-back losing seasons, the Saints don't appear on the verge of Repeat Dat or Two Dat. If they never win or even go to another Super Bowl, there's something extra beautiful about the one they did win. At the end of the movie *The Commitments*, about a rag-tag Irish band, the often sparring band members pull off the perfect performance one night and then totally fall apart backstage, bickering and breaking up. Trumpet player and the band's sage, Joey "The Lips" Fagan, comforts band organizer, Jimmy Rabbitte, "Sure we could have been famous and made albums and stuff, but that would have been predictable. This way it's poetry." The Saints one and only Super Bowl is poetry.

To take in a game in New Orleans, *The Times-Picayune* highlighted 36 bars to "best" watch a Saints game. I won't list them all.

Cooter Brown's 509 S. Carrolton Ave.

Cooter Brown's is always at or near the top of any list. They have twenty-two TVs, including a large-screen, forty beers on tap, 450 beers in bottles, raw oysters, and will be stuffed with enthusiastic locals on game day. Cooter Brown's is named after a man who stayed drunk the entire Civil War so he'd be unfit for service.

Ale on Oak 8124 Oak St.

Ale on Oak has "only" thirty beers on tap, but serves lamb sliders or Chisesi ham and Gruyère hot pockets, which draws a bit more upscale crowd. You'll definitely see fewer patrons there in face paint and gold lamé stretch pants.

Tracy's 2604 Magazine St.

Tracy's splits the middle between upscale and road house. It'll be jammed and rowdy on game days. They are also known for their po'boys and, unlike most sports bars, they also have raw oysters. By the time Chris 'Boomer' Berman picks the wrong teams to win the day's NFL games, there won't be a seat in the house.

The Irish House 1432 St. Charles Ave.

The Irish House serves patrons a free mini cocktail called a Black and Gold Shot (Guinness stout and butterscotch liqueur) every time the Saints score a touchdown.

Manning's 519 Fulton St.

This is Archie Manning's place. The father of Peyton and Eli, and former Saints quarterback, will (rarely) be seen there greeting and gladhanding. What is always there are fifty-seven TVs with a 13' x 8' wall of screens in a semiprivate leather recliner area. Warning: the recliners come with a cost that varies according to the game. The Manning's outdoor courtyard can accommodate 300 fans and is a carless tailgating party with a large flat-screen TV, a smoker that cranks out barbecue, and a DJ that cranks out the music during commercial breaks.

Walk-On's 1009 Poydras St.

For some reason that escapes me, ESPN chose Walk-On's as the #1 sports bar in America. Maybe it was because the bar is blocks from the Superdome, or that Drew Brees is part owner, or that when ESPN commentators were in town, Todd McShay, Coach Ditka, and Schefty got more swag and free stuff from the place than Congressmen get from big banks or Monsanto. Walk-On's doesn't feel a whole lot different from any Bennigan's or Buffalo Wild Wings.

New Orleans is a football town the way St. Louis is a baseball town or Los Angeles is a basketball town. We have an NBA team, but the Pelicans are an afterthought. It might have been otherwise, except for a series of bad choices and ill-advised moves. The new team, then named the Jazz, began its inaugural season in 1974. They played in the Municipal Auditorium and Loyola Field House, where the basketball court was raised so high that the NBA Players Association made the team put a net around the court so that players wouldn't fall off of the court and get injured.

The team's first major move and misstep was to trade for star player Pete Maravich from the Atlanta Hawks using two first-round draft picks, three second-round picks, and one third-round pick. "Pistol" Pete had been a legendary and local college superstar at LSU. He still holds the NCAA records as the all-time leading college scorer (3,667 points, which is over 400 points higher than any other player in history), most points in a single season (1,381), and highest career points per game average (an astounding 44.2).

Some stats nerd with too much time on his hands went back to recalibrate Pistol Pete's points had the three-point shot been in effect. (There was no three-point line during his career.) His points per game *average* would have gone from an all-time best 44 to a staggering 55 points per game.

Maravich was likewise a star for the Jazz. Opposing players hailed his unique talents. Magic Johnson: "Maravich was unbelievable. I think he was ahead of his time in the things he did."

Pistol Pete

Isiah Thomas: "The best showman of all time? I'd probably have to say Pistol Pete." Rick Barry: "He could do things with a basketball I've never seen anybody do." And Lou Hudson: "This man has been quicker and faster than Jerry West or Oscar Robertson. He gets the ball up the floor better. He shoots as well. Raw talent wise, he's the greatest who ever played."

But, having gone all-in on acquiring Maravich, the Jazz were strapped to surround him with talented teammates. His Jazz teams were hopelessly stuck in mediocrity. While Maravich won the NBA scoring title, the team's best season ever was a woeful 39–43.

In 1978, he was shipped off to Salt Lake City. So was the entire team. Keeping the name, Jazz, in the decidedly least jazzy area of the country, Utah, makes about as much sense as naming a team in Los Angeles for the 10,000 lakes of Minnesota.

Had Pistol Pete been born in the post-Jordan era, he would have been a millionaire many times over. With his rail-thin physique (he was 6 feet, 5 inches tall, and barely 180 pounds), floppy Beatle cut hair style, signature drooping socks around his ankles, and above all, his jaw dropping passes that flew in every direction, behind his back and backwards, over his shoulder, eyes looking one way and the ball heading another, or through his legs, his was a completely unique style Madison Avenue would have loved to use to peddle a huge array of products.

Instead, he's become not much more than a footnote without a ring and subject of a little-watched *30 for 30* segment on ESPN. In an interview in 1974, Maravich said, "I don't want to play 10 years in the NBA and then die of a heart attack when I'm 40." On Jan. 5, 1988, he collapsed after a three-on-three pickup game in Pasadena and died of a heart attack. Pete Maravich was 40.

Twenty-four years after losing the Jazz, New Orleans got a new team in 2002. The Hornets were taken from the city of Charlotte. They would eventually give the name back to Charlotte (as Utah should give back the name Jazz to where it belongs . . . ahem!) and the team became named the Pelicans in 2013. The Pelicans, like the original Jazz, has a star player in Anthony "Unibrow" Davis but a forgettable supporting cast. Their overall record, as of this writing, is an uninspired 534–616.

Unlike the Saints, you can pretty easily get tickets for a Pelicans game at the wretchedly named Smoothie King Center. Now, I like Smoothie King, particularly their Peanut Power Plus Chocolate, and I honor the fact that Smoothie King was started in Kenner, a strip mall suburb of New Orleans, but that is just a terrible name for a sports stadium.

An even easier ticket to get, and probably more fun to use, is for a baseball game. The Zephyrs were the minor league team, a part of the Florida Marlins organization until the 2017 season, when they changed their name to the New Orleans Baby Cakes. Fans were apoplectic. What's a Baby Cake? The new name was announced days after the 2016 Presidential election. Here in New Orleans, more people were tweeting #NotMyTeam than #NotMyPresident. Whether called the Zephyrs or the Baby Cakes, they're not an especially great team. Their most noteworthy record is their striking out in a game the most times (29) in minor league history. They surprisingly won that game against the Nashville Sound in a 24-inning contest (also a record).

Their stadium, nicknamed "The Shrine on Airline," was built next to the Saints' training facility on Airline Highway. Its very unique feature is the Coors Light Party Shack. Right Field is not occupied by bleacher seating, but by a swimming pool and Tiki hut bar where you can watch a game chest-deep in chlorinated water while sipping a beer or cocktail. In annoying fashion, the Arizona Diamondbacks ripped off the idea for their Chase Field, so New Orleans now has the first but not the only swimming pool in the outfield.

For my money, and we're talking $10, the best sports experience in New Orleans is the Big Easy Rollergirls, our female roller derby team. They play home matches at the University of New Orleans Human Performance Center. The matches I have attended were all at capacity, with roughly 1,500 people in the stands. The crowd

Roller Girls out of uniform

was equally divided amongst heavily tattooed and pierced hipsters, families with kids, and rednecks screaming for blood on the tracks.

The music greatly ramped up the evening's entertainment value. My first match was accompanied by the Egg Yolk Jubilee performing totally bizarre brass band cover versions of Johnny Cash's "Ring of Fire" and Ary Barroso's cheezy classic, "Brazil." The most recent time, the music was by bounce superstar, Big Freedia. He/She was there to record his/her music video for the song "Dangerous." If you look closely at the video, you can almost, but not quite spot my daughter in the crowd dancing scenes.

But the main event is watching the Rollergirls skate in a circle of flying elbows and body checks. It looks nothing if not like an R. Crumb drawing brought to fleshy and knee padded life. With players' names like Chestosterone, Bang Crosby, and Porchop Slamwitch, you kind of know what you're in for even before the first whistle blows.

The Fairgrounds Race Track, originally built as the Union Race Course in 1852, is the third-oldest site of horse racing in America. In the early years, it was also used for exhibitions, boxing matches, and baseball games. General George Armstrong Custer raced horses there and President Ulysses S. Grant watched races there. It is today ranked the #12 best horse track in the country by the Horseplayers Association of North America. I have no idea where it ranks among ostrich and camel racing tracks.

The Fairgrounds Track has hosted the Dromedary Dash (camel races), ostrich races, and the local mascot race, where people dressed up as Hugo (the NBA mascot), Boudreaux (the Zephyrs nutria mascot), Bones (representing the arena football team, Voodoo), Havoc (Loyola University), Gold Digga (Xavier University) and other costumed characters have competed.

The horse racing season opens each year on Thanksgiving and runs through the end of March. For Thanksgiving, women (and men) show up wearing their most opulent and outrageous hats. You can purchase a Thanksgiving turkey dinner to be eaten in the clubhouse.

In May, during the Mid-City Bayou Boogaloo Festival, you don't so much bet on as "donate" by buying a plastic yellow rubber ducky to compete in the Rubber Ducky Derby. Your donations go to the Second Harvest Food Bank of Greater New Orleans. Over 10,000 rubber duckies are tossed into Bayou St. John. The first place winner that bobbles across the finish line gets a four-day Carnival Cruise. Second place get two tickets to an NFL Saints game. Third place wins four tickets to an NBA Pelicans game. I wonder how the Pelicans feel about that pecking order.

New Orleans has a soccer team, the Jesters, formerly the Shell Shockers (when initially owned by Shell Oil) and, depending on the year, maybe an indoor football team, the Voodoo. The Voodoo were formed in 2002 but didn't play until 2004. The team suspended operations for two years after the 2008 season. The New Orleans Krewe is/was an all-female tackle football team in the 40 team IWFL. They are currently and hopefully temporarily inactive as they seek funding. There is also the WFA, a sixty-three-team female football league. I'm guessing many readers didn't know there were any pro female football teams, let alone over 100 between the two

Rubber Ducky Derby   Frank L Aymami III

LUMINS OF NEW ORLEANS:
Chris Trew

Chris Trew is the chosen Lumin(ary) for my chapter on sports because he is perhaps the best wrestling manager of whom you've never heard. He was named Newcomer of the Year in 2012 by Anarchy Championship Wrestling fans and Manager of the Year in 2013 by The Wrestling Blog. The blog tagged him "a performance artist at the highest level."

Like Deon Sanders and Bo Jackson, Chris is a multi-sport athlete. He's been waging an ongoing but so far unsuccessful campaign to be elected owner of the New Orleans Pelicans, the city's NBA team. Ownership, at this time, is not an elected office.

If "Air Sex" becomes recognized as a sport or gets included in the Olympics, as tug of war and live pigeon shooting used to be and the steeple chase, hammer throw, and synchronized swimming still are, Chris Trew is the odds on favorite to win the Gold. Air Sex was invented in Japan but brought to high art by Chris. Think air guitar minus the guitar plus sex minus a partner. "While I'm very thankful for the Japanese and their inventing of Air Sex," says Trew, "I'm extremely confident that we can more than hold our own as a nation. The talent in North America is creative and hungry. America needs Air Sex. It's a release, it's high-brow entertainment, and it's the most important sporting event in the world."

After this book is written but probably before you read it, MTV will have aired their new series about Air Sex. I'm assuming Chris will be the sort of Guy Fieri host, only far less obnoxious.

Outside of sports, he was also known as Terp2it, his rap handle. Terp2it has released three albums: *The Freshest Dude*, *My Wiener Touches the Ceiling*, and *Half Man Half Beard*.

Chris Trew is, above all else, a comedian and performance artist in the fuck-with-you spirit of Andy Kaufman.

He first got into comedy as a student at LSU, but found himself unable to pursue his dreams in his favorite city. After Hurricane Katrina, Chris and his partner, Tami Nelson, relocated to Austin, where they started The New Movement in 2009. It was a place to teach improv and sketch classes. "The game plan was always to move back to New Orleans," he said. Finally, in March 2012, they returned to New Orleans to open their dream: an improv school and comedy theater in their home city.

New Movement has a permanent home (2706 St. Claude Ave.) in the Marigny. Here they teach classes, give workshops like Humor Writing for Improvisers, Three Person Scenes, and Stare into the Void, and have regular performances. New Movement puts on more than ten shows a week, and hosts improv and sketch comedy classes every night.

To complement The New Movement and the growth of the comedy scene in New Orleans, Chris also helped start Hell Yes Fest. It has grown to become the biggest comedy festival in the South, with 11 days of non-stop endurance comedy featuring hundreds of national and local acts performing one after another in shows, workshops, and a film festival component.

Comedy blog Splitsider said of the pair's work: "Tami Nelson and Chris Trew have shaped their brand by challenging the expectations of what a comedy show and the scene around it looks like."

The Austin Chronicle's review was more directly to the point, "Chris Trew is out of his fucking mind."

leagues. I think there is a team called the New Orleans Jazz, formerly the Mojo, formerly the Blaze, formerly the Spice, which have been around since 2002. But, clearly, I've never been to a game, and the WFA website makes it impossible to know their current status.

The Freret Street Boxing Gym (1632 Oretha Castle Haley Blvd.) has one ring, no air-conditioning, and a portable toilet out back. It's filled with folks serious about working out—jumping rope, hitting the speed bag, lifting free weights (no machines), and sparring.

In 2005, owner Mike Tata began hosting and promoting a lineup of boxing matches to the public. Staged four times a year, the Friday Night Fights have developed an almost cult-like following that includes attendees of all types, from serious boxing buffs who follow the sport to those who simply enjoy the spectacle. The fights, which take place in the street to accommodate the large crowds, feel as much like a festival as an athletic competition. Spectators are entertained by DJs, drag queens, reggae bands, burlesque performers, hot-dog-eating and bikini contests (not yet both at the same time, but that can't be ruled out), dance troupes, and fans dressed up in costumes that rival Mardi Gras attire. Crowd participation is everything—many "misters" have been crowned Miss Friday Night Fights based on audience applause—and winners are often decided by the drunkest and rowdiest. The matches also attract atypical fighters. Father Kevin Wildes—Jesuit priest, president of Loyola University and holder of four master's degrees and a PhD in philosophy—has stepped into the ring, with the crowd chanting "Father, Father!" to spur him on.

For Tata, the Friday Night Fights are, financially speaking, not much more than a nonprofit event. He claims the ticket price covers little more than the costs. But Tata is in it for the fun, not the dough. Crowds average between 1,250 to 1,500 people, so come early if you want to find a good seat among the encampments of regulars with their folding lawn chairs, ice coolers (the event is B.Y.O.B.), and occasional charcoal grills.

No matter where you live, or what sport captures your interest, you can listen to the amazingly (bizarre) sports podcasts of Chris Trew. He is a self-described full-time comedy person and part-time professional wrestling manager. His weekly show, *Trew 2 the Game*, presents Chris' twisted take on New Orleans sports with a rotating cast of writers, comedians and athletes.

Praise for *Trew 2 the Game* ranges from "energetic and razor sharp" (Goth-amist) to "Chris Trew is out of his fucking mind" (*The Austin Chronicle.*) There are new episodes every Tuesday.

Then there remain plenty of outdoor sports that don't involve buying tickets nor rooting for a particular team. You can go kayaking or paddle boarding on Bayou St.

John. You can go fishing in Lake Pontchartrain, the Gulf, or inland waterways—but if you want the locally renowned Redfish, there are restrictive rules. You can't reel in more than five fish, and no more than one can be over 27 inches in length. The Redfish Rules were put into effect after Chef Paul Prudhomme made blackened redfish so popular, the fish almost went extinct.

If you've watched the reality show *Swamp People*, you might think you can come down to Louisiana, grab a gun at the local Cabela's or Walmart, find alligators, and shoot em. This is not so.

Non-residents can only hunt alligators while accompanied by a local guide. The local guide must have an alligator hunter tag. The hunting season lasts only 30 days, beginning the last Wednesday in August for the eastern hunting zones and after the last Wednesday in September for the western zones. And there's a cap. Usually only 800 gators may be "harvested" in any given year.

You can shoot as many nutria as you please and maybe pay for your airfare and hotel expenses in the process. The state pays out a bounty of $5 for every nutria killed and turned in. I'm sorry to not be fully current on my nutria-kill statistics, but back in 2010, 445,963 tails were turned in, netting over $2.2 million in bounty fees.

As much as they try to deny it, the McIlhenny family, owners of Tabasco Sauce, seem to be the culprits who introduced nutria from subtropical South America to run wild in the Louisiana bayous. Nutria are the second largest rodent in the world. They look most like a beaver except their large front teeth are bright orange, they have a rat's tail rather than beaver's, and the females have nipples on their back where nutria babies cling as their mothers swim around the swamp. All in all, nutria are a pretty disgusting animal.

They were brought here for their fur. However, when the fur industry tanked, they either escaped or were let out of their crates and cages. Nutria now run deep into Texas and all along the Gulf coast through Mississippi, Alabama, and Florida. They're sort of a rat version of kudzu.

At first, area chefs tried ways to make them desirable, but there's just no secret recipe to make large rats taste good. Some dog food manufacturers use ground nutria meat. And there has been a small, very small, recent attempt to again use nutria fur in fashion. Designer Billy Reid pushes his rat fur collection. "I love the masculinity of it. It's sort of the bad-ass fur." I've watched *Project Runway* and *Fashion Police* with my wife and daughter and what I've heard on those shows is no less ridiculous than wearing rat.

The average airfare to New Orleans runs about $350. The average hotel is about $150 a night. So, to come spend a three-day weekend, you need to kill about 160 nutria and your trip is paid for, unless you plan to eat, drink, or donate money to Harrah's Casino.

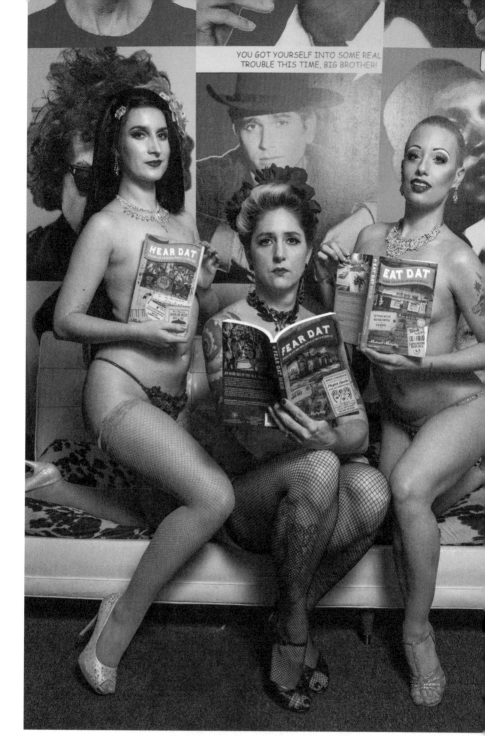

CHAPTER 8

Reading

What We Do When There Are No Festivals Nor Parades and All the Restaurants, Music Clubs, and Bars are Closed, and We Can't Find Someone to Chat Up

---

"I am at the moment writing a lengthy indictment against our century. When my brain begins to reel from my literary labors, I make an occasional cheese dip." —**John Kennedy Toole, *A Confederacy of Dunces***

In New Orleans, "reading" will more often involve Tarot cards, palms, and auras rather than books. There's a saying that New Orleans has vastly more writers than readers. But, our history is jammed with some of the greatest American writers, including our unquestionably greatest playwright, Tennessee Williams, and arguably America's best novelist, William Faulkner.

My college professor for my class on twentieth century American literature said in his lecture on day one, "I respect no man who doesn't love Faulkner." Truth be told, I understand the reverence for Faulkner, but I personally get all Yoknapatawpha'd out in his detailed pastiche of the fictional Mississippi county. Please don't tell Joe DeSalvo and Rosemary James, founders of the Faulkner Society in New Orleans and originators of the Words & Music Festival.

Faulkner lived at 624 Pirates Alley, a home currently occupied by Joe and Rosemary and where they operate Faulkner House Books from the first floor. Faulkner wrote *Soldiers' Pay* and *Mosquitoes* while living there. As a young 20-year-old, his writing often took a back seat to his partying and his habit of shooting at people with his BB gun as they passed under his rooftop.

Faulkner House Books, no bigger than the pets & nature section in a Barnes & Noble, is one of my favorite bookstores. Each book on the shelves has been practically curated. You won't find a single copy of *50 Shades of Grey* here, nor books allegedly written by celebrities David Duchovny, Snooki from *The Jersey Shore*, or James Franco. No, actually James Franco probably did write *Directing Herbert White*, which makes it even more depressing.

Faulkner House also has an underadvertised rare book and signed first edition collection. They've had autographed Lillian Hellmans, Robert Penn Warrens, and of course William Faulkners. Joanne Sealy, who's the ever-present face of the bookstore, said, "The only [Faulkner] first edition I don't currently have is *Absalom, Absalom!* That runs about $3,500."

The Words & Music Festival, created and run by Joe and Rosemary, is, by the way, my favorite writers conference in the country. (A) It's held in New Orleans, and (B) it's set up so that each attending and aspiring writer gets one-on-one sessions with a "real" professional editor and a "real" literary agent. The editors and agents will have read the writer's work before meeting them and may present many detailed criticisms. Several noted writers, like National Book Award winner Julia Glass and Stewart O'Nan were "discovered" at the Festival. As a former literary agent, I signed two writers during the sessions, one published by HarperCollins and the other by St. Martin's Press.

Unlike most cities these days, New Orleans has numerous independent bookstores. The Garden District Books (2727 Prytania St.) is located inside an old roller skating rink turned micro-mall, with maybe four stores and a coffee shop. When she lived in New Orleans, Anne Rice always had her first signing for each new book at Garden District Books. Octavia Books (513 Octavia St.) has a slew of author signings, practically one every night, and a permanent table display near the front door of New Orleans authors and books. Gladden Scott, the store owner, said, "It started as a wake, but it turned into a celebration." The effervescent owner, Elizabeth Berry Ahlquist, is as much a reason to drop by Blue Cypress Books (8126 Oak St.) as her intelligent selection.

And, of course, there are many used or antiquarian bookstores dotting the French Quarter. Choices include Beckham's BookShop (228 Decatur St.), Dauphine Street Books (410 Dauphine St.), and Librairie Book Shop (823 Chartres St.)

Kitchen Witch Cookbooks recently left the Quarter when their rent got jerked up 115 percent. They are one of the country's few bookshops dedicated exclusively to cookbooks. Probably sounding like a broken record, here too the #1 reason to go is to engage with the owners, Debbie Lindsey and retired chef Philipe LaMancusa. Philipe is wizened. Debbie is wacky in the most delightfully engaging way.

Kitchen Witch started with 5,000 cookbooks from Philipe's personal collection and has grown to over 9,500 new, used, rare. and out-of-print cookbooks, priced from $2 to $2,000. They now operate in Mid-City (1452 N. Broad St.), more out of the way for visitors, but now with plenty of parking that could never be found in the French Quarter. Said Debbie, "I never thought I could get so excited about asphalt."

Truman Capote is another favorite son of New Orleans. He always said he was born at the Hotel Monteleone, probably taking a little literary license there. The hotel has named a suite in his honor.

Capote loved New Orleans and New Orleans loved him back. His bitchy-queenie-tongue-in-cheek personality was a perfect fit. While he had many noted quips, my personal favorite was when a man walked up to him during a book signing, whipped out his penis, and said "Why don't you sign this?" Nonplussed and without missing a beat, Capote dismissively looked at the man's junk and said, "I doubt I can do my whole signature. I might have to just initial it."

While most of Capote's adult life was spent in New York, he did return as a young and unpublished writer to work on his first novel, *Other Voices, Other Rooms*. He lived in a rented apartment at 811 Royal Street. Capote returned to New Orleans often as a retreat from the pressures of fame. In a 1981 interview with *People* magazine, he said, "I get seized by a mood and I go. I stay a few weeks and I read and write and walk around. It's like a hometown to me."

Truman Capote has now been dead for 32 years as of this writing. His remains, however, were given new life just in time for the anniversary of Capote's death. Julien's Auctions in Los Angeles announced it will be selling the author's ashes to the highest bidder. The starting price is $2,000. I tried to convince my wife, who bakes cakes and petit fours professionally, to get in on the bidding. I know there are many New Orleanians who'd want to buy a cake with a little Capote baked inside.

Tennessee Williams is the city's #1 favorite son. He came here the day after Christmas in 1938, stepping off a Greyhound bus. He was escaping a series of soul-sucking jobs, working for his father's International Shoe Company in St. Louis, followed by a stint as caretaker on a chicken ranch outside Los Angeles. On his arrival for the first time, Williams wrote in his journal, "Here surely is the place I was made for." Williams also wrote to his mother, "I'm crazy about the city. I walk continually, there is so much to see." He would later issue his more enduring quotation, "America has only three cities: New York, San Francisco, and New Orleans. Everywhere else is Cleveland." As one who grew up in The Mistake by the Lake, or as Cleveland now tries to self-nickname, The Land, I should take offense at that quote.

On literary walking tours, guides can pretty much point to any house in the French Quarter and state, "Tennessee Williams lived there." His first residence was a rented room in the attic of an old boarding house at 722 Toulouse Street, run by Mrs. Anderson. Tennessee dubbed the place "the poetic evocation of all the cheap rooming houses of the world." He wrote on the weekends after working shifts at a local restaurant. Mrs. Anderson has been sort-of immortalized in his lesser read play *Vieux Carré*.

632 St. Peter St. is where he lived and allegedly wrote *A Streetcar Named Desire* in 1946. The original title had been *Poker Night*. Fortunately, an incident where the author had nearly been run over by a city street car (yes, the Desire line) prompted him to choose his far more evocative title. There's a plaque on the side of the building on St. Peter, stating the site as the birthplace of his most famous play, so it must be

true. A Fleurty Girl shop, selling privately designed T-shirts and New Orleans collectibles, occupies the space today.

He eventually bought rather than rented his first home at 1014 Dumaine St. This was the home he said he "wanted to die in." While it remained one of his residences, the peripatetic playwright also lived in New York, Key West, Rome, Barcelona, and London. He actually died in a depressingly banal way. Williams choked to death when a plastic cap of the type used on bottles of nasal spray or eye solution got stuck in his throat. He was in his Manhattan hotel suite, having just returned from his house in Key West.

Tennessee Williams is buried in St. Louis, his childhood home. My guess is that he'd prefer to be in another city he hadn't previously dismissed as a version of Cleveland. In life, he had received four Drama Critic Circle Awards, two Pulitzer Prizes and the Presidential Medal of Freedom.

In late March each year, New Orleans honors him with the five-day Tennessee Williams Literary Festival. Originally drawing only 500 people in 1986, it now attracts over 10,000 attendees each year. The highlight is always the closing "Stella and Stanley Shouting Contest." Men and women, usually attired in Stanley Kowalski-style undershirts, compete to shout the most wrenching and convincing "*STELLAAAAA!*"

2012 winner Nicole Martin revealed on NPR her success came from method acting. "Most of the method was liquid courage." Winners get things like a case of beer, a massage, a hat, T-shirt, or bucket and wine glasses.

While John Kennedy Toole wrote all of one solitary book, his *A Confederacy of Dunces* places him among New Orleans' all-time great writers. Many cities have their signature song: Tony Bennett's "I Left My Heart in San Francisco," Frank Sinatra's "New York, New York," or Randy Newman's ode to Cleveland, "Burn On Big River," about the Cuyahoga River being so polluted, it caught on fire . . . twice.

New Orleans has many signature songs. It's a matter of personal taste if you consider ours Louis Armstrong's "Do You Know What it Means to Miss New Orleans," or any of Professor Longhair's hits from "Go to the Mardi Gras" to "Tipitina's," or Fats Domino's "Walkin' to New Orleans," or Indian songs "Iko Iko" or "Handa Wanda," or any of the hundreds of covers of "When the Saints Go Marching In." But *A Confederacy of Dunces* is far and wide considered our signature novel.

John Kennedy Toole wrote his masterpiece and then killed himself when no one would publish it. His mother took up the cause and forced it upon noted writer and Loyola professor Walker Percy. At first reluctant to read the manuscript, Percy described his discovery as "a prickle of interest, then a growing excitement, and finally an incredulity: surely it was not possible it was that good."

After most large trade houses turned it down (again), Percy convinced LSU

Press to publish the book. It went on to win the Pulitzer Prize as Best Novel and became a permanent fixture on most any critics listing of the best novels of the twentieth century. The novel is the hilarious but spot-on indictments of contemporary culture by the eccentric, idealistic, some might say delusional, and passionately slothful 30-year-old protagonist, Ignatius J. Reilly. Walker Percy, in his introduction for the book, called Ignatius a "slob extraordinary, a mad Oliver Hardy, a fat Don Quixote, a perverse Thomas Aquinas rolled into one."

After Toole's suicide and the later huge success of his novel, his mother, Thelma Ducoing Toole, became a bit of a sensation herself. She was, so to say, a crazy old dame who had a penchant for wearing long white evening gloves, even in the daytime. She booked gigs all over town where she'd play the piano and sing, both quite poorly. Thelma once told an interviewer that she had studied drama for 16 years and piano for 10. There was no evidence of that. Her notoriety as an eccentric spread far enough that the old NBC Tom Snyder TV show in New York, the *Tomorrow Show*, booked her as a guest. After she totally charmed Snyder, he asked her to come back and said he'd provide snacks and drinks. The 80-year-old Thelma replied, "Champagne only, Tom. I'm not just someone you can just drag in off the streets."

I was working in a bookstore when the novel was published. Reading the backstory the week prior to publication, I put five first edition copies of Toole's novel aside for myself, figuring it'd be worth something as a collectible. The first copies on display sold immediately, so I ordered twenty-five more that were to arrive the next day. In the meantime, I slowly depleted my stash by selling them to customers. I hesitated to give up my very last of the five copies, but that last customer looked like a young Cybill Shepherd. I had visions she would, in gratitude, invite me over for live readings, possibly removing an article of clothing every time Ignatius' mom took a snort of muscatel.

When the back-up twenty-five copies arrived at the store, the book was already in its fourth printing. At one point, first editions were worth $2,500 apiece. I never saw the Cybill-look-alike again.

My loss of first editions doesn't compare to the losses of actors cast to play Ignatius Reilly in the film adaptation of *A Confederacy of Dunces*. John Belushi was the first. He died of a drug overdose. John Candy died of a heart attack. Chris Farley died either of a heart attack or drug overdose. Divine was never officially cast, but John Waters was trying to buy film rights to create a vehicle for his outlandish star when Divine too died. Ignoring all "signs," Zach Galifianakis is currently cast to be Ignatius.

At 819 Canal, standing under the clock and in front of what used to be the old D. H. Holmes Department Store and is now the Hyatt French Quarter, stands a bronze statue of the fictional Ignatius J. Reilly.

The statue represents the opening scene in the novel where Ignatius stands outside D. H. Holmes, waiting for his mother under the store's clock in his trademark hunting cap, holding a Schwegmann's grocery store bag, and surveying the street crowd, looking for signs of bad taste.

Walker Percy, who shepherded *A Confederacy of Dunces* to publication, is himself a noted writer and sometimes considered to have written the second-greatest New Orleans novel, *The Moviegoer*. *The Moviegoer* was Percy's first published book in 1961, winner of the National Book Award and honored by *Time* magazine in 2005 as one of the best English-language books published since 1923. Why 1923, I have no idea. Maybe there was a slew of great books published in 1922, making it impossible to narrow it down to just a few all-time greats.

He wrote five other novels and two works of nonfiction, all capable of giving paper cuts of alienation as his books explore the existential search for faith and love in a chaotic world (though Percy himself was not a fan of the word "existential").

After getting degrees from UNC-Chapel Hill (where my wife went) and Columbia University (where my son went), he intended to become a psychiatrist. But contracting tuberculosis, Percy was bedridden for a duration and made the life-altering choice to while away his time reading Dostoyevsky, Tolstoy, and (God-forbid!) Soren Kierkegaard.

The New York Times' uber-critic, Michiko Kakutani, wrote Percy was "one of our most talented and original authors" and that he was "more of a philosophical novelist in the European tradition than a straightforward narrative storyteller." The writer and editor Alfred Kazin called him "the satiric Dostoyevsky of the bayou."

Kate Chopin's *The Awakening*, published in 1899, would be another candidate for Best New Orleans novel. Called "Madame Bovary, Cajun style," the turn-of-the-century novel about a woman's emotional and sexual awakening was considered "inappropriate" and was out of print for decades. The novel is now seen as a seminal work and precursor to twentieth-century Southern greats like Faulkner, Flannery O'Connor, Eudora Welty, Katherine Anne Porter, and Tennessee Williams.

For me, and seemingly not enough others, Valerie Martin's *A Recent Martyr* belongs on that shortlist. Upon publication, *The New York Times* reviewed the novel: "This is a striking book, one with as much depth as the reader dares to plumb. *A Recent Martyr* details the torrid and extraordinary sadomasochistic affair between Emma and Pascal. Through it, Emma tells us, she is 'to discover the sweet and unexpected horror of [her] own nature.'"

The lush writing is filled with sex, faith, death, and decay. What's more New Orleans than that? A GoodReads reviewer best summed up my reactions to reading the novel. "Just finished my reread last night. Emotional, disturbing, cathartic—I'm still in a fog from its clutches." I own three copies just so in case it ever goes out-of-print, I can share it with others.

Sex, faith, death, and decay could also be used as a tagline for New Orleans'

Looking for signs of bad taste

most-read novelist, Anne Rice. With her soon to be fourteenth vampire novel, sixteen other novels about witches, werewolves, castratos, and Jesus as a seven-year-old, plus her five works of erotica written under pseudonyms, Anne has sold well over 100 million books, making her among the bestselling writers on the planet. Her writings have spawned three film adaptations, a mini-series, ten comic books, and a short-lived Broadway play, *Lestat*, with music by Elton John.

She has also, more than anyone alive, revitalized the vampire mythology. She's actually revised vampires from monstrous loners like Dracula into the sympathetic characters like Louis de Pointe du Lac. Anne has said of her first book, "Vampires were these elegant, tragic, sensitive people. I was really just going with that feeling when writing Interview with the Vampire." Some Bram Stoker purists may cringe at the evolution from Dracula to these new "sensitive" vampires like Edward Cullen (*Twilight*) and Bill Compton (*True Blood*). They've become less monsters lurking in the shadows and more desirable boyfriend material.

Being a celebrity vampire novelist is not without complications. Voyeuristic Goth kids started hanging at the fence of her home at 1239 First Street, hoping to get a glimpse of Anne, or trying to spot the giant oak where the fictional Lasher and Emaleth are imaginarily buried, or to merely breathe in the same rarified jasmine and sweet olive-infused air Anne breathed.

Much to the delight of her fans but chagrin of her neighbors, Anne chose to give free Monday night tours of her home. It was as though Greta Garbo had said, "C'mon over everybody, I vont to have a chat." The line on First Street would stretch to St. Charles.

Anne left New Orleans in 2002 following the death of her husband, poet and artist Stan Rice. "I was creatively and emotionally exhausted and craving a fresh start," she said. "I guess I wanted to go to a place with no memories and no history."

Even though Anne hasn't lived at her Garden District home in over a decade, you may still wish to walk by the house on First Street. The front fence plaque (tell me the design in the iron fence doesn't look like little skulls) describes the house as once belonging to both Anne Rice and Albert Hamilton Brevard. The wealthy Brevard brought exotic plants from all over the world, and in New Orleans' subtropical climate, they all flourished. Later, Brevard went bankrupt and attempted suicide on his front porch. While he lay on his deathbed, word spread throughout the neighborhood and his lovely neighbors used the opportunity to rush over and dig up Brevard's plants for their own yards.

My personally favorite *other* vampire writer is Andrew Fox. Fox created Jules Duchon, the obese vampire protagonist in the novels *Fat White Vampire Blues* and *Bride of the Fat White Vampire*. The fictional Duchon was born and bred in the working-class Ninth Ward (or as they would say "Nint Woid") and, even after being bitten and becoming a vampire, he kept his job as a cab driver.

Fox reasoned that "if vampires actually 'lived' in New Orleans and subsisted on the blood of New Orleanians, they'd be sucking down a stew of cholesterol and fatty lipids with every meal. After a century or so, a New Orleans vampire would look a heck of a lot more like John Goodman than Tom Cruise."

I certainly can't cite all the superior books to give you a real sense of the city, but I can list enough to fill your nightstand.

Tim Gautreaux was born in Morgan City, Louisiana, on the banks of the Atchafalaya River. He's a real Cajun, and notes that his family's blue-collar background has been a significant influence on his writing. His father was a tugboat captain and his grandfather was a steamboat engineer. He says, "I pride myself in writing a 'broad-spectrum' fiction, fiction that appeals to both intellectuals and blue-collar types." *The Missing* is largely considered his best work. It is a moody novel set in the 1920s. The oft-troubled protagonist Sam Simoneaux, ironically nicknamed "Lucky," works in a New Orleans department store as the security guard when a little girl goes missing during his shift.

You might better absorb New Orleans through our outstanding crime series. There was a piece written in *The New York Times Review of Books* whose premise was that the best way to get a feel for a city was through its mystery and crime writers. When I read that, I instantaneously felt it to be true. I think Don DeLillo and Jonathan Lethem are great writers. But, if you want to feel the essence of New York City, no one does better portraits than mystery writers Lawrence Block or Andrew Vachss. For Boston, you have Robert B. Parker and Dennis Lehane. Los Angeles has generations from Raymond Chandler and James M. Cain up through Jim Thompson and James Ellroy.

For New Orleans, the Lew Griffin series by James Sallis is a great place to start. There are seven books centered around a bourbon-drinking detective who roams the bleak streets of New Orleans. Garth Cartwright in *The Guardian* wrote, "Subtle and oblique in content, [his stories] are meditations upon America rather than tales of policemen and thieves; this marks them out from much of the crime genre."

David Fulmer's first novel, *Chasing the Devil's Tail*, was published by a small press in Phoenix. He was thereafter "discovered" by Harcourt Books, a national publisher, which published five more novels. *Chasing the Devil's Tail* won the Shamus Award, a major award for mystery writers. His novel *The Blue Door* was also nominated for a Shamus Award. A reviewer noted *Chasing* "is heavy on setting and character development, and if you are inclined to pass this one up because it's billeted as a mystery, don't. You'll really want to visit New Orleans afterwards, which is always a good thing these days."

Many consider our current master to be the transplanted New Yorker, Bill Loehfelm. After two books based on Staten Island, he has set five Maureen Coughlin mysteries in his adopted home. *The New Orleans Advocate* wrote, "Not only has Loehfelm created the most compelling, complex patrol cop in the genre, he has also re-energized New Orleans as a setting for the best in crime fiction, going well beyond the cliché."

Julie Smith has written twenty mystery novels, just as many short stories, and has won tons of awards including the Edgar Allan Poe Award for Best Novel, which is kind of like winning the Oscar for Best Picture. She has two series set in New Orleans, both with strong and utterly unique female protagonists. Talba Wallis, who calls herself the Baroness de Pontalba, is a performance artist, poet, and private detective. She's young, African-American, and, when sleuthing, dresses like a Catholic school girl. Skip Langdon is a cop that's bigger than life—over 6 feet tall and overweight. Prior to being a homicide detective, she was a former debutante and Carnival queen, Tulane flunk-out, boozer, doper, all around screw-up. and daughter of one of the City's most prominent doctors.

Readers, critics, or Julie herself may disagree with me, but I consider *Axeman's*

Jazz her best novel to hook you in. The novel is about a modern day serial killer who's borrowed the name of the Axeman, a serial killer who roamed the city until 1919.

The real life Axeman is sort of New Orleans' Jack the Ripper. Beginning in 1911, a series of people were found hacked to death by an axe, all killed in their homes at night. All cases involved the murder of an owner of an Italian grocery. All had a pattern by which an incredibly small panel had been hacked through the door to gain entry. The police immediately thought they were dealing with the Mafia, without even considering a little person or dwarf who had an unnatural hatred for Sopressata or Mascarpone. Perhaps the victims had not paid "dues" or failed to meet loan payback deadlines.

The axe murders suddenly stopped, only to return seven years later. On May 23, 1918, another Italian grocer and his wife were butchered while sleeping in their apartment above the Maggio grocery store. Again, a small entry hole had been cut into the back door.

The newspaper received a chilling letter dated, "Hell, March 13, 1919." It read:

Esteemed Mortal:

They have never caught me and they never will. They have never seen me, for I am invisible, even as the ether that surrounds your earth. I am not a human being, but a spirit and a fell demon from the hottest hell. I am what you Orleanians and your foolish police call the Axeman.

Undoubtedly, you Orleanians think of me as a most horrible murderer, which I am, but I could be much worse if I wanted to. If I wished, I could pay a visit to your city every night. At will I could slay thousands of your best citizens, for I am in close relationship to the Angel of Death.

Now, to be exact, at 12:15 (earthly time) on next Tuesday night, I am going to visit New Orleans again. In my infinite mercy, I am going to make a proposition to you people. Here it is:

I am very fond of jazz music, and I swear by all the devils in the nether regions that every person shall be spared in whose home a jazz band is in full swing at the time I have mentioned. If everyone has a jazz band going, well, then, so much the better for you people. One thing is certain and that is that some of those people who do not jazz it on Tuesday night (if there be any) will get the axe.

The Axeman

Even if it was a prank, people took the letter seriously. The night of March 19th, the whole city had jazz blaring from every door. No one was murdered that night.

And just like that, the Axeman was gone. He was never seen or heard from in the city again. His crimes remain unsolved. Sorry to disappoint you if you're a *Criminal Minds* fan and need a tidy conclusion followed by a ridiculous quote. As Charles Bukowski once wrote, "Sometimes you just need to pee in the sink."

Confession: Chris Wiltz has become a very dear friend. But I didn't know her when I first read her book *The Emerald Lizard* and felt completely bathed in New Orleans piquancy. She has written three detective novels, *The Killing Circle*, *A Diamond Before You Die*, and *The Emerald Lizard*, which are built around the fictional Neal Rafferty. Her novels *Shoot the Money* and *Glass House* also contain elements of crimes.

But, her signature book is the nonfiction portrait of Norma Wallace, called *The Last Madam*.

Sara Roahen is likewise a personal friend. (We only have 340,000 residents. It's hard not to be in somebody's business.) Sara recently moved from the Gulf Coast to the West Coast. New Orleans misses her greatly. Before leaving, Sara had served as the director of The Southern Foodway Alliance, an organization that documents, studies, and explores the diverse food cultures of the changing American South, and wrote one of the best food memoirs and explorations of New Orleans ever written: *Gumbo Tales*, whose title I don't think conveys the heft and value of the book's contents. I feel Sara's book should be as revered as anything written by noted food/memoir writers A. J. Liebling or M. F. K. Fisher, and Sara's memoir certainly deserves a movie as much as Julie Powell's *Julie & Julia*.

Gumbo Ya-Ya by Lyle Saxon and Robert Tallant is not, as the title might fool you, about New Orleans food. Written in the 1920s, it is a local classic about New Orleans beliefs, superstitions, folklore, and customs, and I would tag it "required reading."

Four newer books I would likewise classify as required reading: *Nine Lives* by Dan Baum I feel is far and away the best post-Katrina book written. *Accidental City: Improvising New Orleans* is Lawrence N. Powell's masterpiece of our early history. As he writes in the book, "The improvisational style was characteristic of many frontier communities. Early New Orleans raised it to an organizational principal." *Empire of Sin: A Story of Jazz, Sex, Murder, and the Battle for Modern New Orleans*, is Gary Krist's definitive portrait of how New Orleans became the epicenter for every manner of vice. *Unfathomable City* by Rebecca Solnit and Rebecca Snedeker is a collection of nearly two dozen essays as utterly idiosyncratic as the city itself. Each piece is accompanied by a colorful map. Wrote one reviewer, "Trying to define New Orleans is like trying to hold water in your hands. And to their credit, they don't even try."

Let me close with a plug for a New Orleans author I represented as an agent. My company, Max & Co., A Literary Agency and Social Club, lasted barely five years.

LUMINS OF NEW ORLEANS:
Bunny Matthews

Among the literary giants of Faulkner, Capote, Tennessee Williams and the seminal classic of New Orleans' literary tradition, *A Confederacy of Dunces*, a strong case can be made that the city's greatest chronicler of our everyday life is the self-taught writer and artist Bunny Matthews. I almost wrote "cartoonist," as he is best known for his 1982 creation of the husband and wife duo, Vic and Nat'ly Broussard, in *The Times-Picayune's* weekly Sunday supplement. Bunny would not want to be restricted by being considered just a cartoonist.

His creation, Vic Broussard, is boorish, overweight, and un-ed-jukated, or as Bunny himself characterized him as "this typical New Orleans asshole, doesn't care what anybody thinks about him." Vic's brassy wife Nat'ly spews an ongoing banter with Vic in the Yat dialect from their fictional working-class corner bar and po'boy joint in the city's Ninth Ward, or what they would say, da Nint Ward.

Here too, Bunny might object to the use of "Yat dialect." He has pointed out, "I've always refrained—I don't think I've ever used it once—the word 'Yat' in any of my cartoons. I don't feel that anyone you would consider a Yat would say the word 'Yat' and then brag about it." Bunny feels the word Yat was coined by lily-white Tulane students who came to New Orleans on their parents' money and are either making fun of, or preciously venerating, locals they encounter in New Orleans.

If you're starting to think Bunny Matthews might be a tad bit bristly, he is unapologetically so. He hates white folks appropriating black traditions like second lining for their parties, weddings, and conventions. In fact, he's not a big fan of white culture in general. He has said, "The way I think American culture works is, and this is very simplified, black people invent things, gay people catch on to it, and then straight hetero white people catch on to it and it's not cool anymore."

Truth is, Bunny Matthews would also strongly object to me and this book. As one born in Detroit, grown in Cleveland, and who spent 27 years in New York City, I'd be dismissed out of hand. If you did not grow up in New Orleans, then you don't really exist to Bunny Matthews. "That is kind of the way I think. I only really care about people from Louisiana. And everybody else, I think that they're temporary."

Bunny began building his reputation in an earlier strip before Vic and Nat'ly. *F'Sure—Actual Dialogue Heard on the Streets of New Orleans* ran in the independent and now defunct weekly, *Figaro*. His signature style has been described as "post-psychedelic baroque."

His only attempt at formal art training was as a child with an Indonesian immigrant woman, but he stopped lessons with her after developing an allergic reaction to the aerosol fixative she used to set pastels.

As a writer, he was the first ever full-time music writer in New Orleans, writing for *The Times-Picayune*. This seems close to incomprehensible that a musical city like New Orleans had none prior. Bunny has written about music in numerous New Orleans publications, including *Gambit* and *Offbeat*, at which he served as editor. In his writing, he brings the same acerbic flare, shocking some, flat-out pissing off others. After he wrote a scathing review of a local concert, one of the show's producers wrote, "A review is indeed one man's opinion only. Thank God there is only one Bunny Matthews."

In addition to an artist and writer, he has been a musician and album cover designer. He composed album liner notes for Smiley Lewis, The Meters, Earl King and James Booker. He's worked as a T-shirt

Bunny Matthews holding court

designer, vinyl record delivery boy, dancer on the John Pela Saturday morning TV show, commissioned mural painter, founding member of Galerie Jules Lafourge. Bunny's an award-winning talk show host whose interviews include Cab Calloway, porn star Marilyn Chambers, James Brown, Brenda Lee, Bob Marley, Professor Longhair, Fats Domino, Ernie K-Doe, Elvis Costello, Suzi Quatro, Al Green, a voodoo priestess, and a couple of dog groomers. If you see a through line there, be sure and let me know.

For many, his seminal classic work is his monumental painting, "Nint'Wardica, or A Roaches History of New Orleans Hurricane Katrina." The massive mural, based on Pablo Picasso's "Guernica," was displayed at the Ogden Museum of Southern Art.

At one time, you could have purchased the Roaches History of New Orleans Hurricane Katrina designer sneakers for $90 (a steal), but these sadly seem to be no longer available and I don't have a pair (size 11, if anyone wants to sell one).

In addition to Leidenheimer delivery trucks, Bunny Matthews' artwork can also be viewed in the permanent collections of the Louisiana State Museum in Baton Rouge, the Audubon Insectarium in New Orleans, and in the private collections of George Clooney and Linda Ronstadt. His original illustrations can be found in the Historic New Orleans Collection, which also commissioned Matthews to create a large mural for the official City of New Orleans Pavilion at the 1984 World's Fair. His exhibitions include "Chihuahua: King of New Orleans Dogs" (Scheurich Gallery), "The Art of Bunny Matthews" (Contemporary Arts Center, New Orleans), "Bunny Matthews: Art For Heterosexuals" (Space Gallery), "Da Eve O'Destruction" (Vega Tapas Cafe), "Too Many Bunnies" (Arthur Roger 434), "Black and White" (Arthur Roger Gallery), and "The People of New Orleans From A–Z" (Arthur Roger Gallery). French travel magazine *I Heart*, titled him the city's "ambassadeur non conformiste."

As much as Bunny Matthews may dislike a Come Here like me, I can't help but love a man who loves New Orleans as fiercely as he does. He has said, "One of the beautiful things about New Orleans is that a lot of it is falling apart, covered with mildew and mold and decaying plaster; that gives it this patina which is beautiful. It's not sterile like the suburbs." And no truer statement has ever been said than, "The way that we live in New Orleans is art. Po'boys, raw oysters and things like that are works of art."

In my short stint, I had represented only one (1) *New York Times* best-seller and one (1) advance of more than $150,000. Sadly for the publisher doling out the six-figure advance, they were not the same book. I shuttered my agency in 2011 because (A) I was barely making a living and (B) I grew just too frustrated when proposal after proposal hooked editors, who shared my passion for the work, but then got shot down in the dreaded gauntlet of Ed Board. Ed Board is a meeting where a publicity director, marketing manager, or the sales rep who calls on Barnes & Noble have their chance to dismiss a book proposal. Sometimes the rejections were for reasons seemingly no better than "We did a book last season with the same number of pages—and it didn't sell."

Barb Johnson is a writer I "discovered" in a very circuitous route. I had fallen in love with a piece by Bern Esposito I read online. Bern was magnificently and fanatically obsessed with plane crashes. She was, at the time, attending the Iowa Writers Workshop. Contacting Iowa, they redirected me to the University of New Orleans writing program, which was sponsoring her sabbatical in France. Joanna Leak, director at UNO, helped me track down the writer I sought but then she also snuck me a short story by one of her students and thereby delivered me the writer I needed. Through this lone story, *St. Luis of Palmyra*, I was utterly blown away by Barb Johnson's talent. She reminded me of Dagoberto Gill, a writer you probably don't know, but should. Gritty yet beautiful, Barb's stories (for me) capture the sights, smells, and rhythms of New Orleans as well as anything I've ever read. Her collection, *More of This World or Maybe Another*, won numerous awards and almost got her a ton of money. Her book was the runner-up as Discovery Book of the Year for Barnes & Noble, which comes with boffo cash attached.

More, much, much more, can be learned about New Orleans literature through Susan Larson's comprehensive overview, *The Booklover's Guide to New Orleans*. For space reasons, I have left out Poppy Z. Brite, a trans man now named Billy Martin, who initially wrote gothic horror and then moved over to dark comedies set in New Orleans' restaurant world; Loyola professor, John Biguenet, the author of an exceptional novel, *Oyster*, and short story collection, *The Torturer's Apprentice;* plus Patty Friedmann, Alexandrea Weis, the historically vital Frances Parkinson Keyes, Lillian Hellman, who split her growing years between New Orleans and New York, Shirley Ann Grau, winner of the 1964 Pulitzer Prize for *Keepers of the House*, Elizabeth Spencer, and I don't know where to fit Robert Penn Warren. I love Robert Penn Warren. I re-read chapter seven of *All the King's Men* every year. I consider it practically perfect writing. However, as one who was born in Guthrie, Kentucky, and lived in Memphis, Prairieville, Louisiana, Fairfield, Connecticut, and Stratton, Vermont, but never New Orleans, can we group him here?

Susan Larson has these and others fully covered. Susan is a local treasure. She was the book editor of New Orleans' *The Times-Picayune* from 1988 to 2009. She now hosts her weekly NPR affiliate radio program, *The Reading Life*. Listening to her calm and gracious voice works for me like the old biofeedback machines of the 1970s, leaving me utterly calm but attentive. In her nonexistent spare time, Susan founded the Women's National Book Association of New Orleans and is a board member of the Tennessee Williams/New Orleans Literary Festival and the New Orleans Public Library. Her house has more books than I've ever seen in a private home. Stacks of books climb the stairway. Other stacks are used as end tables.

CHAPTER 9

Exploring

Out of the Way Spots in America's Most Way Out City

*Our happiest moments as tourists always seem to come when we
stumble upon one thing while in pursuit of something else.*
—**Robert Block, writer**

There are over 2,000 people registered as members of the national tour guide association, the NFTGA-USA. It seems at least twice that number are guides right here in New Orleans alone. At night in the French Quarter, ghost tours are a nearly impassable sea of human bumper cars forever packed six or seven groups deep in front of the Lalaurie mansion.

To be a guide in New Orleans, one has to pass a drug test, an FBI background check, pay $50, and pass a test of their knowledge of New Orleans history and attractions. The test includes several questions about our statues, which I compare to high school algebra. After learning it well enough to pass the test, you'll never use it again.

In spite of all this testing and vetting, I have heard licensed tour guides say the most outlandish things. One told my group that the Lafayette Cemetery is dedicated to Theodore von La Hache, best known as the composer of the song "The Daring Young Man on the Flying Trapeze." The first part is true. The cemetery is dedicated to La Hache and La Hache was a New Orleans musician and founder of the New Orleans Philharmonic Society, but he has no more association with the famous circus song than Pablo Picasso does with fried pickles.

Another guide told my group on a St. Louis #1 cemetery tour that the tradition of marking three X's on Marie Laveau's tomb was started in the 1960s, completely made up by Buddy Ansbacher to sweeten his stories. Buddy Ansbacher was a former cemetery caretaker and tour guide. This is absolutely false. There are mentions in New Orleans' newspapers of the three-cross practice dating back 25 years before Buddy was born. Fieldworkers from the WPA Federal Writers' Project interviewed elderly New Orleanians (born in the 1850s and 1860s) who remembered Marie

Laveau devotees began making cross marks and leaving offerings at her tomb in the 1880s.

Drawing cross-marks is, in fact, rooted in African and Haitian tradition. In Haiti the practice is called chasten, and is used to establish contact with voodoo gods and with the dead. The X indicates the crossing of the world of the living and the afterlife.

In the same cemetery, another guide pointed out the grave of William Clark of Lewis & Clark. I was surprised no one in the group called the guide on this complete fabrication.

Somewhere in the French Quarter, there's an idiot concierge telling guests that it's still legal to duel in the city. You just need to obtain a permit from City Hall and choose your weapons. This is outlandishly not true

And then, almost every time I have taken a city tour or a French Quarter walking tour, the guide has paused in front of the bright gold statue of Joan of Arc on Decatur Street and has said, "*We here in New Orleans call this statue Joanie on the Pony.*" I have lived here 10 years. I have been coming to New Orleans once or twice every year for 35 years and I have never, not once, heard anyone call the statue Joanie on the Pony, other than tour guides.

This chapter will largely ignore the places just mentioned, where most tour companies take you, and instead profile the out of the way, non-touristy spots. Some will be hiding in plain sight and are passed by tourists and locals literally hundreds of times each day without notice.

If you want to take a "normal" tour with Gray Line, Louisiana Tour Company, VIP Tours, Cajun Encounters, or any of the literally hundreds of tour companies, I believe it's the tour guide and not the tour company that makes all the difference. One company just mentioned gives generally good tours, except for one guide. I consider him the #1 worst guide in New Orleans. His city annotation focuses on our new Costco store or bemoans how his Lakeside neighborhood Baskin-Robbins has been converted into a drug store. I wrote to the company begging them to not let this guide ruin first impressions by making New Orleans seem no more interesting than Bellefontaine, Ohio. (Bellefontaine's claim to fame is the world's shortest street, 15 feet long.) Another company listed above I absolutely despise. They are run by slimeballs, and every tour guide in New Orleans knows exactly which company I mean. However, they have one city tour guide whom I consider among our best.

To choose a tour, I'd suggest just close your eyes and point to one of the brochures spread out in front of you. I'll give a special shout out to Tricentennial Tours (www.tricentennialtours.com), which has twelve exceptional tour guides, including many with advanced degrees in history and archeology, some former heads of radio stations or large book publishers. Several guides, like me, are published authors, and all twelve are excellent storytellers. Tours can be given in French,

Spanish, German, Italian, Russian, Korean, and Chinese. I hype Tricentennial Tours because I was invited to be one of the three founding principles and am one of the twelve guides.

Self-promotion aside, this chapter highlights lesser-known places you can go on your own. I profile about a dozen of my favorite spots. I could have listed hundreds. In fact, I did list 111 in another book, *111 Orte in New Orleans Die Man Gesehen Haben Muss*, for a German publisher.

I am not going to list nor suggest hotels as I have a sense "you got this." Well, I will mention just one, and it's one where I am fairly certain you will not stay. The Buckner Mansion (1410 Jackson Ave.) is located on the edge of the Garden District and is a landmark amongst landmarks.

Henry Sullivan Buckner was a cotton king. He wanted to build a house in New Orleans that would be bigger and more grand than Stanton Hall in Natchez, Mississippi, previously the region's most opulent manor and home to Henry's ex-business partner and ongoing rival.

Built in 1856, the 33,000-square-foot house has forty-eight monumental Ionic and Corinthian fluted cypress columns, galleries on three sides, and three massive ballrooms.

Today, most people recognize the Buckner Mansion from the television show *American Horror Story: Coven*. The mansion was featured as Miss Robicheaux's Academy, which trained witches. You can stay at the Buckner for one night to two weeks. But, at a cost of $4,700 per night, you might want to campaign to pay by the hour.

Well, I might sneak in mention of a second hotel because of its rich history. Louis Grunewald, a prominent New Orleans businessman who started with a single music store, built the Hotel Grunewald in 1893. The hotel was later renamed the Roosevelt in 1923 to honor Teddy Roosevelt. The grand hotel included "The Cave," a subterranean lounge and America's first nightclub. Chorus girls danced to Dixieland Jazz under stalactites and waterfalls. The hotel also housed The Sazerac Bar where the Sazaerac cocktail was allegedly invented. In the 1930s, Huey Long, our beautifully corrupt governor, kept a permanent suite on the twelfth floor, where he undoubtedly did questionable activities to serve both his political ambitions and carnal needs. In 1965 the Roosevelt was bought by Fairmount Hotels and Resorts of Canada and renamed The Fairmont. No locals paid any attention and continued to call it The Roosevelt.

After the 2005 flood, the hotel stayed vacant for over two years because the Canadian corporation didn't want to put a dent in their profits from hotels in Vancouver, Quebec, San Francisco, Newport Beach, Monaco, Singapore, the United Arab Emirates, or other locations, and so left New Orleans with an unrestored and historic eyesore in our post-Katrina landscape. Finally, Sam Friedman, son of Louisiana senator Sylvan Friedman, executed a buy-out with the Waldorf Astoria. They spent over 170 million dollars to restore and reopen the Roosevelt, giving a piece of history back to New Orleans.

Today, it again smells like old money, a place where privileged families of New Orleans society meet Granddaddy & Nana for Sunday Brunch. The lobby each holiday season is beautifully lit and decorated to be sort of New Orleans' version of Rockefeller Center at Christmas. There is also a Teddy Bear Tea each Christmas Season for your young daughter or son, but at a price that makes me question why I even mention it. The lobby still has Huey Long's collection box where you can make a financial contribution to the campaign for our governor, dead for over half a century.

The most hiding-in-plain-sight treasures are our many live oak trees, which dot the entire city, from those bursting through the sidewalks in the Garden District to a good 16,000 in the 1.3-acre City Park. City Park is twice the size of New York's Central Park. Most of the live oaks predate the founding of New Orleans 300 years ago.

There are majestic and iconic live oak trees accented with Spanish moss and resurrection fern throughout the American South, but City Park is home to one of the largest and oldest live oak forests in the world. The park lost roughly 2,000 trees following Hurricane Katrina because they stood in five feet of brackish water for weeks. Otherwise, the live oak is nearly impervious to hurricane-force winds, because the massive trunk and expansive limbs you see aboveground are mirrored by an extraordinary root system underground.

The unusual aspect about the City Park trees is that so many have been given personal names and identities. The massive McDonogh Oak is named after the shipping magnate and philanthropist who donated land to form City Park. It has a circumference of 25 feet and is about 800 years old. The Singing Oak was designed, or rather embellished, by Jim Hart as a post-Katrina tribute to rebuilding the city. Seven wind chimes hang on the tree. The chimes are tuned to the pentatonic scale, used by West-African music, early gospel, and jazz, all of which represent the roots of New Orleans music. The Suicide Oak is so called because in the span of 12 years, 16 men committed suicide under its branches because of broken hearts or busted bank accounts. The best known and most visited is the remaining one of two Dueling Oaks, which stands just to the side of the art museum. Before they were outlawed in the late 1800s, countless duels took place under the two trees, using pistols, knives, and most often swords.

Starting with the French Quarter's hidden treasures, thousands upon thousands have dined at Arnaud's restaurant (813 Bienville) since it opened in 1918. With Antoine's (1840), Tujaques (1856), and Galatoire's (1897), Arnaud's isn't even in the same century as our oldest restaurants. But it is the only restaurant with a tucked-away Mardi Gras Museum.

The original Count Arnaud turned over the running of his restaurant onto his daughter, Germaine Cazenave Wells. She was known locally as just Germaine, in the same way as Madonna, Cher, and Beyoncé. Germaine was famously passionate about alcohol, men, parties, and she adored the spotlight.

She ruled over twenty-two Carnival balls, a record on par with Michael Phelps' gold medals. Germaine started her own Easter parade just to show off her latest hats with her friends, also wearing glitzy Easter bonnets. The carriage parade continues to this day.

When Archie Casbarian took over Arnaud's in 1978, he had the foresight to save many of Germaine's sequined hats and hand-beaded gowns. They are now displayed on the second floor of the restaurant. The small upstairs museum has more than two dozen lavish Mardi Gras costumes, including thirteen of Germaine's as well as four king's costumes worn by Count Arnaud. The museum collection includes more than seventy vintage photographs, Carnival masks, faux jewels, plus intricate krewe invitations and party favors.

Mere blocks away from Arnaud's is James H. Cohen & Sons (437 Royal St.). Opened in 1898, Cohen & Sons spans three centuries and five generations of ownership, making it the oldest family-owned business of any kind in the United States. The shop started out as an antiques emporium, but because of grandson Jimmie's passion for antique weaponry and rare currency, the armoires and rugs were gradually pushed out, nudging the store into the fantastic specialized store you'll find today.

Jimmie's fervor for swords, guns, and especially coins was sparked when a customer showed up one day with a Confederate half-dollar, originally struck in 1861 at the New Orleans Mint and one of only four such coins in the world. Jimmie nervously carried the treasured coin in his pocket for weeks, checking it constantly. He finally sold it for a hefty five-figure price, making him a star among numismatics. Today, the coin is worth over $1 million.

Now in their 60s, Jimmie's sons, Steve and Jerry, began working in the store after school and on weekends when they were kids. The Cohens took the boys on the road to trade shows and on antiquing jaunts in Europe, instilling in them a sense of history and an eye for spotting rare and exceptional relics.

For me, Cohen & Sons is all the more alluring for providing a new home for Don Weil's marvelous creations. For many years, Mr. Weil ran a shop (now closed) in the French Quarter called Le Petit Soldier, where you could buy tiny metal Civil War soldiers or replica members of the Roman Praetorian Guard. But most appealing to me were the little Marie Laveaus, Mardi Gras Indians, and one I bought: a figure of Napoleon and Josephine holding hands, seated on a couch. He also created a series I never quite "got." There were various women wearing Russian Cossack hats—and nothing else.

Since opening in 1929, Bottom of the Cup (327 Chartres St.) has established a reputation of being not just the most venerable place for psychic readings in New Orleans, but also the most reliable and authentic. It started out as a tea room, where shoppers could relax in the middle walking, shopping, and eating their way through the French Quarter. After drinking a cup of tea, a psychic would come by the table and read the leaves. The Bottom of the Cup still serves tea, and they sell over 100 brands, but they're now best known for their metaphysical gift items like hanging charms, crystal balls, tarot card decks, and, above all else, their psychic readers.

While all their readers are noteworthy, some have achieved star status. Former owner Adele Mullen, who passed away in 2007, was one of the more famous psychics. She left her career as a teacher to join the family business and discovered that her gifts for predicting the future exceeded her talents for correcting grammar or teaching multiplication tables. During her ownership of Bottom of the Cup, national TV and radio networks sought her out for annual Super Bowl predictions.

Today's star reader is Otis Biggs. He looks like the love child of Truman Capote and Georgia O'Keeffe, and has been doing readings at The Bottom of the Cup since 1972. Otis is a versatile psychic, reading tea leaves, tarot cards, the ridges and lines of your palm, or straight up pure psychic readings using only his natural ability. He has been featured in numerous print and media specials, with topics ranging from his serious forecast of the economy to offering services as a reader on the TLC's, *Little Couple*.

The Bottom of the Cup provides an audio tape of your session so you can go back to refresh mantras you were supposed to repeat or you can later check the veracity of the predictions their psychics made.

On the Lakeside boundary of the French Quarter is Our Lady of Guadalupe Church, also known as St. Jude, also known as the Mortuary Chapel (411 N. Rampart St.). The church was built in 1826 out of necessity, to hold the many bodies of Yellow Fever victims. Back then, the corpses were (incorrectly) thought to be highly contagious and were therefore heaped inside the church and kept separate from the living, and priests would conduct bodiless funerals outside on the street.

As the more famous St. Louis Cathedral (1718) has burned down and been rebuilt and altered several times, the Mortuary Chapel is actually the oldest intact church in New Orleans. To the side of the church is a small grotto lined with plaster "Thank You" plaques and lit by candles. But the #1 reason to visit is the statue of St. Expeditus inside the church.

Churches used to order their statues of Jesus, Mary, and the saints from Italy or Spain. The statues would arrive in crates marked with the name of the enclosed saint. One crate received by Our Lady of Guadalupe had the word "Expeditus" written on the outside. The intended message was "Open Immediately," but the recipients incorrectly interpreted the label as being the name of the saint packed inside.

And so the statue of "St. Expeditus," in his Roman soldier garb, stands at the back of the church, on the far right immediately as you enter.

St. Expeditus is recognized as the patron saint of quick results. For reasons that are not clear, you're supposed to leave him pound cake after he's interceded on your behalf. While not officially sanctioned by the Catholic Church, St. Expeditus' fame and influence are enjoying a recent surge as computer software and tech workers have been invoking him for faster connections.

Running through Treme, you will find the infamous Claiborne Corridor. Claiborne Avenue is one of longest and most storied streets in the city. The section from Orleans Avenue to Elysian Fields was once a thriving commercial district for African-Americans, who were long denied access to the whites-only shops and movie palaces on Canal Street and much of the French Quarter.

At the time, Claiborne had a wide neutral ground lined four deep with live oaks, almost like a park in the middle of the street, where area residents would congregate. Slowly, under the guise of modernization, the neighborhood was torn apart. The final death knell came in the 1960s with the white flight to suburbia and the need to develop a highway system to serve these outlying communities. Five hundred homes were torn down to facilitate construction of the new route for Interstate 10. The green median along Claiborne Avenue was ripped up and replaced by concrete. Not surprisingly, the business district rapidly declined as the community's center disintegrated.

Today, this stretch of Claiborne is a ramshackle collection of vacant homes, used tire shops, and convenience stores, all under the shadow of the freeway that passes overhead. There is, however, a glimmer of hope to be found in the Restore the Oaks program. In 2002, the African-American Museum issued a call to local artists to create a permanent outdoor exhibit using the large cement pillars that hold up the highway as their canvases. Many paintings depict the grand trees that used to stand there. Others memorialize the people of historic Treme and the Seventh Ward, like gospel singer Mahalia Jackson, musician Fats Domino, and inventor Norbert Rillieux.

In the wake of Hurricane Katrina, there's been a more fervent call to rethink the I-10 and explore the possibility of removing the entire 2.2-mile elevated stretch of highway to free up more than 50 acres of land and restore the vibrancy of the area.

Going further downriver, past the Marigny, past Bywater, and over the Industrial Canal Bridge, there are some sights in the Lower Ninth Ward much better than the Brad Pitt Make It Right homes or a self-guided tour of the pain and suffering caused by Hurricane Katrina. Call me an old-fashioned girl, but I think at least 50 years need to pass before you can properly visit the beaches of Normandy or the battlefield at Gettysburg as though you're checking off Yellowstone National Park or the Statue of Liberty on your bucket list. I was appalled (sickened) when I took a

EXPLORING WITH KIDS

There's no such thing as fun for the whole family.

—Jerry Seinfeld

Families with kids seem to flock to Orlando, which has five theme parks and is a short drive away from Gatorland and Xanadu. Other families go to New York City, which mixes oversized sights like the Statue of Liberty and the Empire State building with massive flagship stores for FAO Schwarz, Disney, and Madame Tussauds Wax Museum. New Orleans is not like that. Before living here, I did bring my son as an 8-year-old. He was hopelessly bored wandering the French Quarter, until he spotted a sign advertising "Toys!" and he raced ahead to get there. When we caught up with him, we realized "not THIS kind of toys."

But there are some spots here for kids to enjoy. New Orleans has a great and highly interactive Children's Museum, currently located at 420 Julia Street, but with plans to move uptown next to the zoo. Kids can pretend to drive a riverboat, or pull on a lever to put them inside a giant bubble. What kid doesn't want to be inside a giant bubble? Then there is, of course, the Audubon Zoo (6500 Magazine St.). The joke here is that each pen in the zoo has signage identifying the animals enclosed and then another posted sign for how to prepare them. Cajuns will eat anything. Audubon also has an aquarium and the insectarium, both on Canal Street near the river. The Insectarium serves bugs in their restaurant. I've heard to avoid the grasshoppers. The legs get stuck on the way down.

City Park has a slightly disappointing miniature golf course. It was built by a company from Wisconsin and looks like any old putt-putt you can play on the Jersey shore. Facing the putt-putt course is Carousel Park Amusement Center with rides geared toward younger kids, like a roller coaster less intense than some of our pot hole-filled streets and the namesake carousel, which locals call "the flying horses." The carousel dates back to 1906 and has been in dozens of movies, most recently *Now You See Me*. Right next to the amusement park is Storyland, where you can climb aboard fiberglass sculptures of things like Monstro, the whale in *Pinocchio*, and Mother Hubbard's Shoe.

Absolutely free entertainment is offered just hanging out on Jackson Square. On sunny days, it will be lined with all types of buskers: palm readers, face painters, brass bands, magicians, mimes, and people pretending to be statues. Hint: do not give a dime to the silver painted statue man, forever seated and with a handle bar mustache. A few years ago, he made some $30,000 in tips tossed into his bucket. People thought he was amazing as he didn't move a muscle. It's not a real person. Some guy just painted a mannequin and sits nearby to watch over his tip bucket.

If your kids are six or under, you need to be prepared to be assaulted by the balloon men. They are laying in wait to make balloon animals, hats, and swords, all of which end up looking pretty much alike.

The best free entertainment is driving on Seventh Street between Prytania and Magazine Streets. For some reason that lurks beneath the asphalt, Seventh Street is always a roller coaster and obstacle course of pot holes, sink holes, and maybe a few underground caverns. My wife and I call driving this street "Riding the High Seas."

group of out-of-town visitors to the gaping wound of the World Trade Center mere months after the tragedy. I had to abandon my guests and leave the area when I saw mindless tourists smiling and taking selfies in front of the wreckage where 2,996 people died.

The House of Dance & Feathers is very high on my Ought-To-See Places (I don't believe in Must-See). Ronald W. Lewis, a retired streetcar worker, president of the Big Nine Social Aid and Pleasure Club, former Council Chief of the Choctaw Hunters, 2008 King of Krewe de Vieux, and a central character in what I consider the best post-Katrina book, Dan Baum's *Nine Lives*, is a lifelong resident of the Lower Ninth Ward. And since 2003, he's been the director and curator of The House of Dance & Feathers, located in his backyard.

One day his wife, Minnie, came home to find his feathers, beads, and memorabilia strewn all over the house. "I can't take this anymore!" she announced. So he took all his "stuff" out back to a shed. Kids in the neighborhood started calling it a museum, and Mr. Ronald christened his outbuilding the House of Dance & Feathers (1317 Tupelo St.), his tribute to the New Orleans parade culture and Mardi Gras Indians.

The museum officially opened in 2003, only to be flooded by Katrina two years later and rebuilt through Mr. Ronald's resolve. Call ahead (504-957-2678) to schedule a time to meet with him. He is as much (or more) the reason to visit as all of his masks, suits, figures, books, photographs, and other quirky curios. As posted on his shed and website, "Come in a stranger, leave a friend!"

The nearby Lower Ninth Ward Living Museum (1235 Deslonde St.) features illuminating exhibits that detail the neighborhood's history of social activism, from when the Lower Ninth was an enclave of former slaves, through desegregation, and up to the devastation caused by Hurricane Katrina.

The other Ought-To-See places in the Lower Ninth Ward are the Steamboat Houses (400 and 503 Egania St.). These are very much hidden treasures. Very few venture there. In fact, current owner, Emile Dumesnil, has said more boats on the river pass by his house than cars or tourist vans on the street.

The first steamboat house was built in 1905 for Milton Doullut and his wife. Both were riverboat captains. Seven years later, their son Paul moved into a new and similar house right across the street. The two houses were designated historic landmarks in 1977.

Both three-story houses could be called Steamboat Gothic, with wrap-around porches accented by huge carved cypress balls that look either like a pearl necklace or a string of white Mardi Gras beads, depending on your orientation. From a distance, they also look like decorative bunting on a ship about to leave port. Oval stained glass windows, like ship portholes, are posted at each corner. The roof has two metal smokestacks instead of chimneys.

The insides of the houses have as many architectural quirks as exteriors. Pocket doors divide all interior rooms; the walls and ceiling are covered in pressed zinc panels in a cross-hatched pattern. But the most interesting, i.e. weird, details are on the ground floor. The entire first floor is coated in ceramic tile. The porch and all first-floor columns are sheathed in white tile casting. This came in particularly handy after the flooding from Katrina left five feet of standing water in the house. Because there was no exposed wood, once the water receded, the first floor could be basically hosed out and moved back into the next day.

Another architectural oddity lies in the opposite direction, along St. Charles in the Lower Garden District. The Eiffel Society (2040 St. Charles Ave.) is very reminiscent of the Eiffel Tower. In fact, it bears more than just a striking similarity. What you see actually is, or was, an actual piece of the iconic Parisian monument.

In 1981, engineers discovered that the famous landmark, built for the 1889 Paris Exposition Universelle, was sagging. They decided that the restaurant, which had been added to the tower in 1937 and perched 562 feet up, was too heavy and had to be removed. A French businessman, Georges Lancelin, acquired the Restaurant de la Tour Eiffel in exchange for dismantling it. He planned to rebuild the restaurant elsewhere in Paris, but when city officials forbade him to reopen it anywhere in France, he instead sold it to American John Onorio and noted French chef Daniel Bonnet. The two paid $1.5 million to ship the disassembled restaurant to New Orleans.

Upon arrival, they were faced with 11,062 small pieces of metal with instructions written in French. The restaurant was painstakingly reconstructed and opened on Thanksgiving Day, 1986, with a charity benefit. Invitations were hand-delivered on the wrappers of freshly baked loaves of French bread to guests, each of whom paid $125 to attend. Yet, just three years after its grand rebirth, the restaurant closed. Over the next couple decades, a revolving door of would-be entrepreneurs would try and fail to install restaurants and nightclubs in the building.

The structure now houses an event space and lounge called the Eiffel Society. Sitting 14 feet in the air, the 6,000-square-foot venue has been used for private and ticketed parties, receptions, art installations, and fashion shows. They hold Tango Tuesdays every week, and on weekend nights, the luxury space is open to the public as a unique nightclub that features dancing, entertainment, and cocktails.

There are over seventy-five tattoo parlors in New Orleans. Electric Ladyland (610 Frenchmen St.) employs the most artists and is the most popular in the city. Art Accent (1041 N. Rampart St.) is the most venerable. Jacci Gresham says, "I had no plan and no thought of ever being a tattoo artist" when she arrived from Detroit to open her shop in 1976.

The New Orleans Tattoo Museum (1915 ½ Martin Luther King Jr. Blvd. in Central City) has both premiere tattoo artists and houses a one-of-a-kind tattoo museum.

Tattoo artist "Doc" Don Lucas is a legendary figure in the field. He spent his long career traveling the world, gathering both stories and artifacts. He started his tattoo apprenticeship in 1972 under "Rangoon" Ricky Bordeaux. In 1983, Lucas moved to New Orleans and opened a studio when tattoos were far more fringe than they are today. He recalls that back then, "the city disliked you, the police hated you, nobody wanted you to move next door—you were a pariah."

Among Lucas' protégés was Henri Montegut, whose son, Adam, followed in his career path. Adam came to share Lucas' passion for preserving the history and traditions of tattoos, and used Kickstarter and other funding sources to create his 2,000-square-foot ode to ink in the form of a tattoo museum. The space is divided into three sections. The gallery displays contemporary tattoo art and the work of cool non-tattoo artists, like Ralph Steadman. The tattoo parlor offers the services of Adam, German artist Rachel Ulm, and other gifted tattoo artists. The museum features rotating exhibits, showcasing items from the collection of Doc Lucas.

"My passion was to document as much of the history I've been blessed to have given to me or bought," Lucas says. "It was undocumented. You go to these old-timers and learn from them, because there was no school or learning text. Now I'm the old-timer." Lucas tracked down tattoo collections from retired or retiring artists, including the 60-year life's work of famed artist George "Doc" Webb. Webb's "flash" paintings—punctured hearts, skulls and tigers, daggers wrapped in banners—line the entrance to the museum. Lucas also bought collections from around the world, including that of renowned Canadian one-armed artist Curly Allen.

Inside display cases you'll find a variety of paraphernalia and vintage objects, from old tattoo guns and pigment bottles to framed photographs of inked carnival sideshow performers and the original paintings and drawings of legendary tattoo artists. There's also a collection of taxidermy animals, which seem to have nothing to do with the museum but are cool nonetheless.

After 90 years of municipal squabbles and natural disasters, the Lakefront Airport (6001 Stars & Stripes Blvd) stands as a stunningly preserved exhibition of the Art Deco Age. When I "discovered" the airport in 2015, I immediately took my daughter there on the same day when she got off from school. Her reaction was as I expected. Mouth agape, she too saw it as the perfect place to hold a *Great Gatsby*-style party.

In 1929, Abraham Shushan, a politician, businessman, and a bit of a shyster, teamed up with then-governor Huey Long, a full-blown shyster, to push through their vision for a modern airport. The two spent $3 million to pump out 6 million cubic yards of water to build the airport on a newly formed jetty where a portion of Lake Pontchartrain had been. The land formerly underwater was in the public domain, which meant that anti-Long political factions had no say or control.

Christened the Shushan Airport when it opened in 1934, it was the first combined land and seaplane air terminal in the world. The grand Atrium has a terrazzo floor and is lined with aviation-themed murals by Spanish-American artist Xavier Gonzalez. There are ornamental touches everywhere you turn, from the neon arrow pointing to the Walnut Room to a retro bank of wooden phone booths.

A controversial sculpture/fountain by Enrique Alférez sits out front and depicts the four seasons as three women and a man, all nude. In 1936 it was deemed indecent and city officials demanded the endowed male statue have his genitalia chiseled off. Alférez refused and stood guard every night with a rifle to ward off vandals. Eleanor Roosevelt finally stepped in and basically declared, "the penis stays put!"

More controversy followed in 1939, when Shushan was indicted and convicted on various charges of theft and fraud. In response, the board changed the name to Lakefront Airport. However, they had a much harder time removing Abe's name from all the surfaces of the terminal. In a Donald Trump-like way, he had crazily etched his name in the lavatories, on the doors, in the wall tiles, and even on the pavement outside. One board member admitted defeat: "We haven't got the kind of money it would take to get Abe off everything."

Not quite as stunning as the Lakefront Lobby, the Greyhound Bus Station (1001 Loyola Ave.) has a couple of beautiful murals depicting the history of Louisiana. These were painted by artist Conrad Albrizio as part of the WPA program. They have the feel of the work of Mexican artist (and husband of Frida Kahlo) Diego Rivera.

I'd love to annotate exploration spots like Animatronic Swamp Puppet Show in Breaux Bridge or the Chicken Yard of Plaquemine's Parish, but those are too distant.

On the other side of the Huey Long Bridge sits a plantation roughly an hour closer than any of the many set up for regular tours. Visitors to New Orleans will spend $60 (or more) to travel more than an hour and 20 minutes each way to tour plantations like Oak Alley, the most visited plantation on the planet. Oak Alley has been the setting of more than 40 movies—and several Beyoncé videos. Nearby Laura Plantation has a richer history, with its original slave quarters still intact. Magnolia Lane Plantation is a mere 20 minutes from the French Quarter and dates back to the 1830s. The dramatic grounds have been used as a location in many films, including *Bad Lieutenant: Port of Call New Orleans* and *Twelve Years a Slave*.

It is also a virtual amusement park of the creepy and paranormal. TV shows *Ghost Hunters*, *Ghost Adventures*, and *Scariest Places on Earth* have all filmed segments there. The property has a hanging tree where, depending on who owned the plantation at the time, both Yankees and rebel troops were strung up during the Civil War. The original owner begged Northern soldiers not to damage his home and was shot to death for his troubles. Voodoo artifacts have been discovered on the plantation, an indication that the slaves of Magnolia Lane cast evil spells on their oppressive masters.

In the main house, there is a room dubbed the "Dying Room." Many of Magnolia's residents passed away in this room under mysterious circumstances. My wife forbade me to enter the Dying Room when I visited. When I asked the owner if he's ever had experiences with "real" ghosts, Richard Naberschnig related stories of frequent noises and furniture being moved around with no greater drama than if I'd asked him, "Have you ever eaten cheese?"

Magnolia Lane Plantation is *not* set up for regular tours. You'll need to call ahead (504-715-1611) to see if you can get an audience with Richard and the assorted ghosts.

Across Lake Pontchartrain, on a tree-lined side street in the town of Mandeville, sits what looks like an old country church. In many ways, it is. The spirits of jazz history are alive in its unpainted wood plank walls. Built in 1895, the Dew Drop is the oldest jazz hall in the United States.

A group of African-Americans created the Dew Drop Social and Benevolent Association to provide for the needy. They built the hall to be their headquarters, but it quickly evolved into a hub for jazz musicians. After playing more traditional music for whites-only audiences throughout the week, New Orleans jazz pioneers began rushing across the lake to cut loose for black audiences. The Dew Drop's alumni represent a virtual who's who of jazz greats, most notably, Louie Armstrong, who played there when he needed a break from the demands of his growing international celebrity.

By the 1940s, an emerging African-American middle class meant there was less need for a Benevolent Association. The Dew Drop sat vacant and silent for decades. It wasn't until 2000, when Mandeville received the building as a donation, that restoration got underway. The first concert in 60 years was held in 2007.

As long as you've crossed the lake, you might want to toddle over to Slidell. Slidell is about as exotic as Paramus, New Jersey. However, nestled in amongst Best Buys and Dollar Stores is a place either called Sideshow Props or MovieSets (400 Garrett Rd., Slidell, LA 70458), depending on the whim of the owner, Lawrence Barattini. He rents or sells a huge variety of props and sets to the great many film companies that use New Orleans. Themes of the props cover the gambit from voodoo, military, and sideshow circus, to 1900s parlors. Barattini had been a junk collector for years, but when word got around that he had some pretty cool stuff, from candelabras to custom cars to faux fetuses in bottles, mummies, and severed fingers, film crews came calling. A business was formed.

Barattini now has thousands of eccentric items in a large warehouse space. Out front, the parking lot displays unusual or vintage vehicles. A "City of Los Angeles" police car sits next to an orange Gremlin, next to a Deco-era Chevy covered in chrome.

MovieSets is not a museum. He does rent it out as an event space. Prop people for films are always welcomed to check out his stuff because they are potential customers. You, on the other hand, may wish to call ahead (985-373-1949) to make sure you won't be turned away at the door.

About an hour outside New Orleans, stands a far more eccentric spot, a shrine to tacky taste. The Abita Mystery House (22275 LA-36, Abita Springs, LA 70420) is also known as the UCM Museum, which stands for Unusual Collections and Mini-town, but I fully suspect John Preble, the creator and proprietor, made up the name to pronounce it the "you-see-em-mu-se-um."

Preble had been a teacher and artist for over 30 years before he finally put a lifetime of odd keepsakes on display for all to see. For most roadside attractions, you look at the 10 Cadillacs at Cadillac Ranch, or Lucy the Elephant in New Jersey, or the life-sized statues of the Cabazon Dinosaurs and then you've fully "done" the entire thing. However, once you've entered the Abita Mystery House through a vintage 1930s Standard Oil Gas Station, your adventures are just beginning.

There are sprawling separate buildings, each with its own thematic exhibits of most anything you've imagined in your roadside dreams or nightmares. You can gaze at the collections of combs and old license plates; play several arcade machines, including one made entirely from popsicle sticks; or use push buttons to animate miniature dioramas of a jazz funeral, a tiny plantation, "Lil Dubs BBQ," and a miniature roadside store called Pinky's What All Store with a little banner that reads "We Got It All."

Out back, there's a silver Airstream trailer that was allegedly hit by a flying saucer and a house covered in thousands of fragments of tiles, pottery, mirrors, and glass called the House of Shards. Inside the House of Shards, there's an assortment of weirdness ranging from a vintage bicycle collection to a one-of-a-kind abomination of nature: Buford the Bassigator, a 22-foot-long half alligator-half fish, and an emergency back-up one-of-a-kind abomination, Darrell the Dogigator, half alligator-half dog.

Up that-a-way is the Whitney Plantation (5099 LA-18, Edgard, LA). The Whitney Plantation is the first and only museum in the United States focused on slavery. It was envisioned by a self-described "rich white boy." John Cummings amassed his fortune as a lawyer and real-estate magnate in New Orleans. He spent 15 years and more than $8 million to create a unique—some might say eccentric—museum for how he personally thought slavery should be presented. Because he used no outside funds, Cummings neither had to appease any board members nor make a single compromise.

The museum was created with unprecedented documentation, including

Visionary John Preble

detailed records of the slaves from the original 1721 plantation, listing them by name, complexion of skin, skill sets, and countries of origin, plus an eight-volume study of the grounds conducted by a previous owner, along with nearly 4,000 oral histories of Louisiana slaves compiled by the WPA in the 1930s.

The grounds are centered upon the Big House, a Creole main building with eleven outbuildings including the original kitchen, believed to be the oldest detached kitchen in Louisiana; a storage shed; an overseer's house; a mule barn; and a plantation store. Cummings also bought and reassembled 20 slave quarters on the premises.

Most moving are the sculpture exhibits. One is dedicated to the largest slave revolt in American history. In 1811, just a few miles from the Whitney Plantation, 125 slaves rebelled. They were quickly suppressed, with 95 killed during the conflict and all others executed. As a warning to other slaves, many were decapitated, their heads placed on spikes. Cummings commissioned Woodrow Nash to make 60 ceramic heads, which are set atop stainless-steel rods.

While largely hailed, Cummings has had to defend the Whitney Plantation

LUMINS OF NEW ORLEANS:
Sidney Smith

Sidney Smith, founder of Haunted History Tours, wasn't the first to offer ghost tours of New Orleans, but his have become the overwhelmingly most popular. He's additionally sort of the Bill Walsh or Bill Parcells of Ghost Tours, where his tree of former Haunted History employees includes those that have created most of his company's competition. Smith spawned a ghost tour industry that, if statistics were to be compiled, would probably dust beignets as far as bringing tourists' dollars into the city's economy.

Sidney was born and raised in New Orleans. His first career was as a photographer of rock musicians, beginning at the tender age of 15. He characterizes Cameron Crowe's *Almost Famous* as virtually his biography. Not old enough to vote or drive a car, Sidney was hanging out with Bruce Springsteen, The Allman Brothers, and local musicians like Ernie K-Doe and seeing his photographs regularly printed in *Rolling Stone*, *Creem*, *Circus*, and all the top rock 'n' roll magazines.

His dream photography project became his nightmare. Like so many of his generation (which is also my generation), The Beatles coming to America and appearing on *The Ed Sullivan Show* on February 9, 1964, rocked his world. The Beatles' sound, their look, everything about them was wildly different from anything that preceded them. They created a cultural revolution the likes of which have not been equaled over the past 50 years.

When Paul McCartney came to New Orleans to record a new album, Sidney received a phone call asking him to bring his portfolio to Le Richelieu Hotel. McCartney's manager, upon seeing and liking Sidney's work, asked him one question. "When you meet Paul, you aren't going to cry, are you?" They had worked with other young photographers who'd been so overwhelmed meeting the musical god (they were "*bigger than Jesus*") they started streaming tears. Assuring the manager he'd remain professional, Sidney was led back to the hotel's swimming pool where sat Paul and Linda and their kids. He got to hang out with his idol while repeating the mantra, "I'm not going to cry, I'm not going to cry."

Sidney was hired on to shoot the album cover and to hang out with Paul to capture some candid shots. This included being the only photographer allowed on board when Paul and his buddies, Duane Allman and Professor Longhair, took a river cruise up the Mississippi. Sidney knew this was a photographer's opportunity of a lifetime. He was in Heaven—until the boat returned to dock in New Orleans. After putting down his camera equipment and bags of undeveloped film on deck, he turned back a moment later to discover everything had been stolen. It was like Carrie being chosen Homecoming Queen only to be doused in pig's blood. The experience was devastating. He dabbled in photography a while longer, but his heart was no longer in it.

Sidney's next and highly successful gig was delivering singing and or stripping telegrams. As he notes, "Everything from Get Well to Go To Hell." Beyond performing himself, he was hiring and training others, plus setting up franchises in other cities across America.

This too came to a dramatic, career changing, moment. Still in shape in his '40s, Sidney was performing at a bachelorette party. Everyone was having a wildly good time until the guest of honor bride whipped out a 20-year-old photograph of Sidney performing for her mother's bachelorette party. While she undoubtedly thought the picture was sweetly nostalgic, for Sidney it was another bucket of pig's blood. Being a second generation strip-o-gram performer had not been his vision nor career goal. It was time to hang up the tear-away pants and thong.

Chef Paul Prudhomme has a wonderful quote, "New Orleans . . . will nudge you to become the person you were meant to be." After successful but short careers as a photographer, then strip-o-gram performer, Sidney was being nudged to be King of Haunted Tours.

About this time, Sidney took a ghost tour from the one and then only person offering them. The guide was a crusty old man carrying a lantern around The Quarter. Sidney felt, "I can do this better." He went out, studied New Orleans' dark history, and scripted what was and still is the city's premier ghost tour, plus a vampire tour, voodoo tour, cemetery tour, and the recently added French Quarter history tour.

When Haunted History launched, there were just the two ghost tour companies. Today, there are well over twenty. And they don't always play nice when competing for tourists' dollars. Tearing up or throwing out each other's brochures from travel kiosks and concierge desks is the least of their offenses.

I asked Sidney if anything truly weird or scary happened during the tours. He started with some well-worn chestnuts you'll hear time and again. That, if you take photographs at haunted places like the Lalaurie Mansion or La Pretre House, in about 90 percent of the pictures, there will be etherial gasses or light orbs will appear. There is a single and specific spot outside the Lalaurie Mansion where Sidney has personally experienced five different people fainting and collapsing into a heap.

But he added he had one experience that truly made the hairs on his arm stand up. For a group he guided one night, there was a woman and her young son. About halfway through the tour, the boy left his mother and came upfront to stand by Sidney for the full second hour. At the end of the tour, the mother in the back started yelling, "My son! Where's my son? He was just here!" Sidney motioned to the boy next to him, causing the mother to rush up, questioning her son, "How did you get here? Why did you leave my side?" He answered, "Because you were holding that other boy's hand." There was, of course, no other boy.

from some criticism. He has been quoted as saying, "It is disturbing. But you know what else? It happened."

For this next exploration, I can't guarantee you'll ever find it. In fact, my money's on that you won't. The Honey Island Swamp is a nature preserve about 45 minutes east of New Orleans that gives four or five swamp tours every day. It has always been a popular tourist destination, but since the huge success of the History Channel's *Swamp People*, it's become a version of our Graceland. Thousands trudge out 45 minutes to Slidell because they want to visualize themselves as Troy Landry striding between curtains of Spanish moss to yell out "Choot 'em! Choot 'em!"

I don't doubt you can find the Honey Island Swamp, but the thing to see is the Honey Island Swamp Monster, or a Louisiana style Bigfoot or Loch Ness Monster.

Below is a description of the Honey Island Swamp Monster from Wikipedia (so it must be true):

> The Honey Island Swamp monster is a humanoid cryptid reported from Honey Island Swamp, Louisiana since 1963 . . . [In Native American culture,] this creature is called Letiche. Cajuns call it the Tainted Keitre. The creature is described as bipedal, 7 feet tall, with gray hair and red eyes. The creature is accompanied by a disgusting smell. Footprints supposedly left by the creature have four webbed toes.

Another local legend tells of a train crash in the area in the early twentieth century. A traveling circus was on the train through the bayou when the crash allowed a group of chimpanzees to escape. The apes supposedly interbred with the local alligator population to create the Honey Island Swamp Monster.

I agree if you are right now thinking it's hard to imagine a chimpanzee and an alligator mating by the pure mechanics alone.

Now, if Bassigators, Dogigators, and Swamp Monsters aren't your thing, and you want your explorations curated, pre-packaged, and with an admissions fee, on the page opposite is a quick list of 50-some New Orleans Museums and Parks.

If you want to go matching T-shirts, disposable camera, and fanny-pack wearing Tourist with a capital T, we do have a number of celebrity homes here where you can walk by and gawk. New York City and Los Angeles are cosmopolitan and tend to leave celebrities alone. New Orleans is languorous and we too tend to leave celebrities alone. I will hold back just a bit and not give you actual addresses.

Brad Pitt and Angelina Jolie had a home in the French Quarter. Recently, it sold for just under $5 million from the asking price of $6 million. Many days, Brad used to walk a block from his house to Verti Marte for lunch, until a national magazine outed that fact. Then, people (hopefully mostly tourists) would camp out at the corner grocer as if waiting for concert or play-off tickets. He had to stop going.

My favorite Brad Pitt story, however, involves a handyman who came inside their home to do repair work. He hadn't been told the identity of the owners, just

New Orleans Museums and Parks

Name	Address	Attraction
1850 House	523 St. Ann St.	period home tour
Alligator Museum	2501 Magazine St.	gators
American Italian Cultural Center	537 S. Peters St.	Italian history
Amistad Research Center	6823 St. Charles Ave.	African-American history
Ashe Cultural Arts Center	1712 O C Haley Blvd.	emerging artists
Audubon Aquarium	1 Canal St.	aquarium
Audubon Park	6500 Magazine St.	walking/jogging path, labyrinth, sculpture, bird sanctuary
Audubon Zoo	6500 Magazine St.	zoo
Backwater Museum	1116 St. Claude Ave.	street culture
Beauregard-Keyes House	1113 Chartres St.	period home tour
Besthoff Sculpture Garden	1 Collins Diboll Cir.	outdoor sculpture
Botanical Gardens	1 Palm Terrace	City Park plants
Cabildo	701 Chartres St.	history
Children's Museum	420 Julia St. (moving near zoo)	Children's interest
City Park	1 Palm Dr.	bayou, amusements, 20,000 Live Oak trees
Confederate Memorial Hall	929 Camp St.	2nd largest Civil War Museum in US
Contemporary Art Museum	900 Camp St.	modern art
Crescent Park	1008 N. Peters St.	public green space by river in Bywater
Degas House	2306 Esplanade	Creole history & art
Diboll Gallery at Loyola University	6363 St. Charles Ave.	Belgian Congo
The Fly	Inside Audubon Park	riverside ball parks, picnics, lounging
Gallier House	1132 Royal St.	period home tour
Hermann Grima House	820 St. Louis St.	period home tour
Historic New Orleans Collection	533 Royal	French Quarter history
House of Broel's	2220 St. Charles Ave.	Victorian & Doll House
House of Dance & Feathers	1317 Tupelo St.	street culture

Insectarium	423 Canal	bugs & butterflies
Irish Cultural Museum	933 Conti St.	Irish history
Jazz Walk of Fame	Algier's Point	great views, jazz tributes
Le Musée de f.p.c.	2336 Esplanade Ave.	free person of color
Longue Vue House and Gardens	7 Bamboo Rd.	extensive gardens
Louis Armstrong Park	701 N Rampart St.	statues, strolling paths, Congo Square
Madame John's Legacy	632 Dumaine St.	period home tour
Mardi Gras Museum	813 Bienville St.	Germaine's stash
Mardi Gras World	1380 Port of New Orleans	Mardi Gras
McKenna Museum	2003 Carondelet St.	African American Art
Museum of Death	227 Dauphine St.	more crappy than creepy
National World War II Museum	945 Magazine St.	huge collection of WWII artifacts
The New Canal Lighthouse	8001 Lakeshore Dr.	ecology; interactive
N.O. African American Museum	1418 Governor Nicholls St.	African American
New Orleans Museum of Art	1 Collins Diboll Cir.	110-year-old art museum
Ogden Museum of Southern Art	925 Camp St.	Southern Art; well curated
Old U.S. Mint	400 Esplanade St.	Mint(1st fl) Music(2nd fl)
Old Ursuline Convent	1100 Chartres St.	"treasure of the archdiocese"
Pharmacy Museum	514 Chartres St.	first pharmacy in America
Pitot House	1440 Moss St.	real if small plantation
The Presbytère	751 Chartres St.	rotating exhibits
Preservation Resource Center	923 Tchoupitoulas St.	architecture
Shrine of Blessed Francis Seelos	2030 Constance St.	almost a Saint
Southern Food & Beverage Museum	1504 OC Haley Blvd.	food & spirits
Tattoo Museum	1915 $\frac{1}{2}$ ML King Jr. Blvd.	tattoos
Voodoo Museum	724 Dumaine St.	voodoo
Women's Opera Guild	2504 Prytania St.	period home tour

the address. Seeing the children, Maddox, Pax, Zahara, Shiloh, Knox, and Vivienne, all of different nationalities, the worker thought he'd entered a school or day camp rather than a family home. Then he noticed all the photographs of Angie on the mantles and walls, and said to the man, whom he did not recognize as Brad Pitt, "Man, someone here has a thing for Angie Jolie!" Brad, probably delighted not to be recognized, responded simply, "Yes, I do."

As Brad and Angie will be leaving New Orleans, Jay Z and Beyoncé recently bought a home in Uptown, joining Beyoncé's sister, Solange, who was married in a vacant Bywater church and now lives in the neighborhood.

Sandra Bullock and John Goodman live practically on top of one another in the Garden District. Sandra's home has been mislabeled as a Victorian mansion. There are actually a good four or five architectural styles going on there. If you look closely at the gingerbread, you'll see it's not traditional Victorian motifs, but serpents and Asian designs. Architect James Freret fell in love with a Far Eastern temple he saw at the Paris International Exposition in 1867 and was inspired to integrate some of what he saw.

I have frankly never seen Sandra Bullock. I don't think she's here that often, as she also has a home in Austin, Texas, and seems to make forty movies a year.

John Goodman was not the first celebrity to own his New Orleans residence. Just prior, Trent Reznor of Nine Inch Nails lived there for 10 years. Reznor moved here from Los Angeles area, where he'd lived in the Roman Polanski-Sharon Tate home of the Manson family murders. He brought with him the front door where a member of the Manson clan had written "PIG" in Sharon Tate's blood. He used the door as the entrance to his Nothing Records studio on Magazine Street. The story is that Trent moved away because he grew weary of his Garden District neighbor pushing through noise ordinances. Today, the studio where Marilyn Manson once recorded has been replaced by Zen Pet, a boutique for your vegan dog. Zen Pet tossed out the door either not knowing what it was, or *knowing* what it was. John Goodman can be spotted regularly, working in the yard or walking his dog. Or as I jokingly say, "If you want to see John Goodman, go to Harry's Ace Hardware on Magazine."

Sorry, I don't know where Harrison Ford will live when he moves here in the near future. And, sadly, Lenny Kravitz has left his Creole cottage in the French Quarter. Kravitz had decorated it in a style he called "bordello modern." The interior was all animal skins, metallic foil wallpaper, steel-beaded curtains, and ebony wood floors with an "artfully distressed" exterior. A female friend of mine, who'd seen photographs of his bachelor pad, said, "You could get pregnant just looking at it."

Our streetcars are hardly hidden treasures. They're our mode of public trans-portation. For $1.25 one way or a $3 all day pass, you can ride them just like the thousands of locals who crawl their way to work or to a court appointment. Hint: fare is cash-only and you do want exact change. They'll take your $20 bill, but you'll

Another means of exploring—kayaking Bayou St. John

get nothing back except a white card printed with your balance. The card is useful to me, I can use up that balance over the next month or two, but is simply a waste of money to you.

The reason public transportation is in a chapter about exploring is because there's a whole lotta history and things to know that are not readily apparent as you wait for your streetcar. The St. Charles line, the green one, is the oldest streetcar in America. The original 1834 train was steam-powered, but residents objected to the loud steam engines as they rode by their homes. For years, engines were removed and the cars were pulled by horses. Then, when San Francisco created their trolley system, we stole their idea for an overhead electrical wire and created the streetcar system you see today.

At one time in the 1920 and '30s, Los Angeles, Philadelphia, Boston, Seattle, and most other major American cities had sprawling electric streetcar rail systems. Then, General Motors, Standard Oil, Phillips Petroleum, and Firestone bought up a controlling interest in National City Lines. Once the monopolizing companies owned the railways, they shut them down, forcing Americans to buy cars or ride GM-manufactured buses, fueled with Standard Oil and Phillips Petroleum, and fitted with Firestone tires. This deliberate campaign to kill the electric-powered streetcars is known as the General Motors Conspiracy.

The historic St. Charles line is green. All others are red, so you'll know you're on the right one. The St. Charles line used to be called "The Green Bullet," but as it only goes at a maximum speed of 18 miles per hour, we dropped the nickname.

CHAPTER 10

Fitting In

Going Native in NOLA

We talk funny and listen to strange music and eat things you'd probably hire an exterminator to get out of your yard. We dance even if there's no radio. We drink at funerals. We talk too much and laugh too loud and live too large and, frankly, we're suspicious of others who don't.
— **Chris Rose, *1 Dead in Attic***

There's a popular phrase on local T-shirts and bumper stickers, "Be a New Orleanian, Wherever You Are." This chapter is to hopefully help you become a New Orleanian wherever you're from.

To do so, there are certain things you need to do if you don't want to hang a figurative large sign across your back saying, "Kick me, I'm a tourist." Not that New Orleanians are in the habit of kicking tourists. Tourism and the shipping industry are neck and neck as far as how we financially stay afloat.

As a visitor, you first need to relax and discount your belief that we are a dangerous city where most any night you can be robbed, shot, or disfigured. Very few visitors actually get disfigured. In truth, proportionately fewer visitors get robbed or shot here than Philadelphia, Detroit, Chicago, Memphis, Baltimore, Tampa, Oakland, Oklahoma City, Baton Rouge in our own state, and I could go on. For some reason, maybe our voodoo past or Bourbon Street present, New Orleans has an image as a dangerous place. Visitors often ask "Is it safe to walk around at night?" or "Where should I not go?" Now, there's no question you can get in trouble here. We're a city in America. You can get in trouble almost anywhere, including Happyland, Oklahoma; Pie Town, New Mexico; or Loafers Glory, North Carolina (all real places).

You simply need to keep your wits about you. Stumbling around Bourbon Street three sheets to the wind at 3:00 a.m. is not keeping your wits. I reserve a fair bit of rage for idiots in the media who feed the fears of tourists coming to my glorious city.

Several years ago, the *USA Today* ran a headline on November 1st about two people being shot to death on Halloween night in New Orleans. The same night, five were shot dead in Washington, DC, where the newspaper is based. Nothing. More recently, one person was shot and killed over the Thanksgiving weekend, and that seemed to be all anyone could talk about. I don't mean to diminish that person's death, but I looked up other cities the next day and discovered at the same time, three were killed in Washington, DC, nine people in Chicago, and 13 in Memphis. If you can't handle our humidity, or you just don't like great food and music, I can understand staying away. Otherwise, fear should not be a factor. *Laissez les bons temps rouler.*

Now, to avoid being spotlighted as a total tourist, you need do something so simple as pronounce pralines correctly. We don't care if you call our streetcars trolleys, trams, or trains. Remember it was *A Streetcar Named Desire* not a Tram Named Desire, but say whatever you like. However, say "PRAY-leenz" and we'll act like you insulted our mamma and get all up in your face. It's pronounced "PRAH-leenz."

The TV series *NCIS New Orleans* was roundly criticized by locals after the first few episodes because of their complete butchering of the New Orleans accent. The character, Christopher LaSalle, had the worst attempt at a local accent since Dennis Quaid incinerated one in the movie, *The Big Easy*. Quaid's character, Remy McSwain, stuffed his dialog with way over-the-top and much too frequent use of Dems, Dats, and Doz tossed vigorously with his sobriquet "*Cher*," which he inserted every third or fourth word.

After getting so much bad press in town, the *NCIS* TV show wrote into the script of a later episode someone asking Monsieur LaSalle, "Where you from?" His reply, "Alabama," was supposedly a save for the show from further embarrassment as though we'd ever believe the show named a character LaSalle and stuck them in New Orleans because they're a Roll Tide boy. However, in the same episode, another character delivered the line, "Whoever came up with PRAY-leenz should get an award," and locals all went back to shaking their heads in disgust.

Now good luck to you trying to correctly pronounce our street names. Years ago, David Letterman took a trip to New Orleans, and held a contest when he went back to New York. He held up signs in front of his studio audience and challenged them to pronounce the streets. No one could. Burgundy is "Bur-GUN-dee." Chartres becomes the very un-French like "CHART-Ters." And for Tchoupitoulas you need to take off the opening "T" that's causing your anxiety and the word opens itself up, CHOP-a-TWO-luss." It's a Native American word meaning "River People." There's a locally famous, and probably completely made up, story about the police finding a dead body on Tchoupitoulas. This was back in the day when policeman had to fill out five copies of hand-written incident reports. Rather than writing Tchoupitoulas five times, they dragged the body over to Camp Street.

A Quick & Handy Pronunciation Guide To Other Streets

BURTHE STREET	Pronounced <BYOOTH>
CADIZ STREET	Pronounced <KAY-diz>
CALLIOPE STREET	Pronounced <CAL-lee-ope>
CARONDELET STREET	Pronounced <ka-'ron-da-LET>
CHEF MENTEUR HIGHWAY	Pronounced <SHEF man-TOUR>
CONTI STREET	Pronounced <CON-tye>
DECATUR SCREET	Pronounced <da-KAY-ter>
DERBIGNY STREET	Pronounced <DER-ba-nee>
DORGENOIS STREET	Pronounced <DER-zhen-WAH'>
DRYADES STREET	Pronounced <DRY-ads>
DUFOSSAT STREET	Pronounced <DOO-faucet>
EUTERPE STREET	Pronounced <YOU-terp>
IBERVILLE STREET	Pronounced <IB-ber-'vil>
MARIGNY STREET	Pronounced <MA-ra-nee>
MAZANT STREET	Pronounced <MAY-zant>
MELPOMENE STREET	Pronounced <MEL-pa-meen>
MILAN STREET	Pronounced <MY-lan>
POYDRAS STREET	Pronounced <POY-dras>; or if you want to go hard core local, <PER-dras>
SOCRATES STREET	Pronounced <SO crates>
TERPSICHORE STREET	Pronounced <TERP-sa-core>
TONTI STREET	Pronounced <TON-tee>. And here you start to realize you are perhaps being messed with. Why is TONTI pronounced TON-tee while CONTI is CON-tye? I have no answer for that one.
TOULOUSE STREET	Pronounced <TOO-loose>
VETERANS HIGHWAY	Pronounced <VET-tranz>; make it three syllables, and y'all a tourist

If one of these streets is wide enough to have a meridian, in New Orleans it's not called a meridian but "neutral ground." The phrase dates back to earlier times when the French, Spanish, and Creole residents lived on the Vieux Carré side (down river) of Canal Street and the incoming Americans lived on the other (up river) side, called the American Sector.

They couldn't stand one another. And we're talking much more than hipsters in New York disdaining to ever cross above 14th Street.

The neutral ground was the one place where they agreed not to spat. Otherwise and elsewhere, it was ongoing contempt.

The more established Vieux Carré residents loved the opera, fine dining, and midday naps. No proper French gentleman would ever accept employment where he'd have to remove his jacket during business hours. Manual labor was déclassé. The nouveau New Orleanians, or Americans, who came to the American Sector in the early 1800s, were, in comparison, rude, crude, and ate fast food. The Creoles were Catholic. The American Sector was mostly Protestant. The Americans had little appreciation of the arts, seemed to care mostly about money, and had the nasty habit of blowing holes in each other with pistols. In other words, they were much like Americans today.

Prior to the Americans' arrival, duels in New Orleans made use of swords, not pistols. The cause of duels were often slights no more than one gentleman pulling his chair too close to another man's wife or the time visiting Frenchman, Chevalier Tomasi, said the Mississippi River was "a mere rill" compared to rivers back home in France. So, of course, Chevy had to be slapped across the face and taken out back.

"Out back," before the Americans showed up, was the courtyard behind the St. Louis Cathedral.

The duels ended when one participant drew first blood with a flick of his saber causing a mere nick on the hand or cheek. Winning the humiliation of the opponent was the point. It was never intended to *kill* the opponent. The Americans never quite got the concept. They brought out their guns and blew holes in each other.

Because of this, dueling was banished from New Orleans and occurred thereafter in what was then outside the city, in what is now City Park. The Dueling Oak, identified with a plaque, lives just to the left of the Art Museum (if facing the front).

More than merely being disgusted by the crass Americans, the French have a long history of battling England, dating back to the French-Norman Conquest in 1066. Since most of the Americans flooding into New Orleans were of British descent, it was guilt by association. The two countries fought the Breton War, the Vexin War, several Anglo-Norman Wars, the Hundred Years' War (which was actually 116 years), and also met at Napoleon's defeat at Waterloo in 1815.

After the British defeat of the French in Canada came the Acadian Exodus also known as the Great Upheaval, the Great Expulsion, the Great Deportation, and Le Grand Dérangement. The French Canadians refused to sign a mandatory pledge of loyalty to the King of England, and so were kicked out of the country.

Just under 12,000 Acadians were deported. Frenchman Henri Peyroux de la Coudreniere concocted a plan, some would say a scheme, to transport the exiled Acadians to

Louisiana, making many residents in New Orleans the actual participants in the Great Upheaval. Their hatred for those new Anglos moving in was fresh, personal, and intense. The French still hate the British, but in more of a musty and moderate way. Contemporary French author Jose-Alain Fralon described the British as "our most dear enemies."

The incoming Americans were overtly not welcomed into the Vieux Carré, which the French Quarter was called back then. The name "French Quarter" was hung on the Vieux Carré by those arrogant American intruders.

You'll probably note all street names change at Canal. Bourbon Street becomes Carondolet, Royal turns into St. Charles Avenue. The French and the Americans thought each other were idiots. They certainly weren't going to share a street name.

Canal Street is also known for being the widest street in America. If you're about to argue, "Hey, wait a minute . . ." we'll grant you there are wider avenues and boulevards in America, just no wider streets. New Orleans loves itself, I think quite justifiably. We will find a way to be the biggest, oldest, and best by how we phrase the claims. Antoine's is the oldest restaurant in America (1840) . . . owned by one family. There's an older restaurant in Boston, the Union Oyster House (1826), but that one has had multiple and unrelated owners. The St. Louis Cathedral, built in 1727, is the oldest Catholic church in America . . . in continuous use. The San Miguel Mission in Santa Fe dates back to 1610, but it's been repaired, rebuilt, and out of commission many times. The Lake Pontchartrain Causeway bridge is the longest bridge over water in the world . . . that is a continuous bridge. The much longer Jiaozhou Bay Bridge in China is the longest bridge (sometimes) over water, but it's an aggregate bridge, at points tunneling below water. The Potomac Bay Bridge is probably as long, but it dips below water at several points.

If you're visiting a friend or relative living in New Orleans, let me help them out by pleading with you to please don't ask them to take you across the world's longest (continuous) bridge. As a proper host, they will have to grant your wish. As a local, they've probably *had* to cross it a few times, where once is enough. After the first 2 miles is just another 22 more miles of completely uninteresting water and concrete, and then 24 miles of water and concrete to come back.

Visualize it. Don't do it.

Lake Pontchartrain is also one of New Orleans' cardinal points of direction. Rather than East, West, North, and South, here we have Riverside (the Mississippi), Lakeside (Pontchartrain), Down River (toward the Gulf), and Up River (away from the Gulf). Because the city runs along a twisting double crescent of the Mississippi, giving New Orleans "Crescent City" moniker, the streets are laid out at odd angles and curves. Asking, "Do I go north to get there?" is another way to betray you're a tourist. Normal directions are useless. The West Bank is east of the city, unless you're in Uptown, and then it's south. I live here and practically once a month I will be driving around when struck with the question, "What's the sun doing over *there*?"

Causeway Bridge

About the only place you can be assured of directions is (was) Lee Circle. A statue of Robert E. Lee stands (stood) atop a 90-foot pillar since 1884 in what was formerly called Tivoli Circle or Place du Tivoli. General Lee is (was) always facing North, just in case those Yankees come back. I'm annoying you with present tense (past tense) because the statue remains as I write this book. The General may have been taken down by the time you read this or come to New Orleans. Following the removal of the Confederate flag in South Carolina, the impetus grew to likewise remove our statues of Confederates.

If the statues of Confederates Robert E. Lee, General Beauregard, and Jefferson Davis are gone with the whirlwind, we have plenty of other New Orleans-centric signature sights. Keep your eyes open as you venture around. There are many completely unique to New Orleans things to see.

Perhaps the most beautiful idiosyncratic symbols are our water meters. The nine-pound plates are etched with the words *Sewer & Water Board—Crescent Box*, and decorated with a crescent moon and shooting stars. They are used to cover water meters installed in the streets of New Orleans rather than in our nonexistent basements. Edwin Ford, of the Ford Meter Box Company in Wabash, Indiana, created the Crescent Lid in 1921. His design is now reproduced as coffee coasters, T-shirts, and hundreds of different types of collectibles. But there are fewer and fewer of the actual lids because tourists (and a few nefarious locals) steal them as keepsakes or to sell on eBay. Each year, many stolen lids are returned to the water board after airport security metal detectors outed attempts to fly back home. Hint: You're not going to sneak nine pounds of metal through airport security. Leave them alone. Sadly, the stolen plates are being replaced by the city with unadorned and less desirable ones.

New Orleans is likewise slowly losing the distinctive street signs of blue letters on white tiles that are embedded in the sidewalks. The practice of unglazed tiles as street signs dates back to the 1870s. The blue letters and any design elements in blue were not painted on with dyes or minerals, but dry or dust pressed from clay.

The original tile company, The American Encaustic Tile Company of Ohio, was in operation from 1875 until 1935. Several local ceramic shops still make decorative knock-offs, but they are painted, not meant for outdoor use, and are far less durable than the Encaustic tiles.

A number of street tiles display the older or original street name. Oretha Castle Haley Boulevard, renamed after a Civil Rights leader, still bears the tiled old name, Dryades Street, at the corner on Jackson Avenue. Where Treme and Gov. Nicholls

Streets meet, the tiles in the sidewalk show that Treme Street was once known as North Liberty Street. Some of Jefferson Avenue's tiles still feature the street's original name, Peters Avenue. And for some reason, Hennessey street is misspelled at a few intersections as "Hennessy." Maybe there was a shortage of E's during Reconstruction or the Great Depression.

We are losing our historic tile street signs as Entergy cuts through sidewalks to replace gas lines. Newer laws that require wheelchair access have likewise reduced their number.

If you've got a sharp eye, you may notice some oval plaques on French Quarter buildings that display a horse-drawn fire truck. These showed that the owner had purchased fire insurance. If a fire was to break out, homes displaying the plaque would first get service from firemen before they attended to burning buildings without the plaque.

You can't help but notice most every building in the French Quarter has a balcony, except here most of them are not called balconies. If the balcony comes about half way to the street curb and is held up by brackets, yes, that is a balcony. However, if the balcony overhangs the entire width of the sidewalk and is supported by posts or columns that reach all the way to the ground, that is not a balcony. We call them galleries. We much prefer the cover of galleries when needed to protect us from torrential downpours or the relentless sun on days over one hundred degrees.

Some of the posts will have a metal spider looking nest toward the top of the post. These are called Romeo spikes. Their purpose was to keep amorous young men from shimmying up the post to visit a daughter on the second floor. It's said a boy may go up as a Romeo, but he'll come down as a Juliet. I imagine they work just as well with burglars.

Atop other walls, you'll notice large spikes or menacing arrangements of broken glass. These we call IBU fences as in "I B U, I wouldn't be crawling over that wall."

On wooden houses, particularly the Antebellum homes in the Garden District, you'll notice many underside ceilings on front porches are painted robin's egg or sky blue, or often called haint blue. The practice extends all over the South and now has been adopted by some Yankees. One purpose was to trick bees or spiders into thinking the ceiling was the sky, so they wouldn't bore into the wood. The other was a protection, to keep evil spirits, or haints, away from the house.

If you get out into the country around New Orleans, you might see a bottle tree. Tree branches are adorned with brightly colored bottles, most often cobalt blue. The bottles are hung upside down. The colors attract spirits and then they are trapped in the upside-down bottle, keeping their evil intentions away from the house.

Many houses here are shotgun style. They are long and narrow. An individual shotgun will be only 12 feet wide, but perhaps 40 to 50 feet deep. This style of house comes from the West Indies and became popular here, one reason being that you paid real estate taxes based upon the dimensions of your house at the street. There's also a style known as camelbacks, where the second story of the house was one room back and not right on the street. Once again, this was done to get around having more tax based upon the square footage on the street.

The common story is that shotgun houses got their name from the interior layout. The homes have a center hall that runs straight from the front door to the back. You walk through the living room to get to a bedroom, through the bedroom to get to the kitchen, and so on. The story goes that you could shoot a rifle outside the front door and kill a chicken in the backyard without hitting anything in the house. Now, the African Yoruba word for house is "togun." It is more likely the word togun morphed into shotgun, but shooting a chicken makes a better story.

As you tool around, you may also notice 14-foot-high stick figures made from sandblasted steel. The stick arm is raised as if hailing a cab or pleading with a Mardi Gras float rider, "Throw me somethin', mister!"

These are EvacuSpots. They were designed by Massachusetts sculptor Douglas Cornfield. There are seventeen EvacuSpot figures throughout the New Orleans. If you're staying in the Quarter, the nearest will be at the entrance of Louis Armstrong Park on Rampart Street. EvacuSpots were created after Hurricane Katrina, and mark a pick-up location for the new program where city buses will get residents who don't have the means or the transportation to get out of harm's way when floods or hurricanes threaten.

Rather than seventeen, there's only one Falstaff sign, a towering 108-foot illuminated sign at the corner of Gravier and Dorgenois streets in Mid-City. The 10-foot-tall metal letters, easily seen from I-10, spell out the former brewery's name. Neon red letters forecast changes in weather. If the temperature is expected to rise the next day, the letters will light rising from the bottom to the top. If it is expected to drop, the letters will light from the top to bottom.

A lighted orb, called the weatherball, was added in 1952. When functioning, which can be a hit or miss, the color of the orb also indicates the upcoming weather: green for fair weather, red for clouds, and flashing red and white for approaching storms.

Look down as you walk our streets and you'll see we have small metal circles in our sidewalks, about the size of a silver dollar pancake at IHOP. These are termite catchers. New Orleans has the unique pleasure of Formosan termites, probably brought into the city from a docked ship. Formosan termites, compared to termites in the rest of the country, are like the Ebola virus compared to the common cold. They consume in two days what "normal" termites eat in six months. Their swarms are ten times the size. A queen can produce more than 1,000 eggs per day. And, best of all, Formosan termites are alates or swarmers, i.e. they fly.

My first summer in New Orleans, I was watching my daughter play softball one night under the floodlights at The Fly (a ballpark along the Mississippi River). I asked the dad of another player, "When do those Formosan termites come around?" He replied," Usually about this time a year." Twenty minutes later, it was as though a blizzard burst from the sky. Hundreds of thousands of flying white termites were everywhere, getting into the girls' hair, eyes, and mouths as they tried to play ball. The other dad looked over at me and said, "Thanks for asking."

Fortunately the termites live only two weeks aboveground. During those two weeks, you keep your outside lights off that would otherwise attract a swarm.

At our intersections with traffic lights, you'll see squat box-shaped art galleries. When New Orleans residents, the Tidys, returned from their Katrina-enforced exile in San Diego, they borrowed from a program they saw there called the Urban Art Trail. To make the ugly gray metal electrical boxes less of a visual eyesore, they instituted a project here called the New Orleans Street Gallery. Artists submit designs and, if accepted, they are given a $250 stipend to paint scenes or designs on the utility box. These can be anything from paintings of magnolia flowers, noted musicians, street cars, or stylized gators. So far, about one quarter of the city's 400 light boxes have been turned into public art.

The late George Rodrigue's private paintings might as well be public art. His blue dog paintings are seen everywhere all over New Orleans—as 15-foot-high reproductions in the Sheraton Hotel, 16-foot, 800-pound statues along the neu-

Blue Dog roadkill

tral ground (meridian) on Veterans (Vet-tranz) Boulevard, and on posters in pretty much every gallery in the Quarter, including original art in his own Rodrigue Studio at 730 Royal Street.

George Rodrigue, from New Iberia, Louisiana, began painting in the third grade when he was bedridden with polio. He became a moderately successful artist, rendering scenes of rural Cajun life. I have one of his early lithographs of six Cajun girls eating ice cream cones and seated beneath a moss covered Live Oak tree. Then he was asked to illustrate a book about rural Louisiana folk tales. Struggling to come up with an image for the loup-garou, or ghost dog, sort of a swamp-style werewolf, he fixed on a portrait of Tiffany. Tiffany had been his terrier-spaniel mix and constant companion as he worked in his studio. Her image, rendered in blue, became a part of most of his future paintings. There'd be Robert E. Lee and Stonewall Jackson on their horses . . . with the blue dog. A nude reclining on the couch . . . and the blue dog. Iconic New Orleans musicians Louis Armstrong, Pete Fountain, Al Hirt, each with the blue dog. Drew Brees and the blue dog. Rodrigue's blue dog paintings made him an international icon and a wealthy artist. Blue Dogs have been commissioned for a series of Absolut Vodka ads, the Jazz Heritage Foundation, *USA Today*, and both sides of the political aisle; he's done paintings of George H. W. Bush and Bill Clinton.

More far and wide than Rodrigue's Blue Dog, there are two sign painters whose work you'll see in practically every restaurant and gift shop in New Orleans. Bob Shaffer, more commonly known as Dr. Bob, is best known for his "Be Nice or Leave" signs. His signs were originally meant to keep people from bothering him while he worked in his sculpture studio. But, as he experienced more people stealing his signs than buying his sculptures, Dr. Bob was nudged from sculptor to sign painter. He now sells over 2,000 "Be Nice" signs each year. His work has been shown in art galleries and museums nationwide including the Smithsonian.

His open-air and delightfully ragged gallery and studio, a new addition since Katrina, is housed in a former mule barn at 3027 Chartes Street in Bywater. A hand-painted sign greets you at the front drive-in entrance, "Buy now before the artist dies."

Simon Hardeveld, better known as just Simon (pronounced See-MOAN) moved to New Orleans from France. He was trained as a chef in Cannes. But, in a similar fashion to Dr. Bob, he discovered he had more customers for his hand-painted signs saying things like "Hamburgers $3" than for his actual food. Simon was nudged to give up his pots and pans and become a first-rate dumpster diving artist. His distinctive "naive art" signs painted with squiggles, starbursts, and a predominant "SIMON" can be seen in shops and restaurants all over the city, from Lola's in Bayou St. John to Slim Goodies in Uptown.

Another artist, Randy Morrison, is less known far and wide. Once a Mardi

Gras float designer, he now uses his talent to create fiberglass foam statues of gargoyles, most often holding a severed head. These he tags high up on buildings like 3-D graffiti. The easiest to spot are on a house at 1469 Magazine Street (catty-cornered from Mojo Coffee) and 709 Jackson Avenue. Other street art abounds; there's a group of life-sized bunny men statues standing on the rooftop at 1228 O.C. Haley Blvd. These are portraits of the artist Alex Podesta dressed in bunny outfits. And there is one (1) remaining graffiti design of the internationally famous street artist, Banksy. His Umbrella Girl, where the rain pours exclusively from the underside of her umbrella is thought to be symbolic of the city, protected by a disastrously flawed levee system.

Other things you will see here that may seem visually peculiar include people walking around with dollar bills pinned to their chest. This is a tradition. When it's your birthday, you pin a dollar to your shirt or jacket and locals are supposed to give you a dollar, greet you with "happy birthday," and your single dollar grows into an ever-increasing corsage of cash. When I was a hotel concierge, I used to inform visitors of this practice. Some came back with over $200; more often it was just a few bills. It could be the latter if the birthday celebrant mostly crossed paths with visitors who didn't know this tradition, or locals who were cheapskates, or quite possibly because, even though others knew the tradition, the birthday boy or girl had a face

like Ted Cruz. It helps to be young and cute in order to be tagged with the greatest number of dollars.

Easily the most ubiquitous visual symbol throughout New Orleans is the fleur de lis. It's on our city flag, which depicts three gold fleur de lis on a field of white between thin bars or red and blue. It's on the side of the NFL Saints' helmets. It's seemingly on a good 80 percent of every area business card logo, signage, coffee mug, jewelry, ball cap or T-shirts, cast-iron fence design, dog collar, tattoo, and more.

The fleur de lis is the symbol of French royalty dating back to the Battle of Vouillé in 507 AD. The Franks, commanded by Clovis, who would two years later become the first King of France, battled the Visigoths. One story is that Clovis encountered a swollen river where his troops, dressed in armor, would have drowned if they tried to cross. He then spotted lilies coming up through the water, indicating a shallow point in the river where they crossed and went on to great victory.

The fleur de lis is a stylized representation of the lily flower that guided Clovis.

But true to our style, why have just one story when you can have three? Others have claimed the fleur de lis is symbolic of Clovis' conversion to Catholicism. Here, the three-pronged design represents the Holy Trinity. In another story, they signify perfection, light, and life.

French historian Georges Duby claims the three petals represent the medieval social classes: laborers, soldiers, and the religious sect. I might as well jump in with my own fabricated claim that they represent the three essential career paths for New Orleanians: chefs, musicians, and tour guides.

More than unique sights, we have our own language that you'll need to master if you want to fit in.

In New Orleans, we don't shop for groceries. Here, it's said as "makin' groceries." As a city that values local independents over chains, you are encouraged to go "makin' groceries" at our buy-local stores like Breaux Mart, Langenstein's, Dorignac's, Zuppardo's, or our version of Kroger's and Piggly Wiggly, Rouse's. Rouse's began as one store in Houma, Louisiana. They've since grown to over fifty stores and from four employees to 6,000, but they have maintained a commitment to local farms and local meat and seafood suppliers.

Before you go makin' groceries, you may wish to study up on our local food terms. Below is a partial list.

Alligator Pear: Avocado.
Barbecue Shrimp: A recipe started at Pascale Manales in Uptown and perfected in Mr. B's Bistro in the French Quarter. There is no barbecue sauce in New Orleans BBQ Shrimp—just pepper and butter, and butter, and butter.
Beignet: Deep fried dough, often accompanied with enough powdered sugar to skip over Type 1 and 2, straight to Type 3 Diabetes. Louisiana is actually #1 in the United

States in Diabetes, which is not exactly shocking. A beignet is better than funnel cakes in the northeast, very much like sopapias in the southwest.

Berled Crawfish: Boiled Crawfish, also called Mudbugs. Their season is usually late February until July. If you come for Thanksgiving or Christmas and go looking for a Crawfish boil, you can find one (served up for tourists) where the mudbugs have been kept frozen for half a year.

blessed trinity (lower case): Onions, garlic, and bell pepper, or the basic seasonings in most ev-rey ting we eat.

Boudin: A sausage made from whatever's left over after you butcher a hog—and rice. It's mushy and usually spicy. If you ain't from here, it's about as appealing as that runny chili poured over limp spaghetti noodles and topped with mounds of processed cheese from Cincinnati. If you are from here, it's ambrosia.

Calas: Calas are made of leftover rice mixed into a sugary egg batter, then deep fried, and again covered in an inhuman amount of powdered sugar. Calas has a rich history.

Rich History: In Louisiana, and Louisiana alone, slaves could acquire their freedom. When the Spanish took control of Louisiana in 1762, they brought with them the legal practice of *coartacion*. This gave slaves the right to buy their freedom. As a slave grew older, their freedom buy-out became more affordable because they could do less work.

Some scholars think slaves from rice-growing parts of Africa, Ghana or Liberia, probably brought calas to Louisiana. Back then, and even earlier under the French Code Noir, slaves were given each Sunday off. After church, African women would roam the streets of the French Quarter, touting their fresh baked wares with the chant "Belle Calas! Tout chauds!"—"Beautiful calas! Very hot!"

Through the money made from calas, these women were able to buy freedom for their families. More than 1,400 New Orleans slaves bought their freedom under Spanish rule. Locally famous and passionate chef and food historian, Poppy Tooker, has said, "Once you know the history, who'd want a boring old beignet?"

Creole Cream Cheese: Originally a product of France, a farmer-style cheese similar to a combination of cottage cheese and sour cream. For many years, it was commonly available, but much less so today. Commercial dairies such as Goldseal and Bordens no longer supply the city. Today, Creole cream cheese may be purchased from indie grocers like Dorignac's on Veterans Hwy and Langenstein's in Uptown,

Creole Tomatoes: Large, beat-to-hell-looking tomatoes with, tough, cracked skins that look like James Lee Jones but taste like Scarlett Johansson (if she was a tomato).

Cush-Cush, Kush-Kush, or Couche-Couche: An old French/Cajun breakfast dish. It is prepared by browning or searing cornmeal in an oil-glazed pot 'til light brown, then served hot with sugar and milk in a bowl. It's like cereal, if Special K or Cheerios didn't give a damn about your heart or arteries

Dirty Rice: Rice with debris. Now 'debris' is pulled apart, shredded, beaten to within an inch of its life as a recognizable meat portion of a once living animal that is then thoroughly moistened with pan drippings and/or simmered extra long so it fully absorbs every last dollop of gravy and seasonings.

Dressed: When ordering a po'boy, "dressed" indicates it comes with lettuce, tomatoes, pickles and MYNEZ (mayonnaise) on it. You can order a po'boy as NUTTIN ONIT, which is a po'boy that is not dressed.

Ernge: An orange-colored citrus fruit often squeezed for breakfast juice. Here we also have satsumas, which are a much sweeter cousin of the ernge or tangerine.

Etoufee: A French word meaning smother or suffocate. Crawfish or other seafood are cooked and then suffocated or smothered with roux over rice

Gumbo: Start with a roux, add ya "seasonings," sometimes seafood, or chicken, or Andouille, or sum ting else like Gumbo z'Herbes, a vegetarian gumbo made famous by Leah Chase, and den you eat it.

Hot Sauce: We use hot sauce like you use ketchup. No, make that the way you use salt. Hot sauce goes wit ev'ry ting. But, just as you can't be both a Yankees and Mets fan or Carolina and Duke, you've gotta choose between Tabasco and Crystal. Seriously. Check out the tables in diners and food joints. Most will have a bottle of each set next to the sugar packets and single-serving jelly packs. They don't want to start a fight or have their customers walk out.

Jambalaya: Dem Spanish didn't have no saffron in Louisiana, so dis is what dey came up wit when dey had a hankerin for paella. Jambalaya is not that different from étouffée, only here the rice is cooked in the same pot with the fixing. In étouffée, the fixin's are poured over rice just before serving.

King Cake: A huge Cinnabon-like round cake of breaded dough and frosted with green, purple, and gold sprinkles on top and a su-prise plastic baby inserted in one slice. The colors were chosen by visiting royalty from Russia. The purple is for justice, the green for faith, and the gold for wealth. You're supposed to eat king cakes during Mardi Gras (and no other time). Because of lawyers, the baby Jesus plastic baby is no longer hidden inside the cake awaiting lawsuits for chipped teeth and choking. The host now inserts the baby and takes on all threat of litigation. If you get the slice with the baby, you win the responsibility to bake or bring the king cake to the next party or gathering.

Mirliton: A vegetable pear or chayote squash, which grows wild in Louisiana and in backyards throughout New Orleans. Pronounced "MEL-lee-tawn," it's like a vegetable version of cream cheese or grits. It doesn't have much flavor of its own, but takes on the flavor of the food next to it on the plate. Mirlitons are served stuffed with shrimp, ham, cheese, etc. Dooky Chase restaurant does a particularly good crawfish au gratin stuffed mirliton.

Muffuletta: A quintessential New Orleans Italian sammitch of ham, Genoa salami, mortadella, Provolone cheese, and marinated olive salad with garlic, served on a round seeded Italian loaf. Invented at Central Grocery on Decatur in da Quarter.

Roux: You start with baking powder, water, and animal fat of some kind, then add your blessed trinity as you stir. Some folks like it the consistency of a broth soup. Many more like it dark and thick. There's a brilliant book by Marcelle Bienvenu and first published in 1991 titled, *Who's Your Mama, Are You Catholic and Can You Make a Roux?*

Skrimps: Shrimp.

Yakamein: A spicy beef noodle soup with sliced green onions and a hard-boiled egg half. It was supposedly concocted by soldiers from New Orleans stationed in Vietnam during the war.

Not to be confused with YA MAMA'EN'EM, a New Orleans slang when talking about, "your mom and them."

Zapp's: The most famous and most treasured locally made, kettle-style potato chips. Here, Zapp's has evolved to be the generic term for chips, like Kleenex or Xerox.

Zatarain's: Local company that makes all kind a food seasonings and condiments, most known and beloved for their Creole Mustard.

There are hundreds, if not thousands, of other local phrases and usage that could fill a book and a half. One of my favorites that I don't hear nearly enough is our term for apostrophe. When spelling aloud a possessive word, we wouldn't say for Joe's Bar, "J . . . O . . . E . . . apostrophe S" but rather here we say "J . . . O . . . E . . . comma on the top S."

Recently, I had some of New Orleans' best tour guides at my home. During a side discussion, I learned some beautiful phrases, more countryfied than New Orleans proper. Two sensational "From Here's," Libby Bollino and Jackie Bullock, are both tour guides worth tracking down. From them, I learned that "envie" (ON-vee) is used to describe an extreme desire or craving for something, usually a specific type of food. Example: "I has me an envie for french fries lately." Now, if you get your fries with a Baconator and a Frosty at Wendy's, here you'd be swinging by the chain known locally as "Wendy-boy-gars."

The Cajun word Libby and Jackie just taught me that I absolutely most love is *rodailler* (row-DIE-yey), which means to wander aimlessly, to gallivant, to run around without purpose, and a rodailleur (row-DIE-yure) is one who galavants, runs around, or wanders aimlessly. I now want business cards made up *Michael Murphy, Rodailleur.*

The terms you absolutely need to know and to use if you want to come off like a local are how you agree with someone. You need to pepper your conversation with "F' Tru!" (as in "for true") or "Tru Dat," or the most common "Yay, you rite!"

But *'Nuff Bout Dat.*

LUMINS OF NEW ORLEANS:
The 504 Dancing Man

After Hurricane Katrina, Darryl Young felt "gutting homes, landscaping yards, or reconstructing restaurants wasn't what I felt was my way to give back to the city." Then one night he was on Frenchmen Street when a band in the Apple Barrel bar started playing "Do You Know What It Means to Miss New Orleans?" He knew, "Right then and there, the desire to heal us as a city and to bring back pride instead of sadness came to me through movement, which the people call dance."

Someone tagged him "The Dancing Man," to which he added 504 (New Orleans' area code) and he was off and running. Darryl "Dancing Man 504" Young has become an ambassador bringing second line culture and educating people on New Orleans to all ages and all over the world.

He's performed in a variety of major festivals and small clubs throughout the South. He's danced second lines at weddings, jazz funerals, social events, and Mardi Gras parades, including being the Grand Marshal for life with the Krewe of Freret. He's starred in commercials, some international, and has taught New Orleans' unique dance and associated culture curriculum to students, here in New Orleans and internationally, such as at the Josephine Baker Elementary School in Paris. Some of his highlight performances have been at the Ghost Room for South-by-Southwest, with Dirty Dozen Brass Band and Big Chief Monk Boudreaux, Las Vegas for Zappos New Orleans Bourbon St. Experience, live on the NFL Experience and Game Day in New Orleans, and a Jazz Funeral in Coney Island in Brooklyn. The Red Hot Chili Peppers used him in their video "Brendan's Death Song."

His "Heal 2 Toe Project" is a fitness program aimed at kids using the second line dance as way to engage them in physical activity while teaching them about New Orleans culture. While "Heal 2 Toe" is for kids, he has BrassXcise for adults. In these classes, he does exercise using second line dancing and brass band music to get people shaking their butt to get in shape. He's pitched BrassXcise this way: "In these classes since the music is a so celebratory the participants don't really think of it as exercise in the way most workouts are designed. Also, because New Orleans is such a spiritual place and music and dance for us is like medicine to our souls, it has that effect as well. In the way I use the word 'heel,' it actually has a double meaning for what I do is also designed to 'heal.'"

CHAPTER 11

Celebrating

Are We Having Fun Yet?

No other city in the world had a celebration quite like this. It was beautiful precisely because it was so frivolous. —Dan Baum, *NINE LIVES*

When you come to New Orleans, *whenever* you come to New Orleans, there will most likely be a festival or a parade taking place. At the end of this chapter, I show an extensive but forever incomplete listing of our annual celebrations. I annotate about seventy-five events. I accept I'm most likely leaving out another five to ten. I have no doubt there will be a few new ones created after this book is published. New Orleans has many impromptu celebrations. A parade can break out at anytime and for any reason.

I first moved here in December 2009, just before Carnival season. My daughter, then 8 years old, was not happy about the move; no 8-year-old wants to leave their old school, or friends, or backyard. We were driving down Magazine Street one day, no more than a few weeks after we arrived, when a parade broke out. Years later, I still have no idea what the parade was about. But suddenly our car was engulfed in a sea of brass bands and hankie-waving revelers. It was clear we weren't going anywhere, so I inched the car to the curb and we got out, abandoned the car, and joined the parade. Here, you join a parade, not just watch one. It was that day that Ella uttered, "I like New Orleans."

As I began to write this book in January 2016, David Bowie passed away. Win Butler and Regine Chassagne of Arcade Fire, who have lived in New Orleans for two years, decided to throw our traditional second line parade for their idol and one-time collaborator. The Preservation Hall band joined in to turn Bowie hits like "Rebel Rebel," "Suffragette City," and "Heroes" into exuberant brassy covers.

The parade drew a surprisingly massive turnout, basically shutting down the French Quarter for the day. The surprise was why anyone would be surprised that thousands upon thousands would show up on a beautiful spring-like day just before the Carnival season, in a city where Bowie's flamboyant Ziggy Stardust style here would be considered "business casual."

A few months later, a massive pot hole imploded toward the base of Canal Street, nearest the river. This was the first few days of May. When May 5th rolled around, New Orleans had an impromptu festival, Sink Hole De Mayo.

And then, on September 30th, the French Quarter was dotted with kilt-wearing Irishmen with a few bands and a rather weak attempt at throws. I asked a couple of green T-shirt wearing guys what was going on. "It's the halfway point to St. Patrick's Day."

We will use any reason to celebrate. Got your electricity turned back on? Let's have a parade!

Our biggest celebration is, of course, Mardi Gras, when the population of New Orleans doubles each year. Although, if you want to be 100 percent accurate, it's really called Carnival Season. Mardi Gras translates to "Fat Tuesday" and refers to just the one day and last day of the Carnival Season. I will break with propriety and use both terms willy-nilly (just like everyone else). As Mark Twain wrote, "An American has not seen the United States until he has seen Mardi-Gras in New Orleans." If you have not been in New Orleans during Carnival Season, I feel fairly confident saying it is nothing like you think it is. The media likes to portray it as a combination of *Girls Gone Wild* and a frat party. And it is—but just on Fat Tuesday and just on Bourbon Street.

The origins of Mardi Gras goes back to Rome and Venice in the seventeenth century and the fun-loving House of Bourbon in France. The church was trying to deal with those wild and crazy Visigoths, who celebrated the coming of spring with drunken public orgies. Failing to eliminate the debauchery, the church tried to smooth over the roughest edges and turn the party into a religious holiday.

Carnival Season always begins on January 6th, or the Feast of the Epiphany. This is the end of the traditional Christmas Season and is the day that the Magi (three wise men) visited the Christ Child. The season ends on Fat Tuesday, the day before Ash Wednesday or Lent. Because Easter keeps moving, so does Lent, and therefore the Carnival Season. 2016 was a very short season, ending on February 9th. The 2018 season extends all the way to March 9th. It's all based on the Gregorian calendar and the full moon following a spring equinox, which I won't fully explain here, not because it's boring or takes up too much space, but because I don't get it.

Mardi Gras arrived in America on March 3, 1699, when the explorer Pierre Le Moyne d'Iberville camped about 60 miles downriver from what would become New Orleans. Knowing his buddies back in France were celebrating Fat Tuesday, Iberville named the spot Point du Mardi Gras and threw a small party. They probably did little more that first year than wear their cuirassiers backwards and tell off-color

jokes. A few years later, French soldiers and settlers feasted and wore masks as part of Mardi Gras festivities in the newly founded city of Mobile. Ignoring the historical accuracy of Iberville's party, Mobile claims to have the oldest Mardi Gras celebration in the United States.

The first recorded Mardi Gras in New Orleans wasn't until over 100 years later, taking place in 1837. In 1856, six men organized a secret society called the Mistick Krewe of Comus. By holding a far more elaborate parade than years past with the theme of "The Demon Actors in Milton's Paradise Lost" (not exactly catchy by today's standards), and adding a lavish grand ball at the end of the parade, Comus shaped the spectacle that now draws a million visitors to New Orleans each season.

Kids get off school for a week. The city basically shuts down and gives way to seemingly endless parades. There are seventy parades each year in the New Orleans area.

The Krewe du Vieux kicks off each parade season with a satyrical and salty parade. Their floats are drawn the old-fashioned way, by mules rather than tractors, and are immediately followed on the same parade route by the Krewe of Delusion. These two can get a bit risqué. No, make that flat-out raunchy. I took my daughter, then age nine, to the Krewe du Vieux parade. She gracefully pretended to believe me when I said certain floats were rocket ships, huge pink rocket ships. The year following the NFL's suspension of the Saints coach and several players, the parade actually got a little boring when float after float displayed the same theme: NFL Commissioner Roger Goddell getting anally violated.

The rest of the sixty-eight parades the following week(s) are PG-13.

The signature parades each year are Rex and Zulu, which roll on Mardi Gras Day. Rex was organized by New Orleans businessmen to put on a spectacle when the Grand Duke Alexei Alexandrovich of Russia visited New Orleans during the 1872 Carnival season. They also let the Grand Duke choose the "official" Mardi Gras colors. His choices of purple (for justice), green (for faith), and gold (for wealth) remain to this day and are seen each Carnival season on flags, stripped shirts, and splattered across the frosting of King Cakes.

Membership in the Krewe of Rex was secretive and restricted to city residents of European ancestry. In 1991, the New Orleans city council passed an ordinance that required all social organizations, including Mardi Gras Krewes, to certify publicly that they did not discriminate on the basis of race, religion, gender, or sexual orientation. Rex was one of the few long-standing Krewes that chose to comply. Comus, Momus, and Proteus all withdrew from parading rather than adhere to the ruling. Later, federal courts declared the ordinance was an unconstitutional infringement on First Amendment rights, but only Proteus chose to return to parading.

The Zulu Social Aid & Pleasure Club was officially founded in 1918, and its members were African-American. An earlier and more ragtag group headed by John L. Metoyer and called "The Tramps" walked a parade route beginning in 1909. Inspired by a vaudevillian comedy show called *There Never Was and Never Will Be a King Like Me*, members wore grass skirts and dressed in blackface. The king wore a lard-can crown and carried a banana stalk as a scepter. During the mid-'60s, in a time of racial unrest, being a blackfaced Zulu member became decidedly uncool. Membership dwindled to just 15.

Zulu president, Roy E. "Glap" Glapion, Jr., saved the organization from extinction during his reign from 1973 to 1988. He started recruiting professionals, educators, and prominent businessmen from all ethnic backgrounds and made Zulu the first parade to racially integrate. Don't ask me how white guys in blackface somehow made it any more acceptable.

One of the most treasured throws each year is the Zulu golden nugget, a highly decorated coconut. In the early 1900s, other crews threw expensive glass beads to the crowd. The working men of Zulu could not afford such expensive throws and so decided to buy coconuts from the French Market.

In 1987, the organization was unable to renew its insurance coverage, and lawsuits stemming from coconut-related injuries forced a halt to the long-standing tradition of throwing coconuts. In 1988, Governor Edwin W. Edwards signed Louisiana State Bill ≠SB188, the "Coconut Bill," into law, removing liability from injuries resulting from coconuts and enabling the tradition to resume.

I most often mention two annual parades to immediately blow up your preconceived notion of Mardi Gras being total debauchery.

The Krewe of Barkus is a dog parade through the French Quarter. For a $10 fee, you can dress up your dog and join the parade. I used to go. The parade has become so popular that it's grown to over four hours in length. As much as I love Pugs, by the fifth or sixth one dressed up as Yoda, the charm starts to wear off.

"'Tit" in French means small, (pronounced 'tee'). The 'tit Rex parade is residents designing shoe box-sized floats and dragging them behind their bicycles as their peddle through the Marigny.

New Krewes do pop up every few years. The Intergalactic Krewe of Chewbacchus was founded by "Publicity Stuntman" and conceptual artist Ryan S. Ballard and curator/events director Kirah Haubrich. They marched for the first time during Mardi Gras 2011.

From their website, the mission of the Intergalactic Krewe of Chewbacchus is to "Save the galaxy by bringing the magical revelry of Mardi Gras to the poor, disen-

'Tit Rex parade

franchised, socially awkward and generally weird masses who may have never had the opportunity to participate in a Mardi Gras Parade Organization."

The 2,000-member krewe has only three rules. (1) No unicorns (unless they have rocket thrusters), (2) No elves (unless they are cyborgs), and (3) Whinebots will be airlocked into the nearest Black Hole.

The more traditional Super Krewes are Endymion, Bacchus, and Orpheus. They roll on Saturday, Sunday, and Monday nights prior to Mardi Gras Day. Collectively, these three have more than 100 floats and 90 marching bands. Their more than 3,500 members toss more than 2 million plastic to-go cups, 3 million doubloons, and 400,000 gross of beads. A gross is a bag of 144 strands of beads.

While Mardi Gras' Super Krewes may be known for their size and spectacle, it's the smallest Sub Krewes that best give parades their quirky flavor, making Mardi Gras parades so very much unlike Rose Bowl parades, Macy's Thanksgiving, or Anytown America's oompa bands marching down main street on the 4th of July.

Sub Krewes are much smaller troupes that serve as bizarre palate cleansers in between marching bands and floats. Individual Sub Krewes will often march in several parades each Mardi Gras. There are many and there are forever new ones.

I never even heard of the Laissez Boys until I saw them in the 2016 parade, three years after their launch. The Sub Krewe started as twenty-two men riding the parade route in motorized recliner chairs. The La-Z-boys zip along at 5 miles per hour and are customized with special add-ons like reading lamps and mini-bars. The riders tend toward polyester leisure suits.

The most renowned Sub Krewe is the 610 Stompers, an all-male dance(ish) troupe who call themselves "Ordinary men with extraordinary moves." Dressed in sky blue, very short shorts with to-the-knee striped tube socks, nylon red jackets, and wrist & head sweatbands, they look like an acid flashback of 1970s exercise videos (only replace Jane Fonda with seriously out-of-shape men). Their funky chicken, disco finger, and hustle repertoire of moves take them way way beyond mere renditions of YMCA.

The 610 Stompers march in three or four parades each season and have also performed in the Macy's Thanksgiving Day parade in New York, and during the halftime of Saints games.

Almost any parade will feature at least one of the many (and growing) female sub-krewes. The Muff-a-Lottas, performing in their sexy 1950s car hop waitress outfits (with serving trays), have been "serving" New Orleans since 2007. Their banner, website, and Facebook page all announce "All You Can Eat." They perform throughout the year, including the Halloween Parade, St. Patrick's Parade, Southern Decadence Parade, and Krewe of Jingle Christmas Parade, among many others.

The Pussyfooters are over-30 women who toss on pink wigs, pink and orange

610 Stompers

corsets, white boots, and display as much feathers as ample cleavage. They tag themselves, "Majorettes from the Mothership sent here to help the party people get their groove on." Last year the Pussyfooters marched in five Carnival parades, plus they also do parties, benefits, balls, second lines, and fund raisers.

The Camel Toe Lady Steppers, founded in 2003, march exclusively in the Muses parade. They are the only female group that marches with a brass band, and appoint a local "celebrity" grand marshal/queen each year. The NOLA Cherry Bombs claim a passion for New Orleans, dance, and their bright red tutus. The Bearded Oysters don't do choreographed dances at all, though a few might shimmy of their own volition. The Oysters are accompanied by men dressed up in chef costumes who are known as their "oyster shuckers." The Organ Grinders bill themselves as hard-working "sexah monkeys" and are known for non-stop dancing throughout parades. The Chorus Girl Project is a very recent addition to the parades and was inspired by the early twentieth-century chorus line. The Sirens of New Orleans has over 80 members wearing colorful wigs and mermaid-style costumes. The Gris Gris Strut is a group of high energy professional dancers who are accompanied by a flag corp and marching band. Star-Steppin' Cosmonaughties, called "celestial bodies in motion," are the official dance team of Krewe de Lune. Roux La La change their costumes and choreography to a different theme each year.

The Disco Amigos Social Aid & Boogie Club are a co-ed group created to showcase Disco at parties, parades, and to provide classes for anyone who wants or needs to Do the Hustle. They also host the World's Largest Disco Party.

The Krewe of the Rolling Elvi is always a crowd favorite. They are exactly what they sound like: men in pompadours, killer sideburns, glitzy bell-bottomed jumpsuits as Elvis impersonators riding the parade route on pint-sized motorcycles. It almost doesn't need to be said, but if they throw you something, the proper response is, "Thank you . . . thank you very much."

There is a large assortment of traditions associated with Mardi Gras. King cakes I have presented elsewhere. Flashing breasts for beads is no more a tradition than dubsmash or a smiley face emoji. However, throws are an essential Mardi Gras

tradition, beginning in 1871 when a masker costumed as Santa Claus tossed baubles to the crowd from his float in the Twelfth Night Revelers parade.

Ever since, kings and queens for the day toss trinkets from the floats to the unwashed masses. Throws have evolved from fake doubloons and a modest amount of glass beads to modern parades with an opulence of plastic beads, shipped by fleets of ships from China, plastic cups, plush toys, Frisbees, balls, bracelets, and the ever-coveted blinky thingies.

You will also note after each day's parades a huge number of beads will be stuck in our trees. These are errant throws from the parade floats. The city has the good sense not to take them down. Months later and severe storms will eventually bring down most. And they are just painted plastic, which will tend to grow gray with time. But, the weeks following Carnival Season, the colorful trees lining St. Charles Avenue look like a children's storybook brought to life.

There's more than enough for everyone. Enough beads are tossed each season that every single person can go home with 115 strings. Please don't fight over a strand of the next to worthless plastic beads . . . unless of course the string of beads has a light-up blinking thingy. Then it's OK to backhand a nun in broad daylight to wrench the blinking thingy from the outstretched hands of small children with disabilities.

Blinky thingies show best during nighttime parades. Flambeaux are another longstanding tradition. Comus is believed to be the first parade to use these performers—originally slaves, then free men of color—to light the route by marching and twirling with flaming torches. Crowds tossed coins to the fire-wielders to act as small tips for their work. Flambeaux remain a dramatic spectacle in certain parades, but I have to admit the current practice by which the torches remain lit by propane tanks strapped to their backs fills me with visions of accidental explosions and body parts cluttering the parade route. This has never happened.

No tradition is more eye-popping or jaw-dropping than Mardi Gras Indians. Mardi Gras Indians, a unique subculture exclusive to New Orleans, date back nearly 300 years. The most noteworthy (breathtaking) aspect is the costumes. Krewe members spend a year making intricately and intensely designed costumes that will be worn while parading for only one Mardi Gras and one St. Joseph's Day in March (well, some now also parade the Fairgrounds during Jazz Fest, which ends the first weekend in May). Then the labor-intensive costumes are ripped apart and krewe members start on new ones for the next year.

The elaborate costumes are a cross between the beading of West African ritual garments, and the feathery regalia of Native American outfits. Most books and wiki-statements-of-fact-like-things share a commonly held belief that escaped slaves first created these outfits to honor the Native Americans who took them in or otherwise assisted them after they ran away.

Both cultures share a reverence for the spirits of their ancestors and hold a strong belief in celebrations using ritual costumes. It was also a West African tradition to signal respect for one's hosts by dressing like them in rituals; in this case, it made sense for African-Americans to dress like Native Americans.

But here's the thing: you would never see a Choctaw, Natchitoches, or Opelousa tribe member from Louisiana wearing anything so heavy as one of these Mardi Gras Indian outfits. It's much too hot and humid here. The inspiration really came from New Orleans hosting the World's Industrial and Cotton Centennial Exposition in 1884. Among the exhibits and entertainment was the Buffalo Bill Wild West Show. The intent was to show white men's inherent superiority over the Native Americans, displaying a costumed sideshow of manifest destiny. It had just the opposite effect with the blacks of New Orleans, many of whom sided with the oppressed and not the oppressor.

Mardi Gras Indian outfits much more closely resemble the Plains Indian styles on display at the 1884 Exposition. Historically, blacks were not welcomed to participate in Mardi Gras. So the black neighborhoods in New Orleans developed their own style of celebrating. Rather than Rex, Bacchus, and Proteus, their krewes took on names of imaginary Indian tribes like Wild Magnolias, the Golden Star Hunters, Mohawks, Black Eagles, Wild Tchoupitoulas, Golden Blades, Little Red White &

Blues, Wild Squatoolies, and Fi Yi Yi. The very first gang was founded in 1885 by Became Batiste, a Seventh Ward Creole of African-American, French, and Choctaw heritage.

On Mardi Gras Day each year, "tribes" of black Indians parade through their neighborhoods singing and dancing to traditional chants. In the past, this was a violent day for many Mardi Gras Indians. It was a day used to settle scores. The Big Chiefs of two different tribes would cross paths and start with chants, then ceremonial dances, and threatening challenges to "Humba," or a Big Chief's demand that the other Chief bow and pay respect. Often these confrontations would get violent.

Those practices changed, due largely to the leadership of Big Chief Allison "Tootie" Montana of the Yellow Pocahontas tribe. He redirected the confrontations so that they were not about knives or guns. They became more of an "I'm prettier than you!" *Project Runway* meets the Slam Dunk contest. The krewes with the best outfits were hailed the mightiest.

The culture has survived despite being forced underground twice, first banned by fearful whites after the 1811 Slave Revolt, and later when Jim Crow laws were put into effect in the 1890s.

The Mardi Gras day routes for Indians are not published anywhere. Some sources say that you will see the Creole Wild West tribe at the corner of LaSalle and 2nd Streets sometime between 9 a.m. and 11 a.m. after the Krewe of Zulu passes by. Other tribes meet at the corner of Claiborne and Orleans following the Zulu parade. But there is a shroud of secrecy covering all of the ritual of Mardi Gras Indians.

Today, many wear masks during Mardi Gras. In fact, float riders are required to wear masks by law. While many masks are simple, there are those who put a lot of pride into creating elaborate and beautiful ones. Maskarade (630 St. Ann St.) carries an extensive collection of masks from local and national artists. They also have some handmade Italian masks created in the old traditional Venetian style.

For visitors, the parades are the main event of Carnival Season. For many locals, the real show is at the after-hour balls. These are invitation-only black tie events, often huge productions inside the Superdome with superstar entertainers. The King and Queen of each krewe work all year long for the big, spectacular ball. Their identities are a closely guarded secret and part of the mystique until the night of the Ball.

Debutantes are introduced at the Ball Tableau as a formal introduction to society. In climbing the social ladder, children start by serving as pages to the court. Women dress in ball gowns and hope to be issued a "call-out" card. If a debutante is fortunate enough to receive one, she is seated in a select area and waits her turn to be "called out" for a dance by the krewe member who sent the card. It's a Cinderella-like night of dining and dancing with a masked prince in formal attire.

It's all rather old-school and aristocratic (with a whiff of white privilege). Filmmaker Rebecca Snedeker explored the insular world of the elite, white Carni-

val societies and debutante balls in her documentary, *By Invitation Only*. The film was both highly praised and viciously attacked. The intense criticisms calling it a "hatchet job" might reveal more about the critic than the film.

My favorite part of the film focused on Lynn Watkins. Miss Lynn, who passed away at the end of 2014, was for over two decades a "scepter & courtesy coach." This is a career with no equivalent in Portland or Pittsburgh. She was a lifelong New Orleanian who loved Carnival and was steeped in its nuances, protocol, and lore. It was said she was "the lady behind the scenes who made it all happen." The Krewe of Rex even gave her a scroll proclaiming Miss Lynn the official Royal Court Trainer.

In the weeks leading up to each ball, Ms. Watkins would meet frequently with the make-believe kings and queens, plus maids, dukes, and pages from thirteen organizations, to ensure they learned every bit of the ritual that is as old as Carnival itself. Her students would practice scepter wielding with billiard cues and wooden kitchen spoons to which she'd hot glue cheap rhinestones "because a regular wooden spoon would not do." She'd then encourage or berate her students, yelling at them "You're not stirring a pot of gumbo or trudging through the desert," or snap them to attention with her constant refrain, "Kodak!" That meant it was time to turn and smile at the imaginary crowd for your Kodak moment.

Secrecy is a sacrosanct component of Carnival. You are not supposed to know the identity of the kings and queens ahead of time. During training season, she would have kings from one Krewe running out of her back door as another was walking in the front door to practice. Said Hardy Fowler, a former Rex King, "As I was pulling up to Lynn's home, another car was rapidly speeding away. There was so much traffic in front of Lynn's home, I am surprised the police didn't think she was a drug dealer."

January

Carnival Season or Mardi Gras

Discussed in detail earlier in this chapter. As said by Mark Twain, "An American has not seen the United States until he has seen Mardi-Gras in New Orleans."

The Sugar Bowl

The first few days of January each year (most often January 1st, unless that falls on an NFL Sunday) bring a blooming of tourists in scarlet and gray (Ohio State), blue and orange (Florida), and other colors to (a) support their team in The Allstate Sugar Bowl and (b) act ways on Bourbon Street they would never act back home in Columbus, Gainesville, or Happy Valley.

We actually love the green (money) these uni-clad fans spend in New Orleans. My only real complaint is that the Sugar Bowl has been yoked with Allstate. Some of us, well at least I do, find it rather galling to see a big banner raised outside the Superdome with Allstate printed in twenty-foot-high letters. Aren't these the same guys who covered their good hands in boxing gloves to deny insurance claims following Katrina? Allstate agents were paid incentives for keeping payouts low and following a "sit and wait" policy where they hoped their strategy of dragging out responses would have some customers give up trying to collect. Meanwhile, top executives at Allstate, Thomas Wilson and Edward Liddy, collected $10.7 million and $18.8 million in compensation, respectively, for upholding profits for investors rather than helping customers in desperate need. As Wilson is quoted as saying, "Our obligation is to earn a return for our shareholders."

The Phunny Phorty Phellows

Each January 6th, the Epiphany is also the beginning of the Carnival Season each year (what you call Mardi Gras). The Phunny Phorty Phellows is a krewe that will phorcibly phlex any words into alliteration as they herald the arrival of carnival. On that first evening, the krewe loads up on street cars and rides all way the down St.

Charles Ave. and back. The Phellows, who first took to the streets in 1878, then took a 100-year break between 1898 and 1981, but are now back with a satirical vengeance. Krewe members often dress in costumes, drink champagne, eat king cake, and throw the first beads of the season.

Joan of Arc Parade

January 6th is both the epiphany and Joan of Arc's birthday. Joan of Arc is both a saint and the maid of Orleans. The parade is strictly a walking one. Many who join are dressed in gold, like the statue, which was given to New Orleans by France and moved to the triangle at Decatur and St. Phillip Streets after being unrooted from its original spot by Harrah's Casino.

King Cake Festival

This is the first of a smorgasbord of food festivals each year. Local bakeries offer their best king cakes, and live music enlivens the event. All money raised goes to benefit babies and children at Ochsner Hospital.

February

More Carnival Season or Mardi Gras

Tet, or Vietnamese New Year

With the largest Vietnamese population in North America, their three-day celebration here is much larger than in other U.S. cities. The event features food, carnival games, dragon dances, concerts and other surprises to celebrate the Lunar New Year and ancient traditions of Vietnamese heritage.

Rock 'N' Roll Marathon

The Rock 'n' Roll Marathon course offers runners (and walkers) a virtual guided tour of the most historic and scenic high points of New Orleans. Starting and finishing outside the storied Louisiana Superdome on Poydras Street. The course takes in the French Quarter and lively, a.k.a. smelly, Bourbon Street, scenic St. Charles Avenue, which daily serves as joggers' most-used running route, the stately Garden District, and both major parks, Audubon Park and City Park.

March

Some Years even more Carnival Season or Mardi Gras

Spring Fiesta

The one time each year where many of the posh homes in the Garden District throw open their cast-iron front gates for home and garden tours.

Tennessee Williams Festival

The annual literary festival each March draws noted authors like Edward Albee and Dave Eggers, but also refreshingly non-mainstream celebrities like Tab Hunter and John Waters, to speak on panels and sign books. The unquestionable highlight of each year's festival is the Stella and Stanley Shouting Contest, where T-shirt clad contestants drop to their knees in Jackson Square screaming "Stelllaaaa!"

BUKU Music and Art Project

Under the shadow of the old power & light plant, BUKU has become a celebration of the creative, funky subculture of New Orleans. The music has a different, edgier vibe from most music festivals in New Orleans, with performers like the Flaming Lips, Kid Cudi, and Zed's Dead. The festival's goal is stated as "creating a head-spinning immersive experience." BUKulture curators handpick dozens of street performers, musicians, artists, and interactive exhibits, where the aim is to serve up sometimes unscheduled "pop-up" fashion special moments.

Congo Square New Worlds Rhythms Festival

The festival is presented by the New Orleans Jazz & Heritage Foundation in conjunction with the Tom Dent Congo Square Symposium. The late Tom Dent was a noted poet, essayist, oral historian, dramatist, cultural activist, and Executive Director of the New Orleans Jazz and Heritage Foundation. I had the pleasure of signing him to a contract to write the follow-up to his brilliant book, *Southern Journey*, in May of 1998. He died a month later of a heart attack and that book was never born. This day-long festival celebrates the historic role of Congo Square as the birthplace of American music. The Tom Dent Symposiums feature panel discussions in topics relating to the mixture of world cultures that took place at Congo Square. The festival features African drumming and dance, together with music from Africa, the Caribbean, and the American South.

St. Patrick's Parade

The parade stumbles down Magazine Street through the Garden District and the Irish Channel. Confession: I am not a fan of St. Patrick's Day in any city. They give people who are no more Irish than Geronimo the one-day-a-year license to get totally drunk, try to steal Kiss-Me-I'm-Irish slobbering smooches, and otherwise act like Shane MacGowan. The New Orleans parade comes with a word of caution. In addition to giving out fake green, orange, and white flowers and tossing beads, plush toys, and green panties, there will also be coming-at-you uncooked potatoes, carrots, cabbage, and the occasional canned ham. You can get seriously hurt if you don't see a canned ham coming your way.

St. Joseph's Day

Because of the wave of Italians and Sicilians that came into New Orleans in the 1880s, this has become one of the city's major holidays. The day commemorates the relief St. Joseph provided during a famine in Sicily. New Orleans becomes awash with lush altars displaying statues of St. Joseph surrounded by candles, flowers, medals, and overflowing food. Altars are found inside New Orleans churches, especially those with strong Italian roots, but they are also in private homes, halls, Italian restaurants, and public spaces throughout the city. Cookies, cakes and breads, often in the form of shellfish, are common decorations for altars. Fava beans, or "lucky beans," are particularly associated with St. Joseph because they sustained the Sicilians through the famine. The fava bean was the only crop that survived a drought and saved many from starvation. The legend goes if you carry a fava bean or lucky bean in your pocket or purse, you will never be without money, and the pantry with a fava bean in it will never be bare.

The evening of March 19th begins with food, wine, and Italian music, followed by the parade, where marchers dressed in black tuxedos parade until dark. Paraders give out silk flowers and fava beans as they dance and sing the hours away with enthusiastic bystanders. If you happen to see a fresh green branch over a doorway, it means you're invited to come into their home, participate in the ceremony, and share the food.

Mardi Gras Indians Super Sunday

For reasons that are unclear, St. Joseph's Day has also been adopted as an important day for the Mardi Gras Indians. Their festivities begin at noon in A.L. Davis Park (at Washington & LaSalle Streets) where the Mardi Gras Indians once again dress in their feathers and suits and take to the streets to meet other "gangs." Before 1969, the Indians celebrated by coming out at night. In 1969, the first parade was created and rolled through town at night. In 1970, it was switched to a day parade on Sunday afternoon.

Easter Parades

My first Easter living in the city, my daughter asked what time the parade was. I got to reply, "Do you mean The Historic French Quarter Easter Parade, which begins at 9:45 a.m. in front of Antoine's, or the 1:00 p.m. Chris Owens French Quarter Easter Parade, or the 4:00 p.m. Official Gay Easter Parade?"

Crescent City Classic

Another fun run, this one a 10K. I'd act more enthusiastic, but running events are received by many here, or at least by me, as welcome as getting stuck behind a mule-drawn carriage in the narrow streets of the French Quarter. Streets are closed off for the runners, making it difficult for the rest of us to get around.

Nola Pyrates Week

From the last week of March to the first week of April, people who love and sometimes think they are pirates gather in New Orleans, a city with a rich pirate heritage. In addition to 10 days of pirate music and song, pirate food (whatever that is), and general swashbuckling, the attendees rally around their credo, "Take what ye can . . . GIVE something back!" Their volunteerism and generosity to rebuilding projects provides New Orleans with roughly $10,000 each year. Hard to ARRGGue with that.

Wednesdays at the Square

From March until mid-June each year is a free concert series on Lafayette Square. There are also tents where local artists show, and hopefully sell, their work, plus food tents. But the music takes center stage with some renowned musicians. One time, when visiting New Orleans, I wandered by the square and happened upon Buddy Guy playing . . . for free.

April

Mo Fest

Figuring there just aren't enough parades and festivals in New Orleans, Scott Aiges of the Jazz Heritage Foundation produced "one mo'" festival from 2003 through 2005. The music festival was revived after Katrina in 2007 as the Fan Fest. I'm not really sure of its current status, but you should come to New Orleans just in case it happens.

French Quarter Fest

The decade-old French Quarter Festival occurs before Jazz Fest each year and showcases local musicians and legends like Irma Thomas, Kermit Ruffins, Allen Touisaint. The four days of music is 100 percent free. The food tents allow you to sample

French Quarter Fest

dishes from better restaurants like Drago's, Brennan's, The Court of Two Sisters, and the like for a fraction of what you'd pay inside their walls. What started as a leisurely and lovely weekend, where local residents could pull out a foldaway chair and take in the music has, over the years, drawn more and more notice of tourists. Each French Quarter Festival now draws in more than a half million attendees. Most recently, it topped 700,000.

Hogs for the Cause

Hogs for the Cause is a non-profit annual fundraising barbecue competition and music festival that raises money for families with children fighting pediatric brain cancer. More than ninety pit-master teams compete in the Ben Sarrat, Jr. Cook Off Presented by Children's Hospital of New Orleans for the High on the Hog Grand Champion title.

Freret Street Fest

A large parking lot on Freret Street is used for a once-a-month street fair with food, music, and locals selling everything from T-shirts to sculptures made from cypress roots (which I thought was illegal), to jewelry, dreamcatchers, tiny decorative hats, to dogs up for adoption. I often display, sign, and sell my books there. In April each year is the much larger version, where vendors and music stages spill out from the parking lot to close off the street and occupy six city blocks. Instead of one or two bands as usual, the April fest will have over 20 bands.

Brunch Fest NOLA

The festival serves up brunch foods, breakfast cocktails, brunch-inspired costumes, and a Bloody Mary Contest. All money raised goes to benefit the Louisiana SPCA.

FoodFest

FoodFest started in 2009 as the New Orleans Roadfood Festival, spun out of Jan and Michael Stern's Roadfood Good Food. Whenever I travel by car, the two websites I always go to are roadsideamerica.com, which highlights all the pullover sites like the World's Largest Ball of Yarn (Cawker City, KS) and Adolf Hitler's typewriter (Bessemer, AL), plus roadfood.com for regional diners, small-town cafes, seaside shacks, drive-ins, barbecues, and bake shops. FoodFest is the one food festival that does not focus on local dishes, but other regional fare such as New England clam chowder, Tucson tamales, Memphis barbecue.

Jazz Fest

The New Orleans Jazz & Heritage Festival, a.k.a. Jazz Fest, is always the last week-end in April and the first weekend in May. It was born, like so many things in New Orleans, when opportunity met up with people crazy enough to just go with it and jump in. Miss Mahalia Jackson returned to her native New Orleans in April of 1970, and while visiting Congo Square, The Eureka Brass Band struck up a second line. As revelers passed by Miss Mahalia, George Wein shoved a microphone in her hand. Miss Mahalia just went with it and jumped in, creating a moment of improv brilliance. Wein, creator of the Newport Jazz Festival in 1954, had been looking to create an annual event in New Orleans that would pay tribute to our deep musical heritage. Jazz Fest has grown from 350 people attending to a record 650,000. Moved from Congo Square to the Fairgrounds, Jazz Fest has twelve stages of continuous music in all styles from traditional Cajun music at the Fais Do Do stage to internationally known superstars like Bob Dylan, Miles Davis, Aretha Franklin, James Brown, and a Simon & Garfunkel reunion. When Springsteen comes (quite often), he delivers three-hour sets. I tell people the Gospel Tent alone is worth the price of admission.

Jazz Fest

My first time attending Jazz Fest, in one day we saw & heard Lenny Kravitz, John Hiatt, and Lyle Lovett, all for just $20 (daily tickets have since grown to $85). But the real treat was none of these three stars, but rather the local groups like Big Chief Monk Boudreaux & The Golden Eagles, Los Po Boy Citos, Leroy Thomas & the Zydeco Roadrunners, and New Leviathan Oriental Foxtrot Orchestra, none of whom we knew before hearing them at the festival and then watched in amazement.

Almost every year, one weekend will be stunningly beautiful weather, and the other will be full of torrential downpours. Almost every year, we are treated to Facebook postings of visitors doing their best Woodstock renditions of rolling and dancing in the muddy lakes that form at the fairgrounds. Locals then wonder, "Should we just let them have their fun, or tell them that's not mud, but largely horse shit?"

May

Chaz Fest

Chaz Fest was born when Jazz Fest canceled their Thursday venue one year. A number of local musicians not invited or dis-invited to perform at Jazz Fest got together in a Mister Ferguson's barn kind of way and created their own music festival. The name comes from the irrepressible washboard virtuoso "Washboard" Chaz Leary. Their rough-hewn guidelines are to use local musicians fitting the description, "Nobody here is a huge star, but everybody has been around the block many times." In addition to Washboard Chaz, performers have included Kirk Joseph's Backyard Groove, Tin Men, Happy Talk Band, and Ingrid Lucia, an amazing singer who for the life of me I cannot figure out why she isn't an international star.

New Orleans Wine and Food Experience

This May festival brings together world-renowned winemakers, celebrated chefs, and food industry insiders for the food equivalent of the Cannes Film Festival for cinema buffs or ComiCon for 30-year-old men living in their mom's basement (that's a terrible cliche—having been to ComiCon, I can confirm it's only about 25 percent 30-year-olds living in the basement). The Wine & Food Experience is tastings, seminars, and nothing is "experienced" in New Orleans without music.

Ponderosa Stomp

The Ponderosa Stomp is sponsored by The Mystic Knights of the Mau Mau, a charitable organization dedicated to preserving and presenting the rich history of

American roots music. Held at the House of Blues in the French Quarter, the event celebrates unsung heroes and heroines of rock and roll, rhythm and blues, and other forms of American roots music while those artists are still alive. Past Stomps have showcased Sam the Sham, The Sun Ra Orchestra, Robert Jr. Lockwood, Roy Head, Bobby Rush, and Elvis's drummer.

The Mid-City Bayou Boogaloo

Like so many, what started as a neighborhood thing has grown into an "event." Held along Bayou St. John, the Bayou Boogaloo is billed as the last major music festival before the dog days of summer. It now draws 20,000 people each year to hear music, eat food, play games, buy stuff. The Boogaloo is hosted by the MotherShip Foundation, a nonprofit dedicated to encouraging social change. The venue includes solar powered stage lighting, bio-diesel generators, locally grown & organic food tents, and a recycling education to toss off ticket stubs and containers of stuff. It also has a Rubber Ducky Derby.

Whitney Zoo-To-Do

The event, now in its 40th year, brings out party animals looking like penguins in a black tie to benefit the Audubon Zoo. In addition to food and entertainment, there's a silent auction and raffle for a luxury vehicle.

Greek Fest

The Greek Fest is, as yet, one of the lesser known and thus better festivals in New Orleans.

There's wine, dancing, spit-roasted lamb, and plenty of baklava.

June

The Oyster Festival

Don't ask me why our Oyster Festival takes place the first week in June, when you aren't supposed to eat raw oysters in months without Rs at the end. Maybe it's simply the open weekend between Jazz Fest and The Essence Festival. The celebration of our Gulf shore oysters features live and free music, food tents, and oyster competitions not to be missed. On Saturdays is the oyster shucking competition. Sundays is oyster eating. Displaying more athletic prowess than Michael

Jordan with a basketball or Muhammed Ali in the ring (and clearly possessing no gag reflex), Sonya Thomas, a.k.a. the Black Widow, downed 47 dozen oysters . . . in eight minutes. I was there to bear witness, or there is no way in hell I'd believe what I just wrote. Sonya Thomas also holds the world records for eating hard boiled eggs (52 in 5 minutes), tater tots (250 in 5 minutes), and jalapeños peppers (43 in 1 minute).

Creole Tomato Festival & Cajun-Zydeco Festival & Louisiana Seafood Festival

After years of taking a backseat to crawfish, oysters, and gator on a stick, the Creole tomato demanded a festival of its own. The French Market hosts the Creole Tomato Festival in June with tomato tasting, tomato cooking demos and lectures, and music . . . only now, in the same weekend, in the same area of the French Market, the Creole tomato has to share the spotlight with the Cajun-Zydeco Festival's music & fun, plus the Louisiana Seafood Festival. While triple the fun for festival goes, sometimes life just ain't fair for the beleaguered Creole tomato.

Wednesdays on the Point

For a $2 ferry ride, you can cross the Mississippi River to partake of a free concert series that runs from June through August. Performers are all big-name musicians. A recent lineup included Amanda Shaw, Rebirth Brass Band, and Big Chief Monk Boudreaux.

New Orleans Pride Festival

New Orleans Pride is listed as one of the fastest growing LGBT pride celebrations in the nation and is the only "Official" Pride Festival in New Orleans. *Travel & Leisure* chose it as the #6 best gay festival in the country.

Zombie Pub Crawl

The pub crawl is a night of zombie-themed bar hopping. Hundreds of undead friends will stagger and shuffle from bar to bar. In addition to killing brain cells, the pub crawl also helps the lives of animals in need by partnering with the Louisiana and Jefferson SPCAs.

Bat wielding Bulls getting ready to run

July

The Running of the Bulls

Mickey Hanning, a.k.a. "El Padrino" (the godfather) started the San Firmin in Nueva Orleans Festival in 2007 as a NOLA-skewered version of Encierro, Pamplona, Spain's annual running of the bulls. In our case, it occurs one day in July and is designated to begin at 8:00 a.m. with "bulls" (girls on roller skates, dressed in red with long-horned helmets) chasing after runners (anyone who wants to dare run the streets of the French Quarter dressed all in white with one article of red clothing) as the bulls try to smack the runners on the butt with plastic baseball bats. The run is followed by an all-day-long street party.

The Essence Festival

Sponsored by Coca Cola and *Essence* Magazine, the music festival showcases national acts like Janet Jackson, Usher, Kanye West, and Mary J. Blige, rather than locals. The events take place at the Superdome and the convention center. It's possibly the least New Orleans-y of New Orleans annual events, but we love it because it brings in A LOT of tourists, coming here for the sole purpose of having a good time and willing to drop A LOT of money. If you want to secure a hotel room during the intense Essence weekend, I'd do so right now and finish this book after you have your confirmation number.

4th of July

New Orleans has been rated, by people who waste time rating such things, as a top city in America to watch a 4th of July fireworks celebration. The way we do it is dueling barges on the river, pretty much in front of Wollensky Park in The French Quarter. Some of the best views can be had from large windowed banquet rooms on the top floors of river-facing high-rise hotels like The Westin, Marriot, Sheraton, Hilton, and The Hotel Monteleone. On the 4th, these hotels don't seem to care if you're a guest or a local, so long as you aren't drunk or smelly. Loud is OK.

What we got that Washington, D.C. and New York don't got, is much better music. Rather than patriotic oompa band music being played stiffly, our music on the 4th is more R&B or Reggae Funk. The live music blares from noon until the fireworks start around 9:00 p.m. outdoors at The Spanish Plaza. I'll take our music over John Philip Sousa any day.

Bastille Day

The 4th of July is just the first of two Independence Days celebrated in this French-iest of cities. The storming of the Bastille and French Independence Day comes just over a week later, on July 14th. The several-day celebration includes French films being shown by the New Orleans Film Society, a block party in the Bayou St. John neighborhood where the upper crust French Creoles used to live, plenty of petanque (a French game that resembles Bocce or lawn bowling), the laying of the wreath and singing of "La Marseillaise" at the foot of the golden Joan of Arc statue on Decatur, and the Waiters' Race, which has about twenty waiters from area restaurants racing at high speeds through the Quarter while trying not to spill the contents from their tray. The festivities are concluded with a mock storming of the Bastille at Molly's on the Market. Everyone is encouraged to put on their peasant wear and grab their plastic swords and non-threatening pitch forks.

Tales of the Cocktail

In late July, the French Quarter hosts new chapters in Tales of the Cocktail. The event has many "spirited" seminars about the history and modern practice of the mixing of drinks with plenty of attending mixologist offering intoxicating samples. Even for non-drinkers, or at least less passionate drinkers, the festival is worth a visit for its collection of bar paraphernalia, accessories, and T-shirts. Tales' organizers teamed with Lauren Thom, owner of Fleurty Girl, to create a lineup of shirts to immortalize classic New Orleans cocktails. There's the Ramos Gin Fizz, created in 1888 by Henry C. Ramos; the Vieux Carré, a cognac and whiskey drink born in 1938 at the Hotel Monteleone; and, of course, the Sazerac.

Zombie Run

Not to be confused with the Zombie Pub Crawl, The Zombie Run: Extreme is a mud-filled 5K obstacle course. In addition to climbing over walls, under tunnels, and up ropes, the #1 obstacle is a horde of flesh-eating zombies. Runners will have three "life" flags attached to their waist at the start of the run. If you make it to the finish line with at least one flag still attached, you win absolutely nothing. But you should end up feeling more self-confident that if there ever really is a doomsday, post-nuclear, end of the world, apocalypse with zombies, you have a solid chance of surviving.

Nyctophilia's Mirror Masquerade

Just a few years old, the July event is a live music and DJ'd dance at the Dragon's Den (435 Esplanade). BTW, nyctophilia means a preference or love for darkness, not where your dirty little mind just took you.

Festigals

Billed as "The Original New Orleans Girlfriend Getaway Weekend," Festigals is a women-centric event created by women for women.

French Film Festival

Because we are, were, and always will be, how you say?, so *donc très français*, rather than a Sundance- or Tribeca-type film festival, we put on a French film festival. You can get your Truffaut, Godard, or Tati on at the Pyromania Theater, the last of the single-screen movie palaces (with balcony) in all of Louisiana.

August

Satchmo Summerfest

The three-day festival is dedicated to the life, music, and legacy of New Orleans' favorite son, Louis Armstrong. Three stages of live music blend with food and activities such as the annual Satchmo Club Strut and second line performances. There's also a number of things for kids, like Zulu coconut painting and second line umbrella-making activities. The event always ties into Louis' birthday of August 4th, 1901—even though he himself spent a lifetime of not letting the truth get in the way of a good story. Armstrong insisted he was born on the 4th of July.

The White Linen Night and the Dirty Linen Night

Each August, the art galleries in the Warehouse District host The White Linen Night, where attendees dress in white linen for an elegant summer's eve of local music, food, and gallery viewing. Not to be outdone, the galleries of Royal Street and the French Quarter follow up with an Art Fair block party of sixty-some galleries. They call theirs DIRTY LINEN NIGHT, and all are encouraged to wear whatever the Hell they want.

Red Dress Run

Coolinary New Orleans

Coolinary is less a festival than a month-long celebration by hundreds of local restaurants serving special prix-fixe menus on the cheap during our S-L-O-W month of August, when it's too hot and hurricane-threatening for many tourists and conventioneers to come to New Orleans.

Red Dress Run

On the second Saturday each August, all participants—men, women, or otherwise bust out their little red dress with their best red wig and other accessories for a 2-mile run, walk, stumble, or crawl charity event. It is sponsored by the New Orleans Hash House Harriers, "a drinking club with a running problem." They boast one of the best after-parties in town. In New Orleans, that's saying something.

New Orleans Sushi Festival

Parking and complimentary shoulder massages are free. Everything else comes with a price: $15 for tickets bought ahead of time, $25 at the door. It's $100 for a VIP ticket that gets you in an hour earlier than the unwashed masses and provides unlimited beer and sake. For that price, I think you should get your own *ookikute gouka na*.

September

Southern Decadence

Begun as a going-away party for Michael Evers thrown in 1972 by his friends and roommates on Barracks Street, Southern Decadence has grown in 40 years to become the largest 24-hour gay street party in the country. The first parade was all of fifteen people marching whilst made up as their favorite decadent Southerner, such as Mary Ann Mobley or Tallulah Bankhead. I wish New Orleans could claim Tallulah as a native daughter, but she was an Alabama girl. Her most New Orleans-like exchange happened when the legendarily lusty Chico Marx met her at a party. In his straight-forward style, Chico said to Talluah, "I want to fuck you tonight." Without missing a beat, Tallulah responded, "And so you shall, my dear old-fashioned boy." Now, every Labor Day weekend, over 10,000 people flock to the quarter to revel in outfits ranging from wildly elaborate to barely visible. Having wandered through once, I don't think I will ever attempt a second visit. A large number of bears (overweight and very hairy gay men) running around in leather chaps and nothing else, so that their hairy dimpled butts are hanging out for all to see is, for me, not the height of fun.

Fried Chicken Festival

The first annual Fried Chicken Festival was held September 25th, 2016. What took us so long to come up with this? In Lafayette Square, twenty-five restaurants compete for the crown as top New Orleans musicians, Tank and the Bangas, Sweet Crude, John Boutte, The Brass-a-Holics, and DJ Mania Fresh perform.

Louisiana Seafood Festival

Rather than separate festivals for shrimp, crab, oysters, gulf fish, and crawfish, this one tosses them all in the same pot. Dishes are prepared by local restaurants Acme Oyster House, Arnaud's, Café Giovanni, Drago's Seafood Restaurant, Galatoire's, Mr. B's Bistro, Ninja, Oceana, Pigeon Caterers, Pontchartrain Point Café, Red Fish Grill, Remoulade, Saltwater Grill, and others. The festival includes live entertainment, celebrity chef cooking demonstrations, and local arts and crafts.

NOLA on Tap

NOLA on Tap draws in an excess of 25,000 beer lovers ready to get a jump on Oktoberfest. For tasting, there are 400 local, national, and homebrewed beers. The festival includes contests, People's Choice Awards, and a Homebrewers Beer Judge Certification Program (BJCP). There is, of course, also live music.

Goodfellas Social & Pleasure Club Annual Second Line

The group of brass bands and revelers strut uptown from 1:00 p.m. to 3:00 p.m. on a Sunday afternoon. The Goodfellas thank the "LORD up above" first and urge those watching or joining the parade to "Leave your guns and troubles somewhere else."

Gleason Gras

The festival, named after Saints player and No White Flags hero Steve Gleason, includes a 3.7-mile run (billed as the World's Longest 5K), live music and dance featuring local groups like The Hot 8 Brass Band, Bonerama, Paul Varisco and the Milestones, The 610 Stompers, and, of course, food.

Where Y'hat

A newcomer to the festival scene, hat designer Margarita Bergen has organized a September Hat Festival with live music and lively hats in The French Market and Dutch Alley setting. The event includes hat making, hat contests and raffles, as well as the buying and promenading of hats.

Burlesque Festival

As our #1 tourist attraction from the 1940s through the '60s, New Orleans is the ideal home to host a new festival (launched in 2009) to showcase classic and traditional burlesque. Showcases, workshops (work?), and panel discussions build to the main event, the competition; to be chosen as this year's Queen of Burlesque. The festival was organized by New Orleans native Rick Delaup, whose life was jumpstarted by a chance meeting with Evangeline the Oyster Girl.

Jazz in the Park

From September to the first week of November, Louis Armstrong Park rolls out their version of Lafayette Square's earlier in the year Wednesdays at the Square. This, too, is a live concert series every Thursday from 4:00 to 8:00 p.m. There are local bands, painting and art displays, food vendors, and again, is absolutely free.

October

Blues & BBQ

With weeks having passed since the last festival in New Orleans, the Jazz & Heritage Foundation comes to the rescue to organize and sponsor the Blues & BBQ Festival held mid-October in Lafayette Park. The not-quite-10-year-old festival focuses on Southern Blues, R&B, and ribs.

Halloween

Not shockingly, New Orleans takes Halloween seriously. We have two parades each year. The Jim Monaghan parade is nearing its 20th year. The parade starts at Molly's Market in the French Market and ends with a costume contest at Erin Rose Bar on Conti. There's also the Krewe du Boo Parade, with floats produced by Blaine Kern, and bands and groups like The Krewe of Rolling Elvi (Elvis impersonators

on motorized bikes) or The Bearded Oysters (kind of self explanatory), but mostly everyday people in costume.

Add at least an hour to posted start time to both. The Halloween Parades tend to be as punctual as Mardi Gras parades or street cars or bands playing at Tipitina's or pretty much everything else in New Orleans (i.e. not at all).

Like every city, town, burb, or boondocks, we have haunted house attractions. The elaborate House of Shock, right outside New Orleans in Jefferson (319 Butterworth St.), is rated the #1 haunted house in the country by people who rate such things. Annually, more than 25,000 people will pay $25 to encounter Phil Anselmo's legendary attraction, with live actors portraying freaks and ghouls amid faux graveyards, butcher shops, swamps, and a cultish church. National acts and pyrotechnics kick it up a notch from the average pumpkin patch or corn maze. The attraction opens September 30th and runs every Friday and Saturday through November 5th.

Every bit as popular with locals is The Mausoleum, because it's located in the city proper (3400 Canal St.), easily accessed straight up the Canal Street car line, which is appropriately named "Cemeteries." The massive mansion is the former P. J. McMahon funeral home. Once inside, the monstrous staff do things I thought were illegal. I'd always heard employees were not allowed to touch you in haunted house attractions. Here, they find ways to distract you and physically separate you from your group. What's scarier than suddenly realizing you are all alone . . . in the night . . . in the dark . . .

In addition to haunted houses, New Orleans has haunted boat attractions. The Creole Queen has live music, an open bar, costume contest, and silent auction, where donations are made to provide services for the homeless. The Jean Lafitte Swamp & Airboat Tours hosts "Boat Rides of Terror," a haunted swamp tour where gators, snakes, and the cornball jokes of your tour guide become even more horrifying and are amplified with live music on the shore. Tours run continuously from 7:15 'til 11:00 p.m.

The Audubon Zoo stays open past their normal hours for Boo at the Zoo, nights of entertainment, food, trick-or-treating, and kid-appropriate not-so scary stories. The Audubon Insectarium (423 Canal St.) offers The Crawloween, which includes bug crafts, trick-or-treating, and lectures about misunderstood arthropods like spiders, roaches, and maggots. The Windsor Court hotel hosts a Creepy Crawly Children's Tea. City Park holds Ghost in the Oaks (usually a week before Halloween) from 6:00 to 10:00 p.m. in the Carousel Gardens Amusement Park, which includes food and music.

The French Quarter each year puts on The Boo Carre Halloween & Harvest Festival with miniature golf, a photo booth, Halloween crafts, a costume contest, and pumpkin painting. The Cabildo sponsors The Ghostly Falavant Fundraiser and walking tour. The Hotel Monteleone hosts an annual ball to honor its many ghosts. Dirty Coast, proprietors of exceptionally designed local T-shirts, hosts a Halloween costume party at Studio 3 (3610 Tchoupitolas) with live music, DJs, and a costume contest. The Museum of Art shows nighttime outdoor screenings of scary movies. Last year it showed *Rosemary's Baby*, which, with its Devil rape scene, might have caused a church lady uproar in other cities. Here, not so much.

For your dog, there's the Howl-o-Ween Pawtay at the Times Grill (1896 N. Causeway), a dog-friendly benefit for the Humane Society with live music and a dog costume contest.

The kiddies and pets would not be welcomed at The AllWays Lounge's Halloween Fun House (2240 St. Claude St.) with performances by regulars Nari Tomassetti, Ratty Scurvics, The Mudlark Puppets, and burlesque aerialist Ooops the Clown. If not an X-rated Halloween performance, The AllWays Lounge is at least a sold R.

If you seek regular old trick-or-treating, the best area for that is State Street in Uptown. The street is lined with very wealthy people who take Halloween very seriously. Some of the front yards have movie-set quality decorations. The most highly regarded is the Bone House on 6000 St. Charles Street at State. Each year the owners, Darryl & Louellen Berger, make up fresh wordplay and puns (Die Hard Saints Fan, Napoleon Bone Apart, Bone Appetit, Saturday Night Femur) to attach

The Bone House

as signage hung on their seemingly endless supply of plastic skeletons. They receive, on average, 1,200 trick-or-treaters each year.

For those of you more seriously or deliriously into vampires or voodoo, Halloween offers several signature events.

The Endless Night Vampire Ball, held at The House of Blues each Halloween, is part of a series of masquerade balls produced by Father Sebastiaan. Father Sebastiaan is perhaps the biggest personality in the current vampire subculture. He is the grandson of an orthodontist and nephew of a dentist. Sebastiaan got his first pair of fangs in November 1993; a year later, he picked up his late Grandfather's dental tools and began his career as a fangsmith, with his first customer being his mother. Since then he has traveled the world hand crafting custom fangs and is unquestionably the world's most famous master fangsmith. He is also an avid lover of vampire mythology, steampunk, wolves, history, nineteenth-century art, French culture, ancient Egypt, NLP, psychology and philosophy. His first Vampire Ball was in New York in 1996. These balls, which have been described as a Venetian Masquerade Ball mixed with a Vampire Court, have the energy of a rock concert and the elegance of a burlesque cabaret. Tripadvisor rated the New Orleans Endless Night

Ball the #1 Big Halloween Party in the world, not that I normally trust a word typed onto Tripadvisor.

The Anne Rice Vampire Ball, established by her fan club, is exclusively a New Orleans event. The idea for the ball was hatched in 1988, when founders Sue Quiroz, Susie Miller, and Teresa Simmons stood in line for two hours at DeVille Bookstore to have Anne Rice sign their books.

I actually attended the inaugural ball, ate from the cakes decorated to look like her book covers, made a little speech, and presented Anne with a real skull with pronounced canines. Later, I went off into the night with a fellow attendee. We ended up at a dark-loud-gothy bar on Decatur Street where one of my new friends took a small vial from her neck and drew an X on the palm of my hand in what she said was human blood. But, that's a story for another time and one I'd just as soon forget.

Each year the ball now draws around 1,500 people, all elaborately made up, I would say "for the occasion," but when I asked one attendee where she got her fabulous fangs, she replied, "at my dentist." She'd had them bonded to her real teeth so she was a 24/7 vampire before, during, and after the vampire ball. The location changes each year, you can check into the upcoming venue at www.arvlfc.com.

The UnDead Con is an outgrowth from Anne Rice's Vampire Ball. It is a weekend of panel discussions, book signings, a cemetery picnic, and the Bizarre Bazaar (vendors displaying vampire-appropriate goods and services) built around the Vampire Ball centerpiece. Both conference and ball are run by Suzie Quiros, one of the founders of the Anne Rice Fan Club, director of the Vampire Ball, and formerly the long-time assistant for Anne, back when Anne lived in New Orleans. The UnDead Con aspires to be ComiCon for vampires, but with an emphasis on providing writing skills, marketing strategies, and publishing insights to aspiring horror and goth writers. Past speakers have included Charlaine Harris, Heather Graham, Laurell K. Hamilton, Sherrilyn Kenyon, and, of course Anne and Christopher Rice.

With three Easter Parades, it's not shocking that New Orleans has more than just two parades and three vampire balls on Halloween. The Anba Dio Halloween Festival at The Healing Center grows closer to being a decade-old event. The night includes an early evening parade starting at Mimi's in the Marigny, followed by psychic readings, face painting, and complimentary massage, plus performances deep into the night by first-rate musicians like Jon Mooney and Little Freddie King, with a little burlesque and acrobatics thrown in for good pleasure. Profits from Anba Dio go to supply low-income residents with education and health care.

Hosts of Halloween is a 30 years and running party geared toward LGBT participants. All monies collected go to provide funding for Project Lazarus, a home in New Orleans for men and women with AIDS. Hosts of Halloween have raised over $4.6 million for Project Lazarus. And, like any good gay party, the spectacle is a little more spectacular. Ordinary costume competitions are turned into thematic krewes. Groups wear similar outfits, like the Puppy Breath Krewe (men carrying large bones, wearing dog ears, and little else) or a Joan Rivers Who Wore It Better? tribute where fifteen to twenty men squeeze into the same hideously garish dress and teased wigs.

Now, if you're into both vampires and zombies, you'll have some hard choices to make each Halloween. In addition to the Anne Rice Vampire Ball, the Endless Night Ball, and others listed, there's also Voodoo Authentica (612 Dumaine St.) sponsoring Voodoo Fest. Voodoo Fest is a FREE annual festival that celebrates, hopes to educate, and preserve voodoo traditions in New Orleans.

Treme Fall Fest

Treme Fest is a donation-based event, created to raise money for the historic St. Augustine Catholic Church. Fridays launch with a patron party. Saturdays are a full day of live music, art, crafts, and food. Sundays close with a gospel mass. If you come late on Sunday, you can use one of my wife's go-to jokes. Question: "Is mass out?" Answer: "No, but your hat's on crooked."

Art For Arts' Sake

Created by the Contemporary Arts Center (CAC) in 1980, this annual celebration now draws 30,000 attendees. The downtown art walk includes 20 museums and galleries open late for the event.

Carnival Latino

The festival celebrates Hispanic culture in New Orleans through music, food, and art. In more recent years, it has grown to include a parade and features musicians from all over the world

Oktoberfest

New Orleans' version of Oktoberfest was created in 1928 by Deutsche Gesellschaft von New Orleans, a group that provided support for the numerous German immigrants in the area. It's held at the Deutsches Haus in the Rivertown section of Kenner, where there's always plenty of Kasseler Rippchen with a side of Kartoffelbrei.

New Orleans Film Festival

Founded in 1989, the festival has become one of the more renowned ones in the country. A few years back, the festival was the national premier of *Twelve Years a Slave*, which went on to win Best Picture. In addition to screenings, the festival also presents a series of mentor sessions, workshops, and panel discussions with film industry leaders.

The Words & Music Festival

Each November, Rosemary James, ex-local TV reporter, author, and noted interior designer (you saw her work in the movie version of *Interview With a Vampire*) hosts the Words & Music Festival for local literati and out-of-town writers aspiring to publish. Panels and events are packed with noted authors and publishing executives. Attending writers get one on one sessions with editors and agents to critique their work. National Book Award winner, Julia Glass, Stewart O'Nan, Robin Black, and many other successfully published writers (nearing fifty in all) have been "discovered" at Words & Music. Where the Tennessee Williams Festival has their annual Stella Shouting Contest, Words & Music has their open mic Tall Tales Session, usually hosted by humorist Roy Blount, Jr. and open to anyone who dares to toss out their original tale for immediate public response.

Park(ing) Day

This is an annual, open-source global event where citizens, artists, and activists collaborate to temporarily transform metered parking spaces into "PARK(ing)" spaces, or temporary public art installments. While the event occurs in cities all over the world, it is particularly funky in our peculiar city.

Beignet Fest

Not to be outdone by oysters, po'boys, or creole tomatoes, Amy and Sherwood Collins hatched the idea for this festival to donate proceeds to the Tres Doux Foundation, which they founded to help raise awareness and funds for autism programs in New Orleans.

LUMINS OF NEW ORLEANS:
Ryan S. Ballard

Every city needs an artist like Ryan S. Ballard. New Orleans has hundreds, maybe thousands. The bunnymen of Alex Podesta can be spied on the tops of buildings and in glass-and-chrome-appointed building lobbies. Randy Morrison's fiberglass gargoyles holding severed heads are attached to several buildings. Brandon Odums goes way beyond graffiti to museum quality public art with his murals. And just under a hundred resident artists (so far) have beautified New Orleans by painting scenes and designs on once ugly electrical utility boxes as part of the Street Gallery Project.

CHET OVERALL

Ryan S. Ballard goes a step or three further. As he claims in his mission statement, "I have a dark, satirical sense of humor and a thick subversive streak that tends to find its way into my creations. My work is like cosmic candy that is full of the razor blades of truth."

His art has been displayed in a great many ways. He's a puppeteer who goes by the stage name Dr. Razzamataz. He's posted hand-made handbills around town suggesting that a Bigfoot-style beast stalks City Park. His book, *Faux Teauxs*, is subtitled *Amazing Photographs of Famous Cryptids at All of Your Favorite New Orleans Area Attractions*, and shows images of Bigfoot, Nessy, Chupacabra, Yeti, Sea Serpents, Cattle Mutilations, UFOs, and other mythological monsters creeping around the Crescent City.

As a sculptor, Ryan put on an exhibition where a previously empty church was filled with his electrified creations. There, he displayed a self-lighted, coffin-shaped bed of nails, a giant, throbbing, nail-pierced heart with a requisite glowing digital clock, and a cobbled together manikin with the light-bulb breasts and computer monitor as its head, presenting a film loop of a giant eyeball on screen that winks now and again.

The underlying theme of his art is meant to lampoon what he calls the religion of consumerism.

When not making art, Ryan is a self-declared adventure junky. He's a deep-sea scuba-diving spear-fisher. Three times a year, Ballard leads teenage tour groups on trips to far-flung places like Vietnam and Peru. Most spine-tingling of all, he's been an elementary and middle school art teacher.

I don't know if Ryan considers this a good thing or a bad thing, but he is probably best known and will be longest remembered as the co-founder of the Intergalactic Krewe of Chewbacchus, a Mardi Gras organization dedicated to all things science fiction. His co-founder is Kirah Haubrich. Kirah goes by the code name Overlord Dilithium Crystal Hotsauce. She purports to be an extraterrestrial agent working to subvert the culture of New Orleans on behalf of an elusive race of cat people who hail from somewhere near Beta Alpha Centuri Seven. Clearly, while other krewes may revel in alcohol and debauchery, Chewbacchus is a marching club fully embracing their nerdiness.

"There's a difference between Chewbacchus and a lot of the fandom stuff that happens at, like, Comic-Con," Ryan explains. "We're not going for movie-scale or accurate. There's a whole parody, satire aspect and a heavy Mardi Gras-influenced joke angle that we're going for."

His workspace in Bywater, named Castillo Blanco Art Studios (4321 St. Claude Ave.) also houses the Mardi Gras prop showroom and storage facility of Royal Artists, the HQ of Secret Moonbase Productions, the Den of the Intergalactic Krewe of Chewbacchus, the Shrine of the Sacred Drunken Wookiee, and "a sublimely peaceful space devoted to relaxation," the SPACE Sanctuary Float Tank Experience. Castillo Blanco also has a flying saucer landing zone on the roof, just in case.

Ryan's Facebook page leads with the phrase "Ad Astra per Aspera," which is the state motto of Kansas and a phrase used by Hunter S. Thompson to sign off his letters the same way Louis Armstrong used "Red Beans & Ricely Yours" to close his letters. It was also used by Kurt Vonnegut as the motto of the Martian Imperial Commandos in Ryan's favorite book, *The Sirens of Titan*. "Ad Astra per Aspera" literally means "through hardships to the stars." Why has it been an oft-used and favorite phrase of Ryan S. Ballard, Kurt Vonnegut, Hunter S. Thompson, and Kansas? I can't really tell you.

November

Day of the Dead

The day after Halloween is the Day of the Dead, or Dia de los Muertos, in Mexico. In Mexico, traditions include building private altars, called *ofrendas*, to honor the deceased using sugar skulls, marigolds, and the once-favorite food and drink of the departed. Families visit graves to leave these items as gifts. In New Orleans, it's one more reason to dress up, parade, and party.

Our one-day champion or virtual Mayor of the Day of the Dead is Claudia Gehrke, better known as Mardi Claw. She is a muralist, painter, mask-maker, and whirlwind force in the New Orleans culture of second lines. Her group, Skin n Bonez, has become a fixture in Mardi Gras parades and Halloween parades, but especially in Day of the Dead festivities.

Thanksgiving

There are plenty of places to have a gourmet turkey feast in this city of restaurants, but for many people *the* place to be on Thanksgiving is the Fairgrounds Race Track. It is the opening day of the race season. People come decked out in their most elaborate (and sometimes garish and over-the-top) hats to stuff the viewing stands or common area down by the track, making it sort of a New Orleans-style Kentucky Derby. A complete turkey dinner can be ordered inside the clubhouse.

Leading up to Thanksgiving, you can gorge on the Hoppy Thanksgiving meal offered the Tuesday and Wednesday prior to turkey day at the Audubon Insectarium. For the price of the entrance fee, you can eat their turkey with cornbread and mealworm stuffing, wax worm cranberry sauce, and cricket pumpkin pie. I hear crickets have a nutty taste. I don't plan on ever verifying that claim.

Bayou Classic

Every Thanksgiving weekend since 1974, the Grambling State University Tigers play the Southern University Jaguars in the Superdome. As big as the game are the events with the two school bands, Grambling's "World Famed" Tiger Marching Band and Southern's Human Jukebox. They have a parade down Canal Street the day before the game and a Battle of the Bands, where both groups stage elaborately choreographed performances, on the Friday night before the game.

Celebration in the Oaks

Celebration at the Oaks begins the day after Thanksgiving and lasts into the first few days of January. The glittering light show extravaganza has hundreds of thousands of lights and colorful holiday decorations strung across City Park's centuries-old live oak trees, plus decorations draped over Storyland, the Botanical Gardens, and the Carousel Gardens amusement ride area. Lights shaped like pirate ships, gators, and Tyrannosaurus rexes rise up from the bayou. Over the years, it has become one of the most beautiful and popular holiday lighting displays in the country, attracting hundreds of thousands of people annually.

Congo Square Rhythms Festival

This festival celebrates the music and culture of the African diaspora in Armstrong Park. The free two-day event features the music and dance of Africa, the Caribbean, and the American Gulf South.

Faux/Real Festival

There are roughly thirty Fringe Festivals in the United States, quite possibly hundreds across the world, springing from a festival started in Edinburgh, Scotland. Fringe Fest bills itself as "the festival of the wild, weird, fresh, and original" and showcases previously unproduced playwrights, writers, and performance artists. In New Orleans, where every day is wild, weird, fresh, and original, the festival grew much larger and evolved into Faux/Real. Here, each year, there are nearly 100 separate productions staged, including some with masterful puppetry.

Naughty in N'awlins

In my chapter on Fitting In, I wrote that we'd never make fun of tourists. Tourism is how we survive. I might make an exception in this one case. Any festival that begins by naming itself "N'Awlins" is already charging off in the wrong direction. They write on their website, "Don't be fooled by anyone claiming to have the Biggest event of the year, there can only be one biggest," and then ballyhoo they're the biggest with six whole floats, an entire one (1) Brass Band, and one (1) dance team. A fundraising event in New Orleans for the cheerleaders of Holy Name of Jesus Middle School is bigger than that. And finally, there's the fact that it's a convention for Swingers. Didn't that go out of style in the 1970s?

Boudin, Bourbon & Beer

This food & music festival was created by the Emeril Lagasse Foundation. It's held at Champion Square, right next to the Superdome. In addition to drinking, eating, listening to music from groups as diverse as Grace Potter, Los Bayou Ramblers, The Lone Below, and Sweet Crude, they also have cigar tastings. The festival raises about $3 million each year to benefit nonprofit organizations that provide educational programs and life skills development for New Orleans young people.

Treme Creole Gumbo Festival

The festival, held in Congo Square, celebrates the historic neighborhood with entertainment, mostly brass band and mostly played by musicians who have grown up in Treme, and food, mostly a variety of styles for signature gumbos. You can sample shrimp and oyster, chicken and andouille, Gumbo z'herbes, Creole filé, dark roux, and, if you believe in such things, gluten-free gumbo.

Oak Street Po'boy Festival

Seven years in a row, the Po'boy Festival has been chosen by the annual *Gambit's* poll as the Best Festival in New Orleans. Each year, over forty food vendors serve up their own take on the signature sandwich, while local bands provide the soundtrack. Pets are welcomed. Beer guzzling is encouraged

Mirliton Festival

Let's start with what a mirliton is (pronounce it mel-a-tonn) and why it's worthy of a festival. Mirliton is a member of the gourd family, its technical name is chayote, and it is native to Central and South America. It was introduced here during the French and Spanish settlements of the eighteenth century. It's light green, pear-shaped, wrinkled, and has almost no flavor. It's one of those foods, like cream cheese or grits, that take on the flavors of whatever is next to it on the plate. Mirlitons stuffed with seafood and cheese have been a staple on Creole menus. I often have an *envie* for Dooky Chase's stuffed mirlitons. It deserves a festival, always the first Saturday in November, held at Mickey Markey Park in the Bywater, simply because it's something you eat and we're in New Orleans. I'm surprised we don't have a chapulines festival (toasted grasshoppers) yet.

December

Christmas

There's really only one festival in December, and it's practiced everywhere in the world, but our Christmas celebration, naturally, has a few unique wrinkles.

One tradition, of course, has to revolve around food. The Reveillon Dinners is a Creole feast originated from the early 1800s, when there'd be a massive spread of food laid out following the midnight mass. In French, the word "reveillon" means "awakening." At 2:00 a.m., worshippers would start gorging on chicken and oyster gumbo, game pies, soups, souffles, lavish desserts, brandy, and coffee. It was a tradition the Creoles inherited from Europe as a way of breaking the day-long religious fast leading up to Christmas Eve.

The Reveillon tradition started slowly fading away in the 1940s, but fortunately was revived with some modifications for modern diners. For one, the feasts switched from family homes to our upscale restaurants, and meals are now served at more conventional times rather than the wee hours of past celebrations.

A good fifty New Orleans restaurants—and pretty much all the old classics like Antoine's, Arnaud's, Tujaques, Commander's Palace, and Court of Two Sisters—serve the prix fixe Reveillon dinners.

Both the St. Louis Cathedral and the St. Augustine Church sponsor free concert series, held several evenings during December. The music will be a mixture of jazz, classical, gospel, and pop genres.

Always on the Sunday evening before Christmas, or at least always since 1946, there will be Caroling on Jackson Square. Literally thousands of people will jam into Jackson Square to sing.

Candles and song sheets are provided, courtesy of Patio Planters, a nonprofit group dedicated to the horticultural beautification of the French Quarter. The gates to Jackson Square open at 6:30 p.m. and the caroling begins at 7:00.

Forty-foot bonfires along the Mississippi River are ignited on Christmas Eve to light the way for "Papa Noël," the Cajun Santa Claus, to fly down to New Orleans and deposit his presents. According to some sources, the bonfires may have also been a way of lighting the path to the nearest Catholic church for Midnight Mass . . . or maybe the nearest open all-night bar.

CONCLUSION

Bizarre travel plans are dancing lessons from God. —**Kurt Vonnegut**

Since my first Carnival Season as a resident, I have wanted to form my own troupe of post-50 year olds that we'd call The Sunnydale Nursing Home Low Steppers. We'd march using walkers and wheelchairs, dressed in bathrobes and fuzzy slippers, maybe occasionally flashing some mottled flesh. The Low Steppers would groove to tunes from boomboxes blaring Bobby Darin and Robert Goulet hits. Our throws would include colostomy bags filled with white wine, which I assume no one would ever dare try.

Back before I was a self-employed writer, I had a staff of direct reports and later a gaggle of client authors to bully and bore with my aphorisms. I used to say (far too often), "Ideas are easy, execution is hard." The Low Steppers will most likely remain an unrealized idea.

New Orleans has more than its share of unfulfilled ideas and dreams. There is currently an effort to restore all the movie palaces that once lined Canal Street, making them gilded balconied homes for live theater, sort of a Broadway South. Broadway South was actually the dream of New Orleanian actor and real estate developer Roger Wilson. He is probably best known as Mickey in the first two *Porky's* movies.

The Vitascope on Canal was the first movie theater in America and opened in 1896. NPR radio did a segment on America's oldest movie theater, which they claimed was the 1905 opening of the Nickelodeon in Pittsburgh. I'm pretty sure 1896 pre-dates 1905. I already know not to trust Fox News, CNN, and The Weather Channel, but I'd previously always counted on NPR.

The Joy Theater and the Saenger have been gloriously made over. But the Broadway South dream seems to have ended there. We are currently stuck at being sort of the Belasco Theater South.

Canal Street itself is an unfulfilled dream. The thought back in 1831 was to cut a waterway from Lake Pontchartrain through the swamps, all the way to the Mississippi River for a more convenient trade route. Canal Street was literally meant to be a canal, but never served that purpose. Slaves were considered too valuable to risk working in snake-infested swamps with yellow fever carrying mosquitos. The Irish, however, were pouring into New Orleans daily during the Potato Famine and worked for a dollar a day. They were a replenishable resource, simply dumped in the mud as they got off the boat. If they died on the job, they could always be replaced by fresh Irish immigrants. Over 8,000 Irish lost their lives digging from the lake to

LUMINS OF NEW ORLEANS:
Ruthie the Duck Lady

For the final Lumin(ary) of New Orleans, I will again dip beyond the world of the living and into an historical luminary. There are so many iconic New Orleanians to choose from. When I hear people compare New Orleans to Charleston or Savannah, I try not to show the immediately flared-up rage I normally reserve for Facebook posts or Fox News. When *Travel & Leisure* magazine chose Charleston as their 2016 top travel destination in America, I had to put up with the ludicrous bragging of a dear friend who lives there. When I hear or read such nonsense, inside I think "When Charleston or Savannah produce a Louis Armstrong, Tennessee Williams, Marie Laveau, Blaze Starr, Paul Prudhomme, Jean Lafitte, Truman Capote, Delphine Lalaurie, Professor Longhair, Lady Pontalba, and so many more, then we'll talk." In my mind, comparing Savannah and Charleston to New Orleans is like comparing Taylor Swift and Kelly Clarkson to Edith Piaf.

With all the late greats, I choose a luminary you probably don't know: Ruthie the Duck Lady.

Before Ruth Grace Moulon was known locally as Ruthie the Duck Lady, she was known as Ruthie the Duck Girl. She'd been working the French Quarter since she was a child. For some reason we'll never know, her parents did not enroll her in school. Instead, her mother would put her hair in sausage curls to make her look like Shirley Temple, then came up with the idea that little Ruthie should be a duck girl. The mother dressed her in evening dresses and bought her skates. Ruthie skated through the Quarter with these little ducks following . . . for an entire lifetime. In her adult years, Ruthie zoomed from bar to bar, most often on roller skates, wearing a ratty fur coat and long skirt, or sometimes a bridal gown, and trailed by a duck or three. People gave her ducks each Easter. Most didn't live very long.

She made a modest income when she began charging people to take her photograph. Soon, she began selling picture postcards of herself. Ruthie sold the postcards for twenty-five cents each or three for a dollar. She could never quite grasp that maybe she should sell them five for a dollar, since three for a dollar wasn't exactly a bargain.

Ruthie had legendary status in a city that was and is overstuffed with eccentrics like Dave Gregg, who used to perform on the streets strumming the rhythm guitar hanging from his neck with one hand while playing another guitar slung low behind his back with his other hand, and playing a bass guitar with his bare toes.

Street performer Fred Staten, a.k.a. the "Chicken Man," claimed to be a Voodoo King as he ate fire, handled live snakes, and earned his nickname by hypnotizing a chicken, biting off its head and then drinking its blood through its neck.

In this world of tough competition, Ruthie acquired a coterie of people who found places for her to live, paid her bills, and made sure she got home at night. She spent her life drinking for free (Budweiser was her beer of choice) and bumming cigarettes (she liked Kools). Her favorite haunts were sitting atop bar stools at Pat O'Brien's on St. Peter and Crazy Shirley's on Bourbon.

She was a tiny woman with a reported voice like a Cajun Donald Duck and constant grin. But her mood behind that smile could flash from playful to belligerent. A friend of mine recalls the first time he

met and was terrified by Ruthie. She strode into a bar and bellowed, "Which one of you motherfuckers is going to buy me a beer?"

Ruthie alluded to a boyfriend, Gary Moody, whom she supposedly met as a sailor on shore leave in 1963 and to whom she became engaged before he moved away. Most people felt she had made him up until he flew down from Minnesota to dance at her 67th birthday party held at the Rock 'N' Bowl.

Ruthie the Duck Lady died at age 74. Rick Delaup, who made a documentary film about her, said that "she represents something that's uniquely New Orleans. She's really the last of the old French Quarter characters that lived these really colorful lives."

But the best thing ever said about Ruthie, and a statement that could apply equally well to New Orleans itself, was by David Cuthbert, a reporter for *The Times-Picayune* newspaper. He wrote, "Ruthie's not out of touch with reality; she's just not interested in it."

Basin Street. They didn't dig all the way to the river, because someone had the sense to realize the river is higher than the lake. Had they connected the two, the river's water would have rushed in, flooding New Orleans. By 1950, the city filled it all back in with mud, sea shells, and undoubtedly some bones of the Irish.

I have never experienced a city with more multiple, dysfunctional, but absolutely joyous personalities than New Orleans. I loved my 27 years in the New York area. Manhattan's neurotic energy is absolutely intoxicating in your 20s and 30s. But the drive to keep up with the newest and hottest restaurants, plays, artists, or hippest new neighborhood kind of wears you out in your 50s.

New Orleans is close to the opposite of New York. This may be the simple result of New Orleans being a French city. We were, are, and always will be a French city. When Spain owned New Orleans for 40 years, locals refused to learn Spanish or fly the Spanish flag. To this day, a lawyer must learn French law (Napoleonic Code) to practice in Louisiana. There are, today, schools like Ecole Bilingue De La Nouvelle-Orléans, International School of New Orleans, and Audubon Charter School, which have French immersion programs in which not a word of English is spoken.

Americans spend an average of 75 minutes each day eating meals. The French, by comparison, take up 2.5 hours. By now, I hope you know we eat like the French.

In his book *Nine Lives*, New Yorker Dan Baum wrote, "Life in New Orleans is all about making the present—this moment, right now—as pleasant as possible. So New Orleanians, by and large, aren't tortured by the frenzy to achieve, acquire, and manage the unmanageable future. Their days are built around the things that other Americans have pushed out of their lives by incessant work: art, music, elaborate cooking, and—most of all—plenty of relaxed time with family and friends. Their jobs are really just the things they do to earn a little money; they're not the organizing principle of life. While this isn't a worldview particularly conducive to getting things done, getting things done isn't the most important thing in New Orleans. Living life is. Once you've tasted that, and especially if it's how you grew up, life everywhere else feels thin indeed."

My current dream, which I hope doesn't go unfulfilled, is to live to be at least 83 years old. That way, I will have lived in New Orleans longer than my 27 years in New York or 16 years in Cleveland.

If I fail to set my personal record for duration in one city, we can always roll out one more quote, this one from New Orleans newspaper columnist Angus Lind:

If you die of old age in New Orleans, it's your own damn fault.

APPENDIX: JUST SAYING

I always have a quotation for everything—it saves original thinking.   **—Dorothy Sayers**

What follows is a list of assembled quotes that are, in my opinion, the best things ever said about New Orleans or by New Orleanians. Consider it a form of a greeting card for New Orleans' 300th anniversary. The quotes are presented randomly so that each one will be read and received with fresh eyes.

To get to New Orleans you don't pass through anywhere else.   **—Allen Toussaint, musician**

We dance even if there's no radio. We drink at funerals. We talk too much and laugh too loud and live too large and, frankly, we're suspicious of others who don't.   **—Chris Rose, writer**

New Orleans is the city where imagination takes precedence over fact.
   —William Faulkner, writer

The peculiar virtue of New Orleans, like St. Theresa, may be that of the Little Way, a talent for everyday life rather than the heroic deed.   **—Walker Percy, writer**

If I could put my finger on it, I'd bottle it and sell it. I came down here originally in 1972 with some drunken fraternity guys and had never seen anything like it—the climate, the smells. It's the cradle of music; it just flipped me. Someone suggested that there's an incomplete part of our chromosomes that gets repaired or found when we hit New Orleans. Some of us just belong here.   **—John Goodman, actor**

If you die of old age in New Orleans, it's your own damn fault.   **—Angus Lind, columnist**

What I realized is that every place else in the United States is white bread and mayonnaise, and everything here is not—it's spicy and the architecture is so different. You can't control where you were born, but you have a choice where you live.   **—Banu Gibson, musician**

I am just so happy to live in a place where, if a guy rides by on a bike in full red body paint at 2:00 p.m. on a Monday, he isn't considered weird.   **—Meschiya Lake, musician**

This city breeds and attracts unique people. Bedraggled people who are honest enough to consecrate their shortcomings. Innovative people who see opportunity where others see chaos. Transparent people who will share with you whether you like it or not. Enduring people who rebuild when their city or their lives fall apart. Fierce people who protect what they love and love a great deal.

—**Steve Gleason, football player**

This is the Last Bohemia left in the United States. It's real. We have soul! Our architecture has been saved. We celebrate decay. We celebrate death. We celebrate the dark shadows in the French Quarter. We celebrate our history and architecture and food and everything that goes into it. That's part of the tapestry of this old place. It's not like Houston or LA where they tear it down 'cuz it's old. With real estate, if your house isn't old, it's not worth anything here. If it's seventeenth, eighteenth or early nineteenth century, it's worth much more than something that's new.

—**Jacqueline Bishop, artist**

New Orleans is a city where people make eye contact. There's a more open sensuality there as well. I'd take that in my perfect city.

—**David Byrne, musician**

Times are not good here. The city is crumbling into ashes. It has been buried under taxes and frauds and maladministrations so that it has become a study for archaeologists . . . but it is better to live here in sackcloth and ashes than to own the whole state of Ohio.

—**Lafcadio Hearn, writer**

This city is soul, straight with no chaser.

—**Rob Nelson, TV commentator**

Everyone who's chosen this place to live knows how seductive it is; the city has almost a vortex feeling about it—it just sucks you in.

—**Richard Ford, writer**

In New Orleans, I found the type of freedom I had always needed. —**Tennessee Williams, writer**

A part of New Orleans' beauty is that she is a place where many people, stifled elsewhere, feel safe to be themselves: just safe to be. Whether or not we agree with their politics, life choices, or diets, they are "their business."

—**Quo Vadis Gex Breaux, writer**

I was only supposed to stay for the summer. Two weeks into moving here, I had a snowball, got high-fived on the street by a man dressed as a banana, walked through my first Second Line, and I was hooked. New Orleans had me at shaved ice.

—**Kyle June Williams, actor**

New Orleans is like that. It nudges you to be what you need to be. —**Paul Prudhomme, chef**

I've been all over the world. I love New York, I love Paris, San Francisco, so many places. But there's no place like New Orleans. It's got the best food. It's got the best music. It's got the best people. It's got the most fun stuff to do. **—Harry Connick, Jr., musician**

An American has not seen the United States until he has seen Mardi-Gras in New Orleans.
—Mark Twain, writer

It takes 30 seconds to fall into New Orleans and realize you're in a different place.
—Sunpie Barnes, musician

Few people go to New Orleans because it's a "normal" city —or a "perfect" or "safe" one. They go because it's crazy, borderline dysfunctional, permissive, shabby, alcoholic and bat shit crazy—and because it looks like nowhere else. **—Anthony Bourdain, chef**

Seeing a ghost in New Orleans is as common as having a bowl of gumbo. The question is not when, but where best to savor them both. **—Kala Ambrose, psychic**

The city can drive a sober-minded person insane, but it feeds the dreamer. It feeds the dreamer stories, music and food. Really great food. **—Andrei Codrescu, writer**

I came down here about a month ago and am living in the old French Creole Quarter, the most civilized place I've found in America, and have been writing like a man gone mad ever since I got off the train. **—Sherwood Anderson, writer**

America has only three cities: New York, San Francisco, and New Orleans. Everywhere else is Cleveland. **—Tennessee Williams, writer**

If you have to ask what jazz is, you'll never know. **—Louis Armstrong, musician**

New Orleans is the one place in America where cooking is considered an art.
—Count Hermann Alexander Graf von Keyserling, philosopher

Leaving New Orleans also frightened me considerably. Outside of the city limits the heart of darkness, the true wasteland begins. **—John Kennedy Toole, writer**

The first thing you notice about New Orleans are the burying grounds—the cemeteries—and they're a cold proposition, one of the best things there are here. Going by, you try to be as quiet as possible, better to let them sleep. Greek, Roman, sepulchres—palatial mausoleums made to order, phantomesque, signs and symbols of hidden decay—ghosts of women and men who have sinned and who've died and are now living in tombs. The past doesn't pass away so quickly here.

You could be dead for a long time.   **—Bob Dylan, musician**

New Orleans is the heart, soul, and music of America.   **—Lenny Kravitz, musician**

Those who have not lived in New Orleans have missed an incredible, glorious, vital city—a place with an energy unlike anywhere else in the world, a majority-African-American city where resistance to white supremacy has cultivated and supported a generous, subversive, and unique culture of vivid beauty. From jazz, blues, and and hip-hop to Second Lines, Mardi Gras Indians, jazz funerals, and the citywide tradition of red beans and rice on Monday nights, New Orleans is a place of art and music and food and traditions and sexuality and liberation.   **—Jordan Flaherty, journalist**

I came to New Orleans back in 1994 doing the Interview with the Vampire movie, based on the Anne Rice novel, and fell in love with the city. It got under my skin. Everything was sexy and sultry. I'd ride my bike all over the place, amazed by the architecture. I'd return to New Orleans every chance I could. What can I say: it's got the best people, the best everything. It's the most interesting city in America.   **—Brad Pitt, actor**

The minute you land in New Orleans, something wet and dark leaps on you and starts humping you like a swamp dog in heat, and the only way to get that aspect of New Orleans off you is to eat it off. That means beignets and crawfish bisque and jambalaya, it means shrimp remoulade, pecan pie, and red beans with rice, it means elegant pompano en papillote, funky file z'herbes, and raw oysters by the dozen, it means grillades for breakfast, a po'boy with chowchow at bedtime, and tubs of gumbo in between. It is not unusual for a visitor to the city to gain 15 pounds in a week—yet the alternative is a whole lot worse. If you don't eat day and night, if you don't constantly funnel the indigenous flavors into your bloodstream, then the mystery beast will go right on humping you, and you will feel its sordid presence rubbing against you long after you have left town. In fact, like any sex offender, it can leave permanent psychological scars.   **—Tom Robbins, writer**

New Orleans is not in the grip of a neurosis of a denied past; it passes out memories generously like a great lord; it doesn't have to pursue "the real thing."   **—Umberto Eco, writer**

There is a unique bond between the land and the people in the Crescent City. Everyone here came from somewhere else, the muddy brown current of life prying them loose from their homeland and sweeping them downstream, bumping and scraping, until they got caught by the horseshoe bend that is New Orleans. Not so much as a single pebble 'came' from New Orleans, any more than any of the people did. Every grain of sand, every rock, every drip of brown mud, and every single person walking, living and loving in the city is a refugee from somewhere else. But they made something unique, the people and the land, when they came together in that cohesive, magnetic, magical spot; this sediment of society made something that is not French, not Spanish, and incontrovertibly not American. **—James Caskey, writer**

People don't live in New Orleans because it is easy. They live here because they are incapable of living anywhere else in just the same way. **—Ian McNulty, writer**

There were only two places on earth one could be: New Orleans and somewhere ridiculous."
—Tom Robbins, writer

Ask an informed American citizen today to ruminate on Dallas or Atlanta or Phoenix, and you will probably get small talk, lukewarm pleasantries, and a brief conversation. Ask them what they think about New Orleans, and you are in for not only an opinionated retort, but a sentimental smile, or a scolding finger, a treasured memory, a shaking head, or an exasperated shrug over the course of the conversation spanning the spectrum of human experience. **—Richard Campanella, writer**

I am told there are cities where the citizens speak with one voice and are able to achieve progress in an ordered, mature fashion. In these places, the streets are clean, the people are well-mannered, and the humors of the blood are kept in passionless balance.

I am tempted by such places. If only New Orleans could tame the unruly voices within it— if only I could tame the cacophonous conflicts within myself—perhaps we and I could achieve the bland efficiency that responsible outsiders so earnestly wish for us.

But what does music sound like in those places? What spices do they use to season their food? What sort of colors do they paint their houses? When a street parade erupts in their path, do they honk their horns or do they get out of their cars and join in?

It's expensive living here. We pay high taxes for our non-conformity. I would gladly move, but I fear my time here has ruined me for life anywhere else. When a brass band parades in front of my house in the middle of the night, I'm neither surprised nor disturbed.

If you live long enough with these voices, they start making sense.

—Lolis Eric Elie, writer

Descriptions can give the stranger little idea of the peculiar city. Although all on one level, it's a town of contrasts. In no other city of the United States or Mexico is the old and the romantic preserved in such integrity and brought into such sharp contrast to the modern.

—**Charles Dudley Warner,** *Harper's Magazine 1887*

Apparently people have been playing music in the streets as long as there has been a city here. You go to other places and they try to create what we already have here—some cities pay people to create this cultural life!

—**Mary Howell, attorney at law**

Life in New Orleans is all about making the present—this moment, right now—as pleasant as possible. So New Orleanians, by and large, aren't tortured by the frenzy to achieve, acquire, and manage the unmanageable future. Their days are built around the things that other Americans have pushed out of their lives by incessant work: art, music, elaborate cooking, and—most of all—plenty of relaxed time with family and friends. Their jobs are really just the things they do to earn a little money; they're not the organizing principle of life. While this isn't a worldview particularly conducive to getting things done, getting things done isn't the most important thing in New Orleans. Living life is. Once you've tasted that, and especially if it's how you grew up, life everywhere else feels thin indeed.

—**Dan Baum, writer**

There is something about New Orleans that embodies passion; I've never seen that before. There's something tangible about the essence of the city. You can taste and smell it.

—**Blake Lively, actor**

What happens in Vegas may stay in Vegas, but what happens in New Orleans, goes home with you.

—**Laurell K. Hamilton, writer**

"It's the juxtapositions that get you," wrote Willie Morris about the South, and nowhere is that more true than in New Orleans. Think "jazz funeral" or "drive-through daiquiri shops." One of my first apartments was behind a cathedral school and in between two of the city's biggest gay bars, so that I was awakened by an off-key nun singing "My Country Tis of Thee" every morning, and lulled—sort of—to sleep at night by the bass beat of "I Will Survive." When Tammy Wynette died, the bars played dueling versions of "Stand By Your Man" for a week.

—**Julia Reed, writer**

New Orleans is one of our most precious, historic communities: visually, emotionally, artistically.

—**Sandra Bullock, actor**

New Orleans is like the bad-kid island in "Pinocchio."

—**Jonah Hill, actor**

I've lived in N.Y. and L.A. for many years, but I still gravitate to New Orleans—it's so unique and so European. There's nothing else like it in the country. It has its own music, its own food, its own style and its own way of life.   —Bryan Batt, actor

Mud, mud, mud.   —Benjamin Henry Latrobe, architect

We wander through old streets, and pause before the age stricken houses; and, strange to say, the magic past lights them up.   —Grace King, *French Quarter Guidebook*

Through pestilence, hurricanes, and conflagrations the people continued to sing. They sang through the long oppressive years of conquering the swampland and fortifying the town against the ever threatening Mississippi. They are singing today. An irrepressible joie de vivre maintains the unbroken thread of music through the air. Yet, on occasion, if you ask an overburdened citizen why he is singing so gaily, he will give the time-honored reason, "Why to keep from crying, of course!"   —Laura Robinson, *It's An Old New Orleans Custom*, 1948

The dead walk alongside the living here and we talk to them all the time.   —Anne Rice, writer

Hot weather opens the skull of a city, exposing its white brain and heart of nerves.
                                                            —Truman Capote, writer

If you're ever lucky enough to belong somewhere, if a place takes you in and you take it into yourself, you don't desert it just because it can kill you. There are things more valuable than life.   —Poppy Z. Brite, writer

I'm just tired of the L.A. lifestyle and I feel like, at this point in my life, I'd rather just live in a place full of real, genuine people. I've been to New Orleans many times over the years and the people there are real . . . they're genuine.   —Harrison Ford, actor

New Orleans, more than many places I know, actually, tangibly lives its culture. It's not just a residual of life; it's a part of life. Music is at every major milestone of our life: birth, marriage, death. It's our culture.   —Wendell Pierce, actor

How does this city take hold of your soul? Through a song or carnival parade or stolen kisses against the cool iron fence behind the cathedral with the scent of sweet olive swirling around you.   —Patrick Dunne, antiquarian and decorator

Jazz came out of New Orleans, and that was the forerunner of everything. You mix jazz with European rhythms, and that's rock n' roll, really. You can make the argument that it all started on the streets of New Orleans with the jazz funerals.   —The Edge, musician

New Orleans is unlike any city in America. Its cultural diversity is woven into the food, the music, the architecture—even the local superstitions. It's a sensory experience on all levels and there's a story lurking around every corner.   —Ruta Sepetys, writer

New Orleans is like a big musical gumbo. The sound I have is from being in the city my whole life.   —Trombone Shorty, musician

I think New Orleans is such a beautiful city. It looks like a fairytale when you walk through the French Quarter or the Garden District. There is such a lush sense of color, style, architecture— and the people themselves.   —Anika Noni Rose, singer

If I had grown up in any place but New Orleans, I don't think my career would have taken off. I wouldn't have heard the music that was around this town. There was so much going on when I was a kid.   —Pete Fountain, musician

Unless you're broke or sick or blue-nosed, I don't see how you could have anything but a good time in New Orleans. "Unique" is a word that cannot be qualified. It does not mean rare or uncommon; it means alone in the universe. By the standards of grammar and by the grace of God, New Orleans is the unique American place.

—Charles Kuralt, TV commentator

By contrast, New Orleans is a warm and dreamy place, birthplace of jazz, lover of good food, and afternoon naps, America's most feminine city. Perhaps it's appropriate that the Saints' symbol, the fleur-de-lis, is a flower. It's love all the same, a devotion so intense that thousands of screaming fans turn out on Sundays to wildly cheer the team—and that's just at the airport after an away game.   —Douglas McCollam, journalist

Thank God the French got here first. Can you imagine what New Orleans might have been had the Pilgrims gotten off at Pilottown instead of Plymouth? It's frightening . . . we might have been burning witches instead of cafe brulot; or preaching to the quadroon beauties, instead of dancing with them; or spending eons eating boiled beef and potatoes, instead of ecrevisse Cardinal, or pompano en papillote, or gumbo.

—Phil Johnson, TV director, producer, commentator

I'm not sure, but I'm almost positive, that all music came from New Orleans.

—Ernie K-Doe, Emperor of the Universe

Everyone in this good city enjoys the full right to pursue his own inclinations in all reasonable
and, unreasonable ways.   **—The Daily Picayune, New Orleans, March 5, 1851**

New Orleans makes it possible to go to Europe without leaving the United States.
       —Franklin Delano Roosevelt, President

When you go to New Orleans, you're not just going to a city, you're going to an entire culture.
       —James Carville, politician and commentator

In other places culture comes down from up high. In New Orleans, it bubbles up from
the streets.   **—Ellis Marsalis, musician**

We don't hide crazy. We parade it down the street.
       —Debby Bird, Mardi Gras enthusiast from Virginia

There are certain things in life that I love. One is architecture, and music, culture, food,
people. New Orleans has all of that.   **—Lenny Kravitz, musician**

To all men whose desire only is to be rich and to live a short life, but a merry one, I have no
hesitation in recommending New Orleans.
       —Henry Bradshaw Fearon, *Sketches of America*, 1919

New Orleans is the only place I know of where you ask a little kid what he wants to be and
instead of saying, I want to be a policeman, or I want to be a fireman, he says, I want to be a
musician.   **—Allan Jaffe, Founder of Preservation Hall**

The first time Taylor brought me to New Orleans all I could say was, "I'm going to die here."
Like Venice. And that same decadent, romantic, slow sweetness comes over me every time I
return. It's one of the few places that's not precious to the nth degree; it doesn't look as though
its history has been cleaned up by Disney. It's funky and untidy. It's my contact with Europe
in America.   **—Helen Mirren, actor**

New Orleans . . . a courtesan, not old and yet no longer young, who shuns the sunlight that the
illusion of her former glory be preserved.   **—William Faulkner, writer**

Food is a major topic of conversation in New Orleans as in France, and the newcomer is
overwhelmed with advice on what and where to eat.   **—Sarah Searight, writer**

Fuck You, You Fucking Fucks   **—Ashley Morris, blogger and professor,**
his iconic response to the lack of support after Hurricane Katrina

The French Quarter . . . was a place to hide. I could piss away my life, unmolested . . . there was something about that city, though it didn't let me feel guilty that I had no feeling for the things so many others needed. It let me alone . . . being lost, being crazy maybe is not so bad if you can be that way undisturbed. New Orleans gave me that.   **—Charles Bukowski, writer**

There's a spirit to this city. This city has a soul. If you can sense it, you don't want to go anywhere else.   **—Maria Shaw Lawson, psychic**

I liked it from the first: I lingered long in that morning walk, liking it more and more, in spite of its shabbiness, but utterly unable to say then or ever since wherein its charm lies. I suppose we are all wrongly made up and have a fallen nature; else why is it that while the most thrifty and neat and orderly city only wins our approval, and perhaps gratifies us intellectually, such a thriftless, battered and stained, and lazy old place at the French quarter of New Orleans takes our hearts?   **—Charles Dudley Warner, writer**

This town is the first that one of the world's great rivers has seen rise upon its banks . . . this wild and desrt [sic] place that canes and trees still cover almost entirely, will be one day, and perhaps that day is not far off, an opulent city and the metropolis of a great and rich colony."
—Pierre-François Xavier de Charlevoix, priest

Much distortion of opinion has existed . . . respecting public morals and manners in New Orleans. Divested of pre-conceived ideas on the subject, an observing man will find little to condemn in New Orleans, more than in other commercial cities; and will find that noble distinction of all active communities, acuteness of conception, urbanity of manners, and polished exterior. There are few places where human life can be enjoyed with more pleasure, or employed to more pecuniary profit.
—William Darby, *A Geographical Description of the State of Louisiana*, 1816

Here one finds the narrow streets with overhanging balconies, the beautiful wrought-iron and cast-iron railings, the great barred doors and tropical courtyards. Many of these fine houses are more than a century and a quarter old, and they stand today as monuments to their forgotten architects. For it must be remembered that New Orleans was a Latin city already a century old before it became a part of the United States; and it was as unlike the American cities along the Atlantic seaboard as though Louisiana were on another continent.
—Federal Writers' Project, *New Orleans City Guide*, 1938

During the greater part of the first half-century in which Louisiana was part of the United States . . . the more legitimate gayety of the town was concentrated in the Vieux Carré, which, though Spanish in its physical aspects, was still predominantly French in spirit and custom. In that area were located the pits for cock-fighting; the elegantly appointed gambling-houses; the best of the cafés and coffee-houses; the fashionable cabarets and bordellos, which were operated with such circumspection that almost no record of their existence remains; the eating-places which were already developing the cuisine that was destined to spread the fame of New Orleans throughout the world; the ballrooms; and most of the theatres . . .

—**Herbert Asbury, writer**

The banquettes of Royal Street were crowded with the masked and the unmasked, almost everyone moving slowly uptown toward Canal Street. The bars on the corners were already filled. Decorated automobiles rolled past, and now and then more trucks. There was a truck filled with hillbillies, with a little outhouse at the center of it, entitled "Dog Patch," and another filled with boys and girls in striped suits called "The Prisoners of Love." Two voluptuous blondes in pale lavender taffety gowns of the Gay Nineties, wearing no masks, but with their faces heavily painted, came swishing down the banquette, each carrying a bottle of bourbon, from which they took drinks from time to time, and conversing in deep bass voices. They were men.

—**Robert Tallant, writer**

My advice to you is to stay for a while in the old section of the city, sit for a time in Jackson Square and let the old world charm you. Give the atmosphere a chance to lull you. Take your time and wander slowly; look twice at the old houses, they are worth it. Talk to the beggars in the street; talk to any one you chance to meet. The natives of the Quarter are pleasant people and they will gladly tell you anything they happen to know.　　—**Lyle Saxon, writer**

There is a velvety sensuality here at the mouth of the Mississippi that you won't find anywhere else. Tell me what the air feels like at 3:00 a.m. on a Thursday night in August in Shaker Heights and I bet you won't be able to say because nobody stays up that late. But in New Orleans, I tell you, it's ink and honey passed through silver moonlight."　　—**Andrei Codrescu, writer**

New Orleans is unique in the world. This city has a life and a spirit and a soul that's missing in most places. There's this invisible reality that's reflected darkly into the physical world, but that invisible reality is full of spirit and life. Different cultural traits come here and somehow New Orleanians put a spin on it and make it their own, and it comes out in some garbled, wonderful, and re-inventive way that has a whole new flavor.

—**Sallie Ann Glassman, Voodoo Priestess**

The city has burned twice, flooded, survived recession, depression. New Orleans has known who she is for a really long time and changed with the times. But I do think if they fuck around with the go cup, the people will revolt. —**Elizabeth Pearce, drinks historian**

God took off his boots to rest here because he liked the looks and the feel of this special place he created, and then he saw the faith of the people and the love they had for each other. He wanted to hear music while he was resting in this special place and he gave us the gift of music and we have it in our souls for eternity. —**Charmaine Neville, musician**

New Orleans is the most unique of American cities because it is the only city in the world that has created its own culture. With architecture, music and festive ceremonies, it's of singular importance to the United States of America. Moreover, with a mixture of Spanish, French, British, West African and American people living in the same city, New Orleans can be depicted as the original melting pot. The collision of these cultures created jazz, the only art form that embodies the fundamental principles of American democracy. Serving to represent the best of the United States, it eventually swept the country and the world at large.

—**Wynton Marsalis, musician**

In New Orleans, absurdity is like the humidity. It permeates everything, until you stop noticing it. It connects everything and everyone in its oddness and the climate of convention has no place within it. That's how it goes there. You live, breathe, and feel the life that finds you. Thinking's not required. Thinking can come later, when the weather breaks and you need some saner shelter. —**Michael Reilly, writer**

The nights are darker here. Palpably darker. And thicker. You can reach out and stroke the darkness. Touch it. Run your hand over it, like somebody's skin, or a piece of soft cloth. Got a soft feel to it, New Orleans nights. The nights are always softer here. No matter what else has happened. No matter what kind of horror show. The nights are always soft. I can't tell you how many times, how many blood-soaked crime scenes I been privy to, how many murders. I just stepped away, stepped outside, into the night, and been struck by how thick and soft and sweet and downright dark the nights are here. Struck dumb. It's a mystery. —**Eric Overmyer, writer**

Louisiana in September was like an obscene phone call from nature. The air—moist, sultry, secretive, and far from fresh—felt as if it were being exhaled into one's face. Sometimes it even sounded like heavy breathing. Honeysuckle, swamp flowers, magnolia, and the mystery smell of the river scented the atmosphere, amplifying the intrusion of organic sleaze.

—**Tom Robbins, writer**

Don't you just love those long rainy afternoons in New Orleans when an hour isn't just an hour—but a little piece of eternity dropped into your hands—and who knows what to do with it?　　　　　　　　　　　　　　　　　　　　　**—Tennessee Williams, writer**

I'm not going to lay down in words the lure of this place. Every great writer in the land, from Faulkner to Twain to Rice to Ford, has tried to do it and fallen short. It is impossible to capture the essence, tolerance, and spirit of south Louisiana in words and to try is to roll down a road of clichés, bouncing over beignets and beads and brass bands and it just is what it is.

It is home.　　　　　　　　　　　　　　　　　　　　　　**—Chris Rose, writer**

Everything in New Orleans is a good idea.　　　　　　　　　　**—Bob Dylan, musician**

New Orleans food is as delicious as the less criminal forms of sin.　　　**—Mark Twain, writer**

He learned about life at sixteen, first from Dostoevsky and then from the whores of New Orleans.　　　　　　　　　　　　　　　　　　　**—Richard Brautigan, writer**

But the reasons against going to New Orleans—that spicy southern city known for jazz and Mardi Gras and hospitality—were the very reasons we had to go. **—Howard Schultz, businessman**

Any time you discover a place as magical and weird as New Orleans, it doesn't hit you right away. Until you experience it—meet the people, eat the food, breathe that air, drink the water— it's not something you can really understand.　　　　　　　　**—Bo Koster, musician**

Here's the great thing about New Orleans. They were going to throw you a party whether you won or lost.　　　　　　**—David Letterman to Drew Brees, the day after the Super Bowl**

You'd have to be crazy not to want to have New Orleans as a host city for your event.
　　　　　　　　　　　　　　　　　　　　—NBA Commissioner David Stern

The French philosopher René Descartes declared that: "All my life I delighted in the use of reason more than memory." New Orleans is precisely the opposite, a more subjective place, a city that lives on reminiscences and feeling rather than on the cool and objective analysis of reality. In the American brain, New Orleans represents the right hemisphere, not the left.
　　　　　　　　　　　　　　　　　　　　　　—S. Frederick Starr, historian

The biggest challenge in New Orleans is to find a worker who can climb a ladder after lunch.
　　　　　　　　　　　　　　　　　　　　　　—Harry Anderson, comedian

In New Orleans I felt a freedom. I could catch my breath here.   **—Tennessee Williams, writer**

Every time I close my eyes blowing the trumpet of mine—I look right in the heart of good old New Orleans. It has given me something to live for.   **—Louis Armstrong, musician**

All of us from New Orleans have savored that Proust-bites-into-the-madeleine moment when a stray taste, sound, smell, or sight brings remembrances of things past. **—Walter Isaacson, writer**

What I love about New Orleans—trying to understand it is a lifetime of productive bewilderment.   **—Jervey Tervalon, writer**

To the uninitiated, Mardi Gras might seem an act of reckless debauchery. To those who have experienced it and understand it, Mardi Gras is an act of fearless generosity.

—Christopher Rice, writer

New Orleans is the opposite of America. New Orleans is not fast or energetic or efficient, not a go-get-'em, Calvinistic, well-ordered city. It's slow, lazy, sleepy, sweaty, hot, wet, lazy, and exotic.   **—Mark Childress, writer**

There it is—a proper enough American city and yet the tourist is apt to see more nuns and naked women than he ever saw before.   **—Walker Percy, writer**

If New Orleans could be said to have a downside for writers, it would be that there is too much material all around, all the time. If I tried to transcribe half of the peculiar, vivid, outlandish, timeless experiences I've had there I would do nothing else.   **—Haven Kimmel, writer**

New Orleans has figured out how to have its own culture, the fullness of it experienced out of sight of tourists, while also presenting a tasty and not terribly demanding version of that culture in a self-contained, sealed area of the French Quarter, with satellite outposts uptown and in the Garden District. Culturally, New Orleans is healthy.   **—Duncan Murrell, writer**

Look at New Orleans. Part of me hopes that they don't fix the potholes. In the South, it's actually built in—you have to take your time. As for the roads in New Orleans, you go too fast, and you'll burn your lap with coffee and your shocks will be gone. You know what I mean? Just take your time.   **—Matthew McConaughey, actor**

I have been all over and there are no people anywhere like New Orleanians. We're different. We love our city so very much more, we are just nuts about the place. It's the food and the way we enjoy sharing it with each other. It's the music, and that music, it's just always in the air. It's also having something unique to live in, our pretty little shotgun houses, our pretty camelback houses, and our Creole cottages.

—Leah Chase, chef

We let people, our people and our guests, be themselves in New Orleans.
It's a come as you are kind of town, come as you really are or really want to be.
It doesn't matter where you live or who you are married to as long as one of you can cook, come as you are.

—Charmaine Neville, musician

Ever since I was barely in my 20s, I have loved New Orleans the way some men love women, if that means unquestionably. I fell in love with the city eating shrimp cooked seven ways, and riding the ferry across the black, black river where fireworks burned in the air at Algiers Point. I drank so much rum I could sleep standing up against a wall. There is no way to explain to someone who has never lived here why every day seems like a parade. Every time I would swing my legs from under the quilt and ease my toes onto the pine floors of my shotgun double, I would think I am getting away with something here.

—Rick Bragg, writer

Only in New Orleans was a style of music so intertwined with daily life and death as to give not only its sound, but eventually its name to a local funerary custom. **—Ellis Marsalis Jr., musician**

In New Orleans, gluttony is a way of life.

—Morton J. Horwitz, historian

New Orleans is, on the other hand, a comfortable metropolis which has a certain apathy and stagnation which I find inoffensive.

—John Kennedy Toole, writer

No other city in the world had a celebration quite like this. It was beautiful precisely because it was so frivolous.

—Dan Baum, writer

New Orleans, city of roaches, city of decay, city of our family, and of happy, happy people.

—Anne Rice, writer

I wouldn't touch New Orleans with a 10-foot pole. That town is haunted as shit, and all the better for it. Nowhere in the world loves its ghosts more than that city. **—Kendare Blake, writer**

It's just something about the way we, as performers from this city, the way we do things. We hear extra sounds in our heads—extra beats, extra backbeats, extra rhythms that people from other parts of the United States just don't understand or get.

—Irma Thomas, singer

It's a New Orleans tradition that you can take any music and mess with it.

—Bruce Boyd Raeburn, historian

This is one of the great cultural cities of the world. Through the music, New Orleans spoke to the soul of the nation.

—Wynton Marsalis, musician

There have only been five great singers of rhythm and blues—Ernie K-Doe, James Brown and Ernie K-Doe.

—Ernie K-Doe, musician and eccentric

One of the things that's beautiful about New Orleans is how culturally rich we are and how well we have worked together. People call us a gumbo. It's really important that we get focused on the very simple notion that diversity is a strength, it's not a weakness.   **—Mitch Landrieu, Mayor**

We are not a brittle civilization so easily overturned. We are a self-determined, sovereign tribal unit in the depths of an Amazon rainforest. If not the Amazon, then New Orleans certainly lives and thrives in another dimension, historically always amazingly polysemous, and always filling up with curious, new and diverse life forms regularly slipping through the veil into our realm from their definitely dreary worlds.   **—Andy Antippas, art gallery owner**

My duty was to out dance every one of them. I'm just dancing with a spirit.
I'm not just dancing to be dancing.   **—Big Chief Tootie Montana**

Clean living keeps me in shape. Righteous thoughts are my secret.
And New Orleans home cooking.   **—Fats Domino**

Our history is not for museums. We still have a culture that comes from the city, from the neighborhoods; we still have a culture that connects to the past and parades in the streets.

—David Rutledge, professor

I don't think New Orleans is a very American city. It doesn't have the same puritanical drive towards money being the god of all things . . . People live for pleasure in New Orleans."   **—Bunny Matthews, writer & artist**

If you asked me what kind of food we serve in New Orleans, I'd say we serve New Orleans food.

—Emeril Lagasse

I just love me some red beans. This is a red bean city here.   **—Willie Mae Seaton**

The secret ingredient in that treasured recipe called New Orleans is the people who live here—the natives who simply can't stand to be anywhere else for very long and those who came here by choice and stayed forever because they couldn't stand to be anywhere else for very long, and our friends who keep coming back because they get it. They understand why we can't stand to be anyplace else for very long.

—Ella Brennan

It's unique in this country I think, that city. It has this extraordinary ability to live in the past and the present. Time kind of melds. I don't know any other place like that. And so authentic still, to its culture and to the people. You feel on the street what these people feel about this place. I mean, you walk down the streets of New York and everybody just looks so unhappy. But in New Orleans, you get this sense that this is home and we're connected. We're connected through generations and we're connected through the arts and the music and the food and the culture. I mean, it permeates the air . . . not to paint too rosy a picture, because there's a lot of darkness there, but what I find fascinating is how you can be in a place where you sense the decay and the decadence and the elegance and the spirit and everything is just moving together.

—Jessica Lange, actor

Some people don't get New Orleans. They think Mardi Gras, for example, is about breasts and beer. But New Orleans is about fantasy. It's about desire and awareness of mortality. It's a collection of stories, most of which will never be written.

—Elizabeth Dewberry, writer

What is it I can smell, even from here, as if the city has a soul and the soul exhaled an effluvium all its own? I can't quite name it. A certain vital decay? A lively fetor? When I think of New Orleans away from New Orleans, I think of rotting fish on the sidewalk and good times inside.

—Walker Percy, writer

Get off your asses and let's do something!

—Mayor Ray Nagin, in his one moment of glory, yelling at the federal government after Katrina

Nearly every outlaw legend that sprang up in the western territory in the early nineteenth century has some aspect that takes place in, or is related to, New Orleans. There is no legend of the Natchez Trace without New Orleans. The city is where crooks, race-traitors, Catholics, vagabonds, and every other marginalized person could go to hide and, sometimes, recreate themselves. To a great extent, it's still that way.

—Duncan Murrell, writer

We're here to serve people and make people feel they are prettier than they really are.

—Clover Grill menu

Everyone you have known or ever will know eventually ends up at The Old Absinthe House.

—Old Absinthe House motto

It was literally minutes before our scheduled departure. Our driver was in the parking lot, engine running. With the image of those X's forever imprinted in my mind, I looked at my wife and said: "This is where we belong."

—Scott Fujita, football player

My grandmother was extremely strict with me. Believe me, when I got married, I was a virgin. I come from that old school. It was instilled in me, you just didn't sleep with people unless you were married to 'em. That's why I got married so many times.

—Wild Cherry, 1950s stripper on Bourbon Street

No Officers, No Meetings, No Dues . . . Not Bound By Circumstance.

—ordinances of the Bywater Bone Boys Social Aid & Pleasure Club

You can make prostitution illegal, but you can't make it unpopular.

—Mayor Martin Behrman on the federally mandated closing of Storyville

You find as a writer there are certain spots on the planet where you write better than others, and I believe in that. And New Orleans is one of them.

—Jimmy Buffett, musician

The wealth of the world is here unworked gold in the ore. The paradise of the South is here, deserted and half in ruins. I never beheld anything so beautiful and so sad.

—Lafcadio Hearn

What I'm not trying to do is change the world with my food. I'm not trying to recreate the wheel. I'm only here to make people happy, and gumbo does that.

—Frank Brigtsen, chef

I don't see it ever being a clean, efficient, crime-free city. And I think people who live there need to love it for what it is—a celebration of the senses and a place where you can immerse yourself in the creative juices caused by this flow, which can serve as a form of compost for creativity and soul work. New Orleans value to the world lies in its charming dysfunctionality. The world doesn't need more Atlantas. We need a place where 'slow' is accepted as the treasure that it is.

—Lynn Wilson, astrologer

In Ohio, it's just Tuesday. Here, it's Mardi Gras.

—Ella Murphy, my daughter

New Orleans is as far as you can get from America while still being in it.

—Michael Murphy, wrote this book

ACKNOWLEDGMENTS

After at least mentioning my editor, Dan Crissman, my publisher, Ann Treistman, my incredible wife and partner, Marnie Carmichael, my talented, smart-as-a-whip son, Austin, and his wife and child, Jacy and Cadence, I had actually written nearly 500 names of New Orleanians who, for me, make it New Orleans. But, space considerations compel me to reconsider and isolate just one.

Ella Li Genet Murphy grew up in New Orleans and will forever be colored by the city's unique idiosyncrasies. She is an amazing spirit. Ella is fearless. She's also funny as hell, wicked smart (she won first place in the city of New Orleans for her science project "The Effects of Rangia Cuneata Clams on the Turbidity of Lake Pontchartrain"—yeah, I have NO idea what that means either), and quite beautiful (I can say this because she's not from my gene pool). She does, as they say, light up a room. Above all else, Ella has a huge heart that is her essence and not something we ingrained in her.

Recently, I was stuck in Carnival Season traffic while giving a tour, so I texted Ella that I'd be late getting home. Most teens might have texted back "OK" if they responded at all. Ella wrote back to thank me for letting her know and that she was sorry I was stuck. One evening weeks later, she saw a cat snag a bird as we drove by. She yelled to pull over, then shooed away the cat and brought back the injured bird in her palm. After setting up a box with water and birdseed, the bird did pass away during the night and is now buried in our back yard in a faux-jewel-lined cigar box. The attempt to save its life is again rare in a 15-year-old. We like to say Ella is "a citizen of the world."

INDEX